Doing Research *in* Political Science

Doing Research *in* Political Science

an introduction to comparative methods and statistics

• **Paul Pennings** • **Hans Keman** • **Jan Kleinnijenhuis**

SAGE Publications
London • Thousand Oaks • New Delhi

Firt published 1999

SAGE Publications Ltd
6 Bonhill Street
London EC2A 4PU

SAGE Publications Inc
2455 Teller Road
Thousand Oaks, California 91320

SAGE Publications India Pvt Ltd
32, M-Block Market
New Delhi 110 048

British Library Cataloguing in Publication data

A catalogue record for this book is available from the British Library

ISBN 0 7619 5102 4
ISBN 0 7619 5103 2 (pbk)

Library of Congress catalog record available

Typeset by Keytec Typesetting Limited
Printed in Great Britain by The Cromwell Press Ltd, Trowbridge, Wiltshire

Contents

Preface

This book consists of three parts which represent in our view the basic stages of any theory-driven empirical-analytical research in the social and, in particular, the political sciences. The book is written with the purpose of serving as a course-book for undergraduates. In each chapter there is an introduction to its contents, and at the end there is a list of the main topics covered, which may help both teacher and student to find the information she or he needs. In addition, each chapter contains examples which are taken from existing comparative research and are partially based on data that is made accessible by us via the World Wide Web (http://welcome.to/PaulPennings).

In Part I we present our own arguments concerning the comparative approach: namely, that any empirical research needs to be theory-driven and must be formulated in a well-elaborated Research Design. Part II is essential reading for those who wish to understand the use of (advanced) statistics in order to be able to conduct an explanatory analysis (including its caveats and pitfalls!). Part III can be seen as our attempt to pull together the threads of our way of doing comparative research and will be interesting for any reader, whether a freshman or an advanced student of comparative politics and sociology.

Without claiming that this approach and its elaboration is the one and only way to teach comparative methods and statistics in political science, we feel that it offers a valuable 'springboard' to judging the comparative information with which modern students are confronted. It also helps to shape a theory-inspired research design in such a way that it leads to plausible and adequate results. These are valuable skills that are lacking in too many course-books on methodology.

During the process of writing the book, we have benefitted from many institutions, scholars and students, whom we wish to thank for their contributions. First of all, the *Essex Summer School in Social Science Data Analysis and Collection* has given us the chance to test the draft version of the manuscript on an international group of undergraduate students. This opportunity has been very helpful to us in completing and improving the manuscript. The same goes for the comments of Dutch students in political science and public administration at the Vrije Universiteit Amsterdam. We thank copy-editor Colin Macnee for his detailed and helpful corrections to the manuscript. Ian Budge, Kaare Strom, Ross Burkhart and Michael S. Lewis-Beck kindly permitted us to use their data in this book. Other valuable advice on the whole or parts of the manuscript have been given by Francis G.

Castles (ANU, Canberra), Arend Lijphart (UCSD, San Diego), Peter Mair (RUL, Leiden) and Michael McDonald (SUNY, Binghamton). We are grateful for the help of Manfred G. Schmidt and Uwe Wagschal (University of Bremen) who provided us with some crucial data. We wish to thank the Dutch student Arjan Widlak for gathering and analyzing the data on democratization and its determinants. Furthermore, support for this project was given by the *Netherlands Institute for Advanced Study in the Humanities and Social Sciences* (NIAS) and the *Vrije Universiteit Amsterdam*. Any suggestions to improve the book will be welcome.

Finally, we wish to note that this book has been a genuine 'collective action', but at the same time that the 'order of appearance' of the authors reveals the input given by Paul Pennings as stimulator and organizer.

Class material is available on:
http://welcome.to/PaulPennings and on http://www.scw.vu.nl/~pennings

Paul Pennings,
Hans Keman,
Jan Kleinnijenhuis,
Amsterdam

Part I

COMPARATIVE METHODOLOGY

1 The comparative approach and political science

CONTENTS

1.1 INTRODUCTION

Almost everyone watches daily TV, regularly reads a daily newspaper and often discusses what goes on in the world. These activities shape our views on society and, in particular, influence our views on and perspective of the role and impact of politics on societal developments. In this era of easy access to electronic communication (e.g. Internet), worldwide TV-coverage of events (e.g. CNN) and rapid changes in the political mapping of the world (globalization), one is not only confronted with a multitude of bits and pieces of information, but also with various and often conflicting opinionated views of what events may mean and what consequences they may have for our lives and for the society of which we are part and in which we live.

Although we do not realize it all the time (or not at all) we use this information in its multifarious forms in a comparative way. Both the 'messengers' (e.g. journalists, political spokesmen and so-called opinion leaders) and the 'receivers' (readers, TV-watchers, person-to-person communicators) are, more or less consciously, using the 'art' of comparing in order to come to a, more or less, well-founded interpretation of what goes on in public life.

The *first* point of departure of this book is therefore that not only students of social and political sciences are in fact comparing information to form an opinion, but that everyone is doing this in assessing the facts of life around him or her. For instance, how often do you use the words 'more' and 'less' or 'bigger' and 'smaller', and this is 'different' or 'similar' to that, and so on and so forth? All these expressions used by everyone in their daily conversation basically imply that you (seem to) have a comparative idea about what occurs in reality. And not only that – most of the time if not always – you do deliver a statement about, for instance, politics and society that is, more or less, implicitly of an evaluative nature. To give an example: in New Zealand in 1996 the first elections were held under a new system (it used to be 'First-Past-the-Post' and it is now a variation of the Proportional Representation electoral system). The electoral outcome necessitated the formation of a coalition government instead of a one-party government. Apart from the fact that this type of government and the related procedure of forming it was new to both the public and the politicians, everyone could now evaluate what the change of the electoral system implied in reality. One could now evaluate what goes on by means of comparing the 'old' with the 'new' situation.

The 'art of comparing' is thus one of the most important cornerstones of the development of knowledge about society and politics and insights into what is going on, how things develop and, more often than not, the formulation of statements about why this is the case and what it may mean to all of us. In short, comparisons are part and parcel of the way we experience reality and, most importantly, how we assess its impact on our lives and that of others.

Yet, and this is our *second* point of departure, the use and application of the *comparative method* is often not systematic, nor is it applied rigorously in most cases. This may not only result in unfounded opinions or flawed conclusions, but also in biased views of reality as well as in inappropriate generalizations about what goes on in society. In this book we wish to introduce you to the comparative method and related statistical tools in order to help you to reduce these hazards and to develop standards for yourselves and others to gain a more sustainable view on the world.

These simple types of comparison can often be found in newspapers or are delivered by politicians. The following example may give you an idea as to why comparisons are so often made, but also allow you to see that the way it is done or presented may well lead to either biased opinions or misleading perceptions of reality. The Ministry of Social Affairs and Employment of the Netherlands published in 1996 a report on economic competitiveness and its organization of Social Security benefits. It was explicitly organized on a comparative basis (comparing the Netherlands with Denmark, Belgium, Germany, the United States of America and Japan) in order to evaluate the Dutch state of affairs in this respect.

This type of comparison is becoming quite a popular instrument for many government agencies and related bureaus. It is often called 'benchmarking' and is considered to be an important tool of so-called 'thinktanks' to assess the strengths and weaknesses of policy-making and related achievements. The Dutch Minister of

Economic Affairs, for instance, advocated this comparative approach in a leading Dutch economic journal (Wijers, 1998: 73). However, by adjudicating economic parameters in terms of more or less efficient, and social security benefits in terms of more or less expensive (as well as transposing these in terms of good versus bad), the presentation offered a biased and prejudiced view of the Dutch economic performance in relation to the existing welfare state system.

First of all, the report should have made explicit what the leading *Research Question* was (e.g. does the Dutch social security system hamper economic development, or even prevent it from recovery?). Secondly, the Ministry should have made clear – given the relationship under review (namely: the economic development and social welfare system) – that the underlying hypothesis is: is there a trade-off between an extensive and wide coverage of social security in a society, on the one hand, and the flexibility and versatility of the market forces, in particular of the labor market, on the other? Neither was done, however, and therefore the research led to one-sided conclusions about the lack of competitiveness of the Dutch economy in relation to its assumed (over)generous social security system. In combination with an implicitly formulated Research Question, a Research Design had been developed that did not cover all (possible) comparable *cases* nor all (potentially) relevant *variables*. In other words: wishful thinking (social security is negatively affecting the working of the labor market) was corroborated by means of an inadequate Research Design, which was conducive to a probably biased, but politically helpful, 'scientific' outcome.

A Research Design implies the proper *choice of cases* (number and type), the type of *indicators* and the *mode of analysis* that is needed to provide a proper answer to the Research Question(s) asked (this will be elaborated in detail in Chapter 3). In all these respects the Ministry's report showed shortcomings:

1 The choice of cases was meaningless since it did not cover all relevant cases which could be compared, nor did the research demonstrate systematically over time the magnitude of change (lack of external validity).
2 The indicators appeared to be chosen, one may well suspect, to fit the required answers and subsequently the conclusions to be drawn, instead of deriving them from the Research Question and related potential answers, or hypotheses (lack of theory).
3 The analysis was based on either simple dichotomies or straightforward Rank Orders to prove a point, rather than measuring in detail what is under scrutiny (lack of internal validity).

There would have been nothing wrong with such a type of analysis, if and only if it had been based on *valid* and *reliable* indicators covering all relevant cases. If not, it only covers a part of reality, and one has no control over the comparative variation as a whole let alone the possibility of reaching viable generalizable conclusions. We shall deal with this in Chapters 2 and 3.

In summary: without a proper Research Question and Research Design, the 'art of comparing' becomes meaningless and – which is worse – may lead to dubious evidence on which existing policies may be changed that affect many in society.

Max Weber – the famous German sociologist – warned against these practices in his major work, *Economy and Society*, 1918 (Weber, 1972), by discussing value-free science *vis-à-vis* ideologically driven analysis, which would not only harm scientific progress but also jeopardize the correct use and application of social scientific results in practice (see: Bendix, 1977; Giddens, 1971).

To be sure: value-free types of analysis are not to be equated with 'objective knowledge'. The latter is a dream situation in social sciences, where – by definition – the subject of analysis always implies a reference to the study of the interactions between human beings and of related behavior. 'Value free' means, according to Weber, not driven by subjective or premeditated views of how individuals ought to behave or how a state or society *should* be organized. On the contrary: science, including social science, needs to be based on factual description and associative reasoning about reality. If this is not the case then subjective views precede analysis and tend to preserve the status quo in a society, rather than to assess reality, and this is conducive to ideology (Gerth and Mills, 1968).

From this follows, as the *third* point of our presentation, that it is crucial to know from the beginning *what, when and how* to compare. Seemingly, this triad goes almost without saying. Yet, it is vital for any comparative analysis that researchers ask themselves whether or not there is indeed a proper answer to these methodological questions. If not, the chances of coming up with valid and reliable answers will be reduced and the quality of knowledge advanced will be less. Hence, you must know beforehand what the phenomenon is that you wish to research, when – or at what point of time or period under review – the phenomenon can be best studied, and how to do this, i.e. which method must be applied to come up with plausible answers.

For example, if one wishes to know whether the welfare state is indeed a widespread phenomenon that could be seen as a product of modernization, or conversely as a result of political action which promoted its development and scope in a variable way, then one must reflect not only *what* a 'welfare state' is (as a dependent variable), but also which *cases* and *period* (i.e. countries or systems at one or more of points of time) can or must be taken into account to properly assess the question of *how* it develops. Similarly, to continue this example, the 'modernization' thesis requires a Research Design to investigate it, which is different from the 'politics-does-matter' hypothesis, which would test the 'political action' approach. The first requires a conscious time series analysis to inspect social developments which serve to show whether or not similar tendencies are indeed emerging (Pryor, 1968), whereas the second ought to be analyzed by means of comparing political action within various systems simultaneously at a well-chosen period of time (e.g. Castles, 1982). This can be done by means of a cross-sectional analysis, meaning that the comparison of countries is executed at a specific point of time.

Finally, the question of *why* to compare is equally vital. Do we want to know how a welfare state as an 'organization' emerged and developed? Or do we wish to focus on what it delivers as a 'system'? Or are we interested in how it affects the social and economic life of (individual) citizens? These deliberations are essential if we are to give exact answers to the questions raised and to decide the findings to be reported. Hence, what, when and how to compare are questions that need to be reflected on before one can even begin to analyze systematically the events of real-life situations, let alone to interpret the results of the comparison as such. In this book we shall demonstrate systematically how to do this and what is required to do it.

This point is perhaps the most important message we wish to get across. We view the 'art of comparing', or what is generally called 'the comparative approach to political and social science', *not* as an 'art' in itself but as one of the most adequate ways to connect ideas about society and politics with what is actually going on in the world in which we live. In short, we wish to introduce to you the comparative approach in such a way that one can explain convincingly and in a plausible way what is going on in the real world of politics and society – and hence, how one can interpret reality systematically in order to gain knowledge about the society in which we live.

1.2 THE COMPARATIVE APPROACH TO POLITICAL AND SOCIAL SCIENCE: THEORY AND METHOD

It is our contention that the comparative approach and its methodological application must be conducted by means of developing hypotheses. This is to say: a Research Question must be formulated as a point of departure of comparative investigation, which enables the student to reflect on what, when and how to compare and to what purpose. If not, the comparison becomes a recording instrument only. This, however, is not our goal, nor is it in our view scientific. Scientific activities always imply the quest for explanations, which are not only empirically based and yield systematic results, but also lead to results which are plausible. It is vital to realize that throughout this book we shall contend that empirical-analytical analysis is an instrument to develop social and political knowledge that is both scientifically valid and societally plausible.

Valid means here not only whether or not it is devoid of mistakes of the 'Third Order' (Blalock, 1972), i.e. avoiding incorrect operationalizations, incorrect indicators and inadequate levels of measurement and inferring false causal conclusions – these matters will be dealt with extensively in Part II of this book – but primarily whether or not the Research Design is indeed adequately derived from the Research Question which underlies the comparative research. The above-mentioned example of the Dutch research by the Ministry of Social Affairs and Employment into the relation between economic development and social security is an example of *in*valid comparative research. And although the results may well have been plausible as regards its political use, they are not plausible from a scientific point of view.

Validity in comparative (and other types of) research is a very central concept. However, more often than not, it is used in different ways and its use may well confuse the student. Throughout this book we shall employ the concept as follows:

- *Internal validity* concerns the question whether or not the measurements used in a given research project are properly, i.e. correctly, operationalized in view of the theoretical concept as intended. For instance: can, in a research project on western political parties, all the parties under review be considered to be identical in terms of their properties, and can they be seen as unique entities and not be confused with other types of social and political movements (like interest groups or new social movements). Hence research results are internally valid if and when they are *truly* comparative, i.e. yield the *same* results for all cases under review.

- *External validity* presupposes that the concepts used in a given research, and the related outcomes, apply not only to the cases under review but to *all similar* cases that satisfy the conditions set out in the Research Question and related Research Design. Similarity implies here comparable through space or time. For example, the factors found to explain the variations in government formation in terms of the resulting types of government (e.g. majority or minority and one-party versus multi-party governments) should also apply to those cases which were not included or in periods that were not covered in the original analysis. Obviously this requires careful and qualified arguments and spills over into the quality of conceptualization and operationalization (i.e. internal validity!). Hence, research results are viewed as externally valid when they yield *truly* comparable results for *similar* cases that have (yet) not been under review. This implies that one should expect that a replication of such a research with other countries or at another period would produce more or less the same results.

It should be realized that the concepts of internal and external validity are of an *ideal-typical* nature: in a perfect world with complete information the standards of validity may well be met, but in practice this is not a realistic goal. Yet, and this is what we put forward, one should try to get as close as feasible to these standards (see: Mayer, 1989: 55; Whiteley, 1986).

With plausibility we mean that the results are both empirically sound and societally relevant, i.e. they are neither counterintuitive nor inapplicable in reality. We do realize that this concept is a double-edged one and open for discussion. Yet we feel that political and social research, aiming to analyze reality, should be contributing to knowledge that is scientifically valid and is at the same time instrumental to understanding, i.e. developing plausible knowledge of society (see also: Giddens, 1971; Keman, 1988). Hence the concept of plausibility implies not only scientific rigor and flawless methods, but also concerns whether or not the knowledge generated is relevant and applicable in 'real life' situations.

The answer to this question depends in part on the question asked and the underlying goal of the research undertaken. If one, for instance, wishes to find out how to solve a societal problem like criminal behavior, pollution, or unemployment, the plausibility of the research results is assessed by the question whether or not these results can be translated into viable public policies. On the other hand, if the primary goal of a given research (question) is to enhance our knowledge of the 'quality of life' then it suffices if and when the results (can) demonstrate to what extent this varies across nations, within a population or over time in relation to a number of conditions and factors. Here, plausibility is not aiming at a finding that points to a solution (by means of a policy measure), but at understanding how, when and where 'happiness' does occur and why. The more convincing the results are from a scientific perspective, the more plausible the knowledge generated will be.

In summary: we argue that one needs to formulate a Research Question (*RQ*) first, in order to be able to decide what, how and when to compare. This leads logically to the development of a Research Design (*RD*) in which these matters are addressed and elaborated in such a way that the research results will be valid, reliable and plausible. Only then is it proper to choose and select the correct techniques to perform the analysis in order to reach correct research results. And only then is it possible to decide which data must be collected to carry out the empirical and statistical analysis for a meaningful comparison that may produce substantial explanations of *why* societal and political events and developments have taken place. In short: substance comes before method, questions come before answers, and theory always precedes comparative analysis.

In Chapter 2 we begin therefore with an outline of what the role of theory is in political and social science. We shall elaborate this more specifically by asking what is the substance of 'comparative politics'. This is a much-contested topic of late (see: Ragin, 1987; Almond, 1990; Dalton, 1991; Keman, 1993d; Rogowski, 1993; Chilcote, 1994; Lane and Ersson, 1994b; Mair, 1996a). Yet our purpose is not to add another view concerning this (ongoing) debate, but rather to exemplify what the relationship is between theory and method – that is: between Research Question and Research Design – and thus how to conduct comparative analysis in a meaningful way. Central to this enterprise is to understand the vital ingredients of the comparative method. In Chapter 3 we shall therefore introduce some important concepts of how to organize your research. What is a unit of variation *vis-à-vis* a unit of observation and measurement? What is the relation between these concepts and why are they crucial for a proper Research Design?

In addition we shall elaborate on the core subject of the comparative approach to political science, namely on the triad '*Politics, Polity, Policy*' (Almond et al., 1993; Keman, 1993c; Schmidt, 1995), which can not only be considered as the core of political science, but concerns also the second dimension structuring Part III of this book.

Recall that the first dimension is what, when and how to compare. As the relation between politics and society is not only dynamic, but also obviously a process, we need a clear and systemic *model* that can be applied to various situations and related questions that cry out for explanatory analysis by means of the 'art of comparing'.

The formulation of a Research Question in relation to a Research Design, and thus in particular what, when and how to compare, is up-front in Chapter 3. The focus is on how to consciously make correct choices to allow for proper answers to question(s) asked in a systematic fashion; this is conducive to furthering theory as well as valid answers and plausible results. We shall demonstrate that, on the basis of one Research Question, it is possible and sometimes inevitable to give different answers, or working hypotheses, which all can be considered as equally plausible. We shall elaborate on this by introducing central concepts of any political analysis

– namely: actors, institutions and performances – and these will figure prominently in Part III of this book.

These concepts are essential components of the triad 'politics, polity and policy' and are at the same time consequential for the direction of the analysis in terms of the Research Design that is developed. For instance, the type of actor that is studied determines the type of analysis (e.g. the question of whether it concerns a voter, a party or a state makes a difference in terms of what is observed). This is important and shall be elaborated in Part II of the book. If, for instance, we study actors, by definition we deal with behavior. This implies that, depending on the Research Question under review, we must decide what kind of behavior is considered to indicate the actor we study. What is crucial then is that we take good note of the relationship between the level of measurement (e.g. actions of a voter, a party or a party system) and the unit of observation (i.e. a spatio-temporal entity, e.g. the properties of a nation, or of an individual or a group of individuals). If it concerns a study of voting behavior, the level of measurement and unit of observation are *both* directed to the individual (mostly on the basis of a sample across populations). Information on various individuals with respect to their preferences, background, and attitudes form the core of investigation. However, if we wish to research into the behavior of parties then the unit of measurement is not the individual any more but rather organizations that aim at participating in elections, by putting forward candidates for electoral offices, having a program for policy action, being involved in, making and breaking governments and so on.

In short, organized action turns a party into a collective actor and thus the unit of observation, i.e. an aggregate of individuals, who are considered as a unitary actor, measured at the organizational level. Finally, it should also be taken into account that, of course, different types of actors can be included in an analysis, meaning that they are observed at different levels of measurement (e.g. parties and voters). This implies that we are confronted with the possibility of *multi-level* analysis. Yet, in most cases it will depend on the Research Question, which defines the *Units of Variation*: the (theoretical) concepts used which are seen to establish the relations between variables employed, at what level the units of observation are to be measured. If we are interested in the interactions between parties as regards government formation we shall conceptualize actors as unitary (aggregated) actors and investigate the party's behavior on the level of a party system. Hence the unit of measurement is the type of interaction within a party system and the units of observation are parties.

The same principle applies to the type of *institutions*, or the 'rules' of the political and social game, and affects choices made rather than behavioral characteristics (see: Laver, 1983; Ostrom, 1990; Keman, 1997). Yet, here the choice concerns the level of political and social organization where the rules of the game apply and not so much the question whether or not the actor is an aggregate of individuals (e.g. a party, movement or government); likewise the variables representing policy-making are related to the type of political organization which can be held responsible (e.g. does it concern policy-making by an international, a national or a subnational organization?). All these options must be consciously considered beforehand on the basis of the Research Question under scrutiny. Hence before jumping to matters of measuring and modeling politics in relation to society and discussing related matters like the use of statistics, we must and shall discuss dilemmas of comparative methodology.

In Chapter 3 the delicate problem of elaborating the Research Question in relation to the Research Design in terms of the Units of Observation and the Units of Variation will be discussed. *Units of Variation* can be seen as those elements or dimensions in the empirical analysis that are the building stones for a meaningful comparison. These units can be divided into *dependent* and *independent* variables. The dependent variable is dependent since its magnitude or shape and type co-varies with at least one other variable. Note that the latter must not have the same meaning, content, or be measuring the same phenomenon. Hence the Units of Variation, together with the Units of Observation are central to any type of comparative analysis (see also: Przeworski and Teune, 1970; Mayer, 1972; Lijphart, 1975; Janoski and Hicks, 1994). The relation between these units becomes not only relevant for the choice of the cases to be included in terms of units of measurement (e.g. parties or governments) but also with respect to the question of whether these cases *represent* the so-called 'universe of discourse' or can be considered as the total population. That is to say: the difference between all relevant cases and all cases present in reality.

The term 'cases' is again often used in the comparative literature in various ways. On the one hand, cases may simply refer to the units of observation in a data-matrix. This is the general meaning of the term and is used in most course-books on methodology. On the other hand, the comparative approach generally uses cases to refer to the combination of the level of measurement employed (e.g. individuals, parties, or government) and the Units of Variation or variables employed (e.g. electoral attitudes, party programs, or government policies). The problem which arises from this kind of formulation boils down to the difference in seeing cases as an *empirical* entity (fixed in time and space; see: Ragin and Becker, 1992: 4–5; Lijphart, 1975: 160) or as a *theoretical* construct or convention. An example of the first kind are representatives of any type of system, like countries, parties, voters, years, decades, etc. This type of case defines the boundaries of investigation. The second type refers to theoretical properties from which the researcher derives the Units of Observation, i.e. cases. Welfare states, left-wing parties or coalition governments are examples. Whatever way one argues, however, we feel that cases are always defined as empirical entities in relation to the Research Question asked. Hence we shall define cases as those *Units of Observation* that are:

- identically defined by time and place
- logically connected to the Research Question under review.

Cases are then 'carriers of information' which must and can be collected by translating concepts into empirical indicators, such as having a written constitution or not, having a certain type of multi-party system, the size of the electorate, etc.

The general use of the term case will tell you how many political or social entities (in the broad sense of the word) are included and represent simply the *row*-scores of a data matrix, whereas the number of variables (operationalized theoretical concepts) are the *columns* of the same matrix (and the total Number of Cases is thus Variables × Units of Observation). However, in comparative research the term cases is reserved for the Units of Observation that are compared, be it voters in different countries or regions, parties in various political systems, or welfare states across nations. Here the information in each row of the data matrix is two-dimensional: it concerns the voter in country A, B or C or it refers to a party family X, Y or Z (if we wish to compare differences between party families and/or within party families). Or, for example, the row displays information on welfare states as a whole (equals one country). In the same vein, variables may well represent conceptual information *over time* (e.g. years), but the number of cases is still Variables × Units of Observation. Hence the term case basically refers to the units of observation that are compared. The following rule of thumb may be of help to the reader: if the Research Question is elaborated in terms of an international comparison, the number of cases is identical to the number of nations included; if the Research Question is said to be *cross*-national the number of cases is defined by the Units of Observation, like parties or governments, regardless of the number of nations or systems; finally, if the Research Question focuses on change over time (i.e. inter-temporal) then the time-units included indicate the number of cases. In summary: what is compared determines the number of cases rather than the total number of cells in a data matrix. That number (= N) is used in the statistical procedures, in particular for tests of significance, and refers to the total number of observations or *values* under scrutiny (see Figure 1.1).

- *Units of Variation* ⇒ *Variables* = columns of data matrix, indicating the *variation* across the Units of Observation according to empirical features derived from theoretical concepts;
- *Units of Observation* ⇒ *Cases* = objects of comparison with *separate* values for each variable along the row of the matrix representing the universe of discourse;
- *Units of Measurement* ⇒ *Values* = operational *features* (i.e. scores) of each separate case on each variable presented in the cells in the matrix. The total number of values, or cells, represents the statistical N.

Another important matter with regard to the number of cases is thus the question to what extent the cases under review indeed represent the so-called '*universe of discourse*'. As we shall elaborate in Chapter 3, there is quite some variation in various Research Designs as to how many relevant cases can or should be involved. This depends not only on the Research Question under review, but also on the mode of analysis which is considered to be proper for answering it. For example, if we study the development of welfare states, we may opt to compare them all, or a number of them. This choice, i.e. of the number of (relevant) cases involved, is related to the dichotomy – proposed by Przeworski and Teune (1970) – between a 'most similar' and a 'most different' design. In the former instance we seek to analyze a causal relationship by collecting data for all the cases that can be

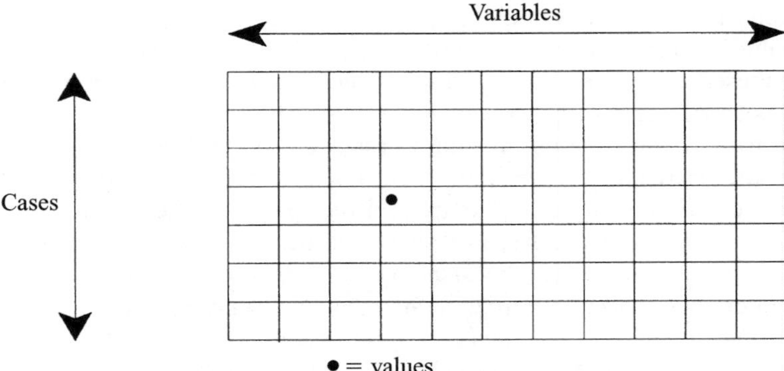

Figure 1.1 *Units of variation, observation and measurement (NB: Cases × Variables = total N of values). Unit of Variation = variable; Unit of Observation = case; Unit of Measurement = value*

assumed to be similar in terms of their contextual features. In the latter case it is assumed that the causal relation under review remains identical notwithstanding considerably-varying systemic differences. Francis Castles has put the difference between the two approaches succinctly as follows:

> A most similar approach implies that . . . the more circumstances the selected cases have in common, the easier it is to locate the variables that do differ and which may thus be considered as the first candidates for investigation as causal or explanatory variables. A most different approach involves . . . a comparison on the basis of dissimilarity in as many respects as possible in the hope that after all the differing circumstances have been discounted as explanations, there will remain one alone in which all the instances agree. (quoted in Keman, 1995: 137)

Hence, the issue is how to control for contextual or exogenous variation given the Research Question. For instance, if we wish to analyze the role of parties in government with regard to welfare statism, we could decide – on the basis of the Research Question – to restrict ourselves to a certain type of party or government. In this case not the system as such, nor its features, are decisive with respect to the Research Design, but the actual unit of variation which is central in the theory underlying the Research Question (i.e. Do parties matter in or out of government?). A basic concern remains the question whether we endeavor to achieve *external* validity of the answers given (i.e. the claim of generalizing conclusions) or strive for *internal* validity (the analysis is valid for the cases under review). The one type of validity is not by definition superior to the other. Again, it depends on the Research Question and on the type of data available (Ragin, 1987; Przeworski, 1987; Mair, 1996b). In addition the cases to be analyzed empirically and the variables to be constructed will have an impact on the type of statistical analysis that can feasibly be conducted. This has led to a number of insights and a related debate on the pros and cons of the so-called 'variable-oriented' *versus* the 'case-based' types of analysis. Some have labeled this controversy in terms of 'quantitative' versus 'qualitative' comparative analysis (O'Donnell, 1979; Ragin, 1987; Rueschemeyer et al., 1992; Keman, 1993c).

We think this latter distinction to be misleading: the debate should not focus on the superiority of number-crunching or nomothetic analysis as opposed to idiographic analysis based on (hi)stories, but rather on what, when and how to compare. Only answering these questions will give us insights into whether or not a Research Design may yield valid and reliable knowledge that allows for *systematic* (i.e. open for external control and replication) and *plausible* (i.e. enlightening for the topic under review and applicable to other related subject-matters) conclusions. If this is not the case, then it is not because numbers or stories lay the foundation for the analysis, but because the link between Research Question and Research Design has not been properly established.

In this section we have discussed a number of items that are vital to developing a proper relationship between a theoretically guided Research Question and a comparatively based Research Design. A number of problems have been mentioned and will be elaborated in the following chapters. These are listed in Table 1.1. All five clusters in Table 1.1 represent choices as regards relating the Research Question to an adequate Research Design. Secondly, the five clusters are steps the researcher must take in order to establish a comprehensive and feasible Research Design.

So, the first step is to assess whether or not we try to find answers to a specific question or a general one. For instance, Lijphart's analysis of the Dutch system (Lijphart, 1975) was based on the explanation of a deviant case (i.e. Consociationalism) within a general theory (of stable democracy). The problem he was confronted with was whether or not his comparative case study allowed for external valid conclusions. Later on he has remedied this problem by using more cases to corroborate his ideas (Lijphart, 1977). Hence, although the Research Question

Table 1.1 *Summary of choices that link the Research Question to the Research Design*

	Research Question	Research Design	Problem or caveat
1	General or Specific	Most similar or Most different	Internal validity and External validity
2	Descriptive Explorative Testing	Truly comparing Selecting cases Causality	Many variables Comparability Galton's problem
3	Units of variation Units of measurement Units of observation	Variables Indicators Cases	External validity Internal validity Selection
4	Qualitative Quantitative	Equivalent information Reliable data	Systematic comparison Ecological fallacy
5	Evaluation Problem-solving Theoretical	Benchmarking Manipulation Comprehensive	Universe of discourse Selection of variables Parsimony

remained the same, a different Research Design was developed to improve the generalizing capacity of his conclusions regarding the occurrence and working of consociationalism as a subtype of stable democracy. This example of Lijphart's work also can serve to illustrate the second step: from a descriptive study the Research Design was changed in the direction of consciously selecting a number of cases to explore the original explanation in order to study its occurrence and working elsewhere. The problem was, however, for Lijphart to enhance the comparability, since the cases selected had less in common than seems admissible. This example on the basis of Lijphart's work (see also: Lijphart, 1984) only shows how important these steps are, for critics of Lijphart pointed out that the internal validity was insufficient because the indicators used as units of measurement were not comparable for the cases involved. In fact, the critics claimed that a qualitative approach should have been pursued rather than a quantitative one.

Step four rests on this choice. For some time a debate has raged around this topic, as mentioned earlier. It is difficult to say which direction, qualitative or quantitative, should be preferred. In fact, this again is a choice the researcher ought to make him/herself depending on the Research Question. Yet, each direction has its hazards, and the problem of data availability *and* its comparability should not be underestimated, regardless of what direction is chosen.

The fifth step can basically be considered as a culmination of the foregoing ones. It draws attention to the question of what purpose the research serves, and with it the plausibility of the results. Actually three possible goals are formulated here which have an impact on the Research Design to be developed. The above-mentioned study of the Dutch Ministry has a typically evaluative purpose: what is the position of the Netherlands *vis-à-vis* neighboring countries in terms of economic performance and social security provisions. Research aiming at problem solving may well be an extension of evaluative oriented research. In the above-mentioned research of the Ministry, it would imply that certain variables are selected (e.g. the level of social security benefits for individuals) and can be compared with those systems where the levels or conditions of receiving benefits are different. In this way, through manipulation of cases, it is possible to compare the effects of a changed condition on the economic performance of a country. This type of research is often used for policy analysis and focuses on discerning the effects of the implementation process, and less on explaining what has happened.

Conversely, if we aim at explanation, the primary goal of the research is then to understand the working of a political and social system by means of modeling politics in a comprehensive but parsimonious fashion. For instance, the debate on 'Does politics matter' had nothing to do with an evaluation of the factual role of politics in democracy, nor was it intended to change this role in reality, but was solely conducted to contest a rival theory, which stated that political decision-making is completely conditioned by non-political factors such as economic development and demographic changes (Castles, 1982; Keman, 1988; Schmidt, 1996). Regardless of the purpose of the study, it is not only crucial to establish a proper relation between the Research Question and Research Design, but also to employ the correct methodology, the proper data, and adequate statistical tools. And that is what this book is about.

1.3 DEVELOPING EMPIRICAL-ANALYTICAL COMPARATIVE ANALYSIS

In Part II of the book we shall introduce and elaborate the tools of comparative *statistical* analysis. In Chapter 4 the issue of organizing data is taken up in conjunction with problems of measurement. In other words, how to transform the proposed theoretical relations as derived from the Research Question into testable propositions. 'Testable' meaning first of all the elaboration of the Research Question in terms of relations between independent (X) and dependent (Y) variables. This important step means the transformation of the Research Question into an empirical investigation by means of the process of operationalization and by means of developing empirical indicators which allows us to start the – often difficult and seemingly tedious – task of collecting the proper data for analysis. Therefore it will be useful for students to become acquainted with how to organize this hunt for the necessary data, including gaining some knowledge of how to find out whether data-sets exist, and if so, how to transform these to suit your own needs.

Equally important is the question of what to do if and when the data do not exist in a ready-for-use format. More often than not one needs to be inventive, if not creative. These activities may imply both the construction of 'proxies' – indicators that are considered to be functionally equivalent to the original concept, e.g. tribal chiefs are functionally equivalent to party elites (Dogan and Pelassy, 1990) – or the reconstruction of existing data into 'composite' variables that resemble the phenomenon under analysis more adequately than do their separate components (Keman, 1993a). Again, like choosing the correct Research Design, this is a delicate and, more often than not, a creative enterprise. Examples of this measurement will be presented in this chapter for the various units of observation as well as the units of measurement utilized.

In Part III of this book we shall demonstrate that there is more than one way to develop variables and indicators of party-behavior. To give an example: political parties perform various functions at the same time, and thus the study of their behavior should be analyzed according to these functions or roles. On the one hand a party is, for instance, striving for maximum influence by acquiring as many offices as possible (like representatives in parliament or ministers in a coalition-government). On the other hand, a party is more often than not the bearer of an ideology by means of a program, which is conducive to its policy-making behavior. When one wishes to analyze the office-seeking potential of a party, one ought to develop indicators that measure its efforts *vis-à-vis* other parties (e.g. campaigning by means of salient issues or communication strategies which help to enhance party identification or personal qualities of party candidates, and thereby enhancing its vote-seeking potential; Budge and Farlie, 1983). On the other hand, however, to analyze the policy-seeking quality of a party we need to know more about its stance on various policies and related issues (e.g. emphasizing state-intervention and welfare statism, or conversely stressing law and order and moral issues like abortion and euthanasia). In this way it is possible not only to compare parties in performing their different functions, but also analyze to what extent parties *per se* do behave differently within a system as well as across systems. Other examples can be given (and will be elaborated in Part III) of party behavior in differently organized democratic systems, such as has been, for instance, distinguished by Lijphart (1984), or the behavior of organized interests, as Schmitter and Lehmbruch (1982) have done.

Another type of comparative investigation in which the importance of a proper operationalization of the Research Question will be highlighted is that in which one shows how existing variables representing public policies and related performances can be developed into proxies and composite indicators (examples of this practice are the Misery Index and fiscal and monetary policy instruments as well as functional expenditures by state agencies; Castles, 1987; Keman, 1993a; Lane and Ersson, 1990). These procedures are vital in order to be able to construct a proper data-set on the basis of the empirical model representing the relation between Research Question and Research Design. Further chapters of Part II will present the statistical techniques available to describe the model in empirical terms (Chapter 5) and how to find out which answers appear adequate to the Research Question posed (in Chapter 6).

This is what is meant by explanations in social and political sciences: how can we account for the variation found in the relationship between X and Y. We shall offer various examples of explanatory analysis and suggest to what extent conclusions can be drawn on the basis of generalizations across the cases studied, be that cross-sectionally, over time, or both.

Finally, we shall discuss in Part III the topic of a 'truly' comparative analysis: instead of endeavoring to explain the 'universe of discourse' *per se*, the mode of explanation is directed to test the theoretical relations as such. In other words: how to develop and test a theory empirically rather than to confirm or falsify a theory as applied to reality. Przeworski and Teune (1970) attempt to make this difference clear by suggesting that 'variables replace proper names' and are meant to explain empirical phenomena by concepts independent from their empirical origins. This step from descriptive comparisons of so-called 'closed' or 'given' sets of cases (e.g. west European Democracies, which is given by the fact that inclusion is geographically determined, or the study of a certain type of party – like Christian Democracy – which is by definition a closed set), however useful and important they may be, to a 'truly comparative' research and analysis, is a crucial one if one wishes to offer explanatory results on the basis of a comparative approach.

Yet, one should be aware of the caveats present and the pitfalls lurking, as we are dealing with social reality and related political action. This implies that the relationship between theory (Research Question) and empirical analysis (Research Design) is not only dynamic, but also that it can only produce 'middle-range' theories. The term *middle-range* indicates here the situation that only in a perfect world could the results of the comparative inquiry be considered as an absolute truth for all times and situations. Of course, this cannot be the case. However, one should always aim at comprehensively analyzed results, which allow for valid and plausible answers. This is superior to 'one-shot' analyses. In other words: we should strive for a result which is optimal in terms of 'true' and 'plausible' knowledge, on the one hand, as well as being valid and applicable to the widest 'universe of discourse' that can be identified as relevant with respect to the Research Question asked and the Research Design applied, on the other.

An example of such an attempt is found in the analysis of the interactions between democratic institutions and political actors and their patterned reactions to societal developments across relevant cases. This type of analysis underlies the structure of Part III (but see also: Budge and Keman, 1990; Castles, 1993; Klingemann et al., 1994; Keman, 1997). In Part III we also turn to what partially could be labeled as the manual to do your own research. We shall then be applying what has been put forward in Part I and II. To this end we take as a point of departure one of the best-known (and often disputed on various grounds) comparative models used in political science: the input–throughput–output model, or the empirical elaboration of the political systems approach (Almond et al., 1993; Lane and Ersson, 1994b: Chapter 1).

This general model, introduced by Easton (1965), places the *polity* (the political-institutional framework of any society) in a dynamic context. The political system receives 'inputs' from its environment (i.e. society) in the form of demands (e.g. issues and conditions that are considered to influence societal development) or support (e.g. allegiance to the leaders, and acceptance of the existing rules of the game by the population). These inputs are subsequently handled by means of the conversion process of the system (e.g. decision-making by means of democratic procedures or binding regulation through a political elite or bureaucracy), resulting in 'outputs' (public actions and expenditures). Eventually, so the argument goes, the *performances*, or effects of the outputs, are monitored back by an information feedback loop, affecting the ensuing societal demands and support for the political system. It is obvious that this model of politics and society can be formulated in terms of *politics* (issue competition and competing preferences for action = input), *polity* (relating inputs to outputs by means of decision-making = throughput) and *policy* (public action by means of regulation and provisions = output).

In essence the model tries to capture the dynamic survival and functional quality of a political order and its public effects on society. Although criticized for its underlying teleological and potentially conservative bias (the theoretical mechanism would only allow for equilibrium situations and not for fundamental change or the deterioration of the existing system), one may well apply this model, if one allows for the view that there is room for transition and adaptation of parts of any system (or even: the more or less radical replacement of a political order, as, for instance, has occurred in post-colonial systems and the communist world as well as in European democracies like Belgium and Italy). Whatever way one looks at this theoretical problem, our concern here is exactly to view it as an empirical-analytical problem that is well fitted for comparative inquiry (Bingham Powell, 1982; Keman, 1997).

In Chapters 7 to 9 of Part III we shall therefore endeavor to demonstrate how to formulate Research Questions and related Research Designs with regard to systems theory, and put them to the test. The main *Research Question* raised is then: to what extent do change and persistence within and between political systems occur, and with what effect on society? We study this by investigating the behavior of political actors operating within the existing 'rules of the game'. In addition we ask: to what extent are the resulting outcomes of the political decision-making and related public policy-making conducive to equilibria or tend to become unstable?

To this end we shall focus explicitly on democratic systems, by means of the 'democratic chain of popular control and political command' (Keman, 1997). Yet, it should be noted that the principal aim of these exercises is not to confirm or to disprove the empirical quality of systems theory, but rather to make the student familiar with doing comparative research in practice. In the last part of this volume we shall therefore conclude with our ideas on why, when and how the comparative approach is not only useful to investigate a variety of theory-driven questions, but also provides an invaluable set of tools for scientific inquiry into the real world and which may well be conducive to the development of 'truly' comparative models of that world. Hence, the world must be decomposed first, before we can start – on the basis of valid and plausible, or convincing, findings – to *integrate* the various answers to Research Questions posed into genuine models that are based on 'truly' comparative knowledge, i.e. that corroborates our intuitions by means of evidence. Such knowledge can be acquired by any student of social and political sciences and can be applied by her or him if, and only if, he or she is conscious of the steps to be taken in the process of developing the relationship between question and answer on the basis of an adequate Research Design and employing the correct statistical tools and methods.

1.4 HOW YOU CAN USE THE BOOK

This book consists of three parts which represent in our view the basic stages of any empirical-analytical research driven by theory in political and social sciences. As the book is written to serve as a course-book for undergraduates, we feel that they should go through the whole text, chapter by chapter. In each chapter there is an introduction to its contents, and in the end matter there is a list of the main topics covered, which may help both teacher and student to find information she or he needs (for instance, whilst doing research). In addition, each chapter contains examples which are taken from existing comparative research that has been published elsewhere and is at least partially based on data that is accessible (provided by us, or we specify where to obtain it). Other students willing to use the comparative approach in their (postgraduate) research may wish to skip parts of the book. Apart from the topics lists in the endmatter of each chapter, which can be used to find the information needed quickly, we would advise postgraduate and other students to read at any rate Chapter 3 of Part I, Chapters 5 and 6 of Part II, and the final Part of the book as a whole.

In Part I we present our own arguments concerning the comparative approach: namely that any empirical research needs to be theory-driven and must be formulated in a well-elaborated Research Design. Chapter 6 is essential reading for those wishing to understand the use of advanced statistics in order to conduct explanatory analysis (including its caveats and pitfalls!). The final part can be seen as our attempt to pull together the threads of our way of doing comparative research and will be interesting for any reader, whether a freshman or an advanced student of comparative politics and sociology.

Part II can also be used independently for anyone who wishes to 'catch up' with the statistical techniques whilst conducting research. Part III can also be used separately and will be extremely useful for those who are investigating the dynamic and interactive processes of politics and society. Without claiming that this approach and its elaboration is the one and only way to do it, we feel that it offers a valuable 'springboard' to judging comparative information with which you are confronted, or to shape your own theory-inspired Research Design in such a way that it leads to convincing results.

1.5 ENDMATTER

Topics highlighted

- Comparing as a tool for political and social scientists to test theories.
- The 'art of comparing' as a theory-driven method for empirical analytical research.
- The types of explanation and the methodology required in relating Research Questions to Research Designs.
- The meaning of cases and variables in comparative empirical research.
- Actor-, Institution-, Performance and systems theory as a descriptive analytical model of politics in society.
- How to use this book on the comparative approach, for different types of students.

Questions

- Why is the 'art of comparing' not only useful but also a necessary part of the toolkit of any social scientist?
- Try to elaborate whether or not the rules of internal or external validity are violated in the following statements:
  1. Political parties and social movements are functional equivalents and can therefore be compared throughout the whole world.
  2. The development of welfare states must be researched cross-nationally.
  3. Party government in whatever political system provides a representative basis for the analysis of the process of government formation.
- Is there a difference between a theoretical proposition and a Research Question? Whatever your answer is, give an example of a proposition and a Question to support your view.

Exercises

If you look up Volume 31: 1–2 (1997) of the *European Journal of Political Research* in your library, you can try to answer the following questions:

1. Reproduce by means of a 'diagram' the Research Design as described by Geoffrey Roberts on pp. 100–1. Ask yourself: what are the *Units of Variation*

and what are the *Units of Observation* (for this, see also: Castles and McKinley, pp. 102–6 in the same volume).
2 Ask the same question by using pp. 159–66 of the same volume in EJPR. However, focus now on the *Units of Measurement*.
3 Now turn to pp. 83–93 of the same volume and describe the *Unit of Observation*, which is central here and is related to a crucial *Unit of Variation*. To what is it crucial? (explain!).

Further reading

- *General*: Mair, 1996b; Wiarda, 1991; Lane and Ersson, 1994a.
- *Specific*: Przeworski and Teune, 1970; Ragin and Becker, 1992; Keman, 1997.

2
The comparative approach: theory and method

CONTENTS

2.1 INTRODUCTION

In this chapter we shall elaborate on the essentials of the 'art of comparing' by discussing the relation between theory and method in the comparative approach. In order to clarify this point of view, we shall first discuss some of the existing ideas about what the comparative approach is in terms of a scientific undertaking (Section 2.2). In addition, in Section 2.3 we shall argue that comparativists should focus on the core subject and processes under review, stressing the inevitable choice between middle-range versus general theories. In this section we shall delve into the matter of whether or not one can distinguish in the comparative approach a 'core subject' of its own, and if so, whether or not this may lead to a theory. In

Section 2.4 we shall enter into the important topic of the comparative approach, i.e. the comparative method and its implications for a 'proper' Research Design. The central argument will be that a coherent framework of theoretical references and a corresponding logic of inquiry are required. If it is not possible to do this, the comparative approach will still remain a valuable asset to political and social science, yet any claim of being a 'scientific' approach should then be put to rest (Mayer, 1989; Keman, 1993a).

There have been several attempts to delineate the boundaries of the comparative approach, yet there is little agreement at present on its distinctiveness. Essentially, one could argue that there exist three different ways of defining the comparative approach: firstly, those who distinguish it from other approaches to political and social science by referring to certain concepts employed which can only be properly understood by means of comparative analysis; secondly, those who take as a point of departure the central features of, for instance, the political process which can be analyzed for all social systems; finally, there are many who define the comparative approach by means of its method: i.e. the art of comparing (Mair, 1996a: 310–12).

Although the last way of delineating the comparative approach is purely methodological, it is the most prevalent one and not the worst description. However, we do not wholly concur with this view, for it would mean that the domain of social science is defined by its method, rather than by its *core subject*, i.e. the study of politics and society, which is then, of course, still in want of a definition itself. Hence, we do not share the idea that a discipline can be defined by its mode of analysis, which is supposed to advance our knowledge of the core subject underlying the discipline. In this chapter we shall therefore demonstrate what the comparative approach can add to the social sciences by means of its use of attributes of macro-social units in explanatory statements (Ragin, 1987: 5). This calls for an elaboration of the core subject in terms of an identifiable object of study and how this relates to various types of comparative analysis. The term core subject denotes a systemic definition of the central features of what we wish to study in reality (here: the relations between politics and society). Hence, it defines the system as well as its components in a heuristic way.

In addition, a second concern will be to develop ideas about theory in connection with comparative methodology that is capable of explaining and interpreting multi-level variations of the core subject (the so-called micro–macro linkage). In social sciences, and in particular if we are investigating relationships on the level of society and politics, we are inevitably confronted with the question of how to combine theories that are conceptualized on the aggregated level of social and political action with the restriction of observing real-world phenomena that are either individuals or constructs, i.e. assuming that a 'thing' can act (for instance, 'parliament decides' or a 'group operates'). Whilst constructing theories one may assume that collectives are actors and that there are rules (in whatever way defined) that 'exist'. In terms of empirical observations one must subsequently make clear whether or not these entities are the result of individuals or not. This epistemological problem refers to 'methodological individualism' (micro-level) on the one hand, and to 'sociological realism' (macro-level) on the other. In this book we do not claim to make a final choice for either of these assumptions. Yet, we contend that *non*-individual observations can and will be useful in social science (see for a further discussion: Stinchcombe, 1968; Giddens, 1971; Smelser, 1976; Ragin, 1987; Mayer, 1989; Braun, 1995; Keman, 1998).

A final concern is a resultant of the preceding ones and involves scrutinizing existing logics of comparative inquiry to account for the observed variation by means of testing empirical hypotheses, thereby either corroborating or falsifying them (Lijphart, 1975: 159; Mayer, 1972; Przeworski and Teune, 1970). Hence we explicitly aim at the relation between proposition and empirical evidence and consider that as the cornerstone of social science. This implies the use of *positive* theory as a stepping stone to advancing our knowledge of politics and society. The central feature of this approach to social science is embedded throughout this book as the relationship between Research Question, Research Design and – empirical – quantitative data-analysis on the basis of statistics.

All these concerns are in themselves worthy of serious discussion and deliberation, yet the main issue at hand is that the comparative approach lacks coherence in terms of a set of theoretical references and related logics of inquiry. In short, this chapter is not only an attempt to delineate the comparative approach, as such, but most of all must be seen as an argument to relate theory and method in order to gain a viable and feasible approach to explaining political and social processes – an argument that will be central throughout this book.

2.2 DELINEATING THE COMPARATIVE APPROACH: SCOPE OF COMPARISON AND RESEARCH QUESTIONS

The comparative approach has grown out of the wish to know more about one's own social system by comparing it with others. In particular, it was believed that knowledge about the institutional framework of society would not only help to understand the peculiar types of interaction among its members, but would also enable one to draw conclusions about the merits and disadvantages of social interaction. However, this approach was dominated by the idea that supplying comparable information on the structure and working of a political and social system *in toto* would be sufficient to further knowledge and that the analysis should therefore remain of a descriptive nature based on facts. For example, James Bryce (1929) stated his task as a comparativist as follows:

> What I desire is, not to impress upon my readers views of my own, but to supply them with facts, and (so far as I can) with explanations of facts, on which they can reflect and from which they can draw their own conclusions. (p. ix)

This empiricist approach – 'it is facts that are needed: facts, facts, and facts. When facts are supplied, each of us can try to reason from them' (Bryce, 1929: 13) – lost its appeal after the Second World War when a more analytical perspective was introduced (Blondel, 1981: 173–8). A good example of this change is offered by Roy Macridis (1955), who argues strongly in favor of a more 'scientific' approach to politics in general and considers the comparative approach as the most promising, if not revolutionary, way to go:

> Comparative analysis is an integral part of the study of politics. The comparative study suggests immediately the laboratory of a scientist. It provides us with the opportunity to discuss specific phenomena in the light of different historical and social backgrounds. It suggests variables of a rather complex order that can be dissociated from the cultural background and studied comparatively. . . . The comparative study of politics is beginning only now to enter a new stage, which reflects in essence the progressive systematic orientation in the study of politics. It is beginning to assume a central role in empirically oriented study. (Macridis, 1955: 1–3)

In sum, Macridis believed that the comparative approach as a distinctive field within political science, as he saw it, would be able to bridge the growing discrepancy between theory and the empirically based study of politics in society. This so-called 'revolution' of political science did not materialize and became a 'stalled revolution' (Mayer, 1989: 20), being reduced to a 'movement' and not a distinctive approach within political science. Gabriel Almond contended that the comparative approach has indeed revolutionized political science, but that this development should be considered as a stage in the development of political science. He concludes:

> It is difficult to see therefore, that comparative politics has a long-run future as a sub-discipline of political science. Rather, it would appear that, like the political behavior movement which preceded it, its promises lies in enriching the discipline of political science as a whole. (Almond, 1968: 336)

Almond's 'developmental' explanation, of course, would mean an integration of the comparative movement into political and social science. His view is not wholly shared by all of his contemporaries such as Macridis, Rokkan, Daalder and Verba (compare: Daalder, 1993). Although they are critical with respect to the development of comparative politics as a distinctive field within political science, they instead stress the fact that the 'stalled revolution' might be seen as the paradoxical result of the growth of comparative research. It is remarkable to note that those who assess the 'state of the art' in comparative politics choose either to view it in an evolutionary or 'positivitist' way, or to see it as one method among others (see: Mair, 1996a: 309–35).

For example, Holt and Turner represent the evolutionary, or a 'positivist' view. In the early 1970s they stressed the pre-paradigmatic situation and sought a solution in 'scientism' in order to move beyond heuristic schemata (Holt and Turner, 1970: 70). Hence the future of the comparative approach to political science depended, according to them (and many others; e.g. Merritt and Rokkan, 1966; Lasswell, 1968; Mayer, 1972), by and large on the development of a proper methodology and genuinely comparable data collections.

Clearly the lack of a theoretical framework, and the continuing debate on both the method and the principal concepts to be used, appear to be most disturbing. This is not necessarily a consequence of using different approaches, or of employing a wide variety of concepts alone (see for this: Sartori, 1970). However, such a pluralistic attitude precisely produces a situation that most protagonists of this field wish to avoid. For this 'live-and-let-live' attitude implies an abandonment of the search for a more coherent approach to comparative politics and, in fact, robs it of any substantial meaning and theoretical rigor. It will only lead to sacrificing substance to method, or to raising only those questions that can be empirically answered, but do not relate to the critical problems of mankind (see also: Mayer, 1989: 21; Castles, 1987: 222). It is also unproductive to focus on partial problems within the field, such as choosing the correct method, selecting the right concepts, and finding the proper data. Yet, we do think that by solving the methodological issues we will strengthen the comparative approach to understanding social reality. To this end we propose the following guidelines to define the comparative approach as a separate way of analyzing and explaining social and political reality:

1 Describe the core subject of comparative inquiry. In other words, formulate the question of what exactly is to be explained and how we recognize a need for comparison – that is: what are the essential systemic features?
2 Develop a view on the theoretical concepts that can 'travel' comparatively as well as measuring what is intended (internal validity) and possessing a unifying capacity for explaining political and social processes in general (external validity).
3 Discuss the logic of the comparative method as a means to a goal, rather than as an end in itself. In other words, which instrument best fits the Research Questions to be answered by means of what type of Research Design?

What is the core subject of an inquiry depends by and large on the definition of political science that is used (see, e.g.: Dahl, 1963; Weber, 1972; Blondel, 1981). Blondel, for instance, argues that politics concerns primarily action-related outcomes (e.g. public policy), whereas Dahl focuses on the wielding of power in decision-making situations, and Weber rather sees politics as a form of political action with societal consequences. The core subject is thus different in essence: in the examples used here it concerns Public Policy – Decisions – Behavior. All these subjects can be operationalized and compared in reality. Without comparison we cannot decide whether or not the subject matter as defined is indeed essential, nor why this is the case within social systems.

The second question we raised was the requirement for specification as well as its comparability *per se*. If we are to study public policy, or decision-making processes, or – as Weber puts forward – the role of leadership in society, we must delineate *what* aspects we think to be most important and how they emerge in reality. In other words: in what way do observations of reality relate to contents under varying conditions? This always implies an uneasy trade-off between reliability and validity (the more specific the operationalization, the more reliable the information, yet the less valid in different contexts and vice versa; this issue will be elaborated more fully in Chapter 3). For example, one cannot study the role of democratic parties in non-democracies. Yet, some may argue that one can do so if one considers concepts in terms of 'functional equivalents', like organized interests in Latin-America, or tribal chieftains in Sub-Saharan Africa (see for this: Dogan and Pelassy, 1990; Macridis and Burg, 1991; Almond et al., 1993).

This is, of course, a rather ambitious agenda, but if we do not at least attempt to investigate the possibilities of new directions in comparative research to journey toward a more or less integrated and distinctive approach within political and social science, we cannot expect to develop adequate and meaningful insights about the development and use of its methodology. Yet, at the same time, we wish to uphold the original motives and intentions of comparativists to develop this approach to political and social science to enhance its rigor and claim as a 'science'. Whatever today's skepticism of the erstwhile protagonists may be, it is worthwhile to investigate thoroughly the possibilities of the comparative approach to politics and society. For, as Mair correctly observes (Mair, 1996a), comparativists often tend to overemphasize the method of research and are primarily concerned with developing rules and standards about how comparative research should be carried out, including the levels of analysis at which the comparative analysis operates, and the limits and possibilities of comparison itself. Precisely because the *art* of comparing is in itself so instinctive to both scientific and popular observers, this element – i.e. its methodology – is all too often assumed to be unproblematic and hence is overlooked or even neglected. And it is this neglect, in turn, which more often than not lies at the root of the more severe problems in the cumulation of research, on the one hand, and in theory building and theory testing, on the other. Let us therefore now turn to the next point on the agenda: the description of the comparative approach as an important instrument of researching the relationship between politics and society.

2.3 COMPARATIVE RESEARCH AND THE RELATION BETWEEN POLITICS AND SOCIETY

Comparative political and social research is generally defined in two ways: either on the basis of its supposed core subject, which is almost always defined at the level of political and social *systems* (Kalleberg, 1966; Wallerstein, 1974; Dogan and Pelassy, 1990), or by means of descriptive features that claim to enhance knowledge about politics and society as a *process* (e.g.: Apter and Andrain, 1972; Roberts, 1978; Macridis and Burg, 1991; Almond et al., 1993). These descriptions are generally considered to differentiate the comparative approach from other approaches within political and social science. Although it is a useful starting point, it is not sufficient. Some authors are more specific in their description and add to this general point of departure that the comparative approach to political and social science concerns societies and their political systems (Wiarda, 1991; Hague et al., 1992), the study of geographic areas, or specific elements of social and political processes (e.g. parties, policies, modernization, behavior, etc.; see for this: Blondel, 1981; Dierkes et al., 1987; van der Eijk, 1993). Finally, some authors deliver a more or less exhaustive definition in which 'the comparative study of political phenomena against the background of cultural, sociological and economic features of different societies' is the focus of comparative political science (Berg-Schlosser and Müller-Rommel, 1987; Lane and Ersson, 1994b).

All these descriptions may be useful up to a point, but they do not help to mark off the field, and they require greater specification. The comparative approach must be elaborated in terms of its theoretical design and its research strategy on the basis of a goal-oriented point of reference, i.e. what exactly is to be explained. A way of accomplishing this is to argue for a more refined concept of 'politics and society' and develop concepts that 'travel' – i.e. are truly comparative – and can thus be related to the political process in various societies (Dogan and Pelassy, 1990; Collier, 1993). In addition, a set of rules must be developed that direct the research strategy, aiming at explanations rather than at a complete description of political phenomena by comparing them across systems, through time, or cross-nationally. At this point most comparativists stop elaborating their approach and start investigating – often, however, without realizing that theory and method are mutually interdependent (Keman, 1993c).

In contrast, the comparative approach should be seen as an approach that aims at explaining processes in a society by means of a (meta-) theoretical framework of reference and where explanations are validated by comparing other units of analysis or units of variation (see also: Roberts, 1978; Przeworski, 1987; Ragin, 1987; Castles, 1989). The goal of comparative analysis is to explain those 'puzzles' which cannot be studied without comparing and are derived from logical reasoning. Hence, there can be no comparative research without an extensive theoretical argument underlying it, nor without a methodologically adequate Research Design to undertake it. An example may help here to make this important point clear. Suppose we wish to know more about the relationship between economic development and the rise of the welfare state, then it depends on the Research Question (RQ) asked which type of Research Design (RD) will be helpful in explaining the relation. If the RQ is: 'Is industrialization promoting welfare policy-making?', then one can elaborate this by studying one (or a few) systems through time. The *units of variation* may be level of industrialization and the contents of welfare-related policy-formation, and the units of observation may be different time periods – e.g. years – so that one is assessing change over time. This may well enhance the internal validation of the explanation (it is 'true' for what has been studied). This is what Lijphart (1971) labels as the 'Comparative Method'. Yet this is a somewhat misleading label. What is meant is that one employs a universe of discourse for which the cases are comparable with respect to their political and social context (i.e. they appear to be more similar than all other countries). Apart from the epistemological problems of this approach (see: Mayer, 1972; Przeworski, 1987), there is the statistical problem of having too few cases and too many variables (we shall return to this in the next chapter). That is to say: other than 'thick description', such an approach only yields randomly distributed variation leading up to 'trivial' knowledge. The RD tends then to be somewhere between the positions (1) and (4) in Figure 2.1. Conversely, if one wishes to know whether or not the degree of industrialization brings about the development of welfare statism, one has to compare more cases simultaneously (i.e. not necessarily at the same point of time!). This is position (3) in Figure 2.1. However, if the RQ is to what extent the welfare state is the result of economic growth, one must take into account both time and space in order to reach viable conclusions, i.e. position (5) in Figure 2.1. Hence, it is the comparison as such that counts but with respect to the answers given, it is the (theoretical) argument that directs the type and necessity of comparison as is illustrated by means of Figure 2.1.

If one examines the literature in the major political science journals (e.g. the *American Political Science Review, Comparative Studies*, or the *European Journal for Political Research*), one can find numerous examples of how a Research Question is indeed translated into a Research Design in which each of the possibilities has been chosen. For instance, the study of Dutch consociationalism is a one case/time series RD ((2) in Figure 2.1), whereas Lijphart's study of democracies (Lijphart, 1984) is a cross-sectional analysis of *all* relevant cases (4). Many studies on welfare states more often than not use a RD in which *all* relevant cases are included and are studied over time albeit for a few period-points only ((3); see e.g.: Castles, 1982; Keman, 1988; Esping-Andersen, 1990). The analysis of the working of coalition governments (see: Laver and Schofield, 1990; Budge and Keman, 1990) is often done by combining as many relevant cases as possible and for as many points in time as feasible. This is what is often called a pooled time series RD (5). In fact, the last example also demonstrates that we are not only interested in countries as cases, but – depending on the RQ – on elements central

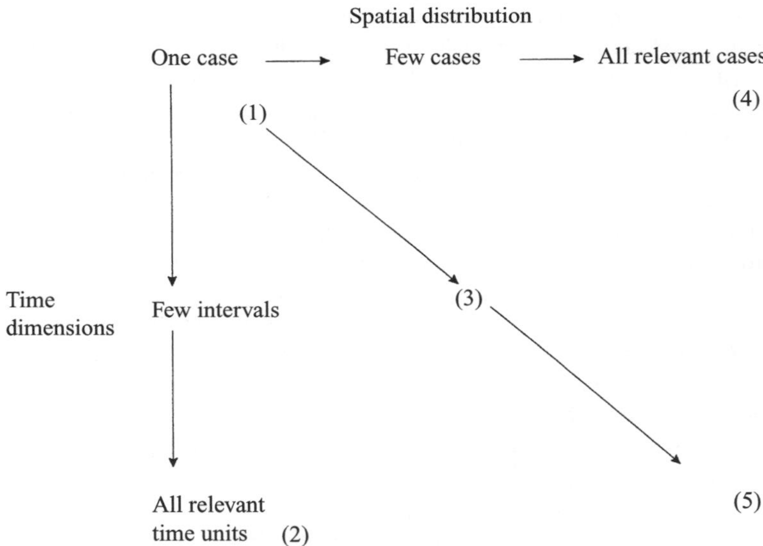

Figure 2.1 *Selecting the number of comparable cases and variables with respect to the Research Question: (1) case study (at one time point); (2) time series (one case over time); (3) closed universe (relevant cases in relevant periods); (4) cross-section (all cases at one time point); (5) pooled analysis (maximizing cases across time and space). NB: these terms are explained in depth in the following chapters*

to the political system, such as: governments, parties, interest groups, voters, institutions and so on. In these instances the number of cases will often be much larger, if and when all relevant cases are included.

The options for choice as depicted here are thus not free. On the contrary, if industrialization is seen as a process it must be investigated over time in order to answer the question of whether this process results in societal change (here) in terms of welfare statism. A good example of employing this type of comparison can be found in the analysis of west European welfare states published in 1981 by Flora and Heidenheimer. Various countries were analyzed from 1848 (when most European states became more or less constitutional liberal democracies) until the present. In effect, the actual number of countries was not important but the number of years was (i.e. situation (2) in Figure 2.1). By comparing the rates of change with the rate of democratization it became possible to demonstrate when and under which conditions the welfare state developed. Studies by Rueschemeyer (1992, ch. 1 in Rueschemeyer et al., 1992) and Lane and Ersson (1990) show respectively RDs of types (4) and (5) in Figure 2.1. Rueschemeyer tried to find out whether or not levels of industrialization were systematically related to levels of welfare expenditures irrespective of when these levels of development coincided. By doing this he was able to show that political variables were subsequently relevant. Lane and Ersson, on the other hand, analyzed whether or not economic growth, when a certain level had been reached, led to the establishment of a welfare state – hence whether or not economic growth was conditional for welfare state development.

In most discussions of the comparative approach, however, it appears that both theoretical and methodological aspects are divorced, or – at least – treated separately. For example, Ragin (1987) and Przeworski (1987) emphasize predominantly the methodological aspects of the art of comparison as a 'logic of inquiry', which is often underdeveloped or incompletely elaborated. At the same time these authors argue their case by means of examples that are seemingly picked at random. Worse even, it seems that some of the examples are selected to demonstrate the tenability of their view. Theoretical progress and explanatory results appear then to emanate from their 'logic' (see: Przeworski, 1987: 45ff; Ragin, 1987: 125ff). Yet, the comparative analysis of the political process must be instead founded *a priori* in theory and then related to the best fitting 'logic of inquiry', or in our terms: a proper Research Design.

Another example of such a separation of theory and method can be found in the study of electoral behavior. This vital part of the political process can be explained fairly well on the basis of deductive reasoning. To validate its micro-level-founded hypotheses regarding individual behavior a comparative Research Design is not necessary. However, electoral behavior or party behavior that is explained by means of the working of electoral systems, features of a party system, or the existing rules of government formation, is in need of a comparative analysis by means of examining the variation in the political properties on both the micro- and macro-level (see, for example: Sartori, 1976; Bogdanor and Butler, 1983; Lijphart, 1984; Budge and Keman, 1990).

This conclusion seems to hold for other types of cross-national research too: since the 1970s the study of 'electoral volatility' in western Europe gained momentum, when it appeared that the division of party systems and the structure of voting patterns was less stabilized than originally assumed (Daalder and Mair, 1983; Crewe and Denver, 1985). It is interesting to note (with the help of hindsight) that most analyses were, in fact, based on country-based descriptions with little comparative information. What was lacking was a *truly* comparative set of theoretical references concerning – in this case – the *explicandum*, i.e. 'political stability', that at the same time are consciously linked to a comparable set of operational terms (see: Bartolini and Mair, 1990: 35–46). In other words: if the *explicandum* is not equal to a system *per se*, but can be considered a subsystem, like governments or electoral results obviously are, we must reflect on the question of whether or not the Research Question is formulated to explain national government or a nation's electoral volatility, or to explain the phenomenon of government functioning or electoral change as such. In the former instance, nations are compared (= inter-national); in the latter case, intra-systemic phenomena are compared (= cross-national; e.g. all governments in all democratic countries after the Second World War; see: Budge and Keman, 1990; or all elections since universal suffrage was in place: in one country this would mean after the First World War, in another after the Second World War; see: Bartolini and Mair, 1990).

The same observation can thus be made with respect to the study of government formation. On the one hand, there are collections of country-studies (more often than not, we must add, developed on a shared list of elements present in each case description; e.g. Pridham, 1986) that stress the idiosyncratic nature of a country's political process, rather than the communality of the development of government for a nation as such. On the other hand, a development can be observed with respect to the politics of coalition-building in which an underlying theoretical argument has been developed that directs the research, where countries are not the principal focus but a collection of comparable cases that show variation concerning what is to be explained (e.g. Laver and Schofield, 1990; Budge and Keman, 1990). Other examples could be mentioned to support this point regarding the relation between theory and method in comparative politics (such as the comparative research into the relation between 'politics and policy'; see: Dierkes et al., 1987; Castles, 1989; Schmidt, 1996; Keman, 1997). Yet, the principal message is that much of the research that is labeled as comparative, either lacks theoretical foundation of *what* mechanisms in various systems have *why* such mechanisms in common or not, or is based on a Research Design that is not comparative but is rather a collection of information about a number of systems. The main lesson that can be drawn from the examples listed here as an elaboration of Figure 2.1 is that the Research Question *per se* directs the Research Design in terms of the central units of variation (like governments, elections, welfare statism, etc.) which imply the theoretical relationships under review and direct as well the units of observation (like years if change is focused upon or all parliamentary governments across the whole universe of discourse if it concerns a cross-sectional design). These choices or decisions – made by the researcher – also dictate, then, the units of measurement, or values, that make up the total number of cases. Given this line of reasoning, which is essential to our approach to comparative research, it is essential, therefore, to develop a theoretical perspective in order to relate systematically the Research Question to possible Research Designs and not simply to gather information about a lot of cases, which are more often than not included for pragmatic reasons.

2.4 MODES OF EXPLANATION BY MEANS OF COMPARATIVE ANALYSIS: THE NEED TO CONTROL THE CONTEXT

Usually the comparative approach to politics and society is defined both by its substance (the study of a plurality of societies or systems, i.e. the cases under review) and by its method (e.g. cross- and inter-national, comparable cases, longitudinal, etc.; see: Lijphart, 1975; see also Figure 2.1). Such a circumscription undermines the necessary link between theory and method as well as the distinctiveness of the comparative approach in terms of what, when and how to compare. Hence, if the comparative approach is indeed distinctive from other approaches in political science in its use, it is only in terms of a combination of theory and method. Theory here equals the propositions concerning the explanation of a relationship between the 'core subject' in social reality and the societal developments that are (seen to be) affected by it. Method is then the most appropriate way to investigate the proposed relationships empirically. As we have stated before, comparing as such is one of the common tenets underlying much if not all research in the social sciences. Yet, one needs to realize all the time that this refers to the 'logic' of systematically finding answers to questions about the complexities of reality. This logic has a long history and was described by John Stuart Mill (1872) as the *methods of agreement and difference* (see also: Janoski and Hicks, 1994: Ch. 1). Comparison is then an instrument to verify or falsify relationships between two phenomena. Yet, here in this book we consider the logic as an integral part of the comparative approach by stressing the crucial nature of the link between the Research Question, on the one hand, and the Research Design, on the other.

In this book we shall therefore confine ourselves to discussing and applying the comparative approach in these circumstances where it is deemed useful or essential. We must first indicate what the core subject is, before we can establish whether or not the comparative method is useful. Hence, the Research Question must be

Table 2.1 *Possible relations between Research Question and Research Design*

Area addressed by theory and Research Question	Method and Research Design	
	Truly comparative	**Implicit comparison**
Politics	1	2
Society	3	4

Note: *Truly comparative* simply means: striving for a systematic and controlled Research Design in which the comparison is crucial for answering the Research Question. *Implicit comparison* indicates the comparative method is not necessary regarding the Research Design, nor is it seen as constitutive for answering the Research Question.
(Adapted from: Mair, 1996b: 3).
The numbers are nominal, to identify the cells (i.e. four options, discussed in the text).

inspected first to decide whether or not it contains political and societal aspects which must be compared in order to establish theoretical relationships that can be observed in reality. If and when this is the case we need to establish the correct Research Design in order to be able to reach valid and plausible conclusions.

Dependent on the Research Question, it is possible to decide whether or not the core subject, i.e. politics and/or society, is in need of a comparative Research Design. If and when one strives for analytical-empirically founded knowledge – as is our point of departure – we assume that it makes a difference whether one investigates a phenomenon (related to the core subject) within or between societies. The only question is whether or not it should be done comparatively. For example, if one studies party-behavior in a country, then one is still comparing parties, unless one is only interested in pure description. The same line of reasoning applies to specific groups or collectives in a society. In short, an implicit comparison may be useful and plausible under certain circumstances, yet one is not able to conclude why the phenomenon under study is behaving or changing, other than by means of explicit or true comparison, i.e. in cells 1 and 3 in Table 2.1.

As Sartori (1990: 244–5) stresses, we need to compare in order to control the observed units of variation or the variables that make up the theoretical relationship. In fact, what the researcher is attempting, is to identify the necessary and sufficient conditions under which the relationship occurs in reality. In fact this would entail that it may be assumed by the researcher that all other things, or conditions, are equal except for the relationship under empirical review. This is what we call the *Ceteris Paribus* clause. The more 'true' the comparison, i.e. the more explicitly the relationship between the Research Question and Research Design is of a comparative nature, the more positive the analytical results will be. If we look, for instance, at the relationship between 'class society' and the emergence of 'welfare states', the relationship is positive if we examine the developments in the UK and Sweden and in New Zealand and Australia (Castles, 1978, 1985). Yet, the answer could be negative to this Research Question if we focus instead on the Netherlands, Germany and Italy (Van Kersbergen, 1995) where the role of religion used to be the central focus of political behavior. Hence, only when we take into account as many relevant and concurrent cases as is possible can we reach a viable and plausible conclusion concerning socio-economic divisions in society and related consequences in terms of welfare regulation. Similarly, the question whether or not economic developments are also dependent on types of democratic governance and interest intermediation cannot be fully answered by studying one country, nor – like Olson (1982) did – by comparing only the states within the USA. The basic message, contained in Table 2.1, is thus that – dependent on the definition of the core subject of investigation – the degree of control of the environment or contextual features necessary to reach sound conclusions can be decided upon. From this point of view, it appears reasonable to conclude – as Dalton (1991) does – that it is almost impossible to conceive of serious explanatory work in political and social science that is not at least implicitly comparative.

Janoski and Hicks (1994: Ch. 1), for instance, point correctly to the distinction between *internal* and *external* analysis in the social sciences. Both types are considered as important for comparative research. Internal analysis refers to the knowledge necessary to understand the cases under review *per se*, whereas external analysis is the analysis of the agreement or differences *between* cases. As we shall see later on, both types of analysis are useful for: (1) selecting the proper Research Design; (2) evaluating the reliability and validity of the data gathered. Hence, from the perspective that the comparative approach is a crucial one in political and social science, depending on the definition of the core subject and Research Question asked (i.e. cells 1 and 3 in Table 2.1) one must also take into account that knowledge of the cases as such, which make up the universe of discourse, is a vital prerequisite for accomplishing good comparative types of analysis. Hence, internal types of comparisons can be useful in carrying out external analysis of the same phenomenon.

The comparative approach to political science is thus not by itself exclusive, but if we follow the idea that concepts derived from theories about the real world need to be investigated by means of controlling variation as observed in the real world, we cannot abstain from this approach (Lijphart, 1971; Smelser, 1976; Mayer, 1989; Sartori, 1991). Actually, we could go even further by saying that the comparative approach is the fundamental point of departure for most theories that figure in political and social science. In addition, the comparative method then is not only preferred, but required in those situations in which there is no possible recourse to experimental techniques or when the number of observations do not allow for the use of statistical techniques that are based on comparable cases. However, as we already saw in Figure 2.1, these situations are rather the exception than the rule, since in most instances we can use more than one unit of variation and a concurrent number of units of observation (see also: Mayer, 1989; Keman, 1993d; Collier, 1993).

An important and crucial step in the use and application of the comparative approach is the issue of *concept formation*, which can travel across time, situations, or societies (Sartori, 1970; Frendreis, 1983; Bartolini, 1995). In other words, we seek to define crucial concepts and subsequently develop a systematic classification of variables that represent the theoretical relationship proposed and which are derived from the core subject of the discipline (which is – as we explained in the Introduction – confined to political science for presentational reasons, but is in essence not different *per se* from other disciplines that are regarded as being part of the social sciences in a broader sense; see also: Przeworski and Teune, 1970; Mayer, 1972; Smelser, 1976; Skocpol and Somers, 1980; Ragin, 1987). We now turn to the conceptual elaboration of the core subject within political science.

2.5 THE CORE SUBJECT AND THE COMPARATIVE APPROACH: POLITICS AND SOCIETY

What is remarkable is that in most contributions to political science the core subject under review is either taken for granted, or assumed to be self-evident (e.g. Blondel, 1981). 'Politics' is what governments do (or do not do), the actions of politicians and (their) parties or of (organized) interests, the institutions that make up a political system and also the process of policy-formation. Yet, little is said about what the nature of the relation between politics and society is, apart from referring to it as an inevitably 'contested notion' (see Connolly, 1988).

We shall not endeavor to put forward here a neatly packaged definition of politics, but rather attempt to show that it is possible to circumscribe it in terms of reference that enable us to distinguish 'politics' from other phenomena in society. We feel this to be necessary, since many of the theories that have been used in comparative politics have failed to recognize that without a coherent circumscription of its core subject, i.e. the 'political', explanations have tended to become depoliticized. Hence, the theory is often not using politics as an *explicandum*, but as what had to be explained by other, non-political, features. This development can be amply illustrated by means of the 'grand theories', which were in essence cultural, or functional explanations of political behavior, or conversely remained 'economistic' in nature (Mayer, 1989; Lane and Ersson, 1994b).

Whatever the merits of these approaches as potential explanations of the relations between politics and society, they do not tell us much about the nature of politics, and therefore are not really theories of the political process, but are instead possible explanations about political phenomena and (series of) political events. How then should we proceed from here if socio-cultural and socio-economic properties are to be considered merely relevant as contextual variables in explaining variations of politics, but not always adding knowledge about the 'political' itself? In other words: how do we control for contextual variation, as stipulated in Section 2.4, by using proper concepts of the 'political', i.e. of what is to be explained?

Generally speaking, comparativists have proceeded from this point either in the direction of focusing on central concepts, or they have resorted to a 'scientific' mode of explanation by applying the canons of empirical-analytical methodology (including high-powered statistical techniques) to political topics.

The first approach, for example, concentrated on various topics like democracy, political regimes, parliaments, revolutions, welfare states, war and peace, interest groups, etc. (see for an extensive list of such topics, including the literature: Berg-Schlosser and Müller-Rommel, 1987: 271–304 and also Lane and Ersson, 1994b: 243–63). The 'scientific' approach did not differ from the first in this respect, but concentrated much more on the question of whether or not hypotheses could be corroborated by available, quantifiable data. Again, this certainly added to the body of knowledge of political situations and societal developments, but hardly answered the question of what politics was all about and how politics itself may have an impact on societal developments. In other words: it appears that we know a lot about politics in the real world and, as a result of comparative research, how different its complexion can be, but at the same time we know precious little about its nature and the extent to which it is an independent explanatory factor with regard to societal developments.

An example of this latter issue is a debate within comparative politics on the question of whether or not 'politics does matter' (see: Castles, 1982: 4–15; Keman, 1988: 71–75; Gallagher et al., 1995: 236ff; Schmidt, 1996). It has been one of the first attempts to re-install the 'political' (in this debate: parties and governments) in comparative politics as a variable influencing societal developments. On the one hand, the debate focused on a topical relation in theory, i.e. democratic decision-making and public policy-formation; on the other hand, it searched for the empirical method to prove right from wrong. Both the theoretical conceptualization and the correct comparative method were at issue. Regardless of the outcome of this debate, it demonstrated that seemingly endless debates were possible on concepts themselves, the way of analyzing them, the data and techniques used and so on. At the end of the day it appeared, dependent on the countries studied, the time-period under review, the level of measurement and the operationalizations employed, that all contenders were sometimes right and sometimes wrong (see also: Castles, 1987, 1989; Keman, 1990, 1995).

Undoubtedly, this debate within the realm of comparative public policy analysis has helped to further our knowledge of political processes and the use of comparative methods. However, it also shows that without a clear view of what the core subject actually is, both the methods used and the data collected cannot really enhance our knowledge of 'politics and society' as such. Moreover, it does not help us to define and describe the comparative approach as being a distinctive approach within the social sciences with the help of properly formulated Research Questions and adequately developed Research Design. Before we turn to this crucial part of doing comparative research, we shall elaborate the concept of the 'political' in society as a heuristic device of social science.

The 'political' in a society can be described – as mentioned in Chapter 1 – on the basis of three dimensions: *politics, polity and policy* (Schmidt, 1996; Keman, 1997). Politics is then what we would like to call the political process. On this level, actors (mostly aggregates of individuals organized in parties, social movements and interest groups) interact with each other if and when they have conflicting interests or views regarding societal issues that cannot be solved by themselves (i.e. deficiency of self-regulation). The process of solving those problems which make actors clash, is more often than not visible through the political and social *institutions* that have emerged in order to facilitate conflict resolution.

Institutions – or the 'rules of political governance' – help to develop coalescence and to achieve a consensus among conflicting actors through compromising alternative preferences. These institutions manifest themselves in the *rules of the game* in a society. This is what is meant by the 'polity'. To put it more formally, rules are humanly devised constraints that shape political interaction. Institutions are then considered to be both formal – as for instance in a constitution, which can be enforced – and informal, i.e. they evolve over time and are respected as a code of conduct by most actors involved. Hence, the rules – be they formal or informal – define the relationship between the 'political and society'. This is important to note since it implies that we can compare and distinguish between rules that define, or limit, social action and those that give opportunities to act politically as a social agent (Braun, 1995; Czada et al., 1998). Examples of this are the access an individual has to the decision-making process by means of elections, joining a protest movement and requiring a judicial review or even a referendum, on the one hand. On the other hand, the 'state' and its related agencies (like parliament and the bureaucracy) define for a society or segments thereof (e.g. youth, elderly, employed and unemployed, women, other 'minorities', etc.) what their rights and possibilities are in social and economic life. All these constraining rules as well as opportunities are by and large shaping the way society is not only developing, but also in what way and to what effect.

In short, a theory of the political process must assume that there exists a mutual and interdependent relation between politics and society, but that its organization is to a large extent independent from society. The issue at hand is then to investigate, by means of comparison, to what extent and in what way this process can be observed and affects social and economic developments of societies.

It should be kept in mind that the triad of 'politics–polity–policy' in itself is *not* a theory of the political process. It is instead a heuristic device to delineate the 'political' from the 'non-political' (and thus to distinguish politics from society). This description of the 'political', however, makes it possible to elaborate on the core subject of the comparative approach. That is to say that all those processes that can be defined by means of these three dimensions are worthy of our attention and are in need of a comparative analysis in order to explain the process. Theories and hypotheses in comparative political science usually refer to units of variation, i.e. political variables, policy variables and polity variables at the macroscopic level. The theories and hypotheses often apply to many units of observation (or 'cases', e.g. nations or parties, governments, etc.) and many time periods (e.g. decades or years).

The next step is to specify what the unit of variation for comparative purposes is. A unit of variation is defined as the relation between reality and the hypothesis under review. As Ragin (1987: 7–8) and Przeworski (1987: 2–4) point out, the unit of variation (or 'concepts', 'properties') is *not* the same as the cases, i.e. units of observation under review. The theory that nations whose economy depends largely on the (ups and downs of) world economy tend to boost public expenditures as an internal buffer against external shocks (see Katzenstein, 1985), for example, clearly designates separate nations in specific time periods as the units of observation. Conversely, the variables (or 'concepts') within Katzenstein's theory are, first, dependency on the world economy and secondly, public expenditures; hence they concern a (presumed) vital relationship which in reality can account for the economic performance of a nation (in this case). A disastrous error in scientific research is to equate a theory with *one* class of observations instead of *all* relevant cases. In medical research this error is often exemplified by (im)possible Research Designs to test the theory that smoking is a cause of lung cancer. If only smokers are considered as the units of observation – i.e. as subjects in medical research – then test results will be inconclusive since non-smokers may suffer even more frequently from lung cancer than smokers. Test results will be inconclusive too when only patients suffering from lung cancer are considered as the units of observation, since patients suffering from lung cancer may smoke less than healthy humans. The hypothesis clearly refers to all human beings as the units of observation, regardless of whether they smoke, and regardless of whether they suffer from lung cancer, which would be the unit of variation.

Things become more complicated, however, when the design of feasible, efficient research is at stake. First, it is often unnecessary to include every possible unit of observation, or case, from the complete population in the actual research. A selection from the population may be enough to answer a Research Question in sufficient detail. Katzenstein's theory, for example, may be tested in sufficient detail by a comparison for the post-war period of a number of randomly selected nations which are largely dependent on the world economy with a number of randomly selected nations which are largely independent from the world economy. Random and non-random samples will be discussed in Chapter 5. Secondly, the concepts of theoretical interest – i.e. units of variation – usually have to be translated or 'operationalized' into empirical 'indicators', which can be observed and measured directly. Two indicators of the dependency of a nation on the world economy are exports and imports, for example. The process of operationalization will be discussed in depth in Chapters 3 and 4. Thirdly, the units of variation are often constructed on the basis of indicators with respect to more easily observable units of measurement. The overall measure of public expenditures in OECD-publications, for example, is derived ultimately from measures of expenditures of separate OECD-nations. The intricate relationship between units of observation and units of measurement will be discussed in more detail in Chapter 3.

In sum, the term 'unit of variation' can therefore have two meanings: on the one hand it signifies an elaboration of the theoretical argument and the related Research Question into meaningful concepts, on the other hand it concerns the translation of the theory into a Research Design where variables are developed that can be observed empirically.

A number of comparative researchers have drawn attention to this confusing way of using the terms 'unit of variation' and 'unit of observation', which easily leads to equating description with explanation. Yet, it is quite important to know exactly what is under discussion, if we wish to validate theoretical statements by means of empirical knowledge. Przeworski and Teune propose a distinction between 'levels of observation' and 'levels of analysis' (1970: 50), whereas Ragin introduces the terms 'observational unit' and 'explanatory unit' (Ragin, 1987: 8–9). Both these distinctions between, respectively, empirical knowledge and theoretical statements appear useful, but may still be confusing to the practitioner. We propose to follow the formulations as used in Chapter 1.

However, whatever term is used for the units of variation and observation, it does not solve an important problem with respect to the comparative approach in political science. The comparative analysis of the 'political' always involves a multi-level type of argument. Hence, it involves the observations of comparable parts that are considered to constitute a conceptual whole. Of course, both Ragin and Przeworski realize this also, but instead of specifying the core subject of comparative inquiry, they resort to a methodological refinement as a solution. Instead we propose to consider the units of variation to encompass every topic that can be formulated in terms of a meaningful relation, either logically in terms of the heuristic triad of politics, polity and policy, or in terms of societal development. The unit of measurement is then simply the operationalization of the 'triad' in comparative perspective. That is, the Research Question under review can only be explained in terms of macroscopic properties which vary from one unit of observation, or one case, to another. In addition, it should be noted that the unit of variation is (almost) by definition formulated on the meso or macro-level (i.e.

politics and society; e.g. the actions of a political party), whereas the unit of measurement, or the properties to be observed, are often directly related to (individual) behavior, or indirectly to actors or institutions as a whole (e.g. the party as an agent of societal interest and as a unitary actor in parliament and government).

In summary: a comparative analysis of politics in society begins with the formulation of the unit of variation by referring to relations at a macroscopic level (i.e. systemic level). By elaborating these units, one must always keep in mind that the units of observation (i.e. the (sub)systems or cases under review) that are employed are not identical, but are considered to be similar. Finally, the unit and level of measurement (like time intervals or institutional or geographic boundaries) are not by definition equal to the analytical properties as defined in properties theory and related Research Questions![1]

To give an example: the study of the development of the welfare state is not, by definition, a topic of comparative political research. In our view, it becomes a comparative topic only if an attempt is made to explain this development by means of macro-political properties such as conflicting interests between socio-economic classes. These conflicts are, depending on the existing institutions of the liberal democratic state, fought out in parliament and other decision-making bodies and subsequently may result in a patterned variation of public policy-formation at the system-level of the state. Hence the core subject is *not* the welfare state, but instead the extent to which politics, polity and policy can be identified as properties of the political process that shapes the welfare state in a country. This being the case, the extent to which elements of this process are relevant, explains the political development of the welfare state.

Alternatively, if one focuses on 'classes' it is not their existence *per se* that matters, but their degree of political action which may, for instance, explain the emergence, or the change, of political institutions (e.g. the rule of universal suffrage, or the role of trade unions in the decision-making process). In the latter case, i.e. institutional change, the 'political' is regarded as consequential, whereas in the first example, i.e. the development of the welfare state, the 'political' is explanatory. In both examples the unit of variation is expressed in terms of macroscopic properties related to the political process, and measured or observed across systems or across time (i.e. cases under review) within a system at a level that represents a coherent political unit. Politics, polity, and policy are thus a set of theoretical references as well as empirical points of reference, which form together the *core subject* of the comparative approach in political science.

To conclude our discussion of the core subject: the *theory-guided* question within any type of comparative analysis is to what extent the 'political', in terms of explanatory units of variation, can indeed account for, and is shaped by, the political actions in one social system compared with another. Conversely, the theory-guided question, or Research Question, needs to be refined so as to define the units of measurement (= indicators) and thus the units of observation (= cases) in social reality. It is this process and the attempts to explain it by systematic comparison that distinguishes the comparative approach from other approaches in political and social science. This conclusion brings us to the next issue we seek to answer: how and when to compare in a methodologically sound fashion? What are the problems and how to cope with them? In other words: what steps must be taken to properly relate the Research Question to an adequate Research Design, i.e. a design that is conducive to plausible conclusions. This is the subject of the next chapter.

2.6 ENDMATTER

Topics highlighted

- Relation theory and method: the benefits of the comparative approach.
- Theory comes before method, Research Questions before Research Designs.
- Dimensions of comparison: time, space and types of analysis.
- The core subject – i.e. the 'political' in relation to 'society' – enables the comparativist to relate units of variation to units of measurement and units of observation.
- The main advantage of the comparative approach in political and social science is to 'test' theories by controlling contextual variation.

Questions

- Can you explain why different Research Questions about welfare statism could well imply different Research Designs? See for this: *European Journal of Political Research*, 31 (1 & 2): 99–114 & 159–68.
- If you look at Table 2.1, can you give concrete examples for each of the four cells given?
- In this chapter we distinguish: time and space, micro and macro-levels and inter and intra-system comparisons. Could you think of a topic of investigation that is solely comparatively researched on:
  1. time without space?
  2. micro-observations without macro-properties?
  3. intra-system features without inter-system references?

Exercises

- If you read Lijphart's article on 'Dimensions of democracy' and Duverger's article 'A new political system' could you then reformulate their Research Question in terms of our triad: politics–polity–policy? You can find abstracts of these articles in *European Journal of Political Research*, 31 (1 & 2): 125–46 & 193–204.
- An important feature of the 'art of comparing' is controlling for the contextual variation, or exogenous variables. More often than not, this is attempted by selecting those (proper) cases which are supposed to be similar except for the variation to be explained. If you take the article of Lijphart again (see above) can you tell from his list of cases *why* he thinks that these countries are indeed more similar than others and thus do increase the degree of internal and external validity?

Further reading

- *General*: Ragin, 1987; Castles, 1987; Almond, 1990.
- *Specific*: Mayer, 1989; Dalton, 1991; Keman, 1993c.

Note

1 This distinction refers to the perennial dispute about whether or not social constructs are the result of aggregated behavior or must be seen as social facts in themselves. Weber and Durkheim, the founding fathers of modern sociology, are representatives of each view. Yet, it suffices here to put forward that both believed that social and political action could be observed at the non-individual or macroscopic level. We take this as a point of departure in this book. See for this discussion: Braun, 1995; Keman, 1998.

3

The art of comparing: developing a research design

CONTENTS

3.1 INTRODUCTION

There is little dispute about the comparative method being the most distinctive feature of the comparative approach to political and social science. Yet, at the same time there has been a continuing debate about what, if and when, why and how to compare (e.g. Lijphart, 1975; Roberts, 1978; Dogan and Pelassy, 1990; Rueschemeyer et al., 1992; Keman, 1993d). Before we go into the comparative method as such in more detail, we shall first focus on the extant methodological controversies which this debate provoked (see also: Collier, 1993).

What to compare? Rather than focusing on 'macro-social', 'societal' or 'contextual' entities, it should be clear from Chapter 2 that we propose to study the 'political' *vis-à-vis* the 'societal'. This further implies that the conceptualization of 'politics, polity and policy' as a heuristic tool is our major methodological concern with respect to using the comparative approach. The social and economic configuration of a situation or society is not the primary goal or meaning of comparison; instead capturing the specific *differentia* of the 'political' across situations and across time will be our concern (albeit within the context of societal developments; Lane and Ersson, 1994b).

By taking this point seriously, there are a number of implications for the controversies on the comparative method. They concern issues such as (see also Table 2.1):

- whether Research Question and Research Design, i.e. the relationship between theory and reality, is embedded in the correct approach in terms of case selection, cross-sectional or time series analysis, variable-oriented (often equated with statistical) or case-oriented Research Designs (e.g. Lijphart, 1971, 1975; Przeworski, 1987; Ragin, 1987; Keman, 1995);
- whether or not causal or conditional explanations can be achieved by means of empirical and statistical corroboration (Ragin, 1987; Lijphart, 1975; Smelser, 1976);
- whether or not comparisons are only meaningful by applying the longitudinal dimension and confining the number of relevant cases to be analyzed (e.g. O'Donnell, 1979; Castles, 1989; Bartolini, 1992; Rueschemeyer et al., 1992).

The first issue is more or less reminiscent of the transition from the 'behavioral' dominance in political science and its attempt to achieve 'scientific' status (Mayer, 1972). The comparative method was considered to be the ideal platform, if executed on the basis of statistical techniques using data-collections, variable construction and causal modeling, to achieve this status (e.g. Holt and Turner, 1970). This position strongly coincided with the search for a 'grand theory' of politics. Apart from the fact that for various reasons 'scientism' in the social sciences has lost its appeal, it simply induced a situation in which we lost track of what the substance or the focus of analysis, i.e. the 'political', is (Mayer, 1989: 56–57). Francis Castles (1987), for instance, has succinctly pointed out that 'the major incongruity is not a matter of theory not fitting the facts, but of the facts fitting too many theories' (p. 198). In other words: 'grand' schemes appear to become meaningless if and when faced with 'facts' which are always derived from macroscopical phenomenona. In effect a 'middle-range' school developed in the 1970s (see, for example: Holt and Turner, 1970; Przeworski and Teune, 1970). In the words of Mayer:

> . . . political science is at what might be called a pre-theoretic stage of development. Most of the existing theoretical work has been concerned with establishing logical relationships between non-empirically defined concepts or imprecisely defined classes of phenomena . . . they have produced a plethora of generalizations that are incapable of being tested in terms of observable data. (Mayer, 1972: 279)

And precisely this tendency led to the idea that 'middle-range' theory was a more adequate and plausible way to go. Middle-range theories are those which claim to be explanatory for a certain class of cases (e.g. industrial societies or welfare states or parliamentary democracies) for which specific hypotheses are developed and specified in terms of variables (e.g. industrialism tends to produce welfare systems, or capitalism is conditional for democracy; see: Lipset, 1963; Rueschemeyer et al., 1992; Lane and Ersson, 1994b). In contrast to grand theories, middle-range theories are bounded by situation, time and location (see also: Bartolini, 1995). Yet, even if one knew what to compare, the refined techniques cannot really help us in deciding what is right or wrong, since what we often lack is an adequate theoretical perspective that is consciously elaborated in proper conceptualizations of the 'political' aiming at middle-range explanations.

The latter point, i.e. the relation between conceptualization and operationalization (Sartori, 1970; Lijphart, 1975; Przeworski, 1987), has been taken up since the early 1970s. Even if one thinks one knows what to compare, the question remains of how to translate it into proper terms for empirical research. Hence, developing a Research Design is a crucial step in applying the comparative method to political and social science. How to do this, is elaborated in this chapter.

3.2 THE PROBLEM OF VARIABLES, CASES AND INTERPRETATIONS

As we pointed out in the preceding chapter the problem of the use of the term 'unit of variation' cannot and should not be solved from a methodological point of view alone, but instead ought to be primarily formulated by means of the core subject of comparative politics in terms of substantial relationships. However, this task remains unresolved by the definition of the core subject of the 'political' alone. It essentially means that one has to choose, on the basis of a topical Research Question that is formulated in terms of the 'political', the correct Research Design (see for this: Roberts, 1978; Schmidt, 1987; Keman, 1988; Rueschemeyer et al., 1992 and Section 3.4 of this chapter). The question of what to compare leads to the matter of how to compare, i.e. how to apply the comparative method.

Generally speaking, the 'logic' of comparative research goes back to the famous predicament of John Stuart Mill (1806–73) which has led to the equally well-known distinction between the 'most similar' and the 'most different' systems Research Design for comparing (Przeworski and Teune, 1970: 32). Most comparativists agree on this distinction, but differ on the question of whether or not the Research Design should be based on as many similar cases as possible, or upon a (small) number of dissimilar cases. First, we should elaborate what distinguishes the 'most similar' from the 'most different' systems design. Let us therefore formulate what a theory-guided Research Design is:

$$C^*[X \rightarrow Y]$$

The relation $X \rightarrow Y$ denotes a substantial Research Question in terms of the units of variation. C denotes contextual factors, which are considered to be more or less constant. Depending on the Research Question formulated, the researcher has to decide to what extent contextual factors can be kept constant by means of a 'most similar systems design' or a 'most different systems design'. Hence, depending on the type of RQ, a research strategy is chosen, which in turn directs the inclusion of contextual factors (denoted by ∗). In other words we have translated a theoretical question into a substantial Research Question, which in turn is characterized by an implicit or explicit causal relationship. For instance: does a difference in electoral system (ES) produce different types of party systems (PS)? Or alternatively: do the socio-cultural cleavages (SC) within a nation produce different types of party systems? These Research Questions are derived from theoretical ideas put forward by two political scientists, namely Duverger (1968) and Rokkan (1970). It should be noted that 'causality' is here implied by conditions present in X. In other words: co-variation is seen as a part of the argument but not as *conditio sine qua non*. If that is the case we speak of explicit causality. Hence, the first step in deciding what to compare and how, is to know the units of variation. In this example it concerns electoral systems, socio-cultural cleavages and party system characteristics. So the Research Design to apply could be represented by Figure 3.1. This design, if answered properly, should lead to answers for all cases concerned, i.e. those political and social systems where there is an electoral system and socio-cultural cleavages do exist (and where political parties are allowed, of course) – this is, what we have called in Chapter 1, 'internal validity': the relationship under review is valid for all relevant cases (or a middle-range theory). Yet, as we all know, in reality the world is much too complex, multifarious and varied for us to expect that one can study this kind of causal relationship in isolation. Hence, we need to make assumptions about the extent to which the cases or political systems under review are either similar or different with respect to their context (= C). For instance: can we presume that socio-cultural differences have the same impact on a party system in the industrialized democracies in Europe as in the agricultural systems in the Third World? Or conversely: can we expect that electoral systems do indeed function in the same way in Asia today as in Europe fifty years ago? In other words: to what extent can we assume that the same variables (ES, SC and PS) will behave identically under varying conditions in different contexts? This question has clearly to do with the 'external validity' of the outcomes of the research, and thus the answer is vital for the direction of the Research Design to be used (i.e.: are the

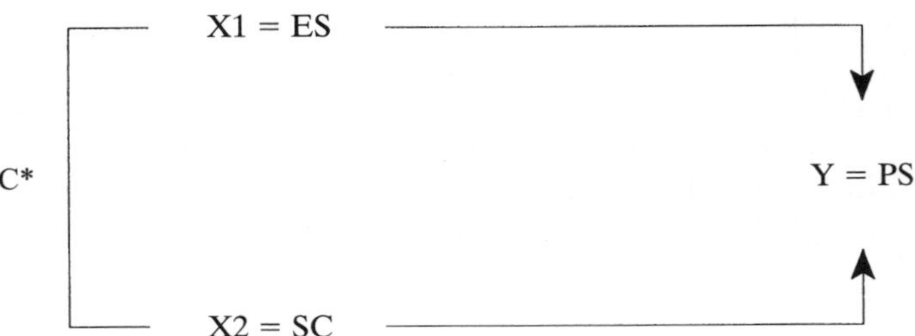

Figure 3.1 *Schematic representation of a Research Design: C, contextual factors; ES, electoral system; PS, party system; SC, socio-cultural cleavages*

results valid for other cases/systems that are not or could not be included). We need to control the context of the units of variation in order to be able to draw conclusions about the X → Y relationship, if and when analyzed on the basis of comparable empirical evidence. The basic assumption underlying this type of comparative Research Design is then that all other things are assumed to be equal (*Ceteris Paribus*).

At this point comparative researchers tend to agree that there is plausible disagreement about what choice to make: on the one hand, one can argue that a few cases will suffice to answer the Research Question [X → Y], since it enables the researcher to include only those cases that have as much context in common as possible. Hence, so it is argued, the control of the context is maximized. Yet, on the other hand, others will argue that the internal validity may be high, but the external validity is not: too few cases are included and too many variables will have come into play in the comparison. Following this line of argument, one will opt for including as many cases as plausible. However, this implies that the number of variables that can be studied simultaneously is limited. In addition, such a choice implies that the context to be controlled is much more varied, and thus the assumed similarity of the cases involved will be in jeopardy.

In short: in order to keep the context under control one has to choose between a large or optimal number of cases/systems that are contextually similar with only a few variables that differ amongst each other, on the one hand, or one can maximize control by using a small number of cases and a higher number of variables which have in fact almost all contextual features in common, on the other. Whatever the choice the researcher makes with respect to the number of contextual comparable cases, it always implies a *most similar systems design* (MSSD) (see also: Przeworski and Teune, 1970; and, about the hazards, Przeworski, 1987). In our example concerning the explanation of the variation of party systems a MSSD-approach implies that we can either include all political systems where these are free elections and parties competing for office, or we start by looking for a couple of systems which have almost all in common except the X → Y relationships under investigation.

The alternative choice concerns the *most different systems design* (MDSD). The crux of the logic of this approach is obviously opposite to an MSSD-approach. Here the researcher is actually hoping that the contextual differences are not only omnipresent, but also that the units of variation – and thus the crucial relationships – do not vary, regardless of the contextual differences. The disadvantage is, then, that one is confronted with Popper's dilemma of the Swans (we will never know whether or not they are *always* white) and this has a negative impact on the 'external validity' of the research.

To sum up: in order to answer a Research Question one needs to make a choice between a most similar and a most different design for comparison. The latter design often leads to problems regarding the external validity of the results, whereas the former strategy has potential implications for the internal validity (due to the assumed control of the context). In addition the MSSD-approach is almost always hampered by the problem of too few variables and too many cases, whereas the MDSD-approach is often hampered by too few cases and too many variables.

The last problem is often called 'Galton's problem' (Lijphart, 1975: 171) – that is: few cases and many variables, which makes it difficult to arrive at conclusions of a causal nature. This is ultimately the result of 'diffusion' (i.e. processes of learning), which may lead to spurious relationships, or to 'overdetermination' (i.e. even if cases are, to a large degree, similar, the remaining differences will be large because of the use of concepts that are broadly operationalized), and in turn this situation will affect the relation between apparently independent variables and the dependent phenomenon (Przeworski and Teune, 1970: 34; Przeworski, 1987: 38–9). As far as we can see, there is, as of yet, no proper solution to this problem. It is by and large due to the dynamic nature of social reality, which cannot be completely captured by means of controlled contexts. The comparative approach can only contribute to reducing the degree of erroneous statements here. Apart from consciously choosing either a MSSD or a MDSD-approach, the reduction of errors is, of course, to be achieved by developing proper measured variables, applying the correct statistical techniques and – last but not least at all – interpreting the results in view of their internal and external validity. This is one of the reasons for writing this book, and even perhaps its mission!

In short, Galton's problem, inherent to the substance of the comparative method in the social sciences, is thus also an inevitable problem of comparative research of the 'political'. Rather than abandoning empirical research aimed at explanatory results altogether (as, for example, MacIntyre, 1978 concludes), we suggest taking into account the limitations and constraints of the comparative method and attempting to develop a Research Design that is suitable for the Research Question under review (see also: Ragin, 1987: 9–10). Hence, it is crucial to develop a proper relation between Research Question and Research Design to promote plausible conclusions regarding a middle-range theory.

All in all, four issues with regard to method are to be observed when a Research Design is developed: firstly, the context of what is compared; secondly, the role of 'time and space' with respect to the problem under scrutiny; thirdly, the level of inquiry, i.e. the micro–macro link; and fourthly, the number of cases involved. These issues are equally important, and decisions made upon them will have a great impact on the plausibility, validity and quality of the outcomes of a comparative research project.

Contextual variables are those variables that make up the environment of the core subject, i.e. of the 'political'. A 'most similar' design – as we stated earlier – is intended to reduce variation in the context to the barest possible minimum by means of selecting cases, or units of observation, that are by and large identical, except for the relations between variables under review that represent the Research Question, i.e. what is to be explained. For example, the debate on 'Does politics matter' to which we referred to earlier, or the analysis of the development of welfare states that was mentioned earlier, are both examples of the importance of the selection of cases in relation to the analytical conclusions based on them. For instance, comparing non-democratic regimes with democratic ones, or 'young' democratic systems with long-established ones could lead to conclusions of whether or not parties do play a role in political decision-making. However, such a comparison would not render information about the question of the extent to which political parties in parliamentary democracies do matter with respect to policy formation in general, or whether party differences are relevant for the development of welfare statism (Castles, 1982; Schmidt, 1987; Keman, 1990).

Moreover, the number of variables not controlled for in a MSSD would be immense and would thus also engender Galton's problem. Obviously, this is an erroneous path to take, although it is worth noting it has been suggested that the problem could be by-passed by using functional equivalents, i.e. assuming that particular actors and institutions in one system are identical to certain phenomena in another system. For instance the role of 'leaders' in the Third World and 'traditional' modes of decision-making could be compared with the ways in which party elite's and concomitant bargaining take place in a parliamentary democracy (Dogan and Pelassy, 1990: 37–43). However, given the already existing problems of comparing on the basis of similarity, we do not consider this a sound trajectory to follow. The number of contextual variables must be low in the eventuality of a Research Question that is akin to the most similar approach, and even in a MDSD the number of 'contextual' variables should not be excessive, otherwise one will end up with conclusions that everything is indeed different and all situations are peculiar by definition. It is the enduring paradox of *Scylla and Charybdis*, and there is no easy solution (see: Skocpol and Somers, 1980; Janoski and Hicks, 1994). Both approaches thus have their drawbacks, but, in addition, it is often the case that their application in practice is also erroneous. Both the 'most similar' and the 'most different' approach are not only developed to control for the context, but also have implications for the 'logic' of interpreting the outcomes of the empirical results. We now turn to this.

Recall that the 'art of comparing' is the fundamental point of departure. This means that the comparison made is considered to deliver the building blocks of the way in which the Research Question can and must be answered. Hence, the 'most similar' and 'most different' approaches are related to an underlying logic or reasoning:

- Most Similar ⇒ Method of Difference
- Most Different ⇒ Method of Agreement.

This 'logic of inquiry', or, in our parlance, the relationship between Research Question and Research Design, runs as follows: in a MSSD, where we compare as many cases as possible, assuming that these cases have more circumstances in common than not, we interpret the research outcomes by concentrating on the *variation across the cases*, focusing explicitly on both the X and Y variables. Often this is called the 'cross-national variation' as the basis for explanation. This type of explanation on the basis of the 'method of difference' can be demonstrated as shown in Table 3.1 (adapted from Janoski and Hicks, 1994: 14). Let X1 be 'PR Electoral System', let X2 be 'Socio-cultural Cleavages', and let X3 be 'Economic Development'. The independent variable (Y) is 'Type of Party System' (i.e. polarized or not). Finally, the cases represent here the political systems under review, i.e. constitutional democracies, warranting universal suffrage and freedom of organization as well as the right to contest elections: the type of democracy

Table 3.1 *An example of a Most Similar Systems comparison*

	Case 1	Case 2	Case 3	Case n
Independent variables				
X1 = PR	yes	yes	yes	yes
X2 = SC	yes	no	yes	no
X3 = ED	no	no	no	yes
Dependent variable				
Y = PS	yes	no	yes	no

PR, electoral system is proportional; SC, socio-cultural cleavages present; ED, economic development is high; PS, party system is polarized.
Adapted from Janoski and Hicks (1994: 14).

which Robert Dahl (1971) has coined as 'polyarchy'. The Research Question is: what causes the differences across polyarchies in the development of party systems? The issue at hand is now: what do the research results tell us? The results tell us that the variation in Type of Party System is – assuming the context to be constant – caused by the existence of Socio-cultural Cleavages (as Rokkan, 1970 contended) since X2 systematically co-varies with the Y-variable (yes/yes and no/no). The other variables X1 and X3 do not co-vary with the dependent variable. To put it differently: the variables X1 and X3 in Table 3.1 are either *invariant* (as is the case with X1, so that it cannot explain the cross-national variation in Y) or not concurrent with Y (as is the case with X3). Apparently, in reality, the type of Electoral System does not systematically produce a concurrent type of Party System (as was put forward by Duverger), nor are differences in economic development an effect-producing condition in this respect. Hence, in a Most Similar Systems Design the focus is on the correspondence between the dependent and independent variables on the basis of their cross-variation.

Conversely, the Most Different Systems approach is based on the Method of (indirect) Agreement. An example of this 'logic of inquiry' can be found in the study of the relationship between capitalism and democracy (Rueschemeyer et al., 1992) and in Barrington Moore's treatise on democracies and dictatorship. In both studies the Research Design started from the idea that the comparison is meant to confront positive (yes, there is a relationship between capitalism and democracy) and negative (no, there is not) outcomes. The Method of Agreement is also called the 'parallel demonstration of theory' (see Skocpol and Somers, 1980) and is demonstrated in Table 3.2. Let X1 be 'Capitalism' present or not (yes/no), X2 be 'Middle Classes' present or not (yes/no) and X3 be 'Economic Development' high or not (yes/no). The dependent variable Y is here 'Polyarchy' or not (yes/no). Although it is easy to infer from the research results that, if X2 and X3 are present, polyarchy appears to have emerged (and would not only support the hypotheses of Rueschemeyer et al. and of Barrington Moore, but also Dahl's theory), the conclusion is not that the variables cause polyarchy, but rather that the independent variables represent favorable conditions for the emergency of polyarchy. In addition, the Method of Agreement is only conducive to internally valid conclusions since the cases hardly ever cover the complete 'universe of discourse' (which

Table 3.2 *An example of Most Different System comparison*

	Case 1	Case 2	Case 3
Independent variables			
X1	yes	yes	no
X2	yes	no	yes
X3	yes	no	yes
Dependent variable			
Y	yes	no	yes

X1, capitalism is present; X2, middle classes are strong; X3, economic development is high; Y, regime type is polyarchy.

would be in this example all the countries of the world, since polyarchy typology can be applied to all political systems). This limitation of the Method of Agreement is implied in its logic since the co-variation is primarily based on the similar situations for the respective cases rather than for separate variables across the cases under review. Finally, since only a limited number of cases can be studied, one should be aware of a functionalist bias in the Research Design, i.e. the case-selection represents comparable but different cases. A way to avoid this problem is, of course, to extend the number of cases without losing too much information. A way to handle this problem is by using Boolean analysis (Ragin, 1987). This type of analysis allows for the handling of qualitative information, or many variables for a relative high number of cases. Boolean analysis will be explained and highlighted in Parts II and III. To recapitulate:

- we are always confronted with the dilemma to choose for a Research Design in which we trade off internal versus external validity due to the problem of many cases, few variables (MSSD) versus few cases, many variables (MDSD);
- if we opt for a MSSD-approach we assume the context to be (more or less) identical across all the cases under review, whereas a MDSD-variables and thus, by limiting the contextual bias different cases or systems can be compared;
- an MSSD-approach follows a logic of inquiry that is based on the co-variation between X and Y-variables, i.e. eliminating cross-system differences, whereas the MDSD-approach induces a logic of inquiry where the parallel demonstration of cases under investigation is based on eliminating cases.

3.3 THE ROLE OF SPACE AND TIME

Often the term cases are confounded with countries in the comparative approach to political and social sciences. This need not to surprise us, since most comparative political research focuses on macroscopical phenomena which are more often than not defined at the national level. Cross-sectional analysis is therefore often considered to mean the same as cross-national. Likewise one will find in course books on the comparative approach that case studies are, by implication, using the historical method. Again, this may well be often the case but not by definition. In this book we therefore argue that comparisons are made across systems – which refers to any type of political and social (sub-)system that has an organizational reference to territorial space. For instance, an analysis of the role of politics with respect to policy-making in the US concerns a cross-sectional analysis of the American states, i.e. the cases are subsystems of the US Federal polity. Conversely, the cross-sectional study of Welfare Statism by Wilensky (1975) comprises the comparison of 66 national welfare states. In this case the cases are indeed nation-states.

The use of the factor time in the comparative approach is also confusingly used in the literature. On the one hand the term Time Series analysis is used, i.e. the cases are time units (e.g. years, days or even decades; see e.g.: Lane and Ersson, 1994b) and the comparative variation across time is the aim of the explanation. On the other hand, periods of time are used as cases. Here we aggregate the information for a number of time units and replicate the cross-sectional analysis on the basis of this division over time (see e.g.: Keman, 1997; Bartolini and Mair, 1990). This combination of sections of time (i.e. periods) and a cross-inspection of systems is commonly called diachronic analysis (see also: Figure 2.1). In this case the comparisons made are intended to observe patterned change over time. Hence, if the cases are defined as time units we see it as 'comparable cases' analyzed on the bases of time series (or to use Castles' metaphor: we look at motion pictures). However, if we compare cross-sections at certain intervals then we have multiple 'snapshots' (Castles, 1987). A combination of the two – using intertemporal and cross-sectional comparable data – is nowadays referred to as Pooled Analysis: variability of time and space is here the aim of the comparative method (e.g.: unit of observation is country and years, i.e. a combination of time/space). What direction is chosen in a Research Design depends, as is by now usual, on the type of Research Question and the related units of variation. If we wish to know whether or not socio-cultural developments have an impact on Party System change we are bound to use time, and if possible, space. However, if we ask ourselves whether or not participation in the EU makes a difference to national policy-making, then we should compare spatial differences and control for time before and after a European nation-state actually has joined the EU (Keman and McDonald, 1996).

In sum: both time and space are important dimensions in any Research Design. Depending on the units of variation (i.e. the $X \rightarrow Y$ relationship) under review, inter-temporal and/or cross-sectional variation will define the type of cases that are needed to organize the comparative data. In addition, if time is the preponderant dimension then, more often than not, the underlying logic of inquiry is based on the Method of Agreement, whereas if space is the dominant dimension of comparison the (indirect) Method of Difference will be the guiding principle of interpretation.

Having outlined the basic problems with regard to space and time in relation to the development of a proper comparative Research Design, we shall now delve into these dimensions a little deeper. This is necessary since both dimensions are crucial with respect to any empirical-analytical studies in the social sciences, in particular when the 'political' as a core subject of the comparative approach is to be researched. First, we shall discuss the historical method – often considered as the 'royal way', since it implies a qualitative design – and thereafter the problems related to spatial analysis, which is most often employed by means of quantitative data.

Time and history

Much comparative research is characterized by a Research Design using the historical method. This poses a number of problems which are related to the consequentiality of time itself, the number of cases that can be studied and, finally, the measurement of time in terms of variation (Flora, 1974; Bartolini, 1995). Bartolini notes that, surprisingly enough, the historical method is rarely disputed by social scientists. However, there exists a large body of literature within historiography that discusses the complexities of temporal variance and its explanatory value (Romein, 1971; Braudel, 1977; Althusser, 1983) and has been discussed by the so-called 'Annals' school. Like the pervasive discussion within social science on levels of measurement, i.e. the micro–meso–macro linkages, the 'Annals' (and Braudel in particular) attempted to differentiate 'time' by distinguishing three levels of diachronic development: the long term (macro), the cyclical movement (meso), and the occurrence of events (micro). The long-term development structures the other levels and makes it possible to relate events to cycles, and, according to Braudel, events can be understood in their proper historical context. In this way, it was claimed, objects of study, such as the political development of a society, can be compared as if they were synchronic. Yet, a problem remains that one is implicitly assuming that the interpretation of time is a result of a few, universal factors (for instance, the impact of processes of 'modernization'). Hence, time remains sequentially defined and is therefore potentially an overdetermining factor in relation to the logic of inquiry applied, i.e. whether or not the Method of Agreement is used.

The alternative route, which is often advocated, is to incorporate time in the Research Design by means of a case study design in order to enhance the internal validity (Abrams, 1982; Skocpol, 1985; Ragin, 1991). Apart from the problem of the time dimension in relation to consequentiality, another problem is contained in the conceptualization of the 'political': are we looking at the same phenomenon through time or merely at functional equivalents? In other words: is the development of a political process captured over time, or does it concern the cross-time variation of a political phenomenon? Barrington Moore (1966) is an example of a study of the development of democracy over time, whereas the analysis of revolutions by Skocpol (1979) concerns a cross-time Research Design. Barrington Moore's research is in search of the consequentiality of a political process. Conversely, Theda Skocpol focuses on the patterned variation in the occurrence of a similar political phenomenon. Both authors ask the same Research Question, namely how to account for a political process, but use a different Research Design regarding the time dimension.

As Bartolini correctly points out, there is no fundamental (or logical) difference between using a synchronical and a diachronical Research Design. In both cases the comparativist has to grapple with the fact of whether or not the observed variation is part and parcel of both the independent and dependent variables. Hence, the so-called qualitative comparative case approach (Ragin, 1991; O'Donnell, 1979) which claims to be superior to the quantitative comparative spatial approach is wrong-headed, as long as its proponents do not supply us with a logical argument that the time dimension can only be applied in a comparative analysis based on case studies. In other words: this type of internal, (or: inside a case) analysis should be complemented by an external (i.e. comparative) analysis.

This type of analysis, employing internal and external analysis is an underused Research Design within the comparative approach. Yet, it is a useful way to amplify the advantages of both types of analysis instead of seeing them as opposite and exclusive instruments of the 'art of comparing'. On the one hand, it can be quite helpful to corroborate findings across the board as a means of validation. On the other hand, it can be quite helpful to generate new hypotheses or to account for deviant cases. In the first use, validation is achieved by first executing a cross-sectional (or a diachronic) analysis and then selecting specific cases to analyze in depth. This crucial case analysis is intended to exemplify, if not to prove, that the multi-case research results are indeed valid. Hence the internal analysis is functional as a 'proof of the pudding' of the outcomes of the external comparative analysis. Conversely, case study analysis, often called critical case analysis, is intended either to function as a kind of pilot study or to see whether or not certain cases deviate from the general outcomes, or trends, as being 'exceptions to the rule' or can be 'explained away' as being idiosyncracies (see also Janoski and Hicks, 1994: 1).

If one investigates, for instance, economic policy-making in OECD countries, one may make use of a periodization which represents a similar incident or event in all the cases under review, at certain intervals. If one wishes to analyze the development of 'welfare statism' one could decide to use time-series analysis, whether or not it concerns one or more countries. A final example of choosing a Research Design may be the study of processes of democratization of a society. To do this on the basis of a single case study is very well justified and useful (e.g. Daalder, 1966; Lijphart, 1968), but a comparative investigation of this process diachronically can be equally justified and useful (e.g. Lipset, 1963; Rueschemeyer et al., 1992). All these examples demonstrate that time can and should indeed be explicitly taken into account with respect to the Research Design. However, the choice of the way in which this is done has more to do with the Research Question than with the superiority of a specific approach of including time in comparative research.

Space and cross-sections

By contrast with the time dimension, as has been pointed out here, the problems with spatial analysis have been discussed at great length. Spatial analysis has to do with the level of measurement in relation to the selection of cases under review. Lijphart (1971) distinguishes three types of spatial analysis, namely: statistically based, case-oriented, and the comparable case approach (see also: Ragin, 1987; Rueschemeyer et al., 1992). Ragin, in particular, overstates the differences between the various methodological approaches. He develops a dichotomy that separates the 'case-oriented' from the 'variable-related' Research Design. The first approach would enable the comparativist to analyze the 'political' more comprehensively than would be possible by means of a 'few variables, many cases' approach. The latter method is, in Ragin's view, inferior to the 'comparable case' approach because the relationships observed are bound to be biased or 'overdetermined' as a result of empirical indicators which are either too generally constructed or measured at a highly aggregated level.

However valuable these insights may be and no matter how important reflection on these issues is, they concern an argument which is false. The differences between Research Designs are often exaggerated and often not based on logical arguments. They concern quality (i.e. historical knowledge) versus quantity (i.e. analytical empiricism), holistic explanations versus parsimonious modeling, interpreting patterned diversity (e.g. on the basis of a 'most different' design) versus judging patterned variation (by means of a 'most similar' design), detailed knowledge of the cases versus theoretical knowledge from relations and so on (Ragin, 1987: Chs 2 and 3). Yet, is there really such a difference between the two approaches that warrants such strong views on the rights and wrongs of either approach? It is obvious that we do not think this to be the case nor that it is necessary (see also: Rueschemeyer et al., 1992: 27ff on this point). Budge and Keman have attempted to clarify this point about applying the logic of comparison to a Research Question as a means to develop a theory within the field of comparative politics, as follows:

> to construct a theory at all one has to simplify and generalize, rather than describe. There is no point in constructing a general explanation clogged up with minutiae of time and place. The purpose of a theory is to catch and specify general tendencies, even at the cost of not fitting all cases (hence one can check it only statistically, and it is no disproof to cite one or two counter-examples). The theory should, however, fit the majority of cases at least in a general way, and provide a sensible and above all an applicable starting-point for discussion of any particular situation, even one which in the end it turns out not to explain – here it can at any rate serve as the basis of a special analysis which shows which (presumably unique or idiosyncratic) factors prevent it from fitting.
>
> A general theory of this kind serves the historian by providing him with an entry point and starting-ideas. These, we would argue, he always brings to the case anyway; with a validated theory he knows they are reasonably founded and has a context within which he can make comparisons with greater confidence. As we suggested at the outset, there is no inherent conflict between historical analysis and general theory. Each can, indeed must, be informed by the other and supplement the other's efforts. Theory is therefore a necessary simplification and generalization of particular motives and influences, not simply a restatement of them, though complete loss of contact with historical reality will render it too abstract and ultimately irrelevant. (Budge and Keman, 1990: 194)

This argument is also aired by others and only demonstrates, once again, the need for a proper Research Design, in which both the time dimension and the spatial dimension are explicitly discussed in view of the Research Question that is under review. We have summarized the discussion of time and space with regard to the requirements of developing a Research Design in Table 3.3.

Table 3.3 *Spatial and temporal aspects of a comparative Research Design*

Dimension	Cases	Type of analysis	Interpretation	Related problems
Space	Territorial units or (sub)systems Case studies (one or a few)	Cross-sectional & quantitative Comparable cases & qualitative	Method of Difference Method of Agreement	– Unit of variation (system specific/unique or not) – Type of data available (qualitative/ quantitative) – Galton's problem and ecological fallacies
Time	Regular intervals (e.g. years) Periodization (e.g. before/after an event)	Time-series Repeated cross-sectional	Method of (indirect) Difference Method of (indirect) Agreement	– Unit of variation (diachronic/event-related or not) – Type of data available (level of measurement) – Sequential or synchronic
Time and Space	(Sub)systems and periods or intervals Multiple case studies	Pooled time-series Time series or QCA	Method of Difference Method of Agreement	– Unit of variation (structural and sequential) – Type of data available (qualitative or quantitative); diachronic Research Question and related causality in X → Y

QCA = Qualitative Case Analysis.

3.4 DEVELOPING A RESEARCH DESIGN

The main argument presented in this chapter has been that the purpose of applying the comparative method in political science is to identify regularities regarding the relationship between societal and political actors, the accompanying processes of institutionalization of political life, and the societal change that emerged simultaneously. In addition the logic of comparison is seen as the 'royal way' to establish theoretical and empirically refutable propositions that explain these regularities in terms of causality.

To this end, the comparative approach to political and social science selects and compares the 'political' in a variety of different societal situations. Comparative analysis is considered to provide a greater opportunity to analyze a greater variety of political behavior and institutions, within and among political systems. Assuming that one knows what to compare and (foremost) why, a proper Research Design must be developed to allow for an analysis that accounts in a plausible way for the Research Question. In Chapter 2 we proposed that the comparative approach to political science may be defined by the use of a particular core subject, i.e. the triad of politics–polity–policy, which involves understanding of the following.

1 How are concepts derived from the 'political' in relation to the Research Question posed; hence: which actors, institutions and types of performance are implied in the Research Question?

   This points to the relation Theory → Evidence → Interpretation.

2 How can these concepts be made to 'travel' from one system (in relation to the unit of analysis) to another; hence: how can one operationalize properly the type of actor, the rules in, and for use of, a system as well as its overall performance?

   This refers to matters of internal and external validity regarding the data analysis.

3 How can a set of units of observation or cases be developed within which systems may be properly compared and classified; hence: which are the comparable cases, rather than maximizing the number of cases beyond the *Ceteris Paribus* clause?

   The question is: what is the adequate 'universe of discourse' in relation to the Research Question asked?

4 How and when does one compare similar and dissimilar systems, synchronically and/or diachronically; hence: how does one take into account time and space as well as promoting the plausibility of making causal statements on the basis of comparison?

   This concerns the range of the theory *per se*.

The understanding of these 'rules' is vitally important for every student of comparative politics and distinguishes it from other approaches within political and social science. In order to develop a proper Research Design by following these 'rules' we need, first of all, to relate the contents or substance of the Research Question to the core subject of the 'political'. Thus are we investigating a problem that is referring to politics–polity–policy altogether or to parts of this triad? For instance, are we employing a Research Question in which both the political determinants and consequences of the welfare state for society form the core subject? This would then imply that the variables are measured on the level of both the political and the social system. In addition the comparativist must decide whether or not it is the process that is questioned or the distinctive features of various welfare states as comparable systems.

This logically leads to the decision on how time and space are part of the Research Design as well as the number of cases that can and should be involved (from 'many' to 'few'). The final decision to be made – in relation to the earlier ones – is then to what extent the context of the variables under investigation is homogeneous or heterogeneous. This means the choice of a 'most similar' or a 'most different' Research Design. If, for instance the Research Question is directed to the internal dynamics of the politics of the welfare state it would imply a homogeneous context. If it concerns a Research Question with regard to the political-economic conditions of the emergence of welfare statism it may well lead to the investigation of regimes throughout the world, which implies a heterogeneous context (see: Keman, 1988 as an example of a MSSD, and Schmidt, 1989 for a MDSD). In summary: the researcher must – on the basis of the Research Question – go through a number of steps in order to develop the proper Research Design. These steps are summarized in Table 3.4.

As has been elaborated in Chapter 1 the 'political' as a core subject of investigation refers to three dimensions: *Politics* = actors and behavior; *Polity* = rules defining the room to maneuver for those actors; *Policy* = outcomes of the decision-making process. As can easily be understood, Politics can be measured on the individual level: for instance voter's attitudes at an election, or the behavior of a party during and after an election. Polity is by definition a feature of the systems under review: for example the type of electoral system or the type of democratic system in which citizens' parties operate (e.g. Lijphart's distinctions of 'consensus democracy' and 'majoritarian democracy'; Lijphart, 1984). Finally, Policy always refers to what has been decided by the political authorities and upon which they act (i.e. public policy-making; Castles et al., 1987; Keman, 1988; Schmidt, 1987). Yet, most important for our purposes here, the student must understand what is central in his/her research. That is: what are the units of variation and their supposed relationship? Is it purely politics, polity, or policy-oriented, or is it a mix? The answer to that question determines the level at which the core subject is to be observed. For example, if we wish to know more about the relations between voters → parties → policy-actions then we strive for observations of individuals (voters), unitary actors (parties), and public policy (e.g. social expenditures) within the rules of the political system. Hence, we use individual observations (micro-level), actor-related ones (meso- or group level) and the system level (the public agency). The main interactions we wish to investigate are then those between politics and society at various levels of measurement. It goes almost without saying that this is quite a complex and delicate matter in terms of operationalization and data-analysis. In general the levels of measurement are more straightforward to determine if the Research Question at stake is directed to the political process itself. These situations refer to rows 2 to 4 in Table 3.4.

Table 3.4 *Choices to be made in developing a Research Design*

Unit of variation of the political	Unit of observation and level	Time dimension	Number of cases	Contextual variables	Type of comparison
1 Politics, polity & policy	Political system & society	(a) Synchronic	Many	Heterogeneous	Cross-sectional
		(b) Diachronic	Few	Homogeneous	Pooled
2 Politics & polity	Intra-system	(a) Synchronic	Many	Homogeneous	Cross-sectional
		(b) Diachronic	Few	Homogeneous	Time series
3 Polity & policy	Inter-system	(a) Synchronic	Many	Heterogeneous	Cross-national
		(b) Periodic	Fewer	Homogeneous	Cross-time
4 Politics	World system	Diachronic	One	Heterogeneous	(Historical) Case study

The second row explicitly refers to Research Questions in which the units of variation are systemic, or intra-system, features related to the behavior of political actors. The study of government formation, for example, is directed by the 'local' rules within a given polity. Hence, we can compare the actual working of these rules over time in one or a few cases from a diachronic point of view. The units of variation concern then the process of government formation, and by definition this occurs within a homogeneous context (Keman, 1995). This implies that circumstances will be more or less constant, and thus deviations can easily be detected and discussed in terms of 'exceptions to the rules' (if not, then we need to reconsider both theory and probably the Research Design!).

The third row points to a Research Design in which the units of analysis are focused at the variation system level: policy-making is then studied at the level of the system *per se* and thus should be compared with other systems. This is why it is called an inter-system comparison which – more often than not – is synchronic in nature (i.e. cross-sectional, if not cross-national). Yet, of course, one may also opt for fewer cases for which it is easier to assume that the context remains constant. This is particularly useful if the researcher aims at the explanation of a complex policy area and uses predominantly qualitative data (e.g.: Héritier, 1993).

Finally, row four is in effect non-comparative, since the 'world system' is by definition unique and singular. Therefore only the change of system components can be studied over time. In fact, this leads to a historical Research Design in which the issue of causality is a contested one (Bartolini, 1992; Keman, 1993d). Hence we work with only one case with features which are difficult to control for.

All in all, Table 3.4 demonstrates that the student – applying the comparative approach to political and social science – is bound to make choices on the basis of the Research Question under review. Therefore the main point of this scheme is that a student of comparative politics learns how to develop his or her Research Design by systematically assessing which options are available on the basis of the Research Question under review. Such a Research Design must thus be conceptualized in terms of the 'political' that is competent not only to answer the specific question under review, but also enhances our (meta-)theoretical understanding of the political process, the 'core subject', such as whether or not conflicting political actors are capable of achieving an optimal decision given the rules of the political game (Keman, 1997).

Examples of comparative research which can be categorized within this framework are the cross-national analysis of political performance (unit of variation 1 in Table 3.4) throughout the world by Bingham Powell (1982), the comparative analysis of the politics of government formation (2), the development of the welfare state (3), and the 'world system' approach (4). In all these instances important choices are to be made relating the Research Question to a Research Design.

Budge and Keman, for instance, consciously choose to explain the process of government formation in terms of actors (i.e. political parties) in relation to their room for maneuver due to existing modes of institutionalized behavior (the 'rules of the game'). The level of observation is 'intra-system' oriented, and they increase the number of meaningful cases within a 'most similar' strategy of comparison (i.e. reducing the number of contextual variables which are assumed to be homogeneous). The diachronic perspective is preferred here to a case-based strategy or a mere country-based comparative approach. Two arguments justify this decision: firstly, countries are not the units of analysis but parties and governments, and the time dimension is considered to be constant; secondly, given the point of departure used as a mode of explanation and the wish to validate the Research Question empirically, as many cases as possible had to be collected as units of observation (Budge and Keman, 1990; Bartolini and Mair, 1990).

Until now we have discussed the basic structural features of developing a Research Design. These features – like units of observation or number of cases, and type of analysis – must be seen as (necessary) steps of reflection in view of the Research Question under review. Recall that a Research Question in our view always implies a relationship (X → Y) representing a (middle-range) theory. In Chapter 1 we defined the unit(s) of variation as the variables (here X and Y) that enable us to develop a data-matrix. Before collecting and analyzing the relevant data one must also take a decision about the kind of data that is called for. Again, as for instance with the issue of many versus few cases, we are confronted with a contested topic amongst comparativists: the constructing of values or indicators (i.e. units of measurement) that are and remain comparable across the 'universe of discourse' (i.e. the units of observation). This debate is now known as the issue of 'concept traveling and stretching' (Sartori, 1970; Dogan and Pelassy, 1990; Collier and Mahon, 1993) and refers to the matter of operationalization. Before turning to this debate we shall first elaborate on the issue of transforming concepts (abstract terms such as politics–polity–policy) into definitions and consequently into operational terms.

3.4.1 Concepts, definitions and operationalization

Within a political system, words to describe the political machinery itself are contested. Judges and bankers quite obviously possess power according to Webster's definition of power as the 'ability to compel obedience' or the 'capability of acting or of producing an effect', for example. Nevertheless many of them would vehemently denounce the assertion 'judges and bankers have great power' as a failure to appreciate that their decisions are not arbitrary but rather based on judicial and financial professionalism.

Therefore, comparative political scientists should neither assume that the same concepts (e.g. 'democracy', 'freedom') used in different political systems have the same meaning, nor that dictionary definitions within a political system overrule the political usage of contested concepts. Concept definitions are needed to deal with ambiguous, abstract and moreover contested concepts. On the other hand too rigid a definition may well be found sterile since it will prevent the application of old concepts to new configurations of facts. Fruitful concepts earn their longevity and their ability to cross national boundaries from the continuous adjustments they manage to absorb (Dogan and Pelassy, 1990: 45). Concept 'stretching' is a necessary phase in the development of constructs. The concept of a 'consociational democracy' was offered by Arend Lijphart (1968) primarily to describe the apparent combination of a fragmented political culture and coalescent elite behavior in the Netherlands prior to 1967. By adapting the concept to exclude historical details concerning the Netherlands, Lijphart was able to apply it to illuminate aspects of (the absence of) democracy in countries such as South Africa and Switzerland (Dogan and Pelassy, 1990: 47–58). Political science rests upon ordinary political language. Its concepts inherit the ambiguities of political life. But definitions may be helpful to clarify the usage of the terms within political science, or at least, the usage of a term by one author. Definitions pave the way to mutual understanding although authors may use different terms and different definitions. Defining concepts is the first step towards measurement. A definition of a concept clarifies which known or unknown persons, objects or states of affairs belong to a certain set. The definition of a concept enables a judgement as to whether the measurements obtained represent the construct in mind to which the concept alludes. Definitions serve to bridge the gap between concepts, which are often vague, abstract or ambiguous, and the units of observation under consideration. They assign cases to concepts. Conversely a definition assigns also conceptual meaning to the raw observations. A concept labels and organizes a vast heterogeneous array of isolated observations (Mayer, 1972: 8, 16). How concepts organize observations is conveyed by their definitions.

3.4.2 Conceptual and operational definitions

A definition provides a cue as to whether a concept applies to an observed case. Definitions are needed to enable judgements of measurement validity. A definition is said to be an operational definition whenever the criteria provided by the definition are unambiguous and apply to all cases under consideration. Operational definitions have often to be adapted to specific techniques of data gathering to allow for such an unambiguous classification. Often, new operational definitions reflect new measurement methods. Operational definitions tend to replace vaguer definitions which are at a higher level of abstraction. The 'issue emphasis of a political party' might serve as an example. Since Budge et al. (1987) came to measure this concept by counting the number of times a party addressed a particular issue in a specific party manifesto, the term issue emphasis has received a far more concrete meaning for political scientists. A conceptual definition or 'analytical definition' clarifies what is meant by a concept without too much operational detail. For the moment we will concentrate on analytical definitions.

Most 20th century readers will take for granted that a definition is merely a social contract proposed by an author with respect to the usage of concepts. Authors ask their audience to use the author's definitions so as to understand what the author intends to say. Definitions can not be 'true' or 'untrue', they just serve to clarify what precisely has been or will be measured (or simply observed) by the author. But ultimately only an analysis based on these measurements and observations adds to our understanding. In the philosophy of science, this social contract view on defining is known as the nominalist view as opposed to the essentialist view that 'true' definitions point to the 'essence' of phenomena. Nominalists interpret a definition like 'politics is in essence a power struggle' as 'if a power struggle has not been observed, then one should not use the label "politics"', whereas essentialists interpret the same definition as 'if A has been labeled as "politics" by observers, then a power struggle must have taken place (whether observed or not)'. Nominalists infer labels from facts, whereas essentialists infer facts from labels. The first are known as prescriptive definitions, whereas definitions reflecting ordinary language use are labeled as descriptive. The latter are to be found in dictionaries. Definitions reflecting the language use in a scientific community are descriptive for that community. They are to be found in scientific textbooks. Definitions in textbooks are designed to communicate the usage of a concept in the scientific community. Since descriptive definitions reflect the obvious, they are neither in need of lengthy comments nor even in need of reiteration.

Authors who prefer descriptive definitions use arguments in discussions over the proper definition of a concept, which come close to the essentialist view. As an example the introduction to 'corporatism' in the textbook of Gallagher et al. (1995) will be discussed. The authors introduce the concept of 'corporatism' as a specimen of 'interest group politics'. Next the authors state that 'Cawson (1986, p. 38) provides a clear-cut definition of the concept:

> "Corporatism is a . . . process in which organizations representing monopolistic functional interests engage in political exchange with state agencies over public policy . . . which involves those organizations in a role which combines interest representation and policy implementation through delegated self-enforcement"'.

Next the authors contend 'The essential features of corporatist decision making are thus as follows:

- Large and powerful interest groups monopolize the representation of the interests of . . .
- Interest groups are organized . . . with a . . . "peak organization" . . . that coordinates strategy . . .
- Interest groups . . . play an important role in both the formulation and the implementation of major political decisions'.

Clearly the authors have shifted here from a descriptive towards an essentialist interpretation of corporatism: the three features above are presented by them as 'essential features' of corporatist decision making, rather than as features of Cawson's definition of corporatism. The textbook quotes in addition Schmitter and Lehmbruch, who wrote that 'Corporatism is more than . . . articulation of interests, rather it is . . . an institutionalized pattern of policy-formation in which large interest organizations cooperate with each other and with public authorities . . .'. Clearly Schmitter and Lehmbruch also adopt an essentialist view, since their formulation suggests that they have revealed the essentials of 'corporatism', rather than having proposed an alternative, prescriptive definition. Prescriptive and essentialist definitions tend to obscure whether facts or labels of facts are at stake in a scientific discussion. They may build up new towers of Babel, since scientific theories tend to become meaningless or untrue when the definitions of their core concepts are replaced, as the debate on corporatism shows (e.g. Woldendorp, 1997). Nevertheless, careful prescriptive definitions are indispensable to communicate the language choices of the author to the audience whenever existing concepts are vague, their usage is contradictory or different definitions are used in different schools of thought.

3.4.3 Extensional and intensional definitions

A definition of a concept clarifies which known or unknown persons, objects or states of affairs belong to a certain set. An enumerative definition exemplifies the set by listing the objects belonging to it. What a democracy is might be explained by the list 'United Kingdom, Germany, The Netherlands, USA, . . .'. One would like to enumerate all the exemplars, but in the social sciences this is usually not possible since the future is unpredictable. Will Nigeria be a democracy by the year 2000? A contrastive definition lists also objects not belonging to the class. The enumerative definition of democracy might be elucidated by a list of states (Indonesia, Cuba, Morocco, . . .) that were not democracies in 1997. Both enumerative and contrastive definitions provide information with respect to the extension of a term. Extensional definitions elucidate the meaning of a concept by listing the objects to which the concept refers. The general format of an extensional definition is: object i is (is not) a member of set X.

The intension of a term describes the criteria which must be met for set membership. The general format of an intensional definition is: X has as property j. Webster's dictionary defines democracy as 'a form of government in which the supreme power is vested in the people and exercised by it directly (as in the ancient Greek city-states or the New England town meeting) – called also direct democracy – or a form of government in which the supreme power is vested in the people and exercised by them indirectly through a system of representation and delegated authority in which the people choose their officials and representatives at periodically held free elections – called also representative democracy'. Intensional definitions presuppose knowledge of related concepts. Webster's intensional definition of democracy presupposes a set of government forms and a subset of them in which the supreme power is vested in the people. The latter subset is divided into a subset in which the people exercise power directly and a subset in which authority is delegated and officials and representatives are chosen by the people in periodically held free elections. Intensional definitions are preferable to extensional definitions because they enable a decision on whether previously unknown entities belong to the defined set. Intensional definitions might be divided further into definitions specifying one criterion for set membership and definitions specifying more criteria. If a definition specifies more criteria to decide on set membership, then the combination of these criteria should be specified. Conjunctive definitions require that all criteria must be met, whereas disjunctive definitions require that at least one criterion must be met. Webster's intensional definition of democracy is clearly disjunctive, since a nation where 'the supreme power vested in the people' is exercised directly only is democratic according to this definition, as also is a nation where this power is exercised indirectly only.

Figure 3.2 gives an overview of various types of definitions. An example of an intensional definition with one criterion is Richardson's early definition of war as any deadly quarrel grouped by an arbitrary cut off point of, for example, 1,000 deaths.

Clearly, Richardson's (1960) definition counted as war incidents that did not involve military combat. Small and Singer (1982) who collected data on wars from 1816 onwards added a second criterion. They went through Richardson's list of wars and eliminated cases they regarded as 'non-wars' because of 'the inadequate political status of the participants'. The definition of Singer and Small of inter-state wars is an example of a conjunctive definition. Both elements must be present: 1,000 deaths and an adequate political status. Of course, inter-state wars will pass the second criterion, but which combinations of famine and tribal hostilities should precisely be classified as wars? Was the political status of various warriors in Eastern Zaire in 1996 adequate enough to warrant the term 'war' for what was going on? Whereas the list of inter-state wars of Singer and Small is accepted as the most definitive to date, their list of intra-state wars is not, because of the vagueness of an 'inadequate political status' (Vasquez, 1993: 21–9).

Related to the conjunctive–disjunctive distinction is the distinction between one-dimensional and multi-dimensional concepts. The reader should first drop the physical connotations of the term 'dimension' here. The number of 'dimensions' of a concept refers to the number of non-compensating criteria for the applicability of the concept, which can be satisfied to a certain degree. Singer and Small's definition of a war specifies two dimensions: the number of deaths in deadly quarrels and the status of the participants. A war might be said to be more 'sincere' when the number of deaths increases, and also when the status of the participants (for example from the status of African farmers to the status of global superpowers) increases. Hence the process of transforming concepts (like Democracy, Power, War) into definitions is an important step in developing an adequate Research

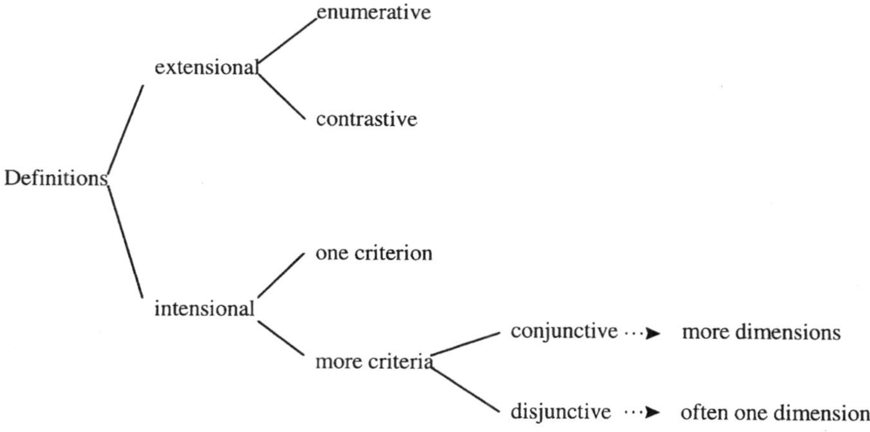

Figure 3.2 *Types of definitions*

Design in comparative politics. Especially crucial here is the degree of comparability in relation to the problem of internal and external validity.

The process of operationalizing means the translation of theoretical concepts into what Sartori (1970) called 'traveling' concepts by means of 'stretching': the units of measurements are too broad to allow for inspecting the 'specifica differentia' across systems or even across time. Hence, the development of 'truly' comparative units of variation is an awkward and often tricky business. Sartori pointed to this problematic as the 'ladder of generality', i.e. either widening the applicability of a theoretical concept by increasing its extension (compared with that of its initial meaning) or constraining it by modifying its intension (limiting observations to specified categories). The latter obviously will reduce the applicability of a concept in actual research but, equally obviously, will increase its internal validity. Increasing extension will have the opposite effect, and here the question is whether or not the wider use (i.e. in number of cases to be compared) impairs the external validity of the analysis. The 'ladder of generality' is depicted in Figure 3.3 (adapted from Collier and Mahon, 1993).

The choice to be made and the matter of dispute is then how broadly (i.e. how great the extension) can we define and measure the units of analysis without a serious loss of meaning (i.e. less-constrained intension)? A good example of how not to do it is the comparative analysis of 'pillarization'. Originally this concept referred to Dutch Society in which, on the basis of the religious cleavage (Catholics versus Protestants), social and political life was organized separately for each group in a vertical fashion (see: Daalder, 1974). By means of this concept Lijphart was able to explain stable government under heterogeneous socio-cultural conditions in the Netherlands (Lijphart, 1968). Other studies used this concept to explain the degree of (in)stability in other segmented societies (such as Austria, Germany, Norway, Italy). The initial operationalization by Lijphart was too strict to apply across western Europe and thus the researchers resorted to the method of categorizing by means of 'family resemblance' (Collier and Mahon, 1993: 846–8). In its simplest fashion this method extends the initial definition, i.e. pillarization, by

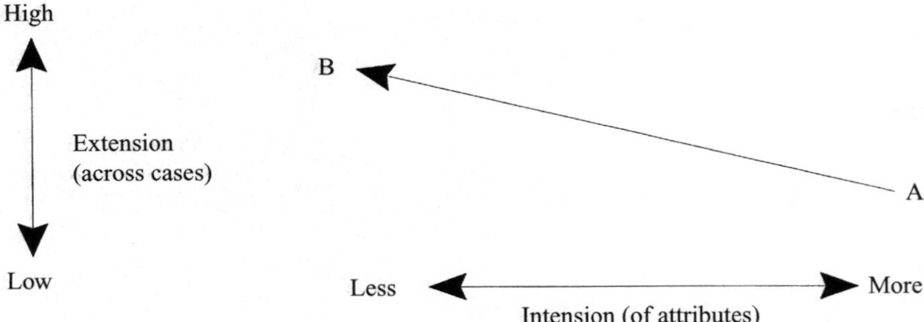

Figure 3.3 *Sartori's 'ladder of generality'. A = initial unit of variation as defined (theoretical concept); B = eventual unit of variation as operationalized (which can 'travel')*

adding cases, which share some (if not most), attributes designated to indicate pillarization. How far this type of widening of extension can go depends, first of all, on the Research Question asked, and secondly on whether or not the remaining contextual features can be kept reasonably constant (in a Most Similar Systems Design, of course), to make use of factor analysis and scalability techniques in general. These will be introduced in Part II.

Another method of going up the 'ladder of generality' is by the use of radial categories. Here the basic idea is that each step of widening extension, and thus including new comparable cases, is defined by a hierarchy of attributes belonging to the initial concept. Take for example the concept of 'polyarchy' as introduced by Dahl (1971). Central to his concept are the degrees to which the population at large is free to participate in political decision-making. Initially Dahl focuses on electoral rights to participate in decision-making and freedom to exercise opposition. In addition he lists a number of attributes that make up the optimal mode of democratization in order to compare the existing democracies in terms of his concept polyarchy (see: Dahl, 1971: Ch. 10). Now, by requiring that the core attributes must be available (opposition and participation), one can develop a categorization of democratic systems in which more or fewer of the other features are available. The fewer the requirements that are fulfilled, the more cases will be included. Hence radial categorization implies widening extension by relaxing the initial definition. Again – as with the method of family resemblances – it depends on the Research Question (X → Y) to what extent this is still valid and will induce viable conclusions.

Figure 3.4 demonstrates the two possible strategies for widening extension. Family resemblance requires commonalities and, in this example, produces three cases in comparison with one under the initial categorization, by sharing two out of the three defining features. The radial method requires that the primary attribute (A) be always included. In Figure 3.4 this produces two cases instead of the initial

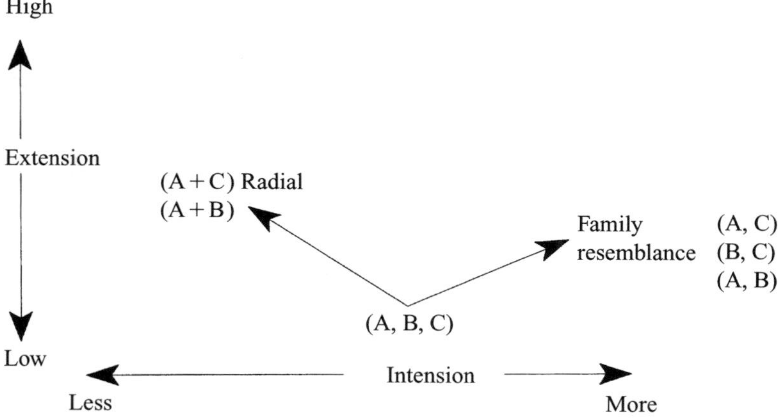

Figure 3.4 *Radial categorization and family resemblance. (A, B, C) = requirements/attributes of the original definition*

one, having in common A and either B or C present in order to increase the number of cases under review.

In summary: the process of operationalization for comparative purposes implies conscious decisions not only on how to develop the proper indicators, but also on the issue of the extent to which the process of operationalization as applied in observable characteristics can be relaxed to increase the units of observation without losing its original meaning or definitions given the Research Question.

3.4.4 Levels of measurement

The process of transforming abstract concepts into empirical definitions in order to develop comparative indicators has its implications for the levels of measurement. Four levels are generally employed in the social sciences: nominal, ordinal, ratio and interval scales (see e.g.: Blalock, 1979).

A *nominal scale* (or 'classification') allows for a great variety of qualitatively different possibilities. In comparative political science, democracies are subdivided further, for example, into 'consensual democracies' and 'majoritarian democracies' on the basis of their electoral system (e.g. Lijphart, 1984). As a further example of a nominal scale the concept of a 'party family', which is used in comparative political science to classify national political parties, may serve as an example. Gallagher et al. (1995: 181–208) classify European parties as 'social democratic', 'communist', 'new left', 'green', 'Christian democratic', 'secular conservative', 'liberal', 'agrarian', 'far right' or 'subnational or regionalist'. A 'party family' is thus conceived as a nominal scale with ten qualitatively different nominal values. From a methodological point of view the assignment of nominal values should be exhaustive and mutually exclusive. The requirement of exhaustiveness has been met when the definitions undergirding the classification scheme enable the assignment of a nominal value to *every* relevant unit of observation. To meet this criterion Gallagher et al. simply introduce an additional party family of 'other parties' which includes all parties that were not included in either of the ten party families mentioned before. Although the family of 'other parties' was apparently indispensable to meet the criterion of exhaustiveness, the recognition of such a family undermines comparative inquiry, since parties belonging to this category do not need to have anything in common. The requirement of mutual exclusiveness has been met when the measurement procedure or classification scheme clearly designates that only one specific nominal value is appropriate. The criterion of mutual exclusiveness entails that it should be clear why the Fianna Fail in Ireland is classified as a 'secular conservative' party, or why 'Green Left' in the Netherlands is classified as a 'new left' party rather than as a 'green' party.

In addition to dichotomous variables, two-dimensional classifications are used to develop a typology. Arend Lijphart, for example, developed a typology of stable democracy in which two dimensions are vital to clarify units of observation: (1) structure of society; (2) elite behavior (Lijphart, 1977: 106). The outcome of his nominal division leads to *four* types, as shown in Table 3.5. This division is not only intended to divide democracies into mutually exclusive types and for all relevant cases (hence, exhaustive), but can also be seen as an empirical instrument

Table 3.5 *Lijphart's typology of democratic systems*

Elite behavior	Structure of society: Homogeneous	Structure of society: Plural
Coalescent	Depoliticized: Austria (1966–)	Consociational: Belgium, The Netherlands, Switzerland, Austria (1945–66)
Adversarial	Centripetal: Finland, Denmark, UK, USA, Norway, Sweden, Germany	Centrifugal: France, Italy, Canada

Source: Lijphart (1977).

to relate units of variation to units of observation by means of nominally measured information.

The next step in this procedure, more often than not, is to develop a refinement in which a 'ranking' of the relevant cases is developed. This is then an ordinal scale.

An *ordinal scale* allows for a ranking of the units of variation. Usually a definition which gives rise to a dichotomy (e.g. either 'democratic' or not) can be extended not only towards a polytomous variable (types of (non-)democracies), but also towards an ordinal scale. One may attempt to rank nations on the basis of their degree of democracy. Switzerland probably has a higher degree of democracy than, for example, Russia, although elections are held in both countries. Parties can be ranked according to their degree of internal democracy, according to the Leftness of their ideology, according to their 'Greenness', or according to whatever ordinal concept applies to parties as the units of analysis. Usually the resulting rankings are 'incomplete', which means that the scale does not give rise to unique ranks, but to ties. It goes almost without saying that an ordinal scale in comparative political science imposes a cognitive ranking, which does not imply an evaluative ranking. The positioning of parties as, say, 'low', 'high', 'extreme' or 'median' on ordinal scales such as 'Leftist', 'Religious', or 'Extremist' depends on qualitative information reported by the researcher and supporting his/her divisions and subsequent rankings.

Further quantitative refinements of an ordinal scale amount to an *interval scale* or a *ratio scale*. A ratio scale of direct democracy, for example, might be obtained by simply counting the number of decisions that were subject to popular referenda within a given time period. A ratio scale has a meaningful zero point (e.g., $0 =$ no popular referenda at all). The Gross National Product of a nation is measured on a ratio scale, since the zero point is meaningful ($0 \Rightarrow$ no valuables were produced). The difference between a ratio scale and an interval scale might also be explained as having a meaningful zero-point or not. In addition an interval scale is the result of manipulating different types of ratio-based information.

The numerical representations of the categories of a nominal scale might be changed in any desired way, as long as different numbers are assigned to different categories (e.g.: $7 =$ male, $10 =$ female, but not $10 =$ male, $10 =$ female). The scores of an ordinal scale might be monotonically transformed, for example by

Table 3.6 *Levels of measurement*

Measurement level	Meaning of numbers assigned to categories	(Examples of) treatment in this book
Dichotomous, binary	Other number ⇒ other category	Either use data analysis techniques for nominal scales or use (eventually adjusted) techniques for interval scales
Nominal		Frequency table (Section 5.1) Cross-tables (5.3, 6.4)
Ordinal	Higher number ⇒ higher rank	Either use data analysis techniques for nominal scales (e.g. if number of categories less than five) or use techniques for interval scales
Interval	Equal interval between numbers ⇒ equal difference between categories	Frequency distribution (5.2) Regression analysis (5.4, 5.7.4)
Ratio	X times as far from zero ⇒ X times more	
Absolute	Number ⇒ number	

The numbers in parentheses refer to the statistics used in combination with the data measured on the level indicated in Chapter 5.

raising all scores to the third power, but the original order must be kept. Only linear transformations apply to interval scales. Only multiplication with a constant is allowed on ratio scales. By a simple multiplication with the exchange rate, a bank account in dollars might be expressed as a bank account in liras, for example. Absolute scales are sometimes distinguished as a special type of ratio scale (e.g. 'number of refugees'). No numerical transformations are allowed on absolute scales. In Table 3.6 the various types of level of measurement are presented.

The levels of measurement of the concepts involved in the analysis determine the choice of the statistical methods to be used for data analysis. Without a proper understanding of the levels of measurement it is impossible to choose the appropriate techniques for data analysis. The available techniques for data analysis will be discussed in Chapters 5 and 6 and will be applied in Part III of this book.

3.5 ORGANIZING AND COLLECTING DATA

As will be clear by now, a comparative Research Design is developed to answer a Research Question by means of empirical data and the use of statistical techniques. We have therefore distinguished units of

- variation, representing theoretical concepts in empirical definitions;
- observation, i.e. the carriers of information that contain empirical indicators;
- measurement, i.e. scales that organize the information into comparable data that can be analyzed.

In political science the units of variation can be properties of (sub)systems, actors or relations between them. Units of variation can never be the same as units of observation, since the cases under review are an empirical entity instead of a theoretical concept. Finally the unit of measurement is the translation of the unit of variation in a way that varies meaningfully across the universe of discourse, i.e. the collection of units of observation. In Table 3.7 we give examples of the three units that are vital to any comparative Research Design.

Many more examples could be mentioned but the point we wish to make is that the units of variation – representing the core argument implied by the Research Question – direct both the selection and type of cases involved and the nature of what is to be derived from these selected units of observation (including the level of measurement, e.g. Democratization is measured as a classification, hence as a nominal scale, whereas Welfare States are based on an indicator measured on interval level). What is important here and should be noted, however, is that the relationship between the Research Question under review may well be conducive to a Research Design that becomes a complex undertaking in terms of type of cases selected and the levels of measurement involved. Take for example the following Research Question:

> To what extent and in what way do organized interests, complexion of government and economic development influence the levels of welfare statism?

In this case the *units of variation* (X and Y) are 'Welfare States' (the dependent variable = Y), whereas 'Corporatism', 'Economic Development' and 'Type of Government' are the independent variables (= X). The selection of the *units of observation* would then be: Nations, Organized Interests, Growth of (e.g.) GNP per Capita, Governments regarding the X-variables and Public Expenditures (on welfare, like transfer payments, health care, etc.) for the Y-variable. So we have an inter-state comparison in combination with intra-state units of observation (parties in government and organization interests) that are *measured* on different levels: Type of Government on the nominal level, Corporatism on the ordinal level, Economic Development on the interval level, and Welfare States on the ratio level.

In short: in developing a Research Design, it is not only vital to choose carefully the proper elements, but also to reflect on the implied consequences for the empirically driven statistical analysis so that we can come up with a valid and plausible answer. If we do not realize that we relate different types of variables

Table 3.7 *Examples of units of variation/observation/measurement*

Unit of variation	Unit of observation	Unit of measurement
Democratization	States	Polyarchy
Welfare states	Nations	Expenditures
Corporatism	Organized interests	Tripartite consultation
Electoral volatility	Elections	Aggregate change of voters
Federalism	States	Constitutional rules
Ideology	Parties	Programs
Type of government	Governments	Party composition
Social movements	Organized groups	Collective behavior
Left versus Right	Parties	Left/Right scales

(some defined on the system level and others on the within-system level) which are based on different types of cases (systems and actors) measured on various levels, then we run the risk of applying the wrong statistical techniques, on the one hand (using, for instance, interval techniques on variables measured on a nominal level), and inferring biased conclusions, on the other (for instance, as a result of Galton's problem: too few cases, many variables).

Hence, before you begin collecting data and then proceed to analyzing them, you must be convinced that the right choices underpin a Research Design which is intended to answer the Research Questions you are asking and are according to the 'rules' of the comparative approach.

3.6 CONCLUSION

It is vitally important that an understanding of these 'rules' for systematically doing comparative research forms an essential part of learning and training – not only in comparative politics in particular, but also in political science in general. Ultimately this is one of the reasons why grounding in comparative politics is so essential to a wider political science education. Political science in general, which has been accurately defined as 'an academic discipline which seeks to systematically describe, analyze and explain the operations of government institutions and overtly political organizations' must necessarily include the comparative approach, if only by virtue of its explanatory intent. Indeed, perhaps the only single circumstance in which a political scientist is not also at least implicitly a comparative political scientist is when he or she remains consistently and exclusively concerned with his or her own national system. However, even then, any attempt to explain one's own system entirely without reference to either the experience of other systems or across time (explicit comparison) or to those theories which have been derived from the experience of other systems (implicit comparison) is almost always doomed to failure.

But if we are to know other countries or systems, and, through this, to begin to understand how politics works, then it is essential that we promote an understanding of how to do comparative political analysis, and of how to become 'conscious' comparativists. And this, more than anything else, requires us to systematically develop a Research Design that enables the student to come to valid, reliable and plausible answers. Vitally important is then – in our view – to relate theory to empirical evidence. And exactly this is a task that requires an adequate knowledge of data-collection and analysis. How to do this is the core of Part II, to which we turn now.

3.7 ENDMATTER

Topics highlighted

- The structure and meaning of a Research Design: $(C * [X \rightarrow Y])$ representing the Research Question.

- The choice of a Most Similar or a Most Different Systems Design: cases and variables to compare.
- Interpreting empirical evidence from a MSSD or MDSD approach: Methods of Agreement and Difference, regarding the interpretation of results.
- Space and time as dimensions of a Research Design: cross-sections, case studies and diachronic approaches.
- Choosing the proper Research Design on the basis of the units of variation (derived from the core subject).
- Conceptualization and operationalization in view of striving for 'truly' comparative knowledge: concept traveling and stretching.
- Levels of measurement and the units of observation.

Question

If you read the article by Lijphart and Crepaz (1991) and the rejoinder by Keman and Pennings (1995) in the *British Journal of Political Science*, can you tell what methodological issues are in dispute? (Think of: reliability and validity; concept stretching and traveling; radial and resemblance.) Whose side are you on regarding the methodological issues raised?

Exercise

We would like you to develop a Research Design of your own using one of the Research Questions listed below. You should do the following:

1 Elaborate the relation between theory and the Research Question.
2 Cast your RQ into ($C * [X \rightarrow Y]$) and infer from that whether or not you intend to use a MSSD or MDSD approach.
3 Develop the requirements of the Research Design in terms of time and space.
4 Specify the units of variation in terms of the 'political' (the core of political science (see also Section 2.4)).
5 Try to operationalize the core of your RQ ($X \rightarrow Y$) and discuss your indicators in terms of concept traveling and stretching (i.e. validity!) and levels of measurement.

The Research Questions from which you can choose are:

1 Does politics matter with respect to the development of the welfare state?
2 Do parties matter with respect to political stability?
3 Do variations in party systems matter with respect to the composition of governments and policy performance?

To answer, you can make use of the following literature:

1 Castles, F.G. and McKinlay, R.D. (1979) 'Does politics matter? An analysis of the public commitment in advanced democratic states', *European Journal of Political Research*, 7 (2): 169–86.

2 Bingham Powell, G. (1982) *Contemporary Democracies: Participation, Stability and Violence*. Cambridge, MA: Harvard University Press. pp. 1–11.
3 Budge, I. and Keman, H. (1990) 'New concerns for coalition theory: Allocation of ministries and sectoral policy-making. A comparative analysis', *Acta Politica*, 25 (2): 151–82.

Further reading

- *General*: Dogan and Pelassy, 1990; Holt and Turner, 1970; Berg-Schlosser and Müller-Rommel, 1987.
- *Specific*: Bingham Powell, 1982; Castles, 1987; Rueschemeyer et al., 1992.

Part II

STATISTICS IN POLITICAL SCIENCE

4

Concepts, cases, data and measurement

CONTENTS

This chapter focuses on the measurement of political concepts. A concept has been measured whenever data have been found that indicate whether, or to what degree, the concept applies to an observed case. A measurement is simply defined as an assignment of a value (or datum) to an observed case (or an observed unit) on a variable (a concept). One measurement of the concept bilateralism, for example, is obtained by assigning the value *yes* to Germany, another by assigning the value *no* to New Zealand.

Most elements of the definition of measurement have already been dealt with in the previous chapter. Whether a concept applies, depends on its definition. Whether it makes sense to ask not only whether a concept applies, but also which degree of the concept applies, depends on its level of measurement. The previous chapter showed also that the units (cases) to which a concept applies are by no means trivial in comparative political science. Political scientists are likely to be interested in nations, in individual voters, and in issue areas as units of analysis, to mention only a few. The units in comparative political science can be time units (e.g. 'Italy 1965', 'Italy 1966', ... 'Italy 1998'), cross-sectional units (e.g. 'Italy 1996', 'Sweden 1996', ...) or a combination of both.

Measurements always presume the availability of data. Various types of available data – e.g. data from statistical agencies, and easily gathered data, e.g. survey data – will be discussed in Section 4.1 Separate measurements might be represented as the entries (or cells) in a rectangular data-matrix with the units (cases) as rows and the variables (concepts) as columns. This rectangular data-matrix which brings together the various measurements for a set of concepts with respect to a set of units is treated in 4.3. The problem of generalizability of research findings, which arises when the available data constitute only a subset of all conceivable data, is introduced in 4.2. Often a variety of data might be used to indicate whether a single concept applies to a given unit. Scalability analysis (Sections 4.4 and 4.5) can be used to test the reliability of multiple indicators.

4.1 DATA AND DATA COLLECTION IN POLITICAL SCIENCE

Political science is in our view an empirical science. Its inspiration may well hinge on philosophies of the good world, or on doomsday prophecies, but more or less irrefutable facts constitute its basis. The relevant facts can be gathered from different sources.

4.1.1 Data obtained from official statistical agencies

An obvious source for comparative information on political processes is the data published on a yearly or quarterly basis by national and international statistical agencies, such as the IMF, the IBRD and the OECD, although the focus of these data is an economic one. The statistical yearbooks from the *Encyclopaedia Britannica*, the Yearbooks from SIPRI on military expenditures and warfare, and the Yale University *World Handbook of Political and Social Indicators* are useful for additional political time series. All types of data sets with respect to political and social indicators compiled by political scientists and sociologists have been made publicly available by the International Consortium for Political and Social Research (ICPSR) in Ann Arbor, Michigan, USA, but most of these data sets are not kept up to date, or refer to one nation only. Some journals in the field of political science, for example the *European Journal of Political Research* will occasionally publish data sets collected by political scientists also. Table 4.1 gives an overview of available data sets for comparative political science.

The compilers of data sets that enable comparisons between nations have usually obtained their data from national statistical agencies. Third world countries in particular do not have the statistical agencies to deliver the required data. When data from national agencies are available, they might not match the definitions of the international agencies precisely. Often the data obtained from statistical agencies do not allow for the distinctions desired by political scientists. The data set NIAS.SAV, which is used throughout this book, was compiled by a group of researchers visiting the Netherlands Institute for Advanced Study in the Humanities and Social Sciences in 1995/1996.

4.1.2 Verbal and visual accounts, content analysis

Verbal accounts from politicians, eyewitnesses, journalists and contemporary historians constitute an important source of information for political scientists. These verbal accounts are accompanied in a growing number of cases by visuals on photographs, films and video. Verbal and visual accounts of the political process might be given by the participants in the process or by observers and interpreters.

Many contributions of the participants in the political process towards decision-making are recorded officially (e.g. party programs, parliamentary proceedings). Politicians will use the media to pursue their ends, and will use press conferences, press reports, and 'sound bites' in television programs to provide additional evidence, or at least additional images, of their daily pursuits.

Table 4.1 *Commonly used datasets from statistical agencies in political science*

Source	Exemplars of comparative periodical datasets
IMF	International financial statistics Direction of trade statistics
OECD	Historical statistics Employment outlook OECD economic surveys (country reports)
ILO	Labour Force Statistics
Encyclopaedia Britannica	Yearbooks, Statistical Addendum (comparative data on government, elections, economics and demography)
Mackie and Rose	Comparative data on parties contesting elections and election outcomes
SIPRI (Stockholm International Peace Research Institute)	Yearbook of world armaments and disarmament
ICPSR (International Consortium for Political and Social Research)	Archive of (party comparative) datasets gathered by political scientists

Professional observers and interpreters of the political process are helpful for the political scientist. Journalists will provide answers to common-sense questions with respect to the political process, especially answers to questions with respect to basic agreements and conflicts between politicians that underlie policy compromises. Collecting newspaper cuttings will be valuable in many research projects, especially when the research question asks for an insight into modes of political conflict and political cooperation. Civil servants, members of advisory councils, and representatives of pressure groups that were involved in a policy process build up the second category of helpful observers and interpreters.

Altogether the amount of available verbal and visual accounts from the political sphere is overwhelming. Citations, paraphrases and sound bites are the traditional means of mastering, or at least reducing, this overwhelming excess of information. Diplomats, journalists, historians and theologians are all masters of the art of citation. It remains often an open question, however, whether the same citations, or even citations with the same purport, would have been selected also by other citation experts when complex policy documents, party programs or parliamentary debates are at stake. The reliability of citations is low.

The term 'content analysis' refers to 'any technique for making inferences by objectively and systematically identifying specified characteristics of messages' (Holsti, 1969: 14). Content analysis thus aims at data with respect to verbal and visual messages that are more reliable than citations and paraphrases. Content analysis data typically enable systematic comparisons of verbal and visual accounts delivered by one actor at various points in time, or between various sources. Two basic types of content analysis can be distinguished: thematic content analysis and relational content analysis (Roberts, 1997).

Thematic content analysis aims at an assessment of the (frequency of the) presence of specified themes, issues, actors, states of affairs, words or ideas in the texts or visuals to be analyzed. Which themes, issues or actors are sought depends completely on the theoretical concepts to be operationalized. The themes, issues or actors sought should be mutually exclusive (no overlaps). The complete set should be exhaustive (no unclassified texts). A mutually exclusive set of themes, issues or actors constitutes a nominal variable, since it does not exhibit a rank order. The frequency distribution of such a nominal variable indicates which themes, issues, facts or actors were mentioned more or less frequently in the texts or visuals being analyzed. In the Manifesto research project (Budge et al., 1987; Volkens, 1994), for example, a thematic content analysis has been performed of more than a thousand party programs from industrialized countries (period 1946 until 1992). Sentences from party programs were classified into 54 predetermined issue areas, such as 'social justice', 'military positive', 'military negative' or 'economic orthodoxy'. Data from this content analysis will be used in this book, amongst others in Section 4.6 to illustrate various types of scalability analysis.

Relational content analysis aims at an assessment of the relations between actors, issues, ideas, etc. according to the texts or visuals being analyzed. As an example the Conflict and Peace Data Base (COPDAB) will be discussed (Azar, 1982). Relations between nations are being sought in this content analysis project. Although newspaper articles are being analyzed, its aim is to reconstruct the 'real events' underlying them. Roughly 350,000 events from the period 1948–1978 were construed on the basis of news reports in 77 international newspapers and news magazines, predominantly from the USA and the Middle East. The data base consists of subject-nation/predicate/object-nation relationships. Each predicate is classified on a ratio scale ranging from extremely negative (full-blown war, represented here as −1) towards extremely positive (voluntary unification, represented here as +1). As an example, six events from this data base concerning the US–Israel relationship in early 1956 are represented below.

yr	mo	da	subj nation	predicate		Value	object Nation
55	11	9	USA	STRESS	STATE DEPT NOT SUPPLY ENOUGH ARMS FOR ARMS RACE	−.1	ISR
55	11	16	USA	REAFFIRM	EISENHOWER GUARANTEE PEACE SETTLEMENT BY PACTS	+.1	ISR
55	11	29	USA	STATE	US THINKS PEACE IS POSSIBLE IN ME	+.1	ISR
55	12	22	USA	PRESENT	RESOLUTION TO CONDEMN ISR ATTACKS ON SYR	−.3	ISR
56	1	6	USA	SPEAK	ON ARMS FOR ISR	+.1	ISR
56	1	11	USA	DENOUNCE	ISR RAID ON SYR	−.3	ISR
56	2	24	USA	DECLARE	US MAY SEND ARMS TO ISR (FOR PEACE)	+.1	ISR

The first sentence indicates a slightly negative event in the relationship of the USA towards Israel: stressing one's foreign policy, e.g. stressing the US policy of restricted arms deliveries towards Israel (presumably to encourage cooperation in the Middle East), is always considered as a mild form of coercive policy according to the COPDAB-coding scheme. The six sentences indicate the ambiguity of US policy on Israel. The USA supported Israel throughout (value +0.1 throughout) although several warnings were issued to prevent a Middle East war (which came about nevertheless in October 1956). The COPDAB data base will recur in Chapter 9.

4.1.3 Questionnaires and surveys

When the personal experiences, perceptions, opinions, attitudes and reported behaviors of still-living persons – either power holders or rank-and-file citizens – are crucial to answering a research question then questionnaires and surveys come into play. In questionnaires and surveys the unit of measurement is usually an individual. Influential individuals might be asked, however, to act as the mouthpiece of their company, their party, or even their nation. In the latter case these organizations will usually become the units of analysis.

Here we will use the term *questionnaire* to denote a set of personalized questions that will be posed to a single actor on the basis of a preliminary investigation with respect to the actor's experiences, policy and world view. Usually the interview design allows for posing subsequent questions that were not foreseen in the interview script. Subsequent questions will depend on the answers of the subject that are the starting point for an interview with a person. Questionnaires and interviews are at the heart of journalism. Political scientists will use them to reveal inside views of the political process. The reliability of answers obtained during an interview relies on an exchange between the interviewer and the respondent. Elite subjects willing to give an interview often want to stress their policy views once more, whereas the interviewer wants to have answers to preconceived questions. Friction in elite interviews is often enhanced by abstract, overarching questions that do not account for the multitude and diversity of daily experiences of elite persons on the basis of which answers to these questions have to be assembled. The question 'how much power has A in your opinion?, for example, is a confusing question. Policy experts might be as confused with respect to the various faces of 'power' as political scientists. Abstract, ambiguous and vague questions evoke abstract, ambiguous and vague answers.

The term *survey* is used to denote a standard list of questions that will be posed to a great number of individuals. Usually not the population of all individuals, but a formal sample from it will be interviewed. Interviews might be conducted by telephone or in a personal setting with an interviewer, usually at the homes of the interviewed persons. Examples of surveys are the National Election Studies in many countries. Commercial marketing agencies conduct surveys on a regular (daily or weekly) basis so as to monitor trends in opinions and behaviors on the basis of which their clients – firms, ministries, and to a minor extent also political parties – might base their marketing decisions. A *panel survey* is a special type of survey where the same respondents are interviewed repeatedly over time. Comparative surveys in several countries are relatively rare. A sociological example, which is useful in the context of comparative research of political values also, is provided by the world value survey designed by Inglehart and colleagues (Inglehart, 1997). The Eurobarometer-data provides comparative data on political attitudes and political behavior in the European Community. Since many textbooks are available on survey research, we will not delve into it here.

4.2 SAMPLING AND THE BASICS OF STATISTICAL TESTING

Usually it is unnecessary to gather measurements on all the empirical cases to which a theory applies. Efficient research bears on a few crucial cases only or on a sample of cases from the population of all cases to which a theory applies. We will start the discussion of sampling here, before the statistics come in (Subsection 5.5.2). Sampling inevitably gives rise to the generalizability question. Is it reasonably safe to infer that the research results with respect to the sample will hold for the population of all cases to which the theory applies? An answer to this question depends of course on known characteristics of the relationship between the sample and the population.

In the *random sample* every individual from a given population has the same probability of being sampled. Most statistics presume random samples, although random sampling is an ideal type only. Research results that hold for a random sample may not hold for the population as a whole. Interesting research results on the basis of a sample are matched against a dull *null hypothesis* maintaining that in the population as a whole the result does not hold. A first type of error (the *type I error*) is to maintain that the interesting result holds for the population as a whole, whereas actually the null hypothesis holds. The aim of statistical testing is to reduce the probability of a type I error to less than a specified level, commonly set as less than 5 per cent. A *type II error* is made when interesting research results on the basis of a sample are discarded in favor of the null hypothesis, but the null hypothesis is false after all. The so called 'power' of statistical tests is their ability to reduce type II errors also. The power of various statistical tests is too complicated a subject to be discussed in this book.

4.2.1 Statistical inference from a random sample

If in the population the numbers '0' and '1' (e.g. representing 'girls' and 'boys') occur with the same frequency, then selecting a sample of 4 elements from this sample will definitely result in one of 16 sequences with equal probability: 1111, 1110, 1101, ... 0000. Each of these 16 sequences has a probability of $1/16$. By counting aspects of these 16 sequences it is easily verified that the probability of getting a sample distribution of either boys only or girls only is $1/8$ ($1/16$ for the sequence $1111 + 1/16$ for 0000). Although girls occur precisely as often in the population as boys, the chance of encountering an equal amount of boys and girls in a sample of four amounts to $3/8$ only (6 of 16 sequences only, namely 1100, 1010, 1001, 0110, 0101, 0011). It is more likely to obtain three times as many exemplars of the one sex than of the second (chance $= 1/2$, corresponding to 8 from 16 sequences, namely 0001, 0010, 0100, 1000, 0111, 1011, 1101, 1110). If one has found either no girls at all or no boys at all in a sample of 4, and one is willing to accept erroneous assertions one out of five times (type I error of 20 per cent), then statistically speaking the conclusion is warranted that boys and girls do not appear equally frequently in the population, since the chance of finding no boys at all or no girls at all amounted to $1/8$ ($= 12.5$ per cent) only. Statisticians are usually more conservative in the sense of accepting erroneous assertions with respect to the population distribution for less than 5 per cent of the possible number of samples only (type I error < 0.05).

Let's emphasize three aspects of the statistician's line of thought in this simple example. First it should be noted that the statistician's tests are based on counts in an imaginary universe of all conceivable samples that might have been drawn. The second aspect to be noticed is that an important ingredient in the calculus of the statistician is the *sample size*. As long as the number of children in the sample is limited, giving birth to children of the same sex only is no reason to falsify the hypothesis that the odds of getting boys and getting girls are equal.

The third aspect to be aware of is that counts in an imaginary population to which the null hypothesis applies mount up to a *probability distribution* of all counts. Selecting at random sets of children from a school class of boys and girls gives a Newtonian or binomial distribution of the numbers of each gender in the sets. Once the probability distribution is known, statistical testing is straightforward from a mathematical point of view. The question of which probability distribution is appropriate under which circumstances will recur in Sections 5.6 and 5.7. Distributions such as the Gaussian or normal distribution, the t-distribution, the Chi-square distribution and the F-distribution play a central role in these sections. Why each distribution applies is the subject of mathematical statistics. We will simply use specific probability distributions on the authority of mathematical statisticians.

4.2.2 Random samples and non-random samples

Most samples are not random. Two types of non-random samples will be discussed here: the stratified sample and the cluster sample. The *stratified sample* intends to be more representative of the population as a whole than a random sample would be. Statistical tests based on random-sample assumptions will be too conservative for a stratified sample. The key to stratified sampling is the use of known population distributions in the sampling plan. If it is known that 50 per cent of mankind are women, and that 20 per cent of men and 22 per cent of women are older than 65, then it is quite natural to draw a stratified sample with 10 per cent of elderly men, 11 per cent of elderly women, 40 per cent of men under 65, and 39 per cent of women under 65. One should keep in mind, though, that the variables of interest are often not the variables on which the sample is stratified. Samples are usually stratified with respect to demographic characteristics, but the advantage of a demographically stratified sample over a random sample vanishes when the variables of interest are related only remotely to demography. If the percentage of the population is to be estimated that perceives a political candidate to be fit for the job, then the advantage of a stratified sample will be negligible, since these perceptions are related only remotely to demographic characteristics.

The *cluster sample*, or multi-level sample, is less representative of the population than a random sample. At the first level, clusters are selected: for example, municipalities within a nation. At the second level, individuals within the first-level clusters, e.g. inhabitants of a selected municipality, are selected. A special type of a cluster sample is the snowball sample, where a set of individuals is sampled randomly and next the population of relatives of the interviewed person is asked to participate in the interview. The statistical inference problem is double-edged now. In principle one has to infer whether results holding for a sample of inhabitants would hold for the municipality as a whole and next whether results that hold for the sample of municipalities hold for the population as a whole. Cluster sampling is often preferred for pragmatic reasons over random sampling. Progress has been made during the last decade with respect to statistics for multi-level samples (Bryk and Raudenbush, 1995) but in this book we will only deal with statistics that assume random samples.

Many economists and political scientists will even perform statistical tests that assume a random sample, when the units of analysis at their disposal mount up to the complete population. Economists studying quarterly data from the 1980s will perform statistical tests that assume a random sample, although the population from which these quarters are randomly drawn is metaphysical. Political scientists using data on all democracies for which data are available (western democracies) will perform statistical tests also. The attraction of statistical tests is their property of taking research results more seriously as the number of units of analysis increases. Since increasing the number of units of analysis will also be a means to cancel out random measurement errors and casual interpretation errors, statistical tests that assume a random sample are often used even when complete populations are being investigated.

4.3 OPERATIONALIZATION AND MEASUREMENT: LINKING DATA WITH CONCEPTS AND UNITS

The *operational definition* of a concept prescribes which measurements are appropriate to measure a theoretical concept. The operational definition of a concept bridges the gap between the general definition of a concept (see Chapter 3) and the available data. Concept definition is the first filter in the funnel from concepts to data, as Figure 4.1 depicts. *Operationalization* is defined as the set of efforts to obtain an acceptable operational definition.

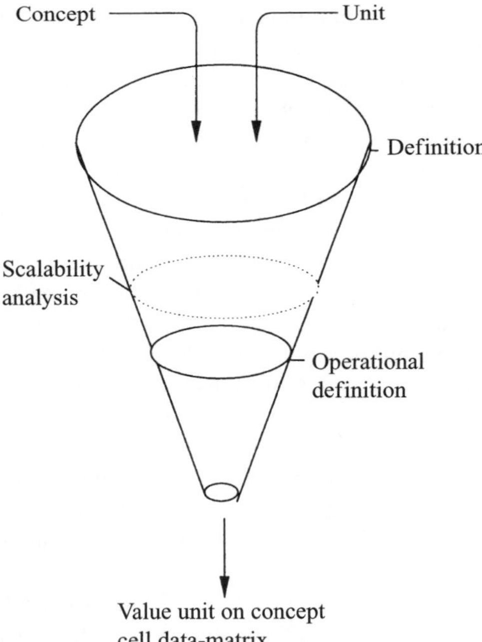

Figure 4.1 *The funnel of operationalization: from a concept and a unit towards a value*

The operational definition embedded in the measurement procedure is the next filter. Separate measurements have to be in accordance with the operational definition, whereas the operational definition has to match the definition of the theoretical concept. The 'salience of an issue for a party', for example, might be defined on a theoretical level as the importance of an issue relative to the importance of other issues according to the policy statements of a party (Budge et al., 1987). If party manifestoes are used as the single source of available data to measure 'issue saliency', then an operational definition might be 'the percentage of sentences in a party manifesto devoted to a given issue'. Usually, various data and, as a consequence, various operational definitions, can be imagined to measure a theoretical concept. Alternative operational definitions of issue salience, for example, could refer to speeches in parliament. As compared with the concept definition the operational definition is restricted to the specific method for data collection to be used. An operational definition of leftist policy viewpoints designated to be used in a content analysis of party platforms will differ significantly from an operational definition designated to perform an elite survey among party officials.

Sometimes operational definitions are provided implicitly in the form of an elaborated measurement procedure, coding scheme, or classification scheme. Operational definitions may well include additional guidelines to apply general definitions to a specific empirical context. Context-specific operational definitions pave the way for sensible 'concept stretching'. Budge and Farlie (1983), for example, apply a general definition of 'bourgeois issues' and 'leftist issues' to categorize campaign news during various specific campaigns in specific countries. Tables with enumerative operational definitions of these broad concepts for specific issues raised in specific elections are provided additionally, so as to prevent coders from making ad-hoc categorizations of news items regarding these issues.

Measurement is defined as the assignment of a value on a variable to a unit of measurement in accordance with an operational definition. The measurements within comparative political science mirror its theoretical concepts into data bases that are accessible for data analysis. The assigned values may be visual (e.g. color graphs on a monitor representing real-time approval of political speeches by members of a focus group), nominal (e.g. 'yes'/'no', 'communist'/'socialist'/. . ./ 'conservative') or numerical. Length, for example, is measured in numbers of meters and centimeters, the gravity of a war is measured by the number of deaths, and political participation by the number of distinct types of activities aimed at political influence. Distinct visual and nominal codes can be represented as distinct numbers also. The visual, verbal and numerical values for separate units of measurement mount up to a measurement scale with nominal, ordinal, interval or ratio level of measurement (see Subsection 4.1.2).

Each measurement fills in a slot in a data-matrix with units (of measurements) in the rows, and variables (indicators of concepts) in the columns. As an example a piece from a data-matrix with 'population' and 'turnout' as variables and stacked country–year combinations is presented in Table 4.2. The value for 'turnout' in Italy in 1990 was measured as 90.5 per cent, for example.

Table 4.2 *Data-matrix of countries (units of analysis) by population characteristics (columns)*

Country	Year	Population (000s)	Turnout (%)
Sweden	1965	7734	78.4
Sweden	1990	8559	85.9
Italy	1965	51 330	91.8
Italy	1990	56 937	90.5
UK	1965	54 595	77.1
UK	1990	57 411	75.4

Putting units of measurement in the rows and not in the columns is a matter of convenience reinforced by statistical packages. Successful measurements result in a completely filled rectangular array, since, for each combination of a unit of measurement and an indicator, a value will be obtained.

The reader should keep in mind that the data-matrix in the final analysis often results from data at a lower level. The value of turnout for the Italian population as a whole (unit of analysis), for example, is actually an aggregation of the voting behavior of individual Italians (unit of measurement in the first stage). The ultimate data-matrix with units of analysis in the rows and concepts in the columns often results from a (row-wise) aggregation of data on units of measurement and/or a (column-wise) combination of indicators of the ultimate concepts (see Table 4.2).

4.3.1 Handling missing data

Measurements should ideally result in a completely filled rectangular data-matrix. However, often many values in the data matrix remain missing.

Many data are simply not available. In the comparative research of nations it may be impossible to retrieve (recent) data on specific economic or political indicators for the complete set of countries. Next, not all indicators may apply to all units of measurement. Survey interviews often have filter questions, e.g. 'Did you vote at the last elections'? The follow-up question – which party was voted for – will be posed only to respondents who answered that they did indeed cast their vote. A third type of missing value results from rest categories in the measurement process. Substantial hypotheses on parties belonging to one of the ten ideological 'party families' distinguished by Gallagher et al. (1995) do not apply to parties which were coded as 'other parties'. A content analysis classification of issues raised in party programs may have 'uncoded' as a category. Many questions in survey research allow for 'don't know' as an answer. Four strategies to deal with missing values will be discussed here.

Inclusion in tables as missing values is appropriate when the number and distribution of missing values is interesting. To answer the simple question 'have the poor a greater propensity to vote leftist' it would be a good idea to include in the cross table to answer this question the percentages of the poor and of the wealthy who abstained from voting, since, for the poor, abstention might be an alternative for a vote to the left.

Listwise deletion means that units of measurement with a missing value on one or more of the variables relevant for an analysis are excluded from the analysis. Listwise deletion is appropriate when the excluded units are not extremely important in the research design. When the number of units of measurement is large compared with the number of missing values, this solution is often preferred.

Pairwise deletion is an alternative to listwise deletion in multivariate data analysis when more than two variables with missing values enter the data analysis. As a first step, the bivariate relationships between separate variables might be based on all the cases with non-missing values for the two variables. Next the multivariate analysis will be performed on the bivariate relationships. The advantage is that fewer units of measurement will be discarded. The disadvantage is its obscurity. It is not always easy to reconstruct which units of measurement bear a special weight for the outcomes of data analysis.

Substitution of the missing values by approximates is a third possibility when it is known that a value for the variable must exist. The missing values might be filled in by predicting the true scores on the basis of causal relationships, by intrapolation and extrapolation, or by cross-sectional mean substitution. If, for example, the exact amount of military expenditures of a specific country is unknown, but the Gross National Product and the number of military personnel is known, and causal relationships between Gross National Product, military personnel and military expenditures are known also, then an estimate of military expenditures might be given. The estimated expenditures might be predicted from Gross National Product and military personnel. Intrapolation and extrapolation are obvious means to fill in the gaps in time series. A warning is, however, in order. Intrapolation and extrapolation may result in erroneous estimates of the statistical properties of time series models: data based on intrapolation and extrapolation give rise to a serious underestimation of the jerkiness of changes (see Subsection 6.7.5).

In sum: missing values create problems. Each treatment has pros and cons. It depends on the research question and the research design which treatment is to be preferred.

4.4 CRITERIA TO EVALUATE THE QUALITY OF OPERATIONALIZATION AND MEASUREMENTS

Many criteria may be applied to judge the quality of the measurements of a concept. The *efficiency* of measurements relates the quality of measurements to the invested time and the costs of getting the data. The *compatibility* of the measurements refers to their usefulness not only in the main research project but also in related research projects that use slightly different data (other nations, other time periods, slightly different data collection methods). The major criteria to judge the quality of measurements are *validity* and *reliability*, however. Measurements that are not valid or not reliable can not be efficient or compatible with other data either.

(Construct) validity

The *validity* of measurements, often labelled as *construct validity*, is defined as the degree to which one actually measures whatever concept (or 'construct') the measurement procedure purports to measure. It refers to the closeness of the correspondence between the measurements and the concept being measured. But how to establish this correspondence?

Measurements possess *face validity* when they are perceived as indisputable facts with respect to the measured concept in the scientific community. Assessments of face validity are often based on the agreement of measurement results with common-sense expectations, regardless of the precise definitions of the concept.

Correlational validity (or 'internal validity') is obtained by using a traditional, but imprecise, measurement device as a yardstick to verify the correspondence between the measurements and the concept being measured. Newer measurement devices, e.g. an electron microscope, should be able to reproduce the measurements of the older ones, e.g. a lens microscope, albeit with greater precision. The refined results should, however, correlate highly with the old results.

The *predictive validity* (or 'external validity') of measurements refers to their usefulness in making correct predictions about real world phenomena. A judgment with respect to external validity presupposes a causal theory with the concept being measured as an independent variable. Let's give an example. One might doubt whether counting the attention given to various issues in party programs (e.g. Budge et al., 1987) renders valid measurements of the party agenda. An empirical demonstration that government expenditures on issues correspond to the attention given to these issues in the programs of the governing party (but not with the attention given in the programs of the opposition parties) renders an external validation for the measurements. Probably, predictive validity is the most important hallmark of validity, since it relates the usefulness of the obtained measurements to the context of prevailing theories.

Students will notice that the word 'validity' is not only used in the context of the validity of measurements, but also in the context of the *validity of theories*. A theory is said to be 'internally valid' when it holds for the cases being investigated. A theory is said to be 'externally valid' when the theory also holds for the cases to which the theory applies which were not included in the data analysis. External validity of research findings is a synonym of generalizability of research findings.

Reliability

Measurements are reliable to the extent that measurements with respect to the same units deliver consistent results. Reliability can not compensate for low validity. The *reliability* of measurements is related to the validity of measurement in the same way as a standard deviation from the mean is related to the mean. Measurements are not reliable when separate measurements have a large variance, i.e. when the precise measurement results for a given unit of measurement at a given time are shaky. It should be noted that a negligible variance of separate measurements does not imply that the measurements are valid: they may be far from the truth collectively. Two varieties of reliability should be distinguished.

- *Intra-observer reliability* refers to the consistency between repeated measurements by the same observers using the same measurement devices with respect to the same units of measurement. Low intra-observer reliability is usually a sign that the interpretation moods of the observer or a less than perfect task performance by the observer have influenced the measurements. Low intra-observer reliability is often reproached to the observers, but is often a result of faulty, ambiguous and contradictory instructions with respect to the observation task.

- *Inter-observer reliability* refers to the agreement between measurements of different observers with respect to the same units of measurement. A lack of inter-observer reliability may indicate that the measurement procedure is too superficial – leaving room for additional interpretations of observers – or too complicated – encouraging personal heuristics – to overcome subjective insights of observers. A mismatch between the phenomena to be observed and the concepts to be measured may also be at the heart of low inter-observer reliability. This type of mismatch will occur when classifications which were appropriate to study one specific country are transferred thoughtlessly to other nations.

Measures for the assessment of intra-observer reliability and inter-observer reliability are available for each level of measurement (i.e. nominal, ordinal, etc.; see Krippendorff, 1985). Reliability measures start from ordinary measures of agreement between observers, but these measures have to be adjusted for agreement on the basis of mere chance. As an example Scott's π (pi), a reliability measure for nominal variables will be considered. As a starting point one can use the percentage of cases agreed upon as a first measure. If 100 cases are observed by two coders and identical observations show up for 98 cases then the agreement according to this intuitive measure would amount to 98 per cent. This intuitive measure does not take into account, however, that agreement may result from chance. If coders have two coding possibilities, then the probability to agree by chance amounts to 50 per cent ($0.5 \times 0.5 + 0.5 \times 0.5$), at least when both coders apply the two coding possibilities equally often. Things are even worse when they do not. Let's give a policy example. Suppose a new law is promulgated with rather vague criteria on special tax reliefs for firms stimulating environmental investments. Suppose that 100 firms demand special tax reliefs, but the civil servants enacting this law judge that only two firms deserve tax relief, because they know that enough money is available to grant two tax subsidies only. Agreement by chance as to whether the 100 firms should be granted tax relief now amounts to $0.96 \times 0.96 + 0.02 \times 0.02 = 0.92$. According to Scott's π the percentage of decisions agreed upon should be adjusted for agreement on the basis of mere chance.

$$\pi = \frac{\%\text{agreements} - \%\text{agreements expected}}{100\% - \%\text{agreements expected}}$$

Scott's π has as its maximum 100 per cent. If the two civil servants pick out precisely the same two firms for tax relief, then this maximum will be reached. If they agree on 96 cases, but disagree precisely on the question of which two firms deserve a tax relief, then Scott's π amounts to near zero. This figure reflects common sense, since the civil servants disagree where the crucial question of which firms deserve tax relief is concerned, notwithstanding their amazing agreement that 96 out of 100 firms do not deserve tax relief.

When multiple indicators are available for one concept, the reliability of the measurements can be assessed by computing one way or another the agreement between these indicators. In the context of multiple-indicator research or 'scalability analysis' or 'item reliability research', which will be discussed in the next sections, the term scalability is used as a synonym of reliability.

4.4.1 Multiple indicators: the scalability (reliability) problem

Often a bewildering variety of related indicators of a concept can be imagined. One may choose one of these indicators as the best indicator on theoretical reasons. Often one will use *multiple indicators* to reconstruct a concept. In party manifesto research, for example, references to 'crime', negative references to 'social security' and references to 'economic orthodoxy' may be considered as signs of a rightist party ideology. In survey research, answers to a number of indicative questions will be combined to arrive at measurements of an abstract concept such as 'political efficacy'. To measure this single concept the survey respondent is asked whether he or she agrees or disagrees with a number of related statements such as 'Members of Parliament do not care about the opinions of people like me', 'Political parties are only interested in my vote and not in my opinions', 'People like me have absolutely no influence on governmental policy' and 'So many people vote in elections that my vote does not matter'. The operational definition of a concept should clarify whether a specific pattern is expected in the data with respect to the multiple indicators of the concept.

Multiple indicators may simply be intended as a *repeated measurements scale* of precisely the same concept. In survey research, several questions can be posed with respect to slightly different aspects of the concept (e.g. questions with respect to newspaper reading, watching television news and participating in political discussions to measure 'political interest'). In the case of repeated measurements one expects that each indicator gives rise to almost the same results.

Indicators may also build up to a *cumulative measurements scale*, however. The concept of 'political participation', for example, can be measured both with 'easy' indicators such as voting at elections (many citizens participate to this degree) and with 'difficult' indicators such as running for a political function (only a few citizens participate to this degree). Cumulative measurement scales resemble long jumping. An 'easy' indicator of one's jumping capacities is whether one can leap over a ditch 1 meter wide (many will pass this easy test), whereas a more 'difficult' indicator would be whether one can leap over a ditch of 3 or even 8 meters (fewer will pass these more difficult tests). Voting is an 'easy' indicator of political participation since many citizens will vote, whereas running for a political function is a 'difficult' indicator since only a few citizens dare take the risk. In the case of a cumulative scale one expects that passing the difficult threshold is a sufficient proof of being able to pass the easy thresholds. It is not to be expected that the world record holder in jumping will fail to leap over a ditch of only 1 meter. It is not to be expected either that those who strive for a political career will not vote themselves.

In the case of an *unfolding measurements scale* or *proximity scale* the multiple indicators tap specific positions of an underlying continuum. If it is assumed that the three indicators 'nationalization of industries', 'no nationalization, no privatization' and 'privatization of government branches' are respectively a leftist, a centrist and a rightist indicator of the underlying left–right scale, then it is to be expected that parties will agree especially with indicators that come close to their own position on the underlying scale. The larger the distance between an indicator and the party position, the larger the disagreement with the indicators. Parties who endorse the centrist position will discard both 'nationalization' and 'privatization', for example. A party in favor of 'privatization' will surely resist the idea of 'no privatization' but will utterly detest the idea of 'nationalization', since the latter indicator of the left–right scale reflects the opposite end of the political spectrum as compared with its own position. In the case of an unfolding scale it is expected that the pattern of responses to indicators reflects the similarities between specific indicators and specific units of analysis.

Scalability analysis is a designation of research techniques to test whether the expectations can be corroborated which follow from the assumptions that multiple indicators build up to a repeated measurements scale, to a cumulative scale, or to an unfolding measurement scale. An overview of available techniques is presented in Table 4.3. Here these techniques will be mentioned only, because scalability analysis is a highly technical area. To test whether indicators can be considered as

Table 4.3 *An overview of techniques for scalability analysis*

Expected relationship between multiple indicators	**Scale type**	**Variety of scalability analysis to test whether expected relationship is corroborated**
Indicators of the same position on an underlying concept	'Repeated measurements scale' with Equal weight indicators	Likert scale; Cronbach's alpha
	'Repeated measurements scale' with Unequal weights indicators	Principal components analysis; (one of the varieties of) factor analysis (e.g. principal axis factoring, maximum likelihood)
Indicators of the 'difficulty' of the position on an underlying concept	'Cumulative scale'	Guttman scale; Loevinger's *H*
Indicators of various positions on an underlying concept	'Unfolding scale'	MUDFOLD (van Schuur, 1984)
Indicators relate to each other in specific ways, not mentioned above	New type of scale	??
Unknown resemblance between indicators		(One of the varieties of) cluster analysis

repeated measurements, a variety of techniques is available, amongst others Likert reliability analysis (with Cronbach's alpha), principal components analysis and an array of variants of factor analysis. To test whether multiple indicators are consistent with an underlying cumulative scale, Guttman scale analysis and Mokken scale analysis are available. To test whether indicators are consistent with an underlying unfolding scale, relatively unknown procedures such as MUDFOLD-analysis are available.

Techniques for scalability analysis should be applied with great care. To test whether a repeated measurements scale holds, when clearly an unfolding scale applies, for example, will give rise to erroneous results. Researchers may even wish to construct their own type of scalability analysis, when the definition of a concept gives rise to an expected pattern in the data on various indicators which corresponds neither with a repeated measurement scale, with a cumulative scale nor with an unfolding scale. Another alternative is to look only at whether various indicators give similar or dissimilar results, without having a precise idea of the origins of (dis)similarity. The aim of *cluster analysis* is simply to cluster indicators which resemble each other, or to cluster units which resemble each other. Cluster analysis combines indicators that resemble each other closely, but it does not result in scores on underlying dimensions. Cluster analysis is useful when the immediate aim is not the construction of a limited number of concept dimensions from data on various indicators, but an explorative investigation into the relationships among indicators of more or less clustered, overlapping concepts.

An introduction to the major techniques of item reliability analysis (or 'scalability analysis') will be presented in the next section. Some of these techniques will recur in Chapters 7, 8 and 9. From the point of view of methodological substance this section should be included as the next section of this chapter indeed, but unfortunately a knowledge of elementary research techniques for exploratory data analysis – which will be discussed in the next chapter – is a prerequisite to understanding techniques for scalability analysis and cluster analysis, even at an introductory level. Readers who are not already familiar with the contents of Chapter 5 should consult the next section after reading that chapter.

4.5 SCALABILITY ANALYSIS AND CLUSTER ANALYSIS

Scalability analysis and cluster analysis deal with the question of whether multiple indicators measure the same concept, or at least – in the case of cluster analysis – amount to similar results. The quite often impressive technicalities of these relatively well-developed approaches easily set beyond doubt rather disputable basic choices. Students may use these technicalities as a pretext for not reflecting upon the appropriateness of the underlying choices. The aim of *item reliability analysis* or *scalability analysis* is to assess whether various indicators 'measure the same'. As can be seen from Table 4.3 a further subdivision is needed to specify what is meant by 'measuring the same'.

If 'measuring the same' is understood as tapping the same position of the same underlying (ordinal, interval or ratio) variable, then a great variety of techniques is available, including Likert scalability analysis using Cronbach's alpha, principal components analysis and (an enormous variety of methods for) factor analysis. All indicators are considered essentially as repeated measurements of an underlying theoretical concept or 'dimension'. In the language of repeated measurement scales the term *dimension* refers to this underlying interval scale, which measures the theoretical concept. If indicators tap the two extremes of an underlying continuum (e.g. nationalization of industries, privatization of government services) then indicators tapping one extreme should be toppled over so as to render equivalent indicators of 'the same' position on the underlying scale. But in the case of more than two positions on an underlying dimension Likert scalability analysis and factor analysis are not to be used.

If 'measuring the same' is understood as tapping various 'easy' and 'difficult' positions on an underlying cumulative variable, then Guttman scales and Loevinger's scalability coefficient H are appropriate. The basic idea is that indicators, for example bar heights for pole-vaulters, vary in terms of their *difficulty*. Some bars are higher than others. The higher the bar, the lower the probability that it will be vaulted over. The world record pole vaulter must be capable of vaulting over all bars at a lower height than the world record. Scales based on this assumption are known as *cumulative scales*.

Techniques for 'unfolding analysis' are appropriate in the case of an underlying (ordinal, interval or ratio) scale on which the indicators occupy a position which may or may not be preferred by the units of analysis. Unfolding scales apply when the underlying concept is a position issue with a left side and a right side. As an example the concept of a left–right dimension in politics might be considered. A leftist indicator of this dimension, such as increasing social security, will be endorsed by leftist voters and leftist parties. High scores (of leftist parties) on leftist indicators are completely compatible with moderate scores on centrist indicators and low scores on rightist indicators. High scores on centrist indicators are completely compatible with low scores for leftist and rightist indicators. A thoughtless application of factor analytic procedures (or other procedures suited for repeated measurement scales) to unfolding scales will result in the erroneous conclusion that at least two left–right dimensions exist (van Schuur, 1993). Unfolding scales are rather common in comparative political science, but have received relatively little attention in the literature.

Cluster analysis is appropriate when the immediate aim is not the construction of a limited number of concept dimensions from data on various indicators, but an explorative investigation into the relationships among indicators of more or less clustered, overlapping concepts.

Why scalability analysis anyway?

If a scale analysis demonstrates that variables do not belong to one dimension, then an addition of the values on these variables will give unintelligible results. The resulting sum will be some random number, almost *independent* of the values on the variables being added.

As an example, the national subsidies for municipalities in The Netherlands might be mentioned. The national law on municipal finances of 1955 opened the possibility for national Ministries to enact Orders in Council which would allow municipalities to receive subsidies whenever they had some specific financial needs. Twenty-five years later, in 1980, more than five hundred Orders in Council dealt with special subsidies for specific financial needs of municipalities. A wicked problem had evolved. The total effect of all these Orders was undesired, although each of the specific Orders had by and large desired effects. Let's rephrase the example in terms of scalability analysis. All subsidies should have been repeated measurements of one (or a few) underlying dimension(s) of legitimate financial municipal needs. But the civil servants on each of the separate Ministries adhered to a faulty philosophy. They reasoned that one should enact a new Order in Council when a municipal financial need was detected that was independent of the remaining financial needs. Thus, a first Order in Council was enacted to subsidize municipalities with inner-city problems, a further one to subsidize municipalities who were in need of money to maintain their forests, a further one to subsidize municipalities who had to maintain their port, and so on, and so on. The problem was that inner-cities, forests, ports, and roads are almost completely independent needs. Not a single municipality suffered from none of the subsidized problems, not a single one suffered from all subsidized problems either. As a result the total amount of money a municipality received as a result of these five hundred subsidies was almost completely independent of any specific municipal need. Accruing a lump sum to municipalities would have had almost the same financial results, with far lower bureaucratic costs (e.g. enacting Orders, implementing subsidies, negotiations on subsidies). The abstract lesson to learn from this policy fiasco is that summing up (non-scalable) indicators which are not repeated measurements of the same (position on the) underlying scale will result in a random number, which is almost independent of the separate measurements. Scalability is thus a prerequisite for combining (adding) multiple indicators. The aim of scalability analysis is to test whether indicators really 'add up'.

Do scalability analysis or cluster analysis always apply to multiple indicators?

Item reliability analysis has been developed primarily by psychologists and sociologists who had scores for respondents on test items, or answers from respondents to survey questions, in mind. The usual presumption is that data with respect to many overlapping tasks or questions are available. Unfortunately the data available to political scientists from content analysis or statistical archives do not usually meet this presumption. In a survey analysis to capture leftist ideas, ten questions with respect to aspects of state intervention might be asked, but a content analysis of a program of a party will probably reveal data with respect to only one of these aspects. It's a matter of interpretation whether opinions with respect to the other nine aspects are deliberately neglected although they were deemed important, whether they simply were not salient for the party, or whether they were perceived as deducible from this one aspect. At any rate, data in political science often do not meet the classical requirements of scalability analysis, especially not the requirements of repeated measurements scales.

Which data to use in empirical illustrations?

The empirical examples to illustrate the use of scalability analysis and cluster analysis will be derived from a subset of the Manifesto research project (Budge et al., 1987; Volkens, 1994) which was discussed in Subsection 4.3.2.

It should be noted that these data do not perfectly match the assumptions of classical test theory. Parties might choose not to address a specific issue area, because they have addressed a related issue area in depth. The data from a questionnaire with respect to opinions on such related (but sometimes neglected) issue areas would show that the various issue areas amount to a strong scale. Since a party may pick up only one issue from a set of related issues in a given campaign, the content analysis data will often show no scales or rather weak scales, although related issues may have been one scale in the minds of the authors of the programs. Therefore the 'strong' criteria for appropriate scales derived from experimental research and survey research should be relaxed.

As an example we will use the indicators for Budge and Laver's concept of 'state intervention' here (Budge and Laver, 1992: 23–5). Five categories from the 54 categories used in the content analysis project are assumed to measure state intervention, i.e. the percentages of programs devoted to 'regulation of capitalism', 'economic planning', 'protectionism: positive', 'controlled economy' and 'nationalization'. The percentages devoted to these categories are simply added to measure 'state intervention'. Such an addition will amount to a random number if these indicators do not 'measure the same'. Budge and Laver assume on the basis of face validity that these indicators 'measure the same'. Budge and Laver use their measure 'state intervention' as one of their 20 measures to predict government coalitions. If the five indicators of 'state intervention' do not belong to the same scale after all, then 'state intervention' as measured by Laver and Budge is really a constant plus or minus a large random component. An even better prediction of future coalitions is to be expected by removing non-scalable items.

Some methods for scalability analysis presume dichotomous items (Guttman scalability analysis) whereas most others do not. To enable a comparison of scale analysis techniques, all of them will be applied to dichotomized items, representing whether or not parties paid any attention in their party manifesto to 'regulation of capitalism', 'economic planning', 'protectionism: positive', 'controlled economy' and 'nationalization'.

4.5.1 The cumulative scale: Guttman scale and Loevinger's H

Because of its intuitive attractiveness, we will start the discussion of scale analysis with a discussion of Guttman's method for cumulative scale analysis. Various advanced scale analysis techniques have been proposed in the literature (e.g. Mokken, 1971) to refine this method.

Presumably the five indicators of 'state intervention' constitute a Guttman scale, since the separate indicators represent various degrees of determination to intervene. The most strong-minded indicator of 'state intervention' is presumably 'nationalization'. In the language of cumulative scales, 'nationalization' may be considered as a difficult indicator of 'state intervention'. Only a few unflinching parties strive for it. Economic planning seems less difficult: even many centrist parties would favor this type of intervention. The crucial assumption of Guttman analysis is the *cumulative assumption*, which implies that strong proponents of state intervention are also stronger proponents of 'weak' forms of state intervention than are weak proponents. Guttman scalability analysis of state intervention in fact assumes that the communists are stronger proponents of a 'weak communist' social-democratic policy than are the social-democrats themselves. Since Guttman scalability analysis presupposes dichotomous items, the percentages of attention for the five issue areas will be reduced to binary indicators whether or not attention was paid to the issue area.

Guttman scale analysis starts with the *difficulty* of dichotomous indicators. The difficulty of an indicator is to be estimated with the percentage of the units of measurement passing the indicator test of state intervention. Table 4.4 displays the 'difficulties' for the five indicators of state intervention used by Laver and Budge. Nationalization is a difficult item indeed. Twenty-eight per cent of the party programs make reference to this code, as compared with 67 per cent for the easiest indicator of regulation. But surprisingly it is not the most difficult item. An even more difficult item is protectionism, which is mentioned in only 24 per cent of the party programs.

A simple measure to verify whether the crucial cumulative assumption of Guttman scale analysis holds is Jane Loevinger's H. H can be computed for each pair of indicators, for each indicator, and for all items combined. If item j is the most difficult item, and i a less difficult item, then the cumulative assumption maintains that units of measurement who failed to pass the less difficult item i should also fail to pass the more difficult item j. Not a single unit of measurement should fall into this 'error cell'. Loevinger's H for two items is computed as one minus the number of units in the error cell (f_{ij}) as compared with the expected number of units in the error cell (e_{ij}).

$$H_{ij} = 1 - \frac{f_{ij}}{e_{ij}}$$

Loevinger's H equals 1 when the error cell is empty, i.e. if $f_{ij} = 0$. As a rule of thumb it is assumed that if $H > +0.30$ a weakly cumulative scale exists. A Loevinger's $H > 0.6$ would indicate a strong cumulative scale.

Table 4.4 *Guttman scale analysis of five items concerning 'state intervention': $H = 0.35$ ($n = 1012$)*

Item	Difficulty (in fact: easiness)	Loevinger's H
Protectionism: positive (406)	0.24	0.25
Nationalization (413)	0.28	0.36
Controlled economy (412)	0.41	0.33
Economic planning (404)	0.49	0.37
Regulation (403)	0.67	0.42

Numbers in parentheses present the code of items according to Volkens (1994).

As an example of its computation a cross table of the most difficult item, 'protectionism', with the next difficult item, 'nationalization', is presented in Figure 4.2. The number of party programs in the error cell is not zero, but 151 (17.4 per cent of all programs). The expected number of party programs e_{ij} when no relationship between nationalization and protectionism exists is computed on the basis of the row percentage (24.2 per cent) and the column percentage (71.9 per cent) of the error cell. When no relationship exists, 24.2 per cent of 71.9 per cent of the party programs would fall into the error cell ($e_{ij} = 0.242 \times 71.9 = 17.4$ per cent). Consequently $H_{ij} = 1 - (14.9/17.4) = 0.14$ only for these two items, which is less than 0.30. Protectionism is a 'difficult' item, but it is not the highest, most difficult rung on the regulation–nationalization ladder. The H_i-measures to compute the position of an item in the midst of the other items, and the H-measure to compute the degree to which all items are cumulative, are based on the same line of thought. Table 4.4 displays these H_i-measures per indicator and the H-measure for the complete scale.

'Protectionism' appears to be the only indicator with an H_i-measure that is (slightly) lower than 0.30 (actually 0.25). This gives rise to the suspicion that protectionism may not be a rung on the regulation–nationalization ladder at all. Protectionism has indeed been a policy of leftist and communist parties to guard their socialist experiments against the evils of the capitalist world market, but the low H-value of 0.25 suggests that protectionist measures have not been promoted exclusively by extremely leftist parties, as one would expect on the basis of a cumulative scale. Apparently rightist parties favored protectionism also, for example to ensure the national balance of trade.

Conclusion on the basis of cumulative scale analysis

Using Loevinger's H the hypothesis was tested that parties adhering to extremist ('difficult') forms of state interventionism such as nationalization of industries

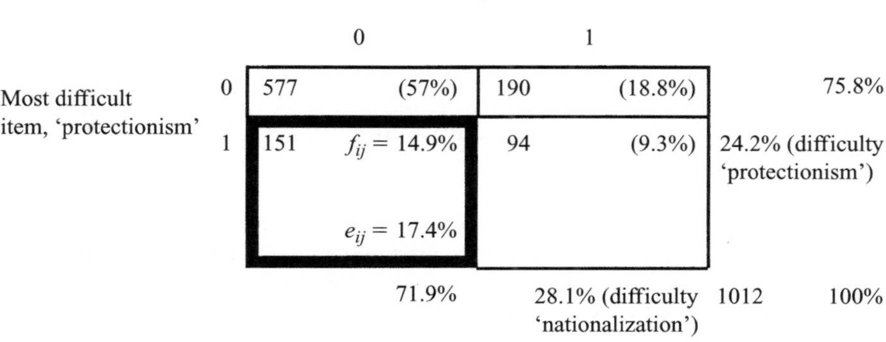

		Less difficult item, 'nationalization' 0	1		
Most difficult item, 'protectionism'	0	577 (57%)	190 (18.8%)		75.8%
	1	151 $f_{ij} = 14.9\%$ $e_{ij} = 17.4\%$	94 (9.3%)	24.2% (difficulty 'protectionism')	
		71.9%	28.1% (difficulty 'nationalization')	1012	100%

$H_{ij} = 1 - (14.9/17.4) = 0.14$

Figure 4.2 *Loevinger's* H *coefficients as a measure of Guttman cumulative scales*

would at least adhere to moderate ('easy') forms of state interventionism such as economic regulation. Cumulative scale analysis suggests that Laver and Budge should not have included 'protectionism' in their ultimate measure of parties' desire for 'state interventionism' on the basis of which these authors wanted to predict future government coalitions. The inclusion of protectionism in the 'state interventionism' scale somewhat blurs the cleavage between leftist and rightist parties, since parties from the left and the right differ from each other with respect to traditional types of socialist state interventionism. The other side of the coin is that by considering 'protectionism' as a specimen of 'state interventionism' the fact remains concealed that parties agreeing on protectionist measures may cooperate in a future coalition, although they differ enormously on more ideological questions regarding 'state intervention'.

4.5.2 Likert scale and Cronbach's alpha

A Likert scale is a summative scale constituted by several unweighted indicators. These indicators are assumed to be identical, parallel, or 'repeated' measurements of one concept. The basic idea of a Likert scale is that a summative scale cancels out the errors in the separate indicators. Therefore the summative scale will discern the units of analysis more precisely than the separate indicators, since measurement errors in the latter hamper their discerning power. Cronbach's alpha is used to test whether an addition of separate indicators adds to the discriminating power of the theoretical concept.

The summative scale should enable distinctions between the various cases that were not enabled by its constitutive parts. In statistical jargon this implies that the *variance* of cases on the summative scale (v_s), i.e. it's power to discern cases, should be larger than the sum of the variances of the separate indicators (Σv_i). The numerator of Cronbach's α is positive whenever this ($v_s > \Sigma v_i$) is the case.

$$\text{Cronbach's } \alpha = \frac{v_s - \sum_{i=1}^{k} v_i}{\sum_{i=1}^{k} v_i} \times \frac{k}{k-1}$$

where v_s = variance of the summative scale, v_i = variance of the ith indicator within the scale, and k = total number of indicators.

The denominator (once more Σv_i) and the multiplicative factor $k/(k-1)$ merely serve to guarantee that Cronbach's α reaches a maximum of 1 in the case of perfect indicators (not to be proved here). To test the reliability of separate indicators, for each item Cronbach's α is computed without the indicator itself. Cronbach's α should not increase by dropping an indicator.

It should be noticed that a proper computation of the variance of the summative scale, v_s, presumes correspondence of the *directions* of the indicators that are summated. If, for example, one dimension is supposed to underlie the answers to the question 'what do you think of the pro-choice movement', as well as the answers to the question 'what do you think of the pro-life-movement' then the answers to one of these questions should be flipped over before summation, i.e. '(strongly) agree' with pro-life should be counted as '(strongly) disagree' with pro-choice.

The value of Cronbach's α tends to increase when the number of indicators increases, since errors are cancelled more easily when the number of indicators increases. As a rule-of-thumb test psychologists and survey sociologists use a minimum value for α of roughly +0.7. Within the context of the Manifesto content analysis of party programs less stringent criteria should be applied, since authors of party programs, as opposed to respondents in survey research, feel free to address only one theme from a set of more or less related themes according to researchers afterwards.

Since Laver and Budge added their five indicators of 'state interventionism' without giving weights to each of them, a test of their scale using Cronbach's alpha would be a good idea. Table 4.5 presents the results. Cronbach's α is positive (+0.59), although too low by the standards for Likert attitude-scales. The moderate value of alpha suggests that parties tend to address issues from the same issue group of 'state intervention' but that they will also often pick only one or a few of them. If one takes into account that parties were not forced in any way to address the themes that were put forward by the Manifesto researchers, the α-score of +0.59 is high enough to warrant unweighted addition of the issues.

To test whether all the indicators indeed belong to the same scale, values for Cronbach's alpha are also computed when specific items are removed from the scale. If Cronbach's alpha increases when a specific indicator is removed from the scale, then that indicator did apparently not belong to the scale. An inspection of the α-values for the scales with separate items deleted shows that the removal of 'protectionism' from the scale would improve Cronbach's alpha. Apparently *protectionism* does not tap the same concept dimension as the other indicators.

Conclusion on the basis of Cronbach's alpha (repeated measurements scale; unweighted)

The computation of Cronbach's alpha rests on the assumption that all indicators measure the same (position on a) concept dimension. Cronbach's alpha measures the degree to which the summative scale discerns the cases being investigated more sharply than the separate indicators, by cancelling out the measurement errors in

Table 4.5 *Cronbach's alpha for five items of 'state intervention'*

Item	Percentage indicators $\alpha = +0.29$ (column below: α with indicator excluded)	Dichotomized indicators $\alpha = +0.59$ (column below: α with indicator excluded)
Protectionism: positive (406)	30	59
Nationalization (413)	18	52
Controlled economy (412)	17	52
Economic planning (404)	31	50
Regulation (403)	25	54

separate indicators. A comparison of Cronbach's alpha for a complete set of indicators with Cronbach's alpha with a specific indicator deleted is required to test whether deletion of that indicator decreases Cronbach's alpha indeed. Computation of Cronbach's alpha shows that the data are in line with an unweighted repeated measurement model of the Likert type, except for the data on 'protectionism'. Cronbach's alpha increased when 'protectionism' was removed from the scale. Thus, the inclusion by Laver and Budge of 'protectionism' in their 'state interventionism' diminishes the discriminatory power – and thereby presumably the predictive power in the context of predicting future government coalitions – of 'state interventionism'. The same conclusion resulted from cumulative scalability analysis, although the assumptions of cumulative scale analysis and repeated measurement approaches are very dissimilar.

4.5.3 Principal components: differently weighted indicators to increase discriminatory power

Principal components analysis is based on the same principle as Cronbach's α. The weighted scale should discern the units of analysis more pregnantly than the separate indicators, since measurement errors in the latter hamper their discerning power. The numerator of Cronbach's α indicated whether the discerning power (the variance) of the summative scale (v_s) exceeded the sum of the variances of the separate indicators (Σv_i). The basic idea of principal components analysis is to find a linear combination S of the indicators with weights for the separate indicators such that the variance of the summative scale (v_s) is maximized. The aim is to find weights – labelled as *factor scores* – $u_1, u_2 \ldots u_k$ for the k indicators of the component S, conceived as a linear combination of the indicators:

$$S = u_1 x_1 + u_2 x_2 + \ldots + u_k x_k$$

such that the variance (discerning power) of this component S, v_s, is maximized. Thus, the factor scores – weights for the separate indicators – are ascertained in such a way that the discriminatory power (variance) of the underlying concept is maximized.

To understand principal components analysis (and factor analysis) one has to know the correct interpretation of the mathematical concepts of *eigenvalues* (*Eigenwerte*) and eigenvectors in this context. The more general interpretation of these concepts, which are used throughout all areas of science where maximization in systems of linear equations is involved, does not concern us here. In effect the first eigenvalue is a measure of the maximum discriminatory power of the underlying concept being sought for. As a first step the variables $x_1, x_2, \ldots x_k$ are standardized so that each of them has a variance of 1. The first eigenvalue, usually denoted as λ_1, reduces to v_s/k, where v_s is the maximum variance (discerning power) of the cases under investigation over the concept to be measured and k represents the number of indicators. If $v_s/k < 1$ then the underlying concept has a smaller discriminatory power than the indicators. The first eigenvalue expresses the discriminatory power of the concept as a multiple of the discriminatory power of separate (standardized) indicators. The larger the first eigenvalue, the higher the discriminatory power. The weights or *factor scores* $u_1, u_2 \ldots u_k$ associated with this value are the elements of the *first eigenvector.*[1]

The question of which indicators qualify as reliable is usually answered by the rule of thumb that each indicator should 'load' on (correspond with) the first component found. As a rule of thumb the correlation coefficient between the indicator and the first component should be +0.35 at least. This requirement implies that roughly one eighth ($0.35 \times 0.35 = 0.1225$) of the variance in the indicator should correspond with variance in the retrieved first component. These correlation coefficients between indicators and the retrieved component are often referred to as *factor loadings* or as the elements of the *factor matrix* (SPSS). From the requirement that each indicator should correlate linearly with the first component follows an overall measure for the reliability of the indicators. The variance in the indicators explained by the first component should be at least 1/8. The proportion of variance in the indicators that is bound by the first component is a simple function of the first eigenvalue, which denotes the variance of the concept starting from indicators with a variance of 1. The proportion of variance in the indicators bound by the first component amounts to the first eigenvalue λ_1 divided by the number of indicators k.

Some variance in the indicators will not be bound by the first component. The process might be repeated. Starting from the second eigenvalue and its associated second eigenvector one might extract a second component which explains the remaining variance maximally. Probably, indicators that did not load on the first factor might load on the second one. In the case of k indicators, a maximum of k components is retrievable, but most computer programs will not extract components with an eigenvalue of less than 1, since such components would have a smaller variance than the indicators on the basis of which the components are constructed. In the context of testing whether indicators represent one underlying concept with an interval level of measurement, the second and higher components do not have any substantive meaning. Output from statistical packages may be confusing because not just one eigenvalue, one eigenvector and one set of factor loadings is printed, but $k - 1$ of them. Only the first series should be used.

The SPSS-output of principal components analysis to our now familiar example of five indicators for 'state intervention' suggested by Laver and Budge is printed in Figure 4.3. SPSS prints only one principal component, since the eigenvalues associated with the remaining ones are less than one. Components with an eigenvalue of less than one are not useful since their variance is lower than the variance of a single (standardized) indicator. The largest eigenvalue is $\lambda_1 = 1.91$. This eigenvalue indicates that the power of the resulting scale of 'state interventionism' to distinguish between the various party programs under investigation is 1.9 times as high as the power of separate indicators to do so. Since five items were included in the component, this amounts to an explained variance in the values of the indicators by the ultimate values on the concept of 'state interventionism' of $1.91/5 = 0.382$, or 38.2 per cent. Since $100 - 38.2$ per cent of unique variation in the indicators remains, it is safe to conclude that the concept 'state interventionism' is not able to capture the larger part of the variation in the

Variable	Communality	*	Factor	Eigenvalue	Pct of Var	Cum Pct
		*				
D403	.37093	*	1	1.90968	38.2	38.2
D404	.46271	*				
D406	.20124	*				
D412	.42838	*				
D413	.44642	*				

PC extracted 1 factors.

Factor Matrix:

	Factor 1
D403	.60904
D404	.68023
D406	.44860
D412	.65451
D413	.66814

Factor Score Coefficient Matrix:

	Factor 1
D403	.31892
D404	.35620
D406	.23491
D412	.34273
D413	.34987

Figure 4.3 *SPSS output from principal components analysis*

attention of parties for each of the separate five indicators of 'state interventionism'.

All factor loadings (the elements of the factor matrix) exceed $r = +0.35$. The worst indicator is D406, the now familiar troublemaker of protectionism. However, still roughly $1/5$ of its variance (0.4486×0.4486) is bounded by the theoretical concept 'state intervention'. The factor scores (interpreted by SPSS as the elements from the first eigenvector divided by $\sqrt{\lambda_1}$), that are given below indicate indeed that D406 should be given a relatively low weight (0.23 instead of roughly $1/3$).

The factor scores represent the optimal weights for the indicators that were sought from the beginning (although the term 'weight' is slightly misleading here since they do not add up to one). The findings on eigenvalues, factor loadings, explained variances, and so on serve only as diagnostic materials. For each case under investigation the ultimate factor scores should be multiplied by the values on the standardized indicators to obtain for each case the values on the standardized concept being sought.

Conclusion on the basis of principal components analysis

Principal components analysis is one of the techniques which starts from the assumptions of the repeated measurements scale: all indicators tap the same position on the same underlying dimension(s). The distinguishing feature of principal components analysis is the assumption that the various indicators of a concept should be weighted according to their contribution to the power of the concept to be measured to discriminate maximally between the cases under investigation: the variance of the resulting concept should be maximized. From the point of view of mathematics, principal components analysis is an extremely straightforward technique, as it rests on the well-known mathematical theory of eigenvectors and eigenvalues. From the point of view of comparative political science, principal components analysis is a good technique when, first, the assumptions of the repeated measurements scale have been met, and the aim is neither to combine indicators in a simple way (use unweighted addition backed up by Cronbach's alpha) nor to combine indicators in such a way that their mutual correspondence is maximized (use one of the varieties of factor analysis), but rather pragmatically to combine indicators in such a way that at least the concepts distinguish maximally between the cases under investigation.

As compared with cumulative scale analysis and Cronbach's alpha, which suggested that 'protectionism' be dropped from the scale of 'state interventionism', principal components analysis is more relaxed. Protectionism is the least convincing indicator of 'state interventionism' indeed, but still some 20 per cent of its variance helps to distinguish between parties with low and high scores on 'state interventionism' (squared factor loading). The ultimate factor scores, which represent the optimal weights of the separate indicators, indicate that protectionism should be weighted only slightly less heavily than the remaining indicators, which all obtained roughly identical optimal weights. Budge and Laver's choice for an unweighted addition of the five indicators of 'state interventionism' is tenable when the assumptions of principal components analysis apply.

4.5.4 Factor analysis

The use of principal components analysis has been criticized because of its failure to signal that some indicators have a very large error component. Principal components analysis tries to capture *all* the variance in the indicators, regardless of whether this variance arises from the unreliability of the indicator or from the 'true' score on the first component. But which scores on an indicator are due to error and which ones reflect the 'true' score? One single answer to this question underlies all variants of 'true factor analysis'. The error part of an indicator does not correlate with the factor, whereas the true part does. The proportion of the variance of an indicator that is not due to errors, but is common with the factors sought, is referred to as the *communality* of an indicator. The communality of an indicator is the percentage of variance in the indicator that could be explained by the factors. The aim of factor analysis is to find weights for the indicators such that the factors to be found do not account for all the variance in the indicators but only for the communalities of the indicators. The use of early computers made a method called *principal axes factoring* (PAF) popular. PAF is still widely used. Principal axes factoring is an iterative method not based on an explicit maximization criterion. Because of its fuzziness from a mathematical point of view it is impossible to render PAF intelligible in a few sentences. PAF resembles principal components analysis except for one important aspect. The variance in an indicator to be explained by the factor(s) is not 1, but its communality (the square of the factor loadings). The problem is, however, that the 'true' communalities are still unknown. A first guess of the communalities is to be made; next, factors will be extracted, which will render an improved estimate of the communalities; factors will be extracted once more, and so on, until the changes in communalities are extremely small.

Figure 4.4 shows SPSS output for PAF. The correlation coefficients between the factor and the indicators now indicate that the reliability of D406, protectionism, is questionable ($+0.30051 < +0.35$). This was precisely what was to be expected. D406 was the weakest indicator according to principal components analysis (PC), and PAF is less optimistic with respect to the reliability of indicators than PC. The explained variance due to the first PAF-factor is 23 per cent only, whereas the first principal component explained 38 per cent of the variance within the indicators.

Since computing power is not a problem anymore, factor analysis variants that are more elegant from a mathematical point of view and therefore more easy to explain than PAF, but computationally more demanding, have gained predominance during the late seventies and eighties. Especially, the *maximum likelihood* (ML) method has gained ground. ML starts from the core idea of item reliability analysis that the values of multiple indicators have to correspond with each other since they are manifestations of the same underlying concept. One expects that the

Variable	Communality	*	Factor	Eigenvalue	Pct of Var	Cum Pct
		*				
D403	.20719	*	1	1.16616	23.3	23.3
D404	.30512	*				
D406	.09031	*				
D412	.27020	*				
D413	.29334	*				

PAF extracted 1 factors. 6 iterations required.

Factor Matrix:

	Factor 1
D403	.45518
D404	.55237
D406	.30051
D412	.51981
D413	.54161

Figure 4.4 *SPSS output from principal axis factoring (PAF)*

indicators are highly correlated, since all indicators tap the same (unmeasured) concept. The amount of correlation to be expected between two specific indicators depends only on their (as yet unknown) factor loadings, i.e. on the correlations between the two indicators and the underlying concept. The correlation to be expected between two indicators is equal to the product of the factor loadings of these two indicators (not to be proved here). In the case of three indicators, it is not too difficult to determine unique factor loadings with paper and pencil. Let's call the factor F and the three indicators x_1, x_2 and x_3. Let's suppose that the correlations between the indicators amount to $r_{12} = 0.24$, $r_{13} = 0.3$ and $r_{23} = 0.20$ (see Figure 4.5). Let's denote the factor loadings of the three indicators as f_1, f_2 and f_3. Since a correlation between two indicators simply is the product of the factor loadings of the two indicators, one can also write: $f_1 f_2 = 0.24$, $f_1 f_3 = 0.3$ and $f_2 f_3 = 0.20$. Elementary high school mathematics can be used to solve this system of three equations with three unknowns, which gives the solution $f_1 = 0.6$, $f_2 = 0.4$ and $f_3 = 0.5$. In the case of more than three indicators no unique solution is guaranteed. The principle remains the same, however. Unweighted least squares factor analysis ascertains the factor loadings in such a way that the sum of the squared differences between the observed correlations between indicators and their expected correlations (i.e. the product of their factor loadings) is minimized. Maximum likelihood (ML) factor analysis adds one complication to unweighted least squares factor analysis, however. Maximum likelihood estimation is a mathematical method to maximize the likelihood that the estimates of *population* characteristics based on sample data reflect the true population characteristics and not only the sample data. Maximum likelihood estimation justifies the general principle that low correlations in a sample should be given less weight, since low observed correlations in a sample are, unlike high observed correlations, easily produced by chance. Thus, maximum likelihood factor analysis is weighted least

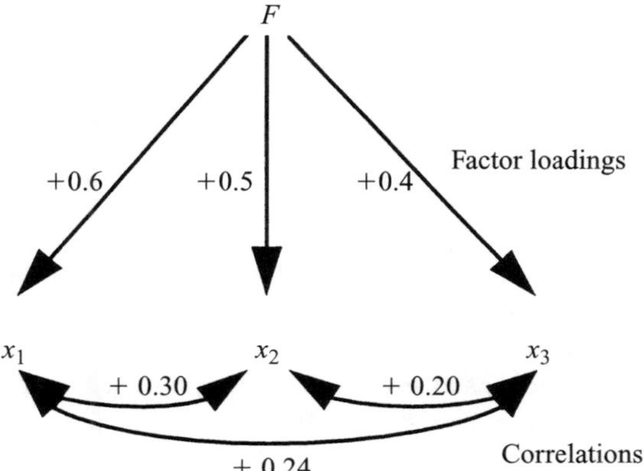

Figure 4.5 *A perfectly reproduced set of linear correlations between indicators.* F, *factor;* x_1, x_2, x_3, *indicators; single-headed arrows, factor loadings; double-headed arrows, correlations*

squares factor analysis with weights dependent on the reliability (the height of the factor loadings) of the indicators. The results of ML factor analysis are usually highly similar to the results of PAF.

The proportion of variance extracted from the indicators by the PAF-factor and the ML-factor is 23.3 per cent only, as compared with 38.2 per cent for the PC-component. In comparison with principal components analysis, factor analysis does a poor job in finding an underlying construct on which the cases under consideration differ from each other. The variance of the cases along the theoretical construct is only 1.167 times the variance of the standardized indicators. Maximum likelihood factor analysis – or PAF, which is less elegant but gives almost the same results – is therefore to be preferred over principal components analysis only when the aim is not pragmatically to contrast the cases under investigation with each other, but the reliability of measurements is a principal concern.

Conclusion on the basis of factor analysis

Factor analysis unequivocally resulted in the same conclusions as cumulative scale analysis using Loevinger's H and Likert scale analysis using Cronbach's alpha. All these techniques suggest that 'protectionism' be dropped from the scale of 'state interventionism'. Only principal components analysis led to a more relaxed conclusion. Principal components analysis detected 'protectionism' also as the least-convincing indicator of 'state interventionism', but suggested pragmatically that protectionism be maintained in the interventionism scale, since the indicator helped on the average to distinguish between parties with low and high scores on 'state interventionism'.

4.5.5 Digression: an unknown number of dimensions

Thus far we have used principal components analysis and factor analysis as confirmatory tools to *test* whether variables are reliable indicators of one concept dimension to be measured.

In the past, factor analysis has been used in a more exploratory, inductive fashion also to reveal how many dimensions and which dimensions would underlie a series of indicators. All variants of principal components analysis and factor analysis are suited for this end.

Procedures and criteria of exploratory factor analysis

The question of how many dimensions underlie indicators should be answered on the basis of the eigenvalues of the extracted factors. As a first criterion, referred to as the *Kaiser criterion* after the psychologist H.F. Kaiser, factors with an eigenvalue of less than one should be discarded, since these factors contain less variance than a single indicator. A more stringent, although mathematically not rigid, criterion is known as *Cattel's scree test* after its inventor, the psychologist R.B. Cattell. In order to apply the scree test the eigenvalues should be plotted in descending order. Factoring should be stopped at the point where the eigenvalues begin to level off, forming a straight line with an almost horizontal slope. As long as an eigenvalue is much smaller than its predecessor, the factor represented by it should be kept. But if an eigenvalue is only slightly smaller than its predecessor, then the factor represented by it, as well as all of its successors should be discarded. Applying the scree test to the series of eigenvalues, for example, a series of eigenvalues such as, 16.8 (1), 7.2 (2), 3.5 (3), 1.5 (4), 1.45 (5), 1.40 (6), . . . (rank orders in parentheses) would result in four factors, since 1.45 is only slightly less than 1.5, whereas 1.5 is much less than 3.5. The rationale of the scree test is that the discarded factors will usually have the variance of one indicator only (Kaiser criterion), plus some noise not explained by the 'true' factors. As a political psychologist Cattell was interested in the causes of wars. In the early 1950s he wrote a then-influential series of articles based on a factor analysis of data from official statistical agencies that revealed twelve cultural dimensions of 69 nations that would render these nations more or less war prone. Fixing the number of factors to be extracted is a prerequisite for answering the next question.

The question of *which* dimensions underlie the indicators is far less easily answered. 'Rotating' the factors that were found by the sequential procedure described above – starting from the complete variance in all indicators, continuing on the basis of the residual variance not explained by the first factor, and so on – might facilitate interpretation from a theoretical point of view. Rotating does not affect the total variance explained by the complete set of rotated factors, but it may redistribute the explained variance over the various factors. The most widely used criterion for an optimal rotation is *(orthogonal) varimax rotation*. The theoretical idea of varimax rotation is that ideally each dimension will have its own subset of (non-overlapping) indicators. Therefore one would expect that some indicators will have high factor loadings on a factor, whereas the factor loadings of the other indicators will be zero. Varimax rotation strives for a maximum variance of the squared factor loadings on each factor. Even the results of varimax rotation – or any other rotation method – might be hard to interpret. The 'low' loadings will not be zero exactly, leaving open the question of whether a poor indicator is an indicator of a dimension or not. Moreover there is no guarantee of course that variables which belong statistically to one factor are really indicators of one theoretical concept. The 'dimensions' found by Cattell in his pioneering work on the dimensions of nations, such as 'conservative patriarchal solidarity versus ferment of release', 'thoughtful industriousness versus emotionality' or 'bourgeois philistinism versus reckless bohemianism' were not very helpful for later generations of comparative political scientists, for example.

Example of exploratory factor analysis

As an example of (the problems with) inductive factor analysis the Manifesto data will be used once more. Laver and Budge (1992) wanted to use the data on party manifestoes to predict government coalitions between parties. They used 20 dimensions to characterize the policy space: 13 were simply the frequencies of the categories that were used in the content analysis; 7 were unweighted scales of these categories. The central dimension in our examples, 'state intervention', was one of the latter 7 dimensions. The question we wish to answer by inductive factor analysis is whether these 20 dimensions can be reduced to a lesser number of dimensions. Maximum likelihood factor analysis will be employed to this end, since the use of this method guarantees that indicators will only be accepted as belonging to one dimension when they correlate predictably.

An explorative factor analysis with all factors extracted, regardless of their eigenvalues, shows that the 20 dimensions might indeed be reduced in number. According to Kaiser's criterion (eigenvalues should exceed 1), 7 factors should be retained. According to Cattel's scree test, only 4 dimensions should be retained. Following the scree test, a factor analysis with a varimax rotation on the four dimensions is pursued. The factor loadings resulting from varimax rotation are given in Figure 4.6. Variable labels and italics for 'significant' factor loadings (absolute value >0.35) have been added manually. The results from varimax rotation are hard to interpret. Only one indicator contributes significantly to the first factor (capitalist economics). The same holds for the third factor (quality of life). The fourth factor can be interpreted as postmaterialism ('democracy' and 'human rights' against 'productivity and technology'), but it's hard to understand why 'the quality of life' is not included in this factor. The second factor makes sense: social conservatism (SOCCONS) against 'state intervention' and social justice (PER503).

Altogether, the first two dimensions seem to reflect the left–right dimension, but why should a factor analysis using varimax rotations result in *two* left–right dimensions? The answer to these questions is that the indicators might not be compatible with the assumption that these indicators tap *the same position* on the

	Factor 1	Factor 2	Factor 3	Factor 4	
STATEINT	.23033	.48165	−.15706	−.02794	State intervention
QLIFE	.08187	.06833	.52864	.01964	Quality of Life
PEACE	.23543	.28417	.14916	.17843	Peace and cooperation
ANTIEST	.16698	.02284	−.19998	.14972	anti-establishment
CAPEC	−.95604	−.23512	−.16838	.03674	capitalist economics
SOCCONS	.10123	−.40294	−.22351	.16506	social conservatism
PRODTECH	−.00993	−.08199	.14894	−.39173	productivity, technology
PER104	−.04777	−.29170	−.07635	−.13787	Military +
PER108	.02065	−.25645	.24322	.10145	European Comm +
PER110	.08940	.24845	−.06688	.09937	European Comm −
PER201	−.04357	−.08673	.01096	.39428	Freedom-Hum Rights
PER202	.11063	.18577	.04089	.38796	Democracy
PER301	−.01439	−.02033	.28026	−.05369	Decentral +
PER303	−.00128	−.28899	.07358	.03803	Gov-Admin Efficiency
PER503	.15640	.40955	.04224	.19976	Social Justice
PER504	.05285	.24732	.21603	−.29257	Welfare +
PER506	.05971	.03154	.31936	−.24690	Education +
PER701	.22702	.13140	−.31572	−.02023	Labour +
PER703	−.06661	−.09280	−.17001	−.34183	Agriculture
PER705	.05788	−.00991	.29658	.11777	Minority Groups

Figure 4.6 *SPSS output (PAF, varimax rotation) of four factors underlying party manifestoes*

underlying (left–right?) scale. Themes in party manifestoes are simply not repeated measurements, but might be more in line with the unfolding model (van Schuur, 1984; see next paragraph).

The future of exploratory factor analysis
During the last decades, scepticism with respect to inductive factor analysis has grown. Especially, the near-zero factor loadings of many indicators on many factors makes interpretation of factors obscure (do low loadings mean anything or nothing?). The scepticism with respect to factor analysis has resulted also in methods to reconstruct underlying cumulative scales and unfolding scales. Cluster analysis, which will be discussed next, has been proposed as an alternative to factor analysis too.

4.5.6 Unfolding analysis

Unfolding analysis starts from the same assumption as cumulative scale analysis: different indicators measure different values (or different positions) on the underlying concept. An unfolding scale assumes that communists oppose social-democrats because they are not precisely communists, although communists will even more vehemently oppose bourgeois parties. An unfolding scale is a bipolar scale. Indicators represent specific values (or 'positions') on this scale, e.g. 'left', 'right', 'centrist', 'extreme right'. The value of a case on an indicator represents whether, or how far, the value of the case on the underlying scale is removed from the position of the indicator on the underlying scale. Thus, if 'state interventionism' is considered to be an unfolding scale, then a party which does not mention a moderate indicator of state interventionism in its program, such as 'economic planning', has either a more leftist or a more rightist position on the bipolar scale of 'state interventionism' than the position of 'economic planning' on this scale. The nasty problem in unfolding analysis is that a separate score on a separate indicator does not give enough cues to determine whether the position of a party is to the left or to the right of the position of the indicator on the scale. This problem can be solved, however, when data on more indicators and on more cases are available.

Let's illustrate the principle of unfolding analysis with a numerical example. Suppose we have three indicators of a political left–right scale, namely I_1 = 'nationalization of industries', I_2 = 'no nationalization, no privatization' and I_3 = 'privatization of government branches'. Suppose three party leaders P_1, P_2 and P_3 are asked whether their party agrees with these items. Responses to the indicators are coded on a three-point distance scale, where 0 represents agreement and higher scores represent disagreement: 0 = 'agree', 1 = 'disagree', 2 = 'disagree vehemently'. Let's make the rather strong assumption that these distance indicators have a ratio level of measurement. Suppose their responses to the indicators amount to the data-matrix depicted in Figure 4.7. Since the entries of the data-matrix represent distances of parties from the indicators, it is easy to see that P_1 and I_3, P_2 and I_2, as well as P_3 and I_1 coincide on the underlying left–right-scale. Apparently I_2 is a centrist indicator, since the (extremist) parties who disagree completely with some indicators do only disagree moderately with I_2. P_2 is apparently a centrist party, because it does not disagree vehemently with the two parties who disagree vehemently with each other. Thus, 'unfolding' the data-matrix of Figure 4.7 results unequivocally in a scale with P_2 and I_2 in the middle.

An enormous variety of variants of methods, each with slightly different assumptions, is available to tackle the unfolding problem. A detailed discussion of variants on the principle of unfolding goes well beyond the scope of this book. Here we will simply apply the default unfolding procedure in SPSS to our example of 'state interventionism'. The current version supports the ALSCAL-family of MDS. The crucial part of the SPSS-output is given in Figure 4.8. The rank order of items obtained by ALSCAL (protectionism, nationalization, controlled economy,

	I_1 Nationalization	I_2 Neither n, nor p	I_3 Privatization
P_1	2	1	0
P_2	1	0	1
P_3	0	1	2

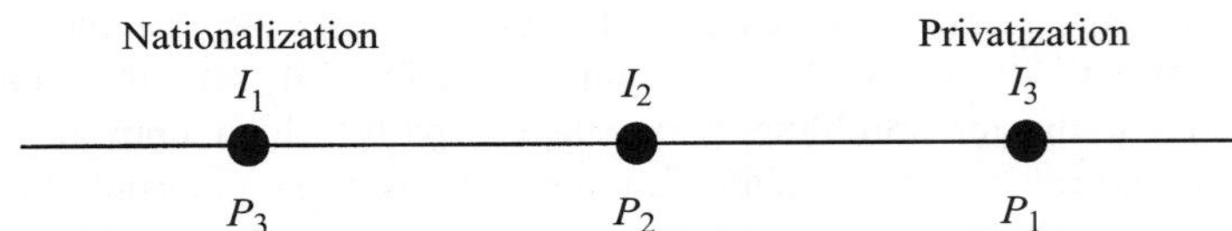

Figure 4.7 *Distance of parties from three indicators on an unfolding left–right scale*

Stress = .01697 RSQ = .99880

Stimulus Number	Stimulus Name	Dimension 1	
3	D406	−1.3653	Protectionism
5	D413	−.4329	Nationalization
4	D412	−.3266	Controlled economy
2	D404	.5218	Economic Planning
1	D403	1.6030	Economic Regulation

Figure 4.8 *SPSS output from unidimensional scaling (ALSCAL, Euclidean distances)*

economic planning, economic regulation) seems to represent indeed a left–right order. Unfortunately the current SPSS version does not render diagnostics to evaluate the quality of the separate indicators. There is no straightforward diagnostic to test the suspicion that 'protectionism' does not really belong to the scale.

Greater acquaintance with factor analysis has led scholars to apply it even when unfolding analysis is appropriate, i.e. when indicators really tap a variety of positions on the underlying continuum. Factor analysis will be misleading if unfolding analysis applies, in two respects. First, factor analysis will underestimate the proportion of variance explained by the underlying dimension. Second, explorative factor analysis with varimax rotation will suggest *two factors* both representing the one underlying (albeit 'folded') dimension which would have been found if unfolding analysis had been applied (van Schuur, 1993, 1994).

4.5.7 Hierarchical cluster analysis

The aim of scalability analysis is to extract 'components', 'factors', 'dimensions' or 'latent variables' that account for the values of the indicators and for the correlations between indicators. The aim of cluster analysis is much more modest. The aim of cluster analysis as an alternative to the scaling methods discussed above is to cluster indicators on which units of measurement have almost identical values. The simplest type of cluster analysis is hierarchical cluster analysis. First indicators are clustered into one group whose members resemble each other extremely closely. The resulting group is considered as a new indicator. The new indicator (or cluster) receives scores by averaging the scores on the clustered indicators. The cluster will resemble some of the remaining indicators. At each point the two 'closest' indicators are combined into a new cluster, a process that is iterated until all indicators take part in one cluster.

Many different measures of 'closeness' have been proposed. Actually, not measures of 'closeness', but opposite measures of 'distances' are used in cluster analysis. The three most widely used measures are probably city block distances, Euclidean distances and correlation coefficients. The *city block distance* between two indicators is equivalent to a simple addition of the *absolute* differences between the values of these indicators on the set of units. The *Euclidean distance* between two indicators is equivalent to the addition of the *squared* differences between the values of these indicators on the set of units. The *correlation coefficient* is one of the most widely used measures of association in the social sciences (see next chapter) and is useful in cluster analysis also. The correlation coefficient has -1 as its value when two indicators are each other's opposite and $+1$ as its value when two indicators do resemble each other perfectly. To use the correlation coefficient r as a distance measure, we have to use the value $d = 1 - r$.

Example: state interventionism

As an example we might apply hierarchical cluster analysis to our now familiar example of 'state interventionism'. The correlation coefficient will be used as the basis for the closeness measure, since the correlation coefficient was also (explicitly or rather implicitly) at the heart of the scaling methods discussed before. An intuitively appealing part of the cluster analysis output is the so-called *dendrogram*. The dendrogram is a horizontal tree. The horizontal axis denotes the (re-scaled) distances between the indicators. The tree indicates which indicators branch together into one cluster given a specific (re-scaled) distance. Figure 4.9 shows a dendrogram. The categories 'controlled economy' (D412) and 'nationalization' (D413) in party programs resemble each other pretty close. 'Economic planning' (D404) seems to belong to the same cluster. 'Economic regulation' (D403) and especially 'protectionism' (D406) are outliers in this cluster. Cluster analysis thus confirms the exceptional status of protectionism.

Digression: clustering units instead of clustering variables

Cluster analysis is also useful to cluster units that have almost identical values on indicators, rather than variables as in the previous example. From a technical point of view the only difference is that cluster analysis is now applied to the transposed data-matrix (considering units as variables, and variables as units). As an example we will use the 20 indicators used by Laver and Budge to characterize party programs to cluster parties in Germany in 1990. Such a cluster analysis reveals the closeness of the German parties in 1990 towards each other. Laver and Budge use these cluster analyses to predict future coalitions. The dendrogram from the relevant SPSS output is presented in Figure 4.10. Since Laver and Budge use *city block distances*, we will use city block distances here also. The use of city block measures to cluster units is recommended because the logic of more complex types of distances does not seem to apply to party programs. The dendrogram indicates that the two green parties ('Bündnis 90' and 'die Grünen') should cooperate immediately. Actually these two parties fused after the election. On the basis of

```
                 Dendrogram using Average Linkage (Between Groups)

  CASE       0        5        10        15        20        25
Label  Num   +--------+---------+---------+---------+---------+

D412    4    -+-----------+
D413    5    -+           +--------+
D404    2    -------------+        +-----------------------+
D403    1    ----------------------+                       |
D405    3    --------------------------------------------------+
```

Figure 4.9 *SPSS output of a dendrogram resulting from hierarchical cluster analysis (Euclidean distances)*

```
  C A S E        0         5        10        15        20        25
Label   Num      +---------+---------+---------+---------+---------+

green     1      -+---------+
green     2      -+         +---------+
pds       3      -----------+         +-------------+
spd       4      ---------------------+             |
fdp       5      -------------------+---------------+
cdu/c     6      -------------------+
```

Figure 4.10 *SPSS output of a dendrogram resulting from hierarchical cluster analysis (city block distances)*

their party program the former communists of the PDS could easily cooperate with the greens. The FDP and the CDU could cooperate also. The SPD, however, seems to be somewhat isolated. The most likely partners would be parties to the left (the PDS and the greens). But the CDU/CSU and the FDP won the election, so a CDU/CSU/FDP coalition came into being.

Conclusion with respect to cluster analysis

The results of cluster analysis with respect to the similarity of indicators or, alternatively, the similarity of the units of analysis being studied, are intuitively appealing. Cluster analysis does not provide clear-cut criteria, however, to decide whether an indicator measures a concept or not.

4.5.8 Summary

Although the combination of various indicators may seem a relatively unimportant problem given the bewildering complexities of the conceptual problems and measurement problems in political science, it has attracted the attention of many scholars. The various methods for scalability analysis are not easily compared, since they are based on a great variety of assumptions whose appropriateness is often hard to verify. As a start the decision tree from Table 4.3 should be used.

The empirical illustrations in this section indicated however that all the methods produced more or less the same outcomes, regardless of their precise assumptions. Of course this is one illustration only. But the suggestion is surely that researchers should not devote the bulk of their energy to the construction of optimal scales. On the basis of the decision tree the most appropriate choice should be made.

4.6 SUMMARY

This chapter provided the linkage between theoretical concepts and units of analysis on the one hand and measurements on the other hand. Concepts were operationalized. Data on units of analysis were eventually found by combining data on units of measurements. Data from content analysis, statistical agencies, and surveys and questionnaires were discussed. To evaluate the performance of measurements the criteria of validity, reliability, efficiency and comparativeness were introduced. Various types of scalability analysis to assess the reliability of multiple indicators were discussed. In the next two chapters the focus will shift from data gathering and measurement towards data analysis.

4.7 ENDMATTER

Topics highlighted

- Data-matrix: a rectangular matrix with cases (units of analysis) in the rows, concepts (variables, or units of variation) in the columns and values (scores) of cases on concepts (variables, units of variation) in its cells.
- Aggregation: combining data on units of measurement to obtain data on the units of analysis, which are of theoretical interest.
- Operationalization: combining data on indicators to obtain data on theoretical concepts (on the variables which are of theoretical interest).
- Validity and reliability of indicators: Do indicators represent the theoretical concept which they purport to measure (validity)? Are measurement errors almost absent (reliability)?
- Scalability of indicators: Are the empirical relationships between indicators consistent with their presumed quality of tapping one and the same theoretical concept?

Exercises

- Operationalize the concept 'mobility' (using indicators from the NIAS data base such as pascarvn, comvehvn, rapakmvn, cakmflvn). Use an appropriate technique for scalability analysis to test whether one dimension of mobility is indeed present.
- Aggregate the concept 'mobility' towards the following units of analysis: (1) Nordic countries; (2) continental Europe; (3) Ireland, United Kingdom and its former colonies; (4) Asian countries.

Further reading

- *General*: White, 1994; King et al., 1994.
- *Scale analysis methods*: *Guttman scale*: Mokken, 1971; van Schuur, 1984; *Likert scale*: Spector, 1992; *Unfolding scales*: van Schuur, 1984, 1993, 1994.
- *Factor analysis*: Kim and Mueller, 1978; Long, 1983; Bollen, 1994.
- *Cluster analysis*: Everitt, 1993.

Note

1 In the SPSS output the term ‘factor scores’ is used slightly differently. On the basis of the SPSS ‘factor scores’ one will not obtain a first component with variance v_s/k but a standardized component with variance 1; mathematically this comes down to printing the elements of the eigenvector $u_1, u_2 \ldots u_k$ divided by the square root of the associated eigenvalue, i.e. by $\sqrt{\lambda_1}$.

5
Explorative and descriptive statistics

CONTENTS

The preceding chapter dealt with data gathering and with the art of obtaining valid and reliable indicators of theoretical concepts for a theoretically interesting set of cases (units of analysis). The next step is to become familiar with the data by exploring them with the help of elementary data analysis techniques. The chapter begins with the analysis of a single variable. Section 5.1 deals with the univariate analysis of nominal variables, Section 5.2 with variables having ordinal, interval or ratio levels of measurement. The distribution of cases along the categories or values of a single variable is the focal point here, for example the distribution of nations as cases over the categories 'yes' and 'no' of the dichotomous nominal variable 'bilateralism'. Considering data from a bivariate perspective means that for each category (or value) of the first variable the distribution of cases along the second variable is studied. Bivariate distributions of one nominal variable with another nominal variable will be discussed in Section 5.3. Bivariate distributions of two interval distributions (e.g. degree of postmodernism and level of economic growth) will be discussed in Section 5.4. In Section 5.5 the relation between a nominal variable and an interval variable will be discussed. The major methods for analysis discussed in Sections 5.3, 5.4 and 5.5 are respectively cross table analysis, regression analysis and analysis of variance. Multivariate extensions of these three data analysis methods will be discussed in Chapter 6.

From Section 5.6 onwards inferential statistics widen the outlook from the data being explored to the universe of data which might have been studied. The focal question becomes whether the findings can be generalized. If data analysis is performed on data with respect to a sample from the population of cases, then the results may not hold for the population of cases. Statisticians have developed various tests to infer whether hypotheses which hold for a sample of cases are also plausible for the total population. Most inferential statistics assume that the sample is drawn randomly, but statistical tests which assume random samples may even be applied when the population of cases is analyzed (see Section 4.2). Statistical significance tests indicate whether findings can be generalized. Section 5.7 presents a short overview of the statistical tests that are used most often in political science research. The subsections of Section 5.7 correspond with the Sections 5.1 to 5.5. In this book on the methodology of political science, statistical tests will only be cursorily discussed. A multitude of voluminous statistical handbooks is available for the interested reader.

5.1 THE UNIVARIATE DISTRIBUTION OF A NOMINAL VARIABLE

The obvious choice to represent a single (univariate) nominal feature of one's cases is the frequency distribution. The frequency distribution displays the actual values of a variable. The frequency of empirical occurrence is rendered for each of these values. A frequency distribution can be changed into a percentage distribution by dividing the frequency of occurrence of each particular value by the total number of occurrences. A pie diagram or a bar graph can be used to visualize the frequency distribution (see, for example, Figure 5.1).

Our example of a nominal frequency distribution bears on the type of macro-economic policy of a country in a given year. The units of analysis are country–year combinations. Four different types of national macro-economic policy were prominent from the Second World War onwards: restrictive policy, monetarist policy, Keynesian policy and austerity policy (Keman, 1988: 101–26). Basically this fourfold typology derives from a cross table of two dimensions: interventions to increase economic welfare and interventions to maintain or increase social welfare. Interventions in *economic welfare* are related to the ultimate pretensions of government policy. Will the central government intervene by means of an active macro-economic policy to neutralize market failures so as to stimulate economic growth? Or is the government just an accounting department looking merely at monetary indicators? Government intervention in *social welfare* is the second dimension of the typology. Does a government support and maintain extensive social security services and related expenditures?

A *restrictive policy* refers to macro-economic aloofness of the central government in combination with the absence of interventions in social welfare. A *monetarist policy*, also labelled as a *supermarket strategy* by Keman (1988), aims primarily at stable monetary indicators (no inflation, low interest rate, avoiding budget deficits), but does not exclude government interventions to maintain social welfare. Macro-economic interventions of the government to adjust the national economy are almost absent. A *Keynesian policy*, on the contrary, strives to provide a governmental stimulus for economic growth. One of the principal means of Keynesian policy is to create a buffer of effective demand due to social security expenditures that are expected to compensate the lack of economic growth. An *austerity policy* is the combination of marginal interventions in social security so as to be able to keep the government expenditures balanced with economic growth.

Data for 18 OECD countries for the period 1965–1990 (26 years) with respect to macro-economic policy were taken from the NIAS.SAV data base. Hence the number of units of analysis amounts to $18 \times 26 = 468$. The type of macro-economic policy is referred to as the variable 'POP' (*p*olicy *o*ut*p*ut) in the NIAS.SAV database.

Table 5.1 presents the frequency distribution of macro-economic policy. What we can learn from the frequency distribution is that the two most discussed macro-economic policies in the economic textbooks of the 1960s and 1970s, namely restrictive policy and Keynesian policy, were pursued less frequently than monetarist policy and austerity policy during the period 1965–1990.

5.1.1 Measures of central tendency for nominal variables: the mode

The *central tendency* of a variable is the value on that variable that 'attracts' most of the cases. The value associated with the central tendency would be the best guess if you were asked to guess which value an unknown case would have on a variable.

Since the values (or 'categories') of a nominal variable have no rank order, the only thing to look for when the central tendency is at stake is the frequency of each category. The most frequently occurring category is called the *mode*. The mode indicates the central tendency of nominal variables. To determine the central tendency of nominal variables the only thing to look for is which value occurs most frequently. Austerity policy, for example, is the mode of macro-economic policy in OECD-countries from 1965 until 1990 since its frequency of occurrence ($n = 157$, see Table 5.1) exceeds the frequency of all other policies.

5.1.2 Measures of dispersion for nominal variables: entropy and the Herfindahl-index

The *dispersion* of a variable indicates to what degree the central tendency is indicative of the values of all cases. Measures for dispersion indicate how confident one can be that the value for a specific case is near to the central tendency of all cases.

Table 5.1 *Frequency distribution of macro-economic policy type (variable POP)*

Policy type	Frequency	Per cent
Restrictive	84	17.9
Monetarist	122	26.1
Austerity	157	33.5
Keynesian	105	22.4
	468	100

Measures of dispersion for a nominal variable are also known as *concentration measures*, because they were used from the 1960s onwards to ascertain the effective number of equally matched firms in a branch industry, i.e. the degree of business concentration. In comparative political science these measures have been adopted by Laakso and Taagepera to measure the 'effective number of parties', i.e. the degree of concentration of voters over parties. Measures of concentration have four aspects in common. A nominal measure of dispersion reaches its minimum when there's only one significant firm or party. Hence the minimum value of a concentration measure (in Number Equivalents) amounts to 1. When each party or firm is equally strong the maximum value of dispersion is reached. Thus, the maximum dispersion for a nominal variable with k values amounts to k.

Two measures of concentration which meet these four criteria have been proposed, namely the *entropy* and the *index of Laakso and Taagepera*, also known as the *Herfindahl-index* in the economic literature. To compute these concentration measures, first 'market shares' or 'frequency proportions' m_i for each of the k values of a nominal variable should be computed. As an example we will discuss once more macro-economic policy (Table 5.1). The four 'market shares' ($k = 4$) of different types of macro-economic policy are $m_1 = 0.180$, $m_2 = 0.261$, $m_3 = 0.334$ and $m_4 = 0.225$. The dispersion will be a number *between* 1 and 4, since the market shares are unequal.

The Herfindahl-index (in Number Equivalents) is defined as the inverse of the sum of squared market shares, thus as

$$Herfindahl_{N.E.} = \frac{1}{\sum_{i=1}^{k} m_i^2}$$

In the 1960s the Herfindahl-index came to be used to measure oligopoly and business concentration.

Since the 'market shares' of different types of macro-economic policy were as given above, the Herfindahl-index for the type of economic policy amounts to $1/(0.0324 + 0.0681 + 0.1116 + 0.0506) = 3.81$. What we learn from this number is that effectively almost four equally matched macro-economic policy types were available throughout the period 1965–1990. In Chapter 8 we will encounter Herfindahl's index again as the index of Laakso and Taagepera to measure the effective number of parties in a democracy.

The Herfindahl-index is more often used in comparative political science than the entropy, but future research may well prefer the *entropy* measure because of its nice statistical features. The *entropy (in Number Equivalents)* is defined as the product of the inverses of market share raised to the power of that market share, thus as:

$$Entropy_{N.E.} = \prod_{i=1}^{k} \left(\frac{1}{m_i}\right)^{m_i}$$

The entropy in Number Equivalents for the type of macro-economic policy is $1.362 \times 1.420 \times 1.442 \times 1.400 = 3.90$.

5.2 THE UNIVARIATE DISTRIBUTION OF ORDINAL, INTERVAL AND RATIO VARIABLES

The frequency distribution is useful also to display the univariate distribution of variables with ordinal, interval or ratio levels of measurement when the number of different categories is small relative to the number of cases. The values should be ordered from the lowest to the highest. If the number of values of a variable is high relative to the number of cases, then the probability that a specific value will occur is zero. To obtain frequency distributions for such variables with an overwhelming number of values relative to the number of cases, the number of values should first be reduced by recoding subsequent values into value intervals.

5.2.1 *Measures of central tendency*

The central tendency is the 'typical' value of a variable. Whereas the mode, i.e. the most frequent value, is typical of a nominal variable, the average value is typical of an interval variable. The *arithmetic mean* $\overline{x}$ is adequate to assess the central tendency of an *interval* or *ratio* variable with values $x_1, x_1, \ldots x_n$. If four persons have lengths of 1.70, 1.85, 1.85 and 2.00 m then their mean length amounts to the sum of their lengths divided by four, which reduces to 1.85 m. Actually, the symbol $\overline{x}$ denotes the *sample* mean. A statistical proof maintains that the sample mean $\overline{x}$ is an unbiased estimate of the population mean, denoted as μ_x. For convenience the symbol $\overline{x}$ will be used in the formulas below.

$$\overline{x} = \sum_{i=1}^{n} x_i$$

where $\overline{x}$ is the arithmetic mean of variable x, n is the number of cases, and x_i is the value of the ith case on variable x. Alternatively, one might first count the frequency of occurrence of each specific value (or category) of the variable. In our example of the lengths of four persons, three different lengths are encountered with frequencies $f_1 = 1$, $f_2 = 2$ and $f_3 = 1$. Next one might compute the mean length as the mean of values weighted by their respective frequencies, thus as:

$$\overline{x} = \frac{\sum_{j=1}^{k} f_j x_j}{\sum_{j=1}^{k} f_j}$$

where k is the number of distinct values, x_j is the numeric value of the jth category, and f_j its corresponding frequency. The mean length is then calculated as $([1 \times 1.70] + [2 \times 1.85] + [1 \times 2.00])/(1 + 2 + 1) = 1.85$. Thus, the mean can also be computed as a weighted mean of means within subgroups, weighted by the frequency of subgroups. The formula for a weighted mean will be used regularly in the next sections. Its denominator is simply the sum of weights. The numerator is a sum of products of weights and corresponding values.

The arithmetic mean is influenced heavily by cases with extreme values. The average length of three persons with lengths 0.50, 1.85 and 2.00 (one baby and two adults), for example is 1.45, although the length of the majority of persons is above this average. A fairly intuitive measure of central tendency would be the *median* length, which is defined as the length of the person in the midst of the queue of persons sorted on the basis of their length. The median length of the three persons is 1.85. For strictly ordinal variables the median should always be preferred over the arithmetic mean also, since the precise numeric values which are used to label the ranks of an ordinal variable lack substantial meaning by definition.

As an example the mean and median of the *public economy*, defined as the amount of public expenditures as a percentage of gross domestic product, will be considered. The cases are once more country–year combinations. New Zealand is excluded since there were no reliable data for many years from the period 1965–1990. Therefore 442 cases (17 countries × 26 years) remain. A *histogram* of public expenditures is presented in Figure 5.1. A histogram is a frequency distribution, with nearby values recoded into classes. The horizontal axis of the histogram or frequency distribution displays public expenditures. The vertical axis displays the relative frequency of specific levels of expenditures. The frequency distribution shows that public expenditures vary between 20 per cent and 67.5 per cent of Gross Domestic Product. Values between 30 per cent and 50 per cent are far more often encountered than values beneath 30 per cent or values above 60 per cent. The *mean* amounts to 41.8 per cent (see Table 5.2). There are no *outliers*, that is to say, no cases with extraordinarily low or high expenditures as compared with the other cases. A best-fitting *normal curve* is imposed on the histogram to display the

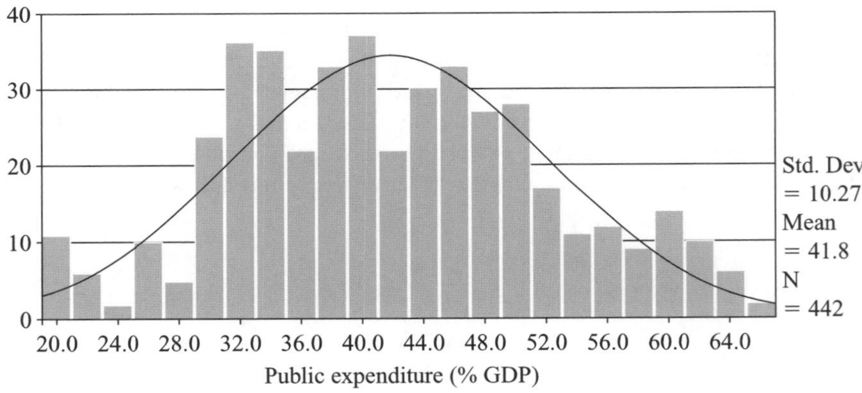

Figure 5.1 *Frequency distribution of public expenditure, with normal curve*

Table 5.2 *Central tendency of public economy*

	N	Mean	Median
Public economy (% GDP)	442	41.8	40.9

dissimilarities of the empirical distribution from a normal distribution. The figure shows that the distribution of public expenditures is slightly skewed to the lower side, since the frequency of percentages near 30 per cent is somewhat higher than expected on the basis of a normal distribution. Therefore we would expect that the median is somewhat lower than the mean. Table 5.2 shows that this is the case indeed. The *median* amounts to 40.9. If the median were to equal the mean precisely, then the distribution would be symmetric rather than skewed. The figure shows that 39–41 years is the mode. If the modal category were to include the mean and the median, then the distribution would be single peaked symmetric.

5.2.2 Measures of dispersion

Intuitively the dispersion of variables with an interval or ratio level of measurement, that are not extremely skewed, and have no outliers, is best measured with the mean deviation from the mean. Because absolute signs are nasty in many types of further statistical calculations, instead of *absolute* deviations from the mean, *squared* deviations from the mean are used. The resulting measure is called the *variance* and denoted as σ^2. The *standard deviation*, denoted as σ, is defined as the square root of the variance.

$$\sigma_x^2 = \frac{1}{n}\sum_{i=1}^{n}(x_i - \overline{x})^2$$

The standard deviation is easier to interpret than the variance. If the values of a variable are multiplied by a factor 2, then the standard deviation will become twice as large also, but the variance will increase by a factor four.

The formulas for the variance and the standard deviation presented here are used to measure the dispersion when the total population is investigated. If a *sample* of cases is analyzed then one should not divide by n but by $n - 1$ to get an unbiased estimation of the population variance. Statistical packages such as SPSS assume that a sample is being analyzed. The sample variance and the sample standard deviation are usually denoted as s^2 and s, respectively.

In a spreadsheet format the computation of the variance and the standard deviation is straightforward. We will perform these calculations in spreadsheet format here, since a good understanding of them is required for the understanding of correlation and regression analysis. Each row represents one case. In Table 5.3 a simple example of five countries is presented. In the first column, fictitious x_i values are represented. The sum of the column divided by n, the number of cases, represents the mean. Next two columns with $(x_i - \overline{x})$ and $(x_i - \overline{x})^2$ are represented.

Table 5.3 *Computation of variance in spreadsheet format*

	x_i	$x_i - \overline{x}$	$(x_i - \overline{x})^2$	x_i^2
	−3	−2.8	7.84	9
	−1	−0.8	0.64	1
	0	0.2	0.04	0
	1	1.2	1.44	1
	2	2.2	4.84	4
$\sum$	−1	0	14.8	15
	$\overline{x} = -0.2$		$\sigma^2 = 14.8/n = 2.96$	$\Sigma x_i^2 = 3$
			$\sigma = 1.72$	$\sigma^2 = 3 - 0.2^2 = 2.96$
			$s^2 = 14.8/(n-1) = 3.7$	
			$s = 1.92$	

The sum of the latter column, divided by n represents the variance. To obtain the *sample* variance one should divide by $n - 1$. The (sample) standard deviation is simply the square root from the (sample) variance. In the example given here the sum of the squared deviations from the mean amounts to 14.8. Therefore $\sigma^2 = 14.8/n = 2.96$ and $s^2 = 14.8/(n-1) = 3.7$. Spreadsheet computations of the type presented above elucidate the logic underlying the formula of the variance. This logic underlies correlation and regression analysis. High-school algebra suffices to simplify the formula of σ^2 further to $(1/n)\sum x_i^2 - \overline{x}^2$. Table 5.3 illustrates that this simplified formula amounts to $3 - 0.2^2 = 2.96$ also.

Standardized variables

The mean and the sample variance of variables are often used to *standardize* variables. Standardized values $z(x_i)$ for a variable are obtained by subtracting the mean value $\overline{x}$ from the original values x_i and dividing the result by the sample standard deviation s. These standardized values are also known as *z-scores*.

$$z(x_i) = \frac{x_i - \overline{x}}{s}$$

Standardized variables have a mean of zero and a sample variance of 1. If the data at hand cover the complete population then σ instead of s should be used to standardize. Most computer programs, amongst them SPSS however, will use s without offering a choice to the user.

The use of standardized variables will often reduce the complexity of statistical computations, and sometimes even the interpretation of data and the interpretation of substantial outcomes of data analysis. For an American statistician the information that Anita from Amsterdam earns a standardized wage of −1.5 although her standardized level of education is +1.5 is easy to interpret. The original data that her net monthly wage amounts to 1700 guilders although she finished the HEAO is rather esoteric, however.

Standardized values should be used to compare the values of variables which would otherwise be hard to compare. But it is often too easily assumed that standardized values are easy to interpret. If the mean and the standard deviation are unknown or unstable because of small sample sizes or fast changes, then standardized values will be even more difficult to interpret than the original values. Comparative indices may be developed which are more easy to interpret (e.g. all expenditures within nations measured as percentages of gross national product; each policy emphasis measured as a percentage of total attention paid to all policy areas).

Dispersion of ordinal variables and variables that are not normally distributed

For strictly ordinal variables, for variables with outliers, and for heavily skewed or otherwise non-normal variables, the variance and the standard variation are often meaningless numbers. The distance between the closures of the first and the third quartile of the frequency distribution is often used as a measure of dispersion for these variables. Computation of this distance presupposes once more that the cases are ordered according to their values on the variable of interest. As an example, measures of dispersion of public expenditures as a percentage of gross domestic product have been included in Table 5.4. The standard deviation amounts to 10.2. If public expenditures had been a perfectly 'normal' variable, then 50 per cent of the observations would have fallen in the range 41.8 plus or minus 10.2, thus in the range 31.6–53.0. The actual range is 33.6–48.9, which indicates that exceptional public expenditures occur less frequently than expected on the basis of a normal distribution.

5.2.3 The shape of the entire distribution of a variable with interval measurement

Numerical indicators of central tendency and dispersion are useful to characterize a variable with ordinal, interval or ratio level of measurement, but a qualitative assessment of the *shape* of the distribution is relevant also. Table 5.5 lists a number of frequently occurring distributions in political science. These distributions are the normal distribution, the skew distribution, the rectangular distribution, the J-distribution and the U-distribution. For each distribution the shape of the *frequency distribution* is sketched. The *cumulative frequency distribution* is derived from the ordinary frequency distribution. The cumulative frequency distribution represents for each value of a variable the proportion of cases with values *lower than or equal* to this value. In the case of a variable x with four values 1, 2, 3 and 4 with respective relative frequencies of 10 per cent, 60 per cent, 25 per cent and 5 per

Table 5.4 *Dispersion of public expenditures*

			Percentiles	
	N valid	Std deviation	25%	75%
Public economy (% GDP)	442	10.27091	33.6	48.9

Table 5.5 *Shapes of ideal-type distributions*

Name	Shapes of probability distribution (left) and corresponding cumulative distribution (right)	Functional form probability distribution
Symmetric		Normal distribution $y = c\,e^{-a(x-b)^2}$ $a > 0;\ c > 0;\ -\infty < x < +\infty$
Skew		Lognormal distribution[a] $y = c\,e^{-a[\log(x)-b]^2}$ $a > 0;\ c > 0;\ 0 < x < +\infty$
J-distribution		Negative exponential distribution $y = ce^{-cx}$ $c > 0;\ 0 < x < +\infty$
Rectangular		Beta(1,1) distribution $y = 1$ $0 < x < 1$
U-distribution		Beta(a,b) function with $0 < \mathrm{a} < 1$ and $0 < \mathrm{b} < 1$ $y = cx^{a-1}\,(1-x)^{b-1}$ $c > 0;\ 0 < x < 1$

[a]Requirements to ensure that probabilities add up to 1 not specified.

cent, for example, the cumulative distribution amounts to 10 per cent, 70 per cent, 95 per cent and 100 per cent.

The *normal* distribution is the work-horse of statistical reasoning. The majority of data analysis techniques in Part II assume that the distributions of all variables have a 'normal' shape. Most of these techniques are fairly *robust*: when the normal assumptions are 'slightly' violated, these techniques and estimators may still produce reliable results. But techniques assuming normal distributions should usually not be applied to J-shaped or U-shaped distributions. This is another reason for a careful visual inspection of the shape of frequency distributions. The *Kolmogorov–Smirnov* test (see Subsection 5.7.2) is useful to determine statistically whether empirical distributions consisting of a few cases only can be considered as drawings from an underlying normal distribution (or as a distribution of any other specified shape).

5.3 RELATIONSHIPS BETWEEN VARIABLES WITH NOMINAL MEASUREMENT LEVELS

Frequency distributions do not tell anything about *relationships* among variables. A simultaneous frequency distribution of two variables is required to examine relationships. We need to know how the empirical cases are distributed over the possible combinations of values on two variables. The *cross table* of two variables displays empirical frequencies for a rectangle of all possible combinations of values on two variables which constitute the upper and left side of the rectangle.

As an example the relationship between macro-economic policy type (POP) and the economic situation will be examined. During the post-war period the world economy flourished until the late 1960s. The first oil crisis of 1973 marked clearly the end of the period in which growth was self-evident. During the late 1970s most economies suffered from inflation, low growth rates and rising interest rates. The second oil crisis of 1979 marked the end of this period. A world recession showed up in the early 1980s, from which most economies recovered only slowly. It might be expected that the economic situation influenced the macro-economic policy, since governments will pursue specific macro-economic policies to restore economic equilibrium when the parameters of the world economy change. A cross table is useful to explore the precise relationship between the economic situation and macro-economic policy.

For three time periods and four types of macro-economic policy a cross table of 12 cells will appear. The cross table registers how the 442 nested units of years within countries are distributed over these twelve cells. It is common usage to display the separate values of the variable that is considered to be the *most interesting one*, or the dependent one, in the *rows* of the table. The columns of the table exhibit the values of the variable that is expected to 'explain' or 'predict' the variable of interest. Therefore the types of macro-economic policy are plotted in the rows, whereas the economic situation is plotted in the columns. The cells of the table contain the absolute frequencies of given policies in specific years. Absolute frequencies are hard to interpret, however. Since the cross table should inform the readers what the distribution of the variable of interest (in the rows) is for each of the values of the explaining variable (in the columns), it is most natural to compute a percentage distribution of the cases for each of the latter (column percentages). Table 5.6 exhibits this cross table.

Since *column percentages* were used, the percentages *should be compared rowwise* to arrive at conclusions with respect to the question of whether the variable of interest depends indeed on the explaining variable. As compared with the earlier and later period, restrictive policy happened to be the most common policy type in the 1970s (23.5 per cent of cases in the 1970s as compared with 5.9 and 17.6 per cent, respectively). Monetarist policies and austerity policies were dominant in the 1960s (35.3, 41.2 per cent) as compared with the 1970s and 1980s (23.5 per cent, 29.4 per cent). Keynesian policies became gradually more prevalent (1960s 17.6

Table 5.6 *Cross table of macro-economic policy type by economic situation (column percentages)*

	Economic tide			
	65–73 prosperity	**74–80 recovery from first oil crisis**	**81–90 recession; slow recovery**	**Total**
Restrictive	6	24	18	15
Monetarist	35	24	24	28
Austerity	41	29	29	33
Keynesian	18	24	29	24
	100 ($n = 153$)	100 ($n = 119$)	100 ($n = 170$)	100 ($n = 442$)

per cent, 1970s 23.5, 1980s 29.4 per cent). The data show that governments responded to the economic problems in either of two ways: either increase the effective demand or reduce the budget deficit. No unidirectional, linear trend shows up. Although Keynesianism as a macro-economic theory was challenged by schools of thought such as monetarism, neo-classicism and rational expectations from the 1970s onwards, the data on economic policy as indicated by public expenditures do not support the belief that Keynesian macro-economic policy vanished. Presumably even governments with a monetarist or neo-classical ideology were forced, by corporatist institutions and Keynesian-inspired arrangements carried over from the previous decades, to raise public expenditures (e.g. legal claims to higher social security expenditures when employment rises).

As a rough measure of the influence of the economic situation the maximum percentage difference in any *row* might be computed (column percentages assumed). In this table the maximum percentage difference amounts to $\varepsilon = 23.5$ per cent $-$ 5.9 per cent $=$ 17.6 per cent in the row of Keynesianism. This value of ε indicates that the changing economic situation corresponded with a change of 17.6 per cent in the pursuit of Keynesianism. No relationship between the variables would have existed were the maximum percentage difference to have been zero.

For exploratory purposes bar graphs might be used instead of cross tables to visualize relationships. As a first example the cross table discussed here is presented as a bar graph in Figure 5.2. The bar graph shows at a glance that conflicting policies arose from the economic crises. Some countries pursued a more Keynesian policy whereas other countries did diametrically the opposite: they pursued a restrictive policy. Obviously, such conflicting policies will tend to cancel each other out in the world economy.

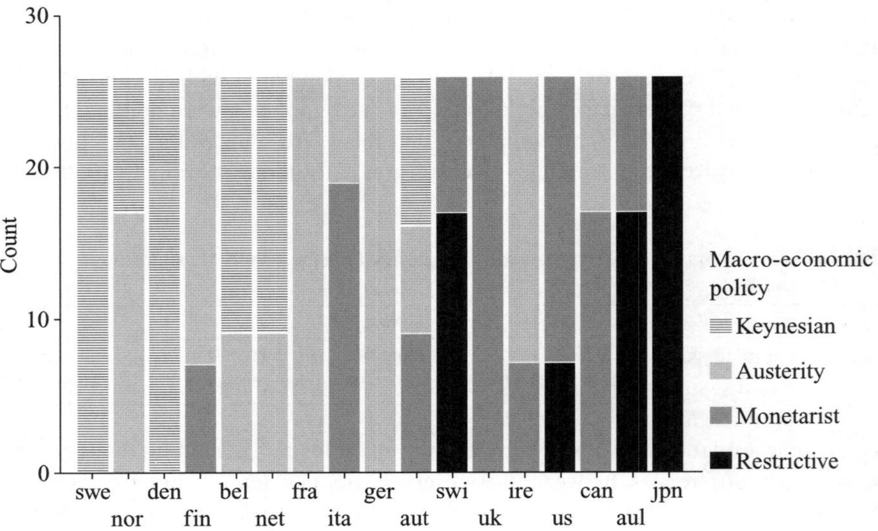

Figure 5.2 *Bar graph of macro-economic policy in various OESO nations*

5.3.1 The Chi-square measure of association in a cross table

A percentage difference as computed above is an intuitively clear measure of association. A percentage difference takes only two columns in one row of the table into account, however. Percentage differences are of little use to express parsimoniously the strength of association in larger cross tables because of their sheer multitude. The number of different percentage differences for a cross table amounts to $(r-1)(c-1)$, where r is the number of rows and c the number of columns, since one row and one column of the table serve as reference categories to compute the remaining percentage differences 'freely'. This number of independent percentage differences $(r-1)(c-1)$, which is known as the *degrees of freedom* of a cross table, will recur in Section 5.6.5 when a statistical test of the association in a cross table is at stake.

A measure of association which takes all differences between rows and tables of the table into account could start from the definition that no relationship between variables exists when the percentage distribution of the first variable is precisely the same for each value of the second variable. The frequencies that would show up when no relationship existed are referred to as the *expected frequencies*. Expected frequencies can be computed from the univariate frequency distributions of the separate variables. As a matter of convenience the univariate frequency distributions of the row and the column variable are often displayed in the margins of the cross table, thus at the right side of the cross table (row variable) and below the cross table (column variable). For this reason the univariate distributions are often referred to as the *marginal distributions*. The expected frequency e_{ij} of the combination of value i on one variable and value j on the other is a function of the marginal frequencies $f_{i.}$ and $f_{.j}$ and number of cases $f_{..}$. Since the percentage distribution of the first variable is precisely the same for each value of the second variable when no relationship exists between the two variables, the ratio $e_{ij}/f_{i.}$ should be equal to $f_{.j}/f_{..}$. Therefore the expected frequency of a cell in a cross table is simply the product of its marginal frequencies divided by the number of cases.

$$e_{ij} = \frac{f_{i.}f_{.j}}{f_{..}} = \frac{f_{i.}f_{.j}}{n}$$

The symbol $f_{i.}$ is used to denote the marginal frequency of value i on the first variable, regardless of the value on the second variable (thus $f_{i.} = \sum_j f_{ij}$). The symbol $f_{.j}$ is used to denote the marginal frequency of value j on the second variable regardless of the value of the first variable (thus $f_{j.} = \sum_i f_{ij}$). The symbol $f_{..}$ denotes the sum of frequencies, regardless of the values of the first and the second variable (thus $f_{..} = \sum_j f_{.j} = \sum_i f_{i.} = n$).

Whether a relationship exists between two variables is revealed by the (absolute or squared) differences between the observed frequencies f_{ij} and the expected frequencies e_{ij}. Chi-square, denoted as χ^2, is defined as the sum of ratios of squared differences between observed and expected frequencies to the expected frequencies. Thus,

Table 5.7 *Frequencies and expected frequencies*

			Y		
			YA value	**YB value**	**Total**
X	XA value	Count	3	1	4
		Expected count	*2*	*2*	
	XB value	Count	2	4	6
		Expected count	*3*	*3*	
Total		Count	5	5	10

$$\chi^2 = \sum_i \sum_j \frac{(f_{ij} - e_{ij})^2}{e_{ij}}$$

Table 5.7 might serve as a simple example. The table consists of 10 cases. For each cell of the table the expected frequency is computed. χ^2 is easily computed as $(3-2)^2/2 + (1-2)^2/2 + (2-3)^2/3 + (4-3)^2/3 = \frac{1}{2} + \frac{1}{2} + \frac{1}{3} + \frac{1}{3} = 1.667$.

Regrettably the value of χ^2 is not easily interpreted, since its value is not restricted to a maximum. But for a 2×2 cross table the square root of χ^2 divided by n, referred to as ϕ (phi), has a maximum of one.

$$\phi = \sqrt{\frac{\chi^2}{n}}$$

For Table 5.7 ϕ amounts to the square root of $1.667/10$, which equals 0.408. For larger tables Cramèr's v should be used, to ensure that the maximum value will not exceed 1. The denominator within Cramèr's v is not simply n, but depends also either on the number of rows or on the number of columns, depending on the question of whether there are fewer rows or fewer columns. In a cross table with one dichotomous variable, v reduces to ϕ.

$$\text{Cramèr's } v = \sqrt{\frac{\chi^2}{n\ (\text{smallest number rows/colums}) - n}}$$

5.4 THE BIVARIATE DISTRIBUTION OF TWO ORDINAL, INTERVAL OR RATIO VARIABLES

Cross tables may also be used to examine the relationships between variables with an ordinal level of measurement. Measures of association have been developed to assess the strength of the relationship between ordinal variables, amongst others Kendall's Tau B, Kendall's Tau C and Gamma. These measures will not be treated here, since the techniques discussed in the previous section suffice to explore relationships between ordinal variables with a few values only, whereas ordinal variables with many values can usually be regarded as variables with an interval level of measurement.

Cross tables are not very useful to describe the relationship between variables with an interval level of measurement, since the ordering of the values on the variables is not taken into account. Many relationships between such variables are of the type 'the higher x, the higher (or the lower) y'. When relationships between variables with an interval level of measurement are examined, the typical question is whether the values of y increase or decrease *monotonically* when x increases. As a matter of convenience it is often assumed that linear relationships can be expected. A perfect linear relationship between a dependent variable y and an independent variable x is represented by the equation $y = \mathrm{b}x + \mathrm{a}$. The complication that relationships in the empirical sciences are usually probabilistic does not need to worry us for the moment. In the language of the empirical social sciences the slope coefficient b in this linear equation is known as the (unstandardized) *regression coefficient*. The regression coefficient indicates how many units y will change on the average when x increases by one unit. Linear relationships are even frequently assumed when ordinal variables with many values are at stake, although for ordinal variables the concept of a slope coefficient is overly precise since the variables can be stretched or shrunken arbitrarily.

As an example we will examine the relation between the level of imports and exports on the one hand and the level of public expenditures on the other. Katzenstein (1985) developed the theory that countries with an open economy, characterized by high imports and exports, such as Belgium or Ireland, are relatively vulnerable to swings of the world economy. Thus the export/import ratio, operationally defined here as IMEX2 $= 50 \times$ (imports $+$ exports)/(gross domestic product), may well serve as an indicator of the economic openness of a nation in a given year. The multiplication by 50 rather than by 100 serves only to ensure that the import/export ratio has 100 per cent as its maximum (the variable IMEX in the NIAS.SAV data base is multiplied by 100, however). Countries with a relatively open economy tend to use public expenditures more extensively than other countries, as a buffer to tone down shocks from outside, David Cameron found. The higher the export/import ratio is, the higher public expenditures will be. The dependent variable Public Expenditures is operationalized as the percentage of central government expenditures as a percentage of GDP. Data are used from the data base NIAS.SAV. The units of analysis in the example are 17 OECD countries in 1988 (New Zealand is left out of consideration because of missing data).

5.4.1 Exploring the bivariate distribution: the scattergram

A feeling for the data precedes any serious data analysis. The 1988 data for seventeen countries on openness of the economy and public expenditures, together with univariate statistics on the mean and the standard deviation, are presented in Table 5.8.

The question to be answered with regression analysis is roughly to what degree countries whose openness exceeds the average (IMEX2 $>$ 31.45) also have public

Table 5.8 *The openness of the economy (IMEX2) and public expenditures (PE) (n = 17)*

Country	IMEX2	PE
swe	31.55	58.10
nor	37.05	52.50
den	30.75	60.20
fin	24.75	44.00
bel	70.75	57.30
net	52.65	56.30
fra	21.45	50.00
ita	19.30	50.30
ger	26.80	46.30
aut	37.50	50.60
swi	36.30	30.40
uk	25.05	37.90
ire	58.40	47.10
us	10.05	32.50
can	26.15	42.50
aul	17.05	33.60
jpn	9.15	31.60

expenditures above the average (PE > 45.95). To answer this question tentatively, one may, for example, first have a closer look at the three countries with either extremely high or extremely low values on each of the variables. Inspection of the data informs us that Belgium, the Netherlands and Ireland have extremely open economies, whereas Japan, the USA and Australia have their economies closed. Sweden, Denmark and, once more, Belgium rank highest on public expenditures, whereas Switzerland and, once more, Japan and the USA rank lowest. Thus, Belgium, Japan and the USA behave according to Katzenstein's theory. Australia behaves according to the theory also, since it ranks as the third country in the list of countries with low expenditures and still as the fourth country in the list of countries with low public expenditures. The Netherlands and Ireland should have high public expenditures. The Netherlands rank fourth on the list of countries with high public expenditures indeed, but the Irish economic model clearly makes an exception. Ireland's public expenditures are roughly on the average (PE = 47.1), in spite of its openness. Another exception is Switzerland, which ranks lowest on public expenditures although it is a relatively open country. Denmark is the country with the highest public expenditures, although its openness is modest. Such casual observations suffice to warrant the conclusion that Katzenstein's hypothesis is a probabilistic one, reflecting a tendency with many exceptions.

The relationship between two interval variables is easily visualized in a scattergram (see Figure 5.3). In a scattergram the variable of primary interest, usually the 'dependent' variable is plotted on the vertical axis (public expenditures, PE), whereas the independent variable (economic openness, IMEX2) is plotted on the horizontal axis. The scattergram reveals at a glance the probabilistic relationship between economic openness and public expenditures. The countries are arranged in

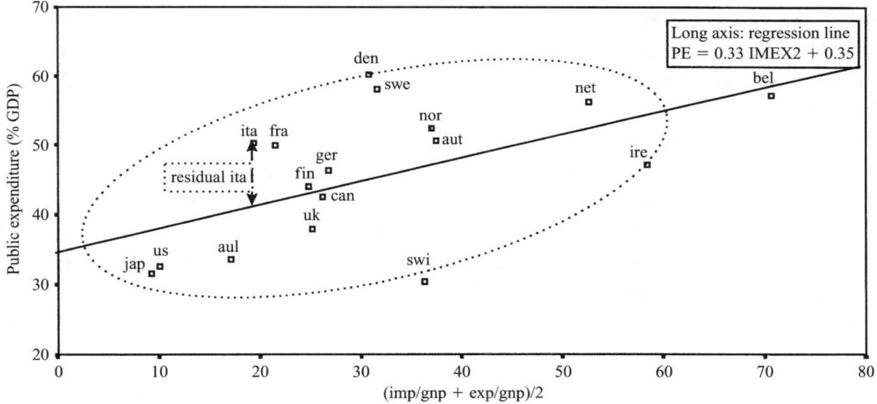

Figure 5.3 *Scattergram of openness of economy (IMEX2) and public expenditures (PE)*

an imaginary *ellipse*. Generally speaking, the long axis of the ellipse, which is known as the *regression line*, represents the rule whereas the vertical distances towards this line represent the exceptions. The long axis of the ellipse suggests a positive relationship between economic openness and public expenditures. The long axis of the ellipse ranges from Japan and the USA (closed, low public expenditures) towards Belgium (open, high public expenditures). Countries like Denmark and Sweden (fairly closed, but high expenditures) and Switzerland (fairly open, but low public expenditures) are located at a large vertical distance from the regression line. The larger the ratio of the length of the long axis of the imaginary ellipse to that of its short axis, the higher the *correlation* between the two variables is said to be. First we will concentrate on the long axis of the ellipse: on the regression line.

5.4.2 Bivariate regression analysis

Regression analysis is a means to assess the slope of the long axis of the imaginary ellipse in the scattergram. It is assumed that for each case i the value Y_i on the dependent variable Y (here public expenditures, PE) is linearly dependent on the value X_i of the same case i (here country) on the independent variable X (here economic openness, IMEX2):

$$Y_i = \beta_0 + \beta_1 X_i + \varepsilon_i$$

The expected values $\hat{Y}_i$ for each case i are precisely located on the regression line:

$$\hat{Y}_i = \beta_0 + \beta_1 X_i$$

The *regression slope coefficient*, or *regression coefficient* for short, β_1 indicates how much the dependent variable Y increases (positive value of β_1) or decreases (negative value of β_1) on the average when the independent variable X increases by one unit. The regression coefficient will be zero when Y does not depend on X. If the imaginary data ellipse in a scatterplot is perpendicular to the X-axis, then the regression coefficient will be zero. The *regression constant* or *intercept* β_0 indicates the average value of Y when X equals zero. If the imaginary data ellipse is centered on the intersection of the axes of the coordinate system – thus, when $X = 0$ and $Y = 0$ – then the intercept will surely be zero. The *regression line* $\hat{Y}$ represents the expected (average) value of Y for each value of X. But some cases will not be precisely located on the regression line. ε_i represents the *residual* or the *error term*. The residual is the *vertical* distance of a case from the long axis of the data ellipse:

$$\varepsilon_i = Y_i - \hat{Y}_i$$

Residuals are perpendicular to the X-axis, not to the long axis of the ellipse. Figure 5.3 highlights the residual for Italy as an example. Since the estimation of the parameters β_0 and β_1 aims at the minimization of the residuals, the parameters β_0 and β_{x1} are derived by minimizing the (sum of squared) differences between the actual values Y_i and the expected values $\hat{Y}_i$:

$$\text{Minimize} \sum (Y_i - \hat{Y}_i)^2$$

Elementary calculus – setting the first partial derivatives of $\sum(Y_i - \hat{Y}_i)^2$ with respect to β_0 and β_1 equal to zero (not to be pursued here) – suffices to derive the least squares estimators of β_0 and β_1:

$$\beta_0 = \bar{y} - \beta_{x1}\bar{x} \qquad \beta_1 = \frac{\sum_i (x_i - \bar{x})(y_i - \bar{y})}{\sum_i (x_i - \bar{x})^2}$$

These estimators are often referred to as the Ordinary Least Squares estimates (OLS-estimates). To get a feeling for a regression analysis it is helpful to understand the formulas of these estimators.

The parameter β_1 represents the slope coefficient of the regression line. The coefficient indicates the number of units that the dependent variable is expected to increase (measured in the units of measurement of the dependent variable) when the independent variable increases by one unit (measured in the units of measurement of the independent variable).

Dividing both the numerator and the denominator by the number of cases n clarifies the regression coefficient further. A formula results with the variance σ_x^2 in the denominator:

$$\beta_{x1} = \frac{\sum_i (x_i - \bar{x})(y_i - \bar{y})}{\sum_i (x_i - \bar{x})^2} = \frac{\dfrac{\sum_i (x_i - \bar{x})(y_i - \bar{y})}{n}}{\dfrac{\sum_i (x_i - \bar{x})^2}{n}} = \frac{\sigma_{xy}}{\sigma_x^2}$$

The fact that the variance appears in the denominator implies that the slope coefficient is measured in units of variance of the independent variable. Increasing the variance of the independent variable artificially (for example by expressing imports and exports not as percentages but as permillages of gross domestic product) will increase the denominator and therefore decrease the slope coefficient, since the change in the dependent variable associated with one unit of change in the independent variable diminishes.

The resulting numerator σ_{xy} is referred to as the *covariance* of the variables. The covariance is the sum of products over all cases of deviations from the mean values on the dependent and the independent variable. The product of deviations from the mean will be positive when the two variables co-vary in the same direction: that is to say, either when both variables are positive, or when both variables are negative (since plus times plus, as well as minus times minus, is plus). The product will be negative when positive deviations from the mean on the one variable coincide with negative deviations from the mean on the other variable. This supports the intuition that the regression coefficient will be positive when x and y move in the same direction, but negative when x and y move in opposite directions.

Related measures I: residual variance, explained variance R^2, F-ratio and adjusted R^2

Since empirical cases will usually not lie precisely on the regression line, the residuals ε_i, defined as $Y_i - \hat{Y}_i$, will usually not be precisely zero. As a measure of fit between the actual values of the dependent variable Y_i and the values $\hat{Y}_i$ predicted on the basis of the regression equation the variance of the residuals σ_ε^2 might be compared with the original variance σ_y^2 of the dependent variable. The explained variance R^2 is based on this idea.

$$R^2 = 1 - \sigma_\varepsilon^2/\sigma_y^2$$

When the ratio of the residual variance to the original variance is small, the explained variance is high. The explained variance has 0 as its minimum and 1 as its maximum. When the ratio of the residual variance to the original variance is high, the explained variance is low.

R^2 is probably the most widely used yardstick to assess the predictive power of a regression model in comparative political science. An R^2 of about zero indicates that it is impossible to predict with any precision *for a specific case* the value on the dependent variable on the basis of the regression model. An R^2 of almost 1 indicates that predictions of the values of separate cases on the basis of the regression model are almost perfect.

R^2 should not be used as the only yardstick of predictive power, however. What predictive power is needed depends entirely on the *Research Question*. A model with an R^2 about zero may still be an extremely powerful predictive model when the Research Question asks for the prediction of an average trend, rather than for a prediction of the values of separate cases. In campaigning research for a political party with a new left ideology, for example, a regression model with a low R^2 maintaining that stressing classical leftist issues rather than environmentalist issues increases the probability of voting for the party is still a powerful predictive model. A party is faced with a political macro question, i.e. how to maximize the sheer number of votes, rather than with a psychological micro question, i.e. how to ensure that citizen A rather than citizen B will vote for the party. A model with an R^2 of almost 1, on the other hand, may hide a failure to predict when some of the variables in the model are uninteresting. In regression models based on time series data the Research Question is often to what degree an exogeneous variable is predictive of the future value of a dependent variable. An R^2 of almost 1 is usually easily obtained by assuming that the value of the dependent variable will resemble as a default the value of the dependent variable from last year, last month, or even yesterday. An R^2 of almost 1 in such an *autoregressive model* (see Section 7.7) is no proof that the Research Question has been answered successfully.

One of the pitfalls of regression is that decreasing the number of cases will usually increase the explained variance, since it becomes easier to fit a straight line. Increasing the number of explanatory variables (thus moving from bivariate regression analysis towards multiple regression analysis) will increase the explained variance even by definition. R^2_{adjusted} is a measure which adjusts R_2 in such a way that – all other things being equal – decreasing the number of cases and/or increasing the number of explanatory variables will not result in an artificially higher R^2. To ensure that an increase in R^2 is not due to a smaller number of cases and/or a higher number of explanatory variables, comparative political scientists routinely report R^2_{adjusted} rather than R^2. Here we will not expound the seemingly odd formula of R^2_{adjusted}, which takes into account that fitting a regression equation becomes artificially easy when *degrees of freedom* (see Subsection 5.6.4) are lost because of a decrease in the number of cases n or an increase in the number of explanatory variables k:

$$R^2_{\text{adjusted}} = 1 - (1 - R^2)\frac{n-1}{n-k}$$

R^2_{adjusted} has 1 as its maximum, just as R^2, but whereas R^2 has zero as its minimum, R^2_{adjusted} will drop below zero when degrees of freedom decrease unduly, thus when n is small and/or k is high.

The *F-ratio* is closely related to R^2_{adjusted}. Whereas the variance explained by regression is divided by the *total variance* to obtain R^2, it is divided by the unexplained variance to obtain the F-ratio. The F-ratio takes the degrees of freedom of the explained and unexplained variance into account. R^2_{adjusted} is easy to interpret, since its maximum is 1, but the F-ratio is useful in statistical tests (see Subsection 5.7.4).

Related measures II: the correlation coefficient

The correlation coefficient is a measure of the strength of a bivariate relationship. It is a measure of association. The 'strength' of a bivariate relationship has to do with the ratio of the short axis of the imaginary data ellipse in the scatterplot to the long axis. If this ellipse is really a circle, then the strength of the relationship amounts to zero. If the two-dimensional ellipse collapses to a one-dimensional regression line – i.e. when all residuals reduce to zero – then the strength of the relationship reaches its maximum.

The correlation coefficient is defined as the *standardized covariance*, as the ratio of the covariance between two variables towards the product of the standard deviations of these variables:

$$r = \frac{\sigma_{xy}}{\sigma_x \sigma_y}$$

Linear transformations of the variables – e.g. using meters instead of inches, or using percentages instead of proportions – do not have any effect on the correlation coefficient, because they have an equal effect on its numerator and its denominator.

One should note that the regression coefficient and the correlation coefficient have their numerator in common. The correlation coefficient standardizes the covariance so as to render a measure of strength which is independent of the original measurement scales, whereas the regression coefficient expresses the covariance in the variance of the independent variable so as to render a measure of the effect, on the dependent variable, of one unit of change on the measurement scale of the independent variable. The correlation coefficient is a measure of association or strength (a measure of the shape of the data ellipse), whereas the regression coefficient is a measure of effect (a measure of the direction of the long axis of the data ellipse). The correlation coefficient varies between -1 and $+1$ whereas the regression coefficient can take any value.

Only in bivariate regression analysis does the correlation coefficient equal the square root of the explained variance: $r = \pm\sqrt{R^2}$. This equality shows that a correlation coefficient of 0.4 corresponds to an explained variance of 16 per cent only. In multivariate regression analysis (see Section 6.7) the relationship between r and R^2 is less simple.

In explorative data analysis it is common usage to inspect the matrix of correlation coefficients between the variables that are of interest in some way or another. Since correlation coefficients are measures of bivariate association only, one should avoid drawing any direct causal conclusions on the basis of such an inspection. Many techniques for multivariate data analysis – amongst others multivariate regression analysis, factor analysis, discriminant analysis and the analysis of structural relationships (see Chapters 6 and 7) – are available to test causal hypotheses accounting for the observed pattern within the correlation matrix.

Related measures III: standardized regression coefficients

A regression coefficient estimates by how many units of measurement the dependent variable will increase when the independent variable is increased by one of the units in which the latter is measured. Regression coefficients are thus expressed in the units of, often rather arbitrary, measurement scales of the dependent and independent variables. Regression coefficients are hard to interpret when the measurement scales which were used are unknown, unfamiliar or contingent upon time or space.

One solution to the problem of incomparable regression coefficients arising from incomparable measurement scales is the use of *standardized regression coefficients*. Standardized regression coefficients express the size of an effect as the number of standard deviations by which the dependent variable will change as a result of a change of one standard deviation in the independent variable. Although it is hard to compare the unstandardized effects of national corporatism as measured by Franz Lehner and the effect of world trade as measured by the OECD on national unemployment directly, a comparison in terms of standardized regression coefficients may still be possible.

One may compute standardized regression coefficients by computing ordinary, unstandardized regression coefficients on the basis of variables that were standardized first (thus by computing regression coefficients from the z-scores). As an alternative one can compute the ordinary, unstandardized regression coefficients first and multiply them by the ratio σ_x/σ_y of the standard deviations of the independent and the dependent variable.

Standardized regression coefficient

$$= \text{unstandardized regression coefficient computed from } z\text{-scores}$$

$$= \text{unstandardized regression coefficient} \times \sigma_x/\sigma_y$$

In bivariate regression analysis the standardized regression coefficient ($\sigma_{xy}/\sigma_x^2 \times \sigma_x/\sigma_y = \sigma_{xy}/\sigma_x\sigma_y$) equals the correlation coefficient ($\sigma_{xy}/\sigma_x\sigma_y$), but this equality does not hold in multivariate regression analysis (see Section 7.7).

Standardized regression coefficients have been used rather thoughtlessly as indicators of effect size. Especially in comparative research and in time series research, effects expressed in units of standard deviations are often harder to interpret than effects expressed in units of the original measurement scales. Standardized regression coefficients have even more pitfalls when the Research Question asks for a comparison of effect sizes in different countries (or different groups). Suppose that it is found that the standardized regression coefficient of the tax level on inflation is 0.5 in Germany and 0.25 in Italy. A thoughtless interpretation would be that higher taxes yield a higher inflation in Germany than in Italy. Policy advice based on this thoughtless interpretation would be that the Italian government should feel more free to increase taxes than the German government. This interpretation is utterly wrong, however: first because taxes were used far more often as a policy instrument in Germany than in Italy (which comes down to a larger σ_x in Germany than in Italy) and secondly because the inflation level varied for other reasons far less in Germany than in Italy (which comes down to a smaller σ_y in Germany than in Italy). When there is reason to expect that standard deviations of the variables of interest will vary through time or between cross-sections, then standardized regression coefficients should not be used. When there is reason to believe that standard deviations of the variables are variable through time or across nations, one should not rely easily on standardized regression coefficients.

A computational example: once more the effect of economic openness on public expenditures

To get a feeling for regression analysis it is instructive to present the required computations in spreadsheet format. Table 5.9 presents these computations. The basic format of Table 5.9 is identical to the format used for the computations of variances and standard deviations (see Table 5.3).

The three basic steps to compute the regression coefficients are:

1 Compute the means of the dependent variable and the independent variable (summation and division by n, represented in an extra row).
2 Compute deviations from the mean (columns $X - \bar{x}$ and $Y - \bar{y}$) and from these the product of deviations (column Covar XY) as well as squared deviations from the respective means (columns Var X and Var Y). Represent the result of summation and division by n in the extra row.
3 Compute the regression coefficients from the results in the extra row.

The correlation coefficient is also computable from the results in the extra row. In the case of bivariate regression the explained variance R^2 is simply the square of the correlation coefficient. An alternative way to compute the explained variance would be to compute the unexplained, residual variance explicitly. The basics steps are:

4 Compute the predicted values of the dependent variable from the original variables and the regression coefficients (column $\hat{Y}$).
5 Compute the residuals by subtracting the predicted values from the original values of the dependent variable (column ε) and from these residuals the squared residuals (column ε^2). Represent the result of summation and division by n in the extra row.
6 Compute the explained variance from the results in the extra row by applying a formula for R^2.

The reader is encouraged to perform these steps – either by hand or using a spreadsheet program – on a data base of four or five cases to learn the steps. At the cost of loss of transparency, the computational efficiency can be increased, amongst other ways, by rewriting the formulas of variance and covariation as functions of original values, squared values and multiplied values.

From Table 5.9 it is evident that the values in the column Covar XY, which

Table 5.9 *Spreadsheet computation in bivariate regression analysis*

	X = IMEX2	Y = PE	$X - \bar{x}$	$Y - \bar{y}$	Covar XY	Var X	Var Y	$\hat{Y}$	ε	ε^2
swe	31.55	58.10	0.10	12.15	1.22	0.01	147.62	45.99	12.11	146.77
nor	37.05	52.50	5.60	6.55	36.68	31.36	42.90	47.82	4.68	21.94
den	30.75	60.20	−0.70	14.25	−9.97	0.49	203.06	45.72	14.48	209.70
fin	24.75	44.00	−6.70	−1.95	13.07	44.89	3.80	43.72	0.28	0.08
bel	70.75	57.30	39.30	11.35	446.05	1544.49	128.82	59.03	−1.73	3.01
net	52.65	56.30	21.20	10.35	219.42	449.44	107.12	53.01	3.29	10.83
fra	21.45	50.00	−10.00	4.05	−40.50	100.00	16.40	42.62	7.38	54.42
ita	19.30	50.30	−12.15	4.35	−52.85	147.62	18.92	41.91	8.39	70.43
ger	26.80	46.30	−4.65	0.35	−1.63	21.62	0.12	44.40	1.90	3.59
aut	37.50	50.60	6.05	4.65	28.13	36.60	21.62	47.97	2.63	6.94
swi	36.30	30.40	4.85	−15.55	−75.42	23.52	241.80	47.57	−17.17	294.69
uk	25.05	37.90	−6.40	−8.05	51.52	40.96	64.80	43.82	−5.92	35.07
ire	58.40	47.10	26.95	1.15	30.99	726.30	1.32	54.92	−7.82	61.20
us	10.05	32.50	−21.40	−13.45	287.83	457.96	180.90	38.83	−6.33	40.05
can	26.15	42.50	−5.30	−3.45	18.29	28.09	11.90	44.19	−1.69	2.85
aul	17.05	33.60	−14.40	−12.35	177.84	207.36	152.52	41.16	−7.56	57.13
jpn	9.15	31.60	−22.30	−14.35	320.01	497.29	205.92	38.53	−6.93	48.01
Sum/n	31.45	45.95	0	0	85.33	256.35	91.15	45.95	0	62.75

$\beta_{xy} = 85.33/256.35 = 0.333.$

$\beta_0 = 45.95 - 0.333 \times 31.45 = 35.48.$

$r = 85.33/(\sqrt{256.35}\sqrt{91.15}) = 0.558.$

$R^2 = 0.558^2 = 0.312$ or

$R^2 = 1 - 62.75/91.15 = 0.312.$

represent the products of deviations from the means of the dependent and the independent variable, are predominantly positive. Thus, the dependent and the independent variable move in the same direction for twelve out of seventeen countries. The Covar *XY* column shows five exceptions (Denmark, France, Italy, Germany and Switzerland). From this observation the sign of the regression coefficient and the correlation coefficient is already apparent, since both regression analysis and correlational analysis are based on the simple arithmetical fact that the product of two deviations from the mean will be positive when both numbers are either both positive or both negative. The further computations serve only to state these observations based on the column of products of deviations from the mean in neat numbers. The regression line becomes PE = 0.333 IMEX2 + 35.48. If a country increases its exports and imports by 1 per cent, then the best guess is that public expenditures will be increased by 0.333 per cent. Exports and imports are by no means the only source of variation in public expenditures, since only 31.2 per cent of the variance in public expenditures is due to imports and exports ($R^2 = 0.312$). In the case of bivariate regression the standardized regression coefficient and the correlation coefficient do not provide additional information, since these coefficients can simply be computed as the square root of the explained variance.

5.5 THE RELATION BETWEEN AN INTERVAL OR RATIO VARIABLE AND A NOMINAL VARIABLE

Many empirical investigations have to do with the relationship between an interval variable and a nominal variable. Political scientists may for example wish to compare public expenditures (interval) before or after the oil crisis of 1973 (nominal), changes in gross national product (interval) after 'treatments' with various macro-economic policies (nominal variable POP, Table 5.1), or public expenditures (interval) in various countries (nominal variable). Most research questions ask for a *comparison of the mean value* of the interval variable between the various categories of the nominal variable. One may, for example, make a cross-country comparison of the *mean* level of public expenditures (interval) within specific countries (nominal) over some time period. More sophisticated comparisons can be made also. A research question regarding the rigidity of public expenditures may require a between-country comparison of the *variance* of public expenditures within these countries over the last thirty years, or even of the *precise time paths* of the levels of public expenditures within these countries. Here we will concentrate on a comparison of the *mean* level of the interval variable for the various categories or values of the nominal variable. Adopting the language of psychologists, biologists and medical scientists, who have developed the explorative research techniques which will be discussed in this section, these values or categories of this nominal variable are also labelled as the 'groups'. The 'groups' in comparative political science do not usually consist of individuals, however, but rather of countries (cross-sectional analysis) or of time points (longitudinal analysis).

5.5.1 An interval variable and a bivariate nominal variable: the comparison of two means

An obvious way to compare the means of *two groups* is to assess the magnitude of the difference between the two means. When this difference is fairly large, as compared with the standard deviation of the interval variable within the two groups, then the two means differ substantially from each other. As a trivial example of this line of reasoning the level of public expenditures within European and non-European OECD countries will be compared. Table 5.10 (produced by SPSS-procedure T-test from the NIAS.SAV data base) presents the basic results. The mean level of public expenditures as a percentage of GDP for non-European countries is 12.46 per cent less than for European countries. A difference between the *means* of these two groups does not imply, however, that each country within the European group has higher expenditures than each country within the group of non-European OECD countries. To determine the degree to which differences between groups hold for all cases within the groups one should compare the *difference between* the means of the groups with the variance (or standard deviation) of public expenditures *within* the two groups. If many exceptions exist to the rule that European countries have higher expenditures than non-European OECD countries, then the variance of public expenditures within the European countries, and the variance of public expenditures within the non-European countries, would be large compared with the difference between the mean expenditures within the two groups. Since the difference between the two groups amounts to 12.46 per cent, which is larger than the standard deviations within the two groups (6.64 and 9.82 per cent, respectively), it appears to be safe to conclude that not many exceptions indeed exist to the finding that European OECD countries have higher expenditures than non-European OECD countries.

Two fairly abstract lessons from this trivial example should be kept in mind. The first lesson is that exploring the relationship between a (dependent) variable with an interval level measurement and a nominal (independent) variable consisting of a few 'groups' (or nominal values, or 'categories') comes down to the comparison of group means. The second lesson is that the difference between the group means serves as a sufficient summary of the differences between the cases from the groups to the extent that the difference between group means is large compared with the variance within groups. The second lesson is essential both to understanding statistical tests of whether group means differ from each other (see Subsection 5.7.2) and to an understanding of more complex types of comparisons between group means, known as the analysis of variance (next Subsection and Subsection 5.7.5).

Table 5.10 *A comparision of two group means*

Variable	Number of cases	Mean	SD	SE of mean
PE public expenditure (% GDP)				
non-European	124	33.6024	6.635	0.596
European	398	46.0586	9.821	0.492
Mean difference = −12.4561				

5.5.2 Analysis of variance: an interval variable by a nominal variable with j values

The label 'analysis of *variance*' is slightly confusing, since its aim is to assess whether group *means* differ substantially from each other. The label expresses that this aim is best achieved by comparing the differences between group means with the variance within groups. The variance between group means is used as an indicator of the mean magnitude of the pairwise differences between the group means, since the number of pairwise differences increases disproportionately when the number of groups increases. J groups would give rise to $\frac{1}{2}j^2 - \frac{1}{2}j$ pairwise comparisons between groups. One would have to compare 136 pairs of means, for example, to test whether public expenditures in a given period differ between seventeen countries. The group means differ from each other when the variance of group means is substantial. Thus, analysis of variance presupposes that group means are different from each other when the variance between groups is substantial compared with the variance within groups. If the variance of group means σ^2_{bt} is substantial compared with the variance within the various groups σ^2_{wh} then there will be only a few exceptions to the rule that, on average, cases from one group have higher (or lower) scores than cases from another group. The *explained variance* R^2, often labeled as η^2 (eta squared) in the context of the analysis of variance, is defined as the ratio of the variance between group means σ^2_{bt} to the total variance of the interval variable σ^2_{tt}

$$R^2 = \eta^2 = \frac{\sigma^2_{\text{bt}}}{\sigma^2_{\text{bt}} + \sigma^2_{\text{wh}}} = \frac{\sigma^2_{\text{bt}}}{\sigma^2_{\text{tt}}}$$

The total variance is simply the variance of the interval variable. The variance between groups σ^2_{bt} is computed as the sum of squared deviations of group means from the grand mean $\overline{Y}$, where the jth group is weighted by its number of cases n_j. Thus,

$$\sigma^2_{\text{bt}} = \frac{\sum_j n_j(\overline{y}_j - \overline{Y})^2}{n} = \frac{SS_{\text{bt}}}{n}$$

where $\overline{Y}$ is the grand mean, the mean value on the dependent variable y across all cases, and $\overline{y}_j$ its mean within the jth group. The variance within groups simply defined as the sum of squared deviations of each value from its own group mean, divided by n:

$$\sigma^2_{\text{wh}} = \frac{\sum_j \sum_i (y_{ij} - \overline{y}_j)^2}{n} = \frac{\text{SS}_{\text{wh}}}{n}$$

This knowledge suffices for the understanding of the principles of the analysis of variance, but it is not sufficient to understand the output of most statistical packages. Instead of using the variance between group means divided by the total variance as a measure of difference between group means, one may also use solely the variance within as the denominator. Since both the variance between means as well as the variance within groups have n in the denominator it is convenient to consider solely the numerators; statistical packages will usually print solely the Sum of Squares Between (SS_{bt}) and the Sum of Squares Within (SS_{wh}).

A further complication concerns the fact that in order to arrive at an unbiased estimator of the variance one should divide the sum of squared deviations by $n - 1$ rather than by n, the number of cases (see Subsection 5.2.2). Since the means of j groups are compared with the grand mean in the numerator, $j - 1$ is the proper divisor of SS_{bt} to arrive at an unbiased estimator of the variance between groups. To arrive at an unbiased estimator of the variance within a specific group j the proper divisor would be $n_j - 1$. Summation over all groups gives $n - j$ as the proper divisor of SS_{wh} to arrive at an unbiased estimator of the variance within. The divisors $j - 1$ and $n - j$ are known as the *degrees of freedom* between and the degrees of freedom within, respectively. The ratio of SS_{bt} divided by its degrees of freedom $j - 1$ to SS_{wh} divided by its degrees of freedom $n - j$ is known as the F-ratio:

$$F = \frac{\dfrac{SS_{\text{bt}}}{j-1}}{\dfrac{SS_{\text{wh}}}{n-j}}$$

In the analysis of variance the F-ratio plays a decisive role in statistical tests (see Subsection 5.7.5).

An example: an analysis of variance of public expenditures in seventeen countries

As an example of the analysis of variance we present a fairly common explorative question in comparative political science. When data on the same cases are available for subsequent days, months, or years the data mount up to pooled time series data. If pooled time series data are available, an important question is always whether the variation in the dependent variables is due to time or due to cross-sectional variation. If the variation through time is negligible then one could just as well employ data on cross-sections at one point in time. If the variation between cross-sections is negligible, then one could just as well study time series data for one specific case.

Here we will explore whether variation in public expenditures (as a percentage of gross domestic product) is mainly longitudinal or mainly cross-sectional. If one believes that global capitalism has reached a phase in which the economies and the economic policies of nations are completely interwoven, then one expects longitudinal variation only. If one believes that national institutions, such as institutionalized corporatist decision making, are hardy enough to allow for incremental policy changes only, then one should expect primarily cross-sectional variation.

For the sake of brevity we will refer to these hypotheses as the global economy hypothesis and the institutional sclerosis hypothesis, respectively.

The graphical tool to split variation in pooled time series data in longitudinal and cross-sectional variation is called the *sequence plot* (available within SPSS) (see Figure 5.4). The sequence plot shows the time path from 1965 to 1995 for each cross-section. It shows at a glance that countries such as Sweden had high public expenditures all along, whereas countries such as the USA and Switzerland had low public expenditures throughout, as was expected on the basis of the *institutional sclerosis* hypothesis. A closer inspection of the time paths shows that in most of the countries public expenditures rose in the 1960s, dropped in the 1980s, but increased once more in the early 1990s. Evidently the public expenditures in all developed countries show up more or less the same changes through time, as was expected on the basis of the rival global economy hypothesis. It is not easy to decipher from the sequence plot the relative strengths of the two hypotheses.

The analysis of variance is the appropriate statistical technique to refine this visual impression. It decomposes the variation in pooled time series into variation through time, variation across cross-sections and remaining 'unexplained' variation due to independent – or idiosyncratic – national policies that result in an independent national time path. First an analysis of variance is pursued to assess the viability of the institutional sclerosis hypothesis, i.e. to answer the question of the degree to which the variance is cross-sectional. What percentage of the variance in public expenditures is maximally due to cross-sectional variation between countries? The results (SPSS output) are presented in Figure 5.5. The SPSS output follows the standard format of analysis of variance output. The columns SS (Sums of Squares), DF (degrees of freedom) and F (the F-ratio) have been discussed before. The column 'Sig of F' must wait until Subsection 5.7.5. Here we will concentrate on the SS column. The figure of 28268.38 in the SS column represents the sum of squared deviations of the mean public expenditures within a country

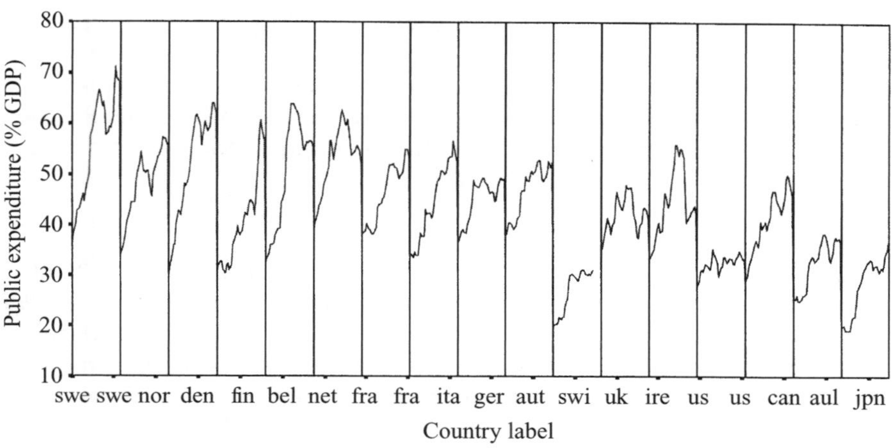

Figure 5.4 *Sequence plot of public expenditure by country and year*

Source of Variation	SS	DF	MS	F	Sig of F
WITHIN CELLS	18253.41	425	42.95		
COUNTR	28268.38	16	1766.77	41.14	.000
(Model)	28268.38	16	1766.77	41.14	.000
(Total)	46521.80	441	105.49		
R-Squared =	.608				
Adjusted *R*-Squared =	.593				

Figure 5.5 *SPSS output for analysis of variance of public expenditure for seventeen countries 1965–1990*

from the overall mean of public expenditures in all countries, where each country is weighted by the number of observations from it (here 26 years). The number 46521.80 represents the sum of squared deviations of the mean public expenditures in specific countries (26 years) from the mean public expenditures in all countries in all years. The proportion of explained variance is obtained by dividing the sum of squares between countries by the total sum of squares. The explained variance amounts to $R^2 = 28268/46521 = 0.608$. Thus, the data clearly support the hypothesis of institutional sclerosis. Some sixty percent of the variation in public expenditures over the period 1965–1990 in OECD countries is due to structural differences between countries.

An analysis of variance with the year as the independent nominal variable reveals that another 30 per cent ($R^2 = 0.297$) is variation through time, independent of the specific country. This implies that the global economy hypothesis is confirmed also, although the explained variance is twice as low. National economic policies in the period 1968–1990 which deviated both from the global trend and from the policies induced by national institutions at an earlier point in time explain merely some ten per cent of the variation in public expenditures. The bulk of the variation in public expenditures was due to the global economic development (roughly thirty per cent) on the one hand and to national constraints on the other (roughly sixty per cent).

Summary

Exploratory analysis of the relationships between variables depends on the level of measurement of the variables. Cross tables and measures such as Chi-square, Phi and Cramèr's v are appropriate when the relationship between nominal variables is at issue. Regression analysis and the analysis of variance assume that the dependent variable has an interval level of measurement. Analysis of variance assumes a nominal independent variable only, whereas in regression analysis the independent variable has interval level of measurement. The concepts of explained and unexplained (residual) variance are central concepts both in the analysis of variance and in regression analysis. The unexplained variance is the proportion of the variance in the dependent variable which is independent of variations in the independent variable.

5.6 POPULATIONS, SAMPLES, AND INFERENTIAL STATISTICS

Unfortunately the results of an exploratory data analysis are almost always based on available data that may not be the only data that can be imagined to mirror the research topic. Therefore statistical tests to assess whether the results may hold for a larger population enter the picture. Whether one feels confident about the results found on the basis of available data depends on the question of whether other results would have been found if other data had been employed. Although the latter question appears to be rather philosophical at first sight, it is precisely this question which is routinely answered by the use of statistical tests. Scientists usually do not feel confident about results of an exploratory data analysis which do not stand against a statistical test. Statistical tests narrow down the philosophical question by asking how likely it is that another sample of data from the same 'population' (or 'reality') would have given rise to completely different results (see Section 4.2). Statistical tests do not question the inherent quality of the available data. Questions of reliability and validity have to be addressed by other means (see Section 4.3).

In the last sections of this chapter we will first repeat the essentials of statistical testing (see Section 4.2). Next, additional concepts such as estimators, desirable aspects of estimators such as unbiasedness and efficiency, and degrees of freedom will be discussed. Commonly used tests will be presented step by step. The chapter concludes with a discussion of the use and misuse of statistical tests.

5.6.1 *The urn model*

The urn model, which provides the basis of elementary statistical testing, was introduced in Section 4.2. The model starts from the assumption that there is an unknown population from which a sample of data has been drawn. Statistical tests are designed to *disprove a null hypothesis* H0 that contradicts an interesting hypothesis H1. The aim is to show that the null hypothesis is untenable as it leads to an unsatisfactorily small probability of being compatible with sample data. Unlike comparative political scientists, statisticians never set out to prove an interesting hypothesis. The best they can do is to demonstrate that the likelihood of a null hypothesis which is not in line with an interesting hypothesis is negligible in the light of the available sample data. This knack is extremely useful, however, to prove that the obtained results are not artefacts of (limited) available data.

A statistical test rests on the thought experiment of drawing *all possible samples* with a sample size precisely as large as the actual sample size from a population in which the null hypothesis holds true. The thought experiment continues with the computation of a *test statistic* for each of these samples. A test statistic is a summary of the sample data that is indicative of the tenability of the hypothesis.

As an example the hypothesis may be considered that proportional electoral systems have higher turnout rates in elections than majoritarian electoral systems, since minorities will not vote in majoritarian countries because the two major parties will seek to please the median voter rather than some extremist minority. Logically the null hypothesis must be that there is no difference between the turnout rates in these systems. Suppose that data on turnout rates in 40 elections – 20 from proportional and 20 from majoritarian systems – are available. The relevant test statistic here is the difference between the mean turnout in proportional electoral systems and the mean turnout in majoritarian electoral systems. The thought experiment of the statistician would be to compute this test statistic, i.e. the difference between the mean turnouts in the two systems, for each possible sample of 40 cases which could have been drawn from a population in which the null hypothesis holds. Most samples will show up negligible differences between the two groups of systems, since such a difference does not exist in the imaginary population from which the samples were drawn. Mere chance dictates, however, that some samples will show up far higher turnout rates in proportional electoral systems, whereas others will show up far higher turnout rates in majoritarian systems. Therefore the thought experiment results in a *probability distribution of the test statistic*. Statisticians have proven that the probability distribution of the test statistic in our example, i.e. the difference between the mean turnouts in the two systems, is a symmetric distribution. Actually it is a 'normal' or 'Gaussian' distribution (see Figure 5.6).

Moreover the mean value of the differences which will be found between the two types of electoral systems in all possible samples will be precisely zero. To put it otherwise, the mean value of the test statistic, i.e. the difference found between the mean turnout in proportional systems and the mean turnout found in majoritarian systems, hits the mark precisely, regardless of the sample size.

However, the variance of the test statistic decreases as the sample size is enlarged. The smaller a sample, the more variant and shaky the results are. If the sample size amounts to 500 elections, then the set of all possible samples will contain only a few samples with large differences between the two types of systems if actually the null hypothesis is true which maintains that in the population the difference between the two systems is zero. If one is drawing all hypothetical samples of only 10 elections then one will find in many samples differences between the groups of electoral systems even when the null hypothesis holds.

Statisticians have proven that increasing the sample size has diminishing returns. Given the sample result that women live 5 years longer on the average, the probability that there is no difference between the mortality rates of men and women in the population decreases sharply when the sample sized is increased from 10 to 1000. A further increase of the sample size to 2000 will decrease the probability that there is no difference in the population only slightly further.

To sum up, statistical testing rests on a thought experiment of mathematical statisticians of drawing all possible samples of a given size from a population in which the null hypothesis holds. The concepts of an estimator, a test statistic and a probability distribution of the test statistic are important in understanding the thought experiment. A few more things have to be said about features of estimators before the general procedure employed in hypothesis testing will be discussed. This additional discussion involves the concepts of (un)biasedness, (in)efficiency and robustness of estimators.

5.6.2 Unbiasedness, efficiency and robustness of an estimator

An estimator is a function of sample data that is used as an approximation of a population parameter. One may use the sample mean as an estimator to estimate the population mean, for example. In comparative political science, as in any other branch of science, estimators should give 'correct' results. The correctness of estimators is operationalized using the concepts of unbiasedness, efficiency and robustness.

An estimator is *unbiased* when its approximations are on the average precisely to the point. An estimator is *biased* when its approximation of the population parameter is consistently besides the point. The sample mean from a random sample is an unbiased estimate of the population mean. In our previous example the difference between the mean turnout in electoral and majoritarian systems according to our sample of 40 elections is an unbiased estimator of the corresponding difference in the population. It is not always true, however, that a sample parameter is an unbiased estimator of the corresponding population parameter. To arrive at an unbiased estimate of the population variance, for example, one should divide the sum of squared deviations from the sample mean by $n - 1$ rather than by n. The reason why an unbiased estimator of the population variance requires division by $n - 1$ rather than by n is that one free observation – one degree of freedom – has to be offered to calculate the sample mean before the actual calculation of squared deviations from it may start. Degrees of freedom will be discussed further in Subsection 5.6.5. An estimator is *asymptotically unbiased* if it is unbiased provided the sample size is sufficiently large. Dividing the sum of squared deviations from the sample mean by n may result in a biased estimator of the variance, but it does result in an asymptotically unbiased estimator, since division by n rather than by $n - 1$ does not make a difference when n is sufficiently large.

Unbiased estimators may still produce faulty approximations of population parameters. Being to the point on average is compatible with being faulty all the time. The variance of the estimates should be taken into account also. Estimators with a small variance are called *efficient* estimators; estimators with a small variance when the sample is large are called *asymptotically efficient*. Whether estimators are efficient depends on contingencies in the population. The ordinary least square estimator of the regression coefficient which was introduced in Section 5.4, for example, is an efficient estimator of population regression parameters in most circumstances. But in Section 6.7 notable exceptions will be discussed (e.g. heteroscedasticity, autoregression).

The third aspect of estimators to be discussed is their *robustness*. The robustness of an estimator refers to its quality of producing more or less the same estimate when small changes in the sample data are introduced. One may perceive the robustness of an estimator also as the quality of being insensitive to violations of the precise assumptions that underlie the estimator. These assumptions regard the randomness of the sample, but also technical aspects of the data, which will be discussed partially in Section 6.7.

A serious statistical problem is that many estimators do not combine the three desirable properties of unbiasedness, efficiency and robustness. Advanced unbiased estimators to deal with (pooled) time series data, for example, have been proven to be less efficient than the Ordinary Least Squares estimator of ordinary regression analysis if they are applied to relatively short time series. (Lack of) Robustness of an estimator is usually demonstrated by executing a great many computer simulations on random modifications of given data sets, whereas unbiasedness and efficiency can be demonstrated by mathematical proofs. Robustness simulations often indicate that elegant estimators produce a variety of utterly inconsistent and extremely shaky results, especially when the sample size is small (e.g. Beck and Katz, 1995; Jackson, 1996). The research on the robustness of estimators suggests a simple conclusion. Estimators that use the complete set of data at once, such as ordinary least squares estimators in regression analysis, or the F-test in variance analysis, are fairly robust. *Hierarchical estimators* tend to be shaky, however. Hierarchical estimators, which first use subsamples of the data to draw inferences from them, are far less robust.

To sum up, the choice of an estimator should depend on its (un)biasedness, (in)efficiency and (un)robustness. Intuitive plausibility and mathematical elegance are additional considerations. The ordinary least squares estimator of the regression coefficient was introduced in Section 5.4 simply because of its plausibility. As an alternative one may derive mathematically which estimator has the maximum likelihood of estimating population parameters correctly on the basis of sample data, given a number of assumptions with respect to the population distribution. Whether an estimator is the maximum likelihood estimator thus depends on the distribution of the data. Most often Maximum Likelihood estimators assume a multi-normal distribution: each variable is normally distributed (see Figure 5.6) and linear interrelationships show up between each combination of variables. If the multivariate population distribution is multi-normal, then the maximum likelihood estimator of the regression coefficient turns out indeed to be the now familiar ordinary least squares estimator. Maximum likelihood estimation is the holy grail of mathematical statistics. One problem with maximum likelihood estimators is that they may not be robust when the precise assumptions on the data have not been met. The assumption of a multi-normal distribution is a strong one, which is seldom warranted by the data. *Parameter-free tests* are designed to keep the number of assumptions with respect to the population to a minimum. But tests that do not rest on any assumption at all do not exist. Many parameter-free tests assume that the rank order of values in the sample reflects precisely the rank order in the population, whereas the values themselves do not. The latter assumption is no less dubious, especially when measurement errors are extant as is usually the case in comparative political science. For this reason we will not discuss parameter-free tests in this book.

5.6.3 The general procedure used in hypothesis testing

Hypothesis testing involves a number of steps (see Kanji, 1994). As a preliminary step the theory at stake should be broken down into testable hypotheses, or, alternatively, testable hypotheses within the theory or testable hypotheses that are implied by the theory should be specified. As a further preliminary step one should decide on the magnitude of the type I error one is willing to make. The error of type I is defined as the chance that the null hypothesis is rejected, although the null hypothesis is true. As a matter of convenience we will abide by the convention that in the social sciences errors of type I that exceed 5 per cent are not acceptable.

For each hypothesis the following steps should be taken.

1a State the *object of an hypothesis* in statistical terms. The object of the hypothesis that a higher income tends to be associated with more right-wing opinions, for example, concerns the magnitude of a correlation coefficient, or probably better, the magnitude of a regression coefficient. Usually the statistical object of a substantial hypothesis is a *population parameter* (e.g. the population mean, the regression coefficient in the population). The example maintains that a specific regression slope coefficient exceeds zero in the population. Its object is the regression slope parameter.

1b Determine whether the hypothesis is one-sided or two-sided. Since the regression slope should exceed zero, the hypothesis in our example is one-sided. A two-sided hypothesis would have been that the regression coefficient equals zero.

1c Formulate a *null hypothesis* which excludes the stated hypothesis. Usually the null hypothesis is less 'exciting' than the hypothesis. The null hypothesis represents usually a standard with which the evidence pointing to the alternative hypothesis can be compared. Typical null hypotheses are that there is no difference at all or no relationship at all. The null hypothesis in our example would be that the regression slope coefficient is zero in the population.

2 Compute a *test statistic* (T), that is a function of the sample data, with a known probability distribution (when the null hypothesis holds). Many test statistics are available. Statisticians have derived what the distribution of the values of the test statistic will be over the infinite number of samples of a given size that might be drawn from the population. Statisticians have derived a test statistic for regression coefficients, for example, that amounts to a t-distribution for the infinite number of possible samples of a given size from a population in which the regression slope coefficients are zero. The t-distribution is one of the four commonly encountered distributions which will be discussed in Subsection 5.6.4.

The construction of the test statistic starts from an *unbiased estimate* of the population parameter which is the object of the hypothesis. Thus, if the object of an hypothesis is a population regression coefficient, then one will compute the sample regression coefficient. To arrive at an unbiased estimator of the population variance, however, one should multiply the direct sample equivalent of the population variance by $(n - 1)/n$.

As a next step the *standard error* of the estimate is usually computed. The standard error refers to the variance of the estimates of the population parameter that would be obtained if the null hypothesis holds and an infinite number of samples of the given sample size were drawn from the population.

As a further step to compute the test statistic the estimate of the population parameter on the basis of sample data is 'compared' with the standard error on the basis of the null hypothesis. The test statistic is a value on the x-axis of the probability distribution of the estimator.

3 Derive from the table of the probability distribution of the test statistic (or from computer output) the *significance level*, i.e. the percentage of the possible samples from the population for which the test statistic is compatible with the null hypothesis. One should take into account whether the hypothesis was one-sided or two-sided when looking up this percentage. Most computer programs will assume that the test is two-sided.

4 Decide whether the null hypothesis should be rejected by determining whether the probability found at step 3 is lower than the accepted magnitude of type I errors (usually set at a maximum of 5 per cent).

5.6.4 Four common probability distributions of test statistics: z, t, χ^2 and F

Consider the probability distribution of the mean age according to samples. Ages in the western world vary between 0 and 120 years. But the mean age according to a sample of 10 humans will not vary that much. It's unlikely, although not impossible, that a random sample of size 10 from the world population will include only newborn babes. In the majority of cases the sample mean will be near to the population mean. Sometimes to the left of it, sometimes to the right of it, but usually not far from it. Although the age distribution is highly skewed, with many babies and only a few old people whose age exceeds 100 years, the distribution of the means of a host of imaginary samples from this skewed population will be symmetric. When the sample size is sufficiently large ($n > 120$) the probability of the sample mean is a *normal* distribution with a standard deviation that is much smaller than the standard deviation of the population distribution, regardless of the precise shape of the population distribution. On the authority of mathematical statistics we accept that the standard deviation of the sample mean, also known as the *standard error*, equals the standard deviation of the population distribution, divided by the square root of the sample size. Thus, if the standard deviation of the population distribution equals 1, and the sample size is 100, then the standard error will be $1/\sqrt{100} = 0.1$. A standard error of the sample mean of 0.1 indicates that on the average the mean of a sample will deviate 0.1 standard deviations from the population mean. To obtain a standard error of 0.01 a sample size of 10 000 is required. Thus, increasing the sample size has diminishing returns. Figure 5.6 depicts a standardized normal distribution. The normal distribution is also known as the Gaussian distribution and as the z-distribution.

The area beneath the standardized normal curve indicates the proportion of cases with specific values. Roughly 68 per cent of the cases are located within one

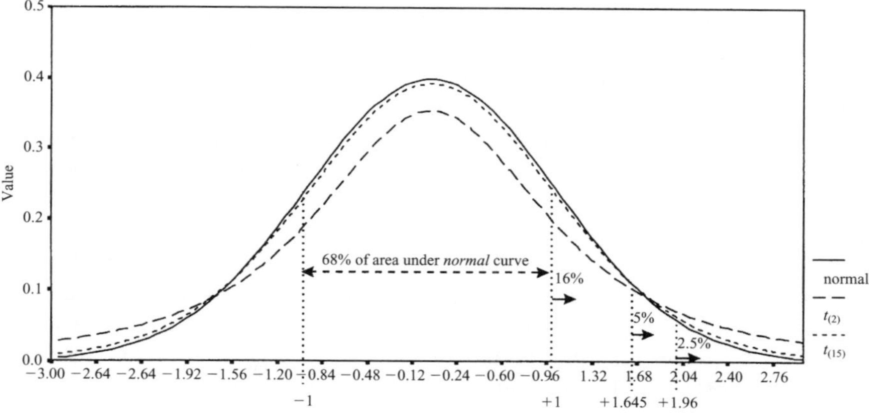

Figure 5.6 *The normal distribution and the t-distribution*

standard deviation from the mean. Five per cent of the cases exceed the mean by more than 1.645 standard deviations. Five per cent of the area beneath the curve is located either to the left of −1.96 or to the right of 1.96. Therefore 1.645 standard deviations is a crucial value in one-sided statistical tests with the normal curve, whereas 1.96 standard deviations is a crucial value in two-sided statistical tests. In our example with a standard deviation of 1 in the population, which resulted in a standard error of 0.1, a sample mean which deviates more than 1.96×0.1 standard deviations from the hypothesized mean in the population would be enough to conclude that the null hypothesis is unwarranted. In the case of a sample size of 10 000, a deviation of the sample mean from the hypothesized mean of $1.96 \times 0.01 = 0.0196$ would have been sufficient to draw the same conclusion.

A slightly different distribution results when the sample size is small: the tails of the resulting probability distribution are somewhat thicker than the tails of a normal distribution. This normal-like distribution is called the *t*-distribution. The top of the *t*-distribution is flatter than the top of a normal distribution, and its tails are thicker. As the sample sizes decrease, or in the language of statistics, as the *degrees of freedom* (df) decrease, the *t*-distribution becomes flatter. Degrees of freedom are related to the sample size, but not identical to them. They will be discussed in the next subsection. Actually there is not a single *t*-distribution, but a class of *t*-distributions depending on the degrees of freedom. When the sample size increases ($df > 100$) the resulting *t*-distributions become almost completely identical to the normal population. Many other test statistics have a *t*-distribution also, for example the sample mean when the sample size is less than 100, or the test statistic of the regression coefficient. Figure 5.6 depicts the $t_{(2)}$ and the $t_{(15)}$ distribution. The $t_{(15)}$ distribution is already indiscernible from the normal distribution by the naked eye. The *t*-distribution applies to many other statistical tests, amongst others to the test whether a regression slope coefficient differs significantly from zero.

The sample variance has quite a different distribution. Suppose that a sample with a size of one is drawn from a population. The variance calculated on the basis of this sample would be zero by definition. To put it more generally, if the sample size is small, then the variance calculated on the basis of sample data will generally be smaller than the population variance. This is the reason why statistical laymen and researchers consistently underestimate the variance of processes on the basis of their limited personal experiences. It is also the reason why case studies should be dealt with cautiously when the research question asks for the assessment of the variability of events, policies, processes or institutions. The distribution of the sample variance statistic, known as the *Chi-square distribution* or χ^2-distribution, is not symmetric, but *skewed*. Again there is a family of Chi-square distributions, each characterized by its degrees of freedom. Figure 5.7 represents as examples the $\chi^2_{(4)}$, the $\chi^2_{(10)}$ and the $\chi^2_{(14)}$ distribution. When the number of 'free' observations increases, the skewness disappears gradually. The $\chi^2_{(14)}$ distribution resembles already a normal distribution, although it is still visibly skewed. When the number of free observations exceeds 100 the Chi-square distribution becomes almost equivalent to the z-distribution. The point at which the χ^2 distribution reaches its maximum increases with the sample size. The $\chi^2_{(df)}$ distribution with df degrees of freedom reaches its maximum for $df - 2$. As can be seen from Figure 5.7, the $\chi^2_{(4)}$, the $\chi^2_{(10)}$ and the $\chi^2_{(14)}$ distributions reach their maximum on the values 2, 8 and 12, respectively. The Chi-square probability distribution applies to many other test statistics, amongst others to test whether a cross table exhibits a relationship.

Many tests involve the comparison of two variances. The analysis of variance (Subsections 5.5.2 and Section 6.6), for example, is based on the comparison of the variance between groups with the variance within groups. Actually the F-ratio in the analysis of variance is defined as the *ratio* between the variance between group means and the variance within groups. The probability distribution of any other division between two sample variances, is known as the F-distribution. Since variances follow a χ^2 distribution the F-distribution is actually the distribution of the division of two χ^2 distributions. Since the F-distribution has a sample variance with its associated degrees of freedom in the numerator, but also a sample variance with its associated degrees of freedom in the denominator, the F-distribution has

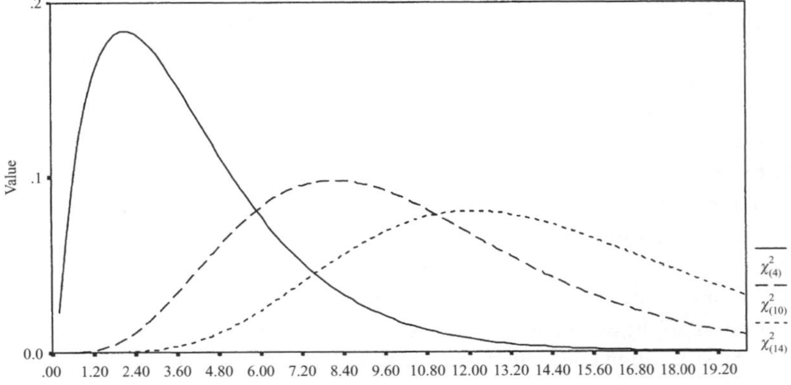

Figure 5.7 *Chi-square distribution with 4, 10 and 14 degrees of freedom*

two different degrees of freedom (df_1 for the numerator and df_2 for the denominator). In the case of the analysis of variance the degrees of freedom in the numerator are related to the number of groups to be compared, whereas the degrees of freedom in the denominator are related to the number of units within these groups.

5.6.5 Degrees of freedom

The t-distribution, the χ^2 and the F-distribution are actually classes of distribution. Figure 5.6 presents the $t_{(2)}$ and the $t_{(15)}$ specimens of the t-distribution, whereas Figure 5.7 presents the $\chi^2_{(4)}$, the $\chi^2_{(10)}$ and the $\chi^2_{(14)}$ distribution. The parameters to specify precisely which distribution is at hand are labeled as *degrees of freedom*. To specify the F-distribution, two degrees of freedom are required: one for the numerator and one for the denominator. Degrees of freedom are derivatives from sample sizes. Degrees of freedom refer to the sample size diminished by the number of units that have to be offered to calculate the test statistic. Degrees of freedom designate the number of units that are still freely available once the required test statistic has been computed from the sample data.

Let's start with the difference between two sample means. To compute a mean, you need at least one unit from the sample. To compare two sample means, two units have to be offered beforehand. The degrees of freedom for the t-distribution of the difference of sample means when variances are known amounts therefore to $n - 2$. As another example the t-distribution of a regression coefficient might be used. At least two units of analysis are required to pin down a regression line since a straight line is defined by two points. Therefore the degrees of freedom for the t-distribution of the regression coefficient statistic amount to $n - 2$ also.

To compute a variance at least one observation is required. The χ^2 (Chi-square) distribution of the sample variance has therefore $n - 1$ degrees of freedom. The χ^2-distribution also applies to the comparison of r samples from a nominal distribution with c values. The degrees of freedom for the χ^2-distribution of differences between samples from a nominal variable amount to $(r - 1)(c - 1)$. This number corresponds precisely with the number of different percentage differences which can be calculated from one cross table. One conception of a cross table of r rows and c columns is that r samples were drawn from a nominal variable with c values. To test whether these r samples might have been drawn from the same nominal distribution, one may choose one sample as the base rate and compare the other $r - 1$ samples with it. To be able to tell something about a sample distribution of a nominal variable, one value of the nominal variable is required as the base rate category, thus leaving $c - 1$ columns freely available. Altogether this results in $(r - 1)(c - 1)$ comparisons.

To test whether two variances are different from each other, the question can be answered whether the ratio of these variances, which follows an F-distribution (see the previous section) differs from 1. The F-test has a number of degrees of freedom for the numerator, as well as for the denominator. The F-distribution of the ratio of two sample variances has therefore $n_1 - 1$ degrees of freedom in the numerator and $n_2 - 1$ degrees of freedom in the denominator. For the outcome of the test the question of which sample is labeled as the first one is irrelevant. The same logic holds for the computation of the degrees of freedom for the F-test in the analysis of variance. This F-test compares the variance between k group means to the variance within these groups. To compute the variance around the mean of the k group means at least one observation is needed to compute the mean of the group means. Therefore the degrees of freedom for the numerator of the test amount to $k - 1$. To compute the variance within these groups, first the means of k different groups have to be computed, which requires k observations. The degrees of freedom for the denominator amount therefore to the number of observations n minus the number of groups k, thus to $n - k$.

5.7 COMMONLY USED STATISTICAL TESTS

This chapter consists of sections on the univariate analysis of nominal variables (Section 5.1) and interval variables (Section 5.2) and on the bivariate analysis of the relationship between two nominal variables (Section 5.3), between two interval variables (Section 5.4) and between an interval variable and a nominal variable (Section 5.5). The tests to be presented in the subsequent subsections correspond with the former sections. Thus, Subsection 5.7.3 discusses a test that might be used to interpret from a statistical point of view the research results obtained by the data analysis methods presented in Section 5.3 on the relationship between two nominal variables.

As far as possible the tests will be presented in the same format. The steps presented in 5.6.3 will recur with each test. For each test a very simple example is given. A practical overview of many more useful tests is provided by Kanji (1994).

5.7.1 The univariate nominal distribution

The most frequently applied test to interpret the proportions of the separate values of a univariate nominal distribution is the z-test of a single proportion. The test applies for example to the question of whether the proportion of voters p intending to vote for a specific party at the next elections according to a survey among 2500 voters differs from the proportion of voters voting for this party in the previous election. The latter proportion is a population proportion, and is referred to also as the expected proportion p_e. The standard error of the proportion estimate is computed as the standard deviation, which amounts to the square root from $p(1 - p)$ for a dichotomous variable, divided by the square root from the number of observations n. The square root in the denominator of the standard error represents the diminishing returns of increasing the sample size. In order to decrease the standard error by a factor f, the sample size should be increased with a factor f^2. The test statistic, to be computed as the difference between the observed and the expected proportion divided by the standard error, has a Gaussian probability distribution.

The example in Table 5.11 shows a worse case. If the expected proportion is 0.5, then even a large sample of 2500 observations is insufficient to render an observed

Table 5.11 *z-test for a proportion*

1	Object	Difference between proportion p and expected proportion p_e
	Assumptions	Random sample, $n > 25$
	H0	$p - p_e = 0$
2	Estimator of object	$p - p_e$
	Standard error of estimate under null hypothesis	$\sqrt{\frac{p_e(1-p_e)}{n}}$
	Test statistic	$z = \frac{p - p_e}{\sqrt{\frac{p_e(1-p_e)}{n}}}$
3	H1	p differs from p_e (two sided); $p_e = 0.5$
	Sample data	$n = 2500$; $p = 0.5134$
	Test	$z = 0.0134/0.01 = 1.34$ Two sided test, significance $= 0.184$ Alternatively: critical value z (two sided, $p = 0.05$): 1.960 Given H0 sample results appear in more than 5% of samples H0 not rejected
4	Conclusion	H1 rejected

deviation from the expected proportion of 1.3 per cent statistically significant. Tests on proportions require fewer observations when the expected proportion is either lower or higher.

No single test is appropriate in all circumstances. The proportion test presented here does not apply when the expected frequency is smaller than 1 per cent (instead of the proportion test the Poisson test should be used to investigate whether 'rare' events occur extraordinarily often). When the number of observations is less than 25 the proportion test presented here should not be used (instead of the Gaussian distribution, which is an approximation of the classical binomial, Newtonian, distribution, the original binomial distribution should be used to get precise results; see Kanji, 1994). The test presented here does not apply to the comparison of proportions from two samples. The χ^2-test to be discussed in 5.7.3 is one of the possible tests for comparing proportions in various samples with each other.

5.7.2 The univariate interval distribution

Three tests regarding an interval variable will be considered: a test of whether its mean conforms to the expected value, a test of whether its variance conforms to the expected value and a test of whether the entire distribution conforms to (normal) expectations.

Tests on (changes in) the mean

The most frequently applied test to univariate interval distributions is the t-test for a population mean. The test applies for example to the question of whether the economy was declining in the early 1980s when data on economic growth for a sample of 25 nations in the early 1980s indicate that the average growth percentage was −1 per cent with a standard deviation of 2 per cent.

As Table 5.12 shows, the standard error is computed as the sample standard deviation s divided by the square root of the number of observations. The test statistic, to be computed as the difference between the observed growth rate and an 'expected' zero growth rate divided by the standard error, follows a t-distribution. When the number of observations is large ($n > 100$) the normal distribution applies. An application of the t-test to our example of a negative growth rate of 1 per cent in 25 nations with a standard deviation of 2 per cent shows that enough data have been compiled to warrant statistically the impression that the economy was declining in the early 1980s.

Test on (changes in) the variance

A second standard test of univariate interval distributions concerns the magnitude of the variance. As an example the question may be considered of whether the economies of the OECD states are converging, when a sample of 10 nations shows that the sample standard deviation s of the economic growth rates in the EC now amounts to 1 per cent, whereas the standard deviation was 3 per cent in the 1960s. A Chi-square test applies, since the magnitude of a single variance is involved.

In a Chi-square test (see Table 5.13) the estimator is expressed as a ratio rather than as a difference. When the sample variance equals the variance under the null hypothesis this ratio will be one. The test statistic is computed as the number of

Table 5.12 *t-test for a population mean*

1	Object	Difference between sample mean $\bar{x}$ and expected mean μ_o
	Assumptions	– Normal population distribution (test is robust for violations) – Population variance unknown (if population variance is known, then use n instead of $n-1$ in formulas below and use z-distribution instead of t-distribution)
	Null hypothesis	$\bar{x} - \mu_o = 0$
2	Estimator of object	$\bar{x} - \mu_o$
	Standard error of estimate under null hypothesis	$\frac{s}{\sqrt{n}}; \quad s = \sqrt{\frac{\sum_i (x_i - \bar{x})^2}{n-1}}$
	Test statistic	$t_{n-1} = \frac{\bar{x} - \mu_0}{\frac{s}{\sqrt{n}}}$
3	H1	$\bar{x}$ lower than μ_o (one sided); $\mu_o = 0$
3	Sample data	$n = 25 \quad \bar{x} = -1 \quad s = 2$
	Solution	$t_{24} = -1/\frac{1}{4} = -4$ Critical value t_{24} (one sided, $p = 0.05$): −1.711 Given H0, sample results appear in less than 5% of samples (actually in less than 0.1% of these samples) H0 rejected
4	Conclusion	H1 not rejected

Table 5.13 *χ^2-test for a population variance*

1	Object	Ratio between sample standard deviation s^2 and expected standard deviation σ_0^2
	Assumptions	Normal population distribution (test is robust for violations when the sample size is large)
	Null hypothesis	$s^2 = \sigma_0^2$
2	Estimator of object	$\frac{s^2}{\sigma_0^2}$
	Test statistic	$\chi^2_{n-1} = (n-1)\frac{s^2}{\sigma_0^2}$
3	H1	s lower than σ_o (one sided); $\sigma_o = 0$
3	Sample data	$n = 10 \quad s = 1 \quad \sigma_o = 3$
	Solution	$\chi^2_{(9)} = (10-1) \times \frac{1}{3} = 3$ Critical value $\chi^2_{(9)}$ (one sided, left-sided, $p = 0.05$): 3.33 Given H0, sample results appear in less than 5% of sample H0 rejected
4	Conclusion	H1 not rejected

observations minus one $(n - 1)$ times the ratio of the sample variance to the variance under the null hypothesis. The value of this test statistic will be $n - 1$ when the two variances are equal to each other. The convergence hypothesis of our example implies that the test statistic should be much smaller than $n - 1$, since convergence means that the current variance is smaller than the original variance. The value of the test statistic of 3.00 is smaller than the critical value of 3.33. Thus, the (fictitious) data in our example are statistically consistent with the convergence hypothesis.

The entire univariate distribution: compatible with 'normal' assumptions?

A further test which is applied often to univariate interval distributions is the test of whether the sample distribution might derive from a population distribution of a given shape. The *Kolmogorov–Smirnov test* can be used to this end. Every possible population distribution of a given shape can be used as the null hypothesis in the Kolmogorov–Smirnov test, but the test is especially useful to assess whether the data at hand are compatible with a normal distribution in the population, since the normal distribution is the work-horse of statistical reasoning. Most of these techniques are fairly robust: when the normal assumptions are 'slightly' violated, these techniques and estimators may still produce reliable results. The Kolmogorov–Smirnov test prescribes comparison of the cumulative distribution of the available data with respect to the variable of interest with the cumulative distribution assumed in the null hypothesis. For each value of the variable the difference is calculated between the actual cumulative proportion and the expected cumulative proportion on the basis of the specified distribution. The maximum difference is the test statistic. For sample sizes of 30 and more the maximum difference at the 5 per cent level of significance is roughly 1.36 divided by the square root of the number of observations, thus roughly $1.36 \div \sqrt{n}$. For smaller sample sizes the

Russian mathematicians Kolmogorov and Smirnov developed a table to test whether the maximum difference found is large enough to warrant the conclusion that the null hypothesis that the sample data were drawn at random from the specified distribution should be discarded.

As an example the question will be considered of whether the sample distribution of answers to an agree–disagree question x (-2 = strongly disagree ... $+2$ = strongly agree) in a sample of 100 respondents might reflect an underlying normal population distribution when the sample distribution of the answers of $n = 100$ respondents over the five values -2, -1, 0, $+1$ and $+2$ is 25, 40, 10, 15 and 10.

The frequency distribution (0.20, 0.40, 0.10, 0.15 and 0.10) is easily translated (see Table 5.14) into the cumulative frequency distribution ($cum(x_i)$: 0.25, 0.65, 0.75, 0.90, 1.00). By standardizing the x_i-values, standardized $z(x_i)$-scores are obtained. If x were normally distributed, then the empirical cumulative frequencies $cum(x_i)$ would correspond with the cumulative frequencies corresponding with the standardized $z(x_i)$-values that are to be found in tables of the standard normal distribution. By taking z-scores the original variable x is transformed into a variable which comes as close as possible to the standard normal distribution. The cumulative probabilities of the standard normal distribution can be found in its table. From the table of the normal distribution it follows that, if x were a normally distributed variable, then the corresponding cumulative frequencies $Z(x_i)$ would be

Table 5.14 *Kolmogorov–Smirnov test to assess whether distribution could be normal*

1	Object	Differences between the cumulative probabilities in the sample $cum(x_i)$ and the cumulative probabilities of a normal distribution $Z(x_i)$ (or the cumulative probabilities according to any other specified distribution)
	Assumptions	Almost none (parameter-free test)
	Null hypothesis	x_i is normally distributed
2	Estimator of object	For each value i of x: $d_i = \|cum(x_i) - Z(x_i)\|$
	Test statistic	Largest d_i
3	H1	Normal distribution
3	Sample data	Frequency distribution of x, see solution
	Solution	(see below)

x_i	$n = 100$	$cum(x_i)$	$z(x_i)$	$Z(x_i)$	$d_i = \|cum(x_i) - Z(x_i)\|$
-2	25	0.25	-1.12	0.13	0.12
-1	40	0.65	-0.35	0.36	0.29 (max)
0	10	0.75	0.43	0.67	0.08
$+1$	15	0.90	1.20	0.89	0.01
$+2$	10	1.00	1.98	0.98	0.02

Critical value when $n > 36$: $1.36 \div \sqrt{100} = 0.136$ (in the case of small n, a table with critical values of the Kolmogorov–Smirnov test should be consulted); largest $d_i > 0.136$
Given H0, sample results appear in less than 5% of sample
H0 rejected

4	Conclusion	H1 not rejected

0.13, 0.36, 0.67, 0.89 and 0.98. The maximum difference between the actual cumulative frequencies and the 'normal' frequencies amounts to 0.29. The critical K–S test value is $1.36 \div 100 = 0.136$. Therefore the hypothesis that the answers are distributed normally is falsified.

5.7.3 The bivariate distribution of two nominal variables

A quite general test for the comparison of two nominal variables is the Chi-square test for cross tables. The test is useful to see whether there is a statistically significant relationship between the row variable and the column variable. As a first step χ^2_{sample} is computed on the basis of sample data (see Section 5.3). This statistic follows a χ^2 distribution with $(r-1)(c-1)$ degrees of freedom, since one column and one row of the cross table have to be offered to compute the remaining expected frequencies freely.

The test applies also to the comparison of two samples from a nominal population distribution. The samples can be considered as different rows in the cross tables, with the columns representing the categories of the nominal variable.

When the cross table is reduced to a 2×2 table the test may also be used to test whether there is an association between two dichotomous variables. This comes down precisely to testing whether two proportions are different from each other. A proportion represents by definition a dichotomous nominal variable, since a proportion might always be considered as a number of 'successes' divided by the sum of 'successes' and 'failures'.

To apply the χ^2 test (see Table 5.15) the number of units of analysis should be a multiple of the number of cells in the cross table. Moreover there should be no row

Table 5.15 *χ^2 test of association in cross table with r rows and c columns*

1	Object	Difference between r independent sample distributions with c nominal values
		Association in cross table with r rows and c columns
	Assumptions	No more than 10% of the cells of the cross table should have expected frequencies e_{ij} of less than 5
	Null hypothesis	No association in cross table of r rows and c columns
2	Estimator of object	$\chi^2_{\text{samples}} = \sum_{i=1}^{r}\sum_{j=1}^{c}\frac{(f_{ij}-e_{ij})^2}{e_{ij}}$
	Test statistic	$\chi^2_{(r-1)(c-1)} = \chi^2_{\text{samples}}$
3	H1	Nominal variables in the rows drawn from different populations (one sided)
3	Sample data	$r = 3 \quad c = 7 \quad \chi^2 = 18.55$
	Solution	$\chi^2_{\text{samples}} = 18.55$ Critical value $\chi^2_{(12)}$ (one sided, $p = 0.05$): 21.03 Given H0, sample results will appear in more than 5% of samples (actually in roughly 10% of these samples) H0 not rejected
4	Conclusion	H1 rejected

or column in the cross table with only a few cases in it. No more than 10 per cent of the cells in the cross table should have expected frequencies of less than 5.

5.7.4 The bivariate distribution of two interval variables

The regression coefficient is the most widely used coefficient to represent the relationship between interval variables. The test statistic compares the magnitude of the regression coefficient with the standard error of the regression estimate. The standard error of the regression coefficient has once more the square root of the number of cases (minus one) in the denominator. The nominator of the standard error relates the standard deviation of the residuals s_ε to the horizontal spread of the data along the x-axis s_x. The example in Table 5.16 derives from the regression example in Section 5.4. The example shows that even in a small sample of 17 nations a moderately strong relationship is statistically significant.

An alternative to the t-test as a test on each specific regression coefficient, is the test on the F-ratio – the ratio of the explained towards the unexplained variance – for the complete regression equation. This F-test is highly analogous to the F-test in the analysis of variance. Its degrees of freedom are $k-1$ and $n-k$ for the nominator and denominator, respectively, where n is the number of observations and k is the number of explanatory variables. Elaborated F-tests, which go beyond

Table 5.16 *t-test for a regression coefficient*

1	Object	The magnitude of the regression coefficient b of variable x on y
	Assumptions	– Normal distribution of the dependent variable y for each value of x (test is fairly robust for violations) – No heteroscedasticity, autoregression, and so on, see Section 6.7 (test will become inefficient)
	Null hypothesis	$b = 0$
2	Estimator of object	Sample regression coefficient, see Subsection 5.4.2
	Standard error of estimate under null hypothesis	$se_b = \dfrac{\frac{s_\varepsilon}{s_x}}{\sqrt{n-1}}$
	Test statistic	$t_{n-2} = \dfrac{b}{se_b}$
3	H1	x influences y; $b <> 0$ (two sided)
3	Sample data	From Subsection 5.4.2; Table 5.9
	Solution	$s_\varepsilon = \sqrt{17 \times 62.75}/\sqrt{(17-2)} = 8.43$ $s_x = \sqrt{17 \times 256.35}/\sqrt{(17-1)} = 16.50$ $se_b = (8.43306/272.372)/\sqrt{(17-1)} = 0.128$ $t_{(15)} = 0.333/0.128 = 2.607$ Critical value $t_{(15)}$ (two sided, $p = 0.05$): 2.13 Given H0, sample results appear in less than 5% of samples (actually in roughly 2% of samples) H0 rejected
4	Conclusion	H1 not rejected

the scope of this book, are useful in comparative tests of whether one regression model explains more variance than an alternative model.

5.7.5 The bivariate distribution of an interval variable by a nominal variable

In ANOVA-models a test is made of whether means from different groups (categories from a nominal variable) differ from each other, by assessing the ratio of the variance *between* groups to the variance *within* groups.

To arrive at an estimate of the mean squared deviations between group means, i.e. at an estimate of MS_{bt}, one starts from the sum over all cases i within each group j of squared deviations SS_{bt} of the group means $\bar{x}_j$ from the total mean over all cases $\bar{x}$ – thus from $\sum_i \sum_j (\bar{x}_j - \bar{x})^2$ (Table 5.17). To obtain an unbiased estimator this sum of squares should be divided by its degrees of freedom df_{bt}, that is to say, by the number of cases that are freely available to compute this sum of squares. Since only j group means are freely available, and one of them must be used as a reference category to calculate the total mean, the degrees of freedom of the variance between groups amounts to $df_{bt} = j - 1$.

To arrive at an estimate of the mean squared deviations of the values from their respective group means, i.e. at an estimate of MS_{wh}, one starts from the sum over

Table 5.17 *F-test in the analysis of variance*

1	Object	Difference between group means $\bar{x}_j$ for j groups (values, categories) of a nominal variable
	Assumptions	– Normal distribution within each group (robust against violations) – Equal variance in each group
	Null hypothesis	The group means are identical; variance between groups is insignificant compared with (divided by) variance within groups
2	Estimator of numerator: mean square between	$MS_{bt} = \frac{SS_{bt}}{df_{bt}} = \frac{\sum_i \sum_j (\bar{x}_j - \bar{x})^2}{j - 1}$
	Estimator of denominator: mean square within	$MS_{wh} = \frac{SS_{wh}}{df_{wh}} = \frac{\sum_i \sum_j (x_{ij} - \bar{x}_j)^2}{n - j}$
	Test statistic	$F_{bt,wh} = \frac{MS_{bt}}{MS_{wh}}$
3	H1	Three group means ($j = 3$) differ from each other
3	Sample data	$n = 63 \quad SS_{bt} = 6 \quad SS_{wh} = 120$
	Solution	$MS_{bt} = 6/(3 - 1) = 3$ $MS_{wh} = 120/(63 - 3) = 2$ $F_{(2,60)} = 1.5$ Critical value $F_{(2,60)}(p = 0.05)$: 3.15 Given H0, sample results will appear in more than 5% of samples H0 not rejected
4	Conclusion	H1 rejected

all cases i within each group j of squared deviations of the values x_{ij} from their own group mean $\bar{x}_j$ thus from $\sum_i\sum_j(x_{ij} - \bar{x}_j)^2$. To obtain an unbiased estimator, this sum of squares should be divided by its degrees of freedom df_{wh}, that is to say, by the number of cases that are freely available to compute this sum of squares. Within each of the j groups, one observation must be offered because the group mean presupposes one observation. Therefore the degrees of freedom of the variance within groups amounts to $df_{\text{wh}} = n - j$.

The final test statistic is the ratio of MS_{bt} and MS_{wh}. Since this is essentially a ratio of variances, an F-distribution results with degrees of freedom df_{bt} for the numerator and df_{wh} for the denominator.

With the use of high-school calculus it is easy to prove that the sum of the sum of squares within and the sum of squares between amounts to the total sum of squares. The degrees of freedom of the total sum of squares amount to $n - 1$ (since only one observation has to be offered to calculate the total mean), which is identical to $(j - 1) + (n - j)$. These identities might be used to check out whether ANOVA computations by hand have been performed correctly.

5.7.6 Sense and nonsense of statistical tests

Statistical tests are often employed although the assumptions that underlie them are violated. Statistical tests are used, for example, when only data are available for successive years, or when the sample consists of data on the complete population of nations. Statistical tests that assume normal distributions of variables are used even though Kolmogorov–Smirnov tests indicate that the variables are not normally distributed.

One should be aware that the unwarranted use of statistical tests renders meaningless significance levels. The decision to discard a hypothesis when the probability that the null hypothesis is true amounts to $p = 0.073$, as well as the decision to maintain an hypothesis when this probability amounts to $p = 0.029$ are completely arbitrary from a mathematical statistician's point of view when the assumptions of the tests are violated.

At least two arguments can be used to make a case for the use of statistical tests even when the precise assumptions of the test are violated. The first justification is that even statistical tests whose assumptions have not been met precisely are based on the common-sense principle that the credibility of research results increases as the number of investigated cases increases. Statistical tests prevent comparative political scientists from jumping to conclusions on the basis of a few cases only. The second justification is the *robustness* of many statistical tests. The outcome of a robust test will still hold when the assumptions are not completely met.

Statistical tests should always be interpreted cautiously. It is an exception rather than a rule that conclusions with respect to the tenability of theories in comparative political science can be based straightforwardly on statistical tests. Nevertheless, statistical tests are important because they are usually more critical than common sense when it comes to an evaluation of theories in the light of available data.

5.8 SUMMARY

This chapter has concentrated on elementary methods for exploratory data analysis. The choice of techniques for data analysis depends crucially on the level of measurement of the variables. The sequence in exploratory data analysis is usually to start with univariate data analysis and to continue with bivariate data analysis. The reason is that one needs to develop a feeling for the separate variables first, before the bivariate relationships which are of theoretical interest can be sorted out.

Univariate analysis centers on measures of central tendency and measures of dispersion. The mode, the median and the mean were discussed as measures of central tendency for nominal, ordinal and interval variables, respectively. The Herfindahl-index, also known as the index of Laakso and Taagepera, and the entropy were discussed as measures of the dispersion of nominal variables. The variance and standard deviation have been discussed as measures of the dispersion of interval variables.

The analysis of cross tables is appropriate for the study of the bivariate relationship between nominal variables. Chi-square, phi and Cramèr's v can be used to express the strength of association in a single number. Correlation and regression analysis were dealt with as the techniques to analyze the relationship between two variables with an interval level of measurement. Measures such as the regression coefficient, the standardized regression coefficient, the correlation coefficient, the explained variance, and the unexplained variance were introduced. The analysis of variance (ANOVA) was introduced to analyze the relationship between an interval variable and a nominal variable. In an analysis of variance the question of association is reduced to the question of whether the mean value of the interval variable varies for the various categories of the nominal variable (which are labelled as 'groups' in the analysis of variance). Concepts such as the variance between groups, the variance within groups, sums of squares between, sums of squares within, the explained variance and the F-ratio were introduced.

Almost inevitably an explorative data analysis will end up in the question of whether the 'findings' are findings indeed. Statistical tests to answer the question of whether theoretical beliefs can stand up in the light of the available data have been discussed in Sections 5.6 and 5.7. Relevant concepts were (unbiasedness, efficiency and robustness of) estimators, test statistics, the normal distribution, the t-distribution, the Chi-square distribution and the F-distribution. Statistical tests prevent one from declaring summer when a swallow has been seen. The ground for statistical tests is often soggy, however, since the precise assumptions of these tests are seldom met in comparative political science.

The next chapter will elaborate on the elementary methods being discussed in this chapter. The methods will be generalized to the analysis of multivariate relationships between variables. The focus will shift from exploratory purposes towards the causal analysis of political processes.

5.9 ENDMATTER

Topics highlighted

- Measures of central tendency (mode, median, mean): assessment of the most likely, typical value.
- Measures of dispersion (entropy, index of Laakso and Taagepera, variance, standard deviation): assessment of the typical departure from the central tendency.
- Measures of association (percentage difference, χ^2, φ, Cramèr's v, correlation coefficient): assessment of the degree to which knowledge of one variable is helpful to predict the value of another variable.
- Explorative univariate data analysis: computation of the central tendency and the dispersion of separate variables.
- Explorative bivariate data analysis (by means of cross tables, analysis of variance, regression analysis): assessment of the degree to which two variables go together.
- Inferential statistics: inferring whether sample data are (in)compatible with a null hypothesis on the population of cases.

Exercises

- Compute measures of central tendency and dispersion for the parties which gained office in agriculture (variable AGRICULT in the NIAS.SAV data base) and social affairs (variable SOCIAL) in Belgium. *Hint*: determine which measures of central tendency and dispersion are appropriate given the level of measurement of the party in office. Use SPSS or another statistical program to display a frequency distribution. Compute the appropriate measures by hand from the frequency distribution.

  Which issues (agricultural or social ones) are more disputed in Belgium? *Hint*: is a low or a high dispersion of the parties holding office a measure of political dispute?

  Which party behaves most vehemently as the 'issue owner' of agriculture in Belgium? *Hint*: What is the central tendency of the parties in office on agriculture?
- Compute measures of central tendency and dispersion of the percentage unemployed in OECD countries in 1965 and 1990 (same steps as above).
- Compute the central tendency and the dispersion of public expenditures as a percentage of GDP (variable PE in the NIAS.SAV data base) in OECD countries in 1965, 1978 and in 1990 and answer subsequently the questions whether:
  - public expenditures were cut down on the average (1) as a reaction to the first oil crisis, (2) as a reaction to the recession of the 1980s;
  - convergence between the economic policies of OECD countries increased (1) as a reaction to the first oil crisis, (2) as a reaction to the recession of the 1980s. *Hint*: convergence is opposite of divergence; divergence = high dispersion.
- Test whether the party group holding office on social affairs (SOCIAL2) has an effect on the type of economic policy (POP).

  - Construe a cross table, and compute Cramèr's v.
  - Interpret the results in the light of substantive theory.
- Apply an analysis of variance to test whether public expenditures (PE) depend on the party group holding the ministry of social affairs (SOCIAL2).
- Use regression analysis to test whether in 1992 the percentage of elderly in a country (variable AGE65 in the NIAS.SAV data base) has an upwards effect on the percentage of public expenditures (variable PE) (e.g. health care, pensions, lower productivity).
- Use appropriate statistical tests to test whether:
  - public expenditures (variable PE) in the twelve EC countries of the 1990s were higher in 1990 than in 1965;
  - convergence of public expenditures has emerged within the EU;
  - the party group holding office on social affairs (SOCIAL2) has an effect on the type of economic policy (POP);
  - public expenditures (PE) depend on the party group holding the ministry of social affairs (SOCIAL2);
  - in 1992 the percentage of elderly in a country (variable AGE65 in the NIAS.SAV data base) has an upwards effect on the percentage of public expenditures (variable PE).

Further reading

- *General*: King et al., 1994; Tacq, 1997.
- *Statistical tests*: Hoel, 1971; Kanji, 1994.

6
Multivariate analysis and causal inference

CONTENTS

The research methods discussed in this chapter are useful for a causal analysis of political processes. The univariate and bivariate methods of Chapter 5 will usually be applied as a first step in data analysis, and the multivariate analysis techniques of this chapter will be applied afterwards. Many research questions can be answered simply by using the techniques discussed in the previous chapters, but multivariate analysis is indispensable to answer research questions concerning the disentanglement of the effects of several variables on a political phenomenon of interest. Examples will be presented in Chapters 7, 8 and 9.

Starting from the discussion of most different and most similar cases (see Part I) the concept of causality will be discussed and applied in the context of multivariate relations in Section 6.1. The introduction of more variables makes data-analysis more complex. Variables can be interwoven in many ways, even when only three variables are considered. A third variable may simply add to the explanation of what is to be explained, but it may also determine the nature of the relationship between the other two variables (an interacting variable). Section 6.2 presents an overview of methods for multivariate analysis, which will be elaborated in the remaining sections. First a distinction is made between methods for many variables but a limited number of cases (units) and methods for the analysis of many cases but a limited number of variables. If the number of cases is limited – e.g. less than 15 units of analysis – then a researcher will strive for a complete deterministic, albeit complex, explanation for most if not all cases. The approach is *case oriented.* But no meaningful deterministic explanation might be found to be consistent with the data on a large set of cases. Simple (although probabilistic) reasoning, dealing with a limited number of variables, dominates the discussion over the explanation of patterns found in large datasets. The typical research question for a limited number of cases – how to account completely for the data on these cases – often shifts towards the question of whether the role of a few crucial variables in a huge variety of cases can be understood *parsimoniously.* The approach shifts towards a *variable-oriented* one. The case-oriented approach will be dealt with in Section 6.3. The four subsequent sections focus on the variable-oriented approach. The choice of the research method depends not only crucially on the number of cases and the number of variables, but also on the level of measurement of the variables (nominal or higher). The research techniques used most often in political science, i.e. cross table elaboration (nominal variables only) will be elaborated more thoroughly and multivariate regression analysis (interval variables only), than the less frequently used techniques. Special attention will be given to variants and extensions that are especially useful for comparative political science, e.g. pooled time series analysis for the analysis of nations whose political characteristics change through time.

6.1 CAUSALITY AND MULTIVARIATE RELATIONS

The relation of cause and effect to which the concept of *causality* refers is a complex one. Yet it appears to be a simple type of relation because we make use of it in almost every instance of our daily and political lives. Our daily activities are aimed at the causal production of results. Causes are manipulated in order to achieve desired effects after a while. Concepts such as action, production, consumption, political power, political influence and political authority all presume the ability to harvest desired future effects above mere chance. They all presume a sequential timely order between a means and an end, between a cause and an effect. These and other observations led John Stuart Mill to state that causation 'is but the familiar truth that invariability of succession is found by observation to obtain between every fact in nature and some other fact which has preceded it'. Unfortunately, invariability of succession is rarely observed in political science. But some timely successions are far more likely than others in a probabilistic sense. The fundamental assumption of the comparative method is that the only baseline to assess whether a cause produces an effect above chance in a given case is provided by comparable cases to which the same cause does not apply. Causal statements in comparative political science rest on a comparison in time, in space or in both.

Causal assertions and levels of measurement

If particular combinations of values on two separate variables occur more frequently than expected on the basis of the frequency distributions of the separate variables then these variables are related to each other in a statistical sense. A causal relationship assumes not merely a statistical relationship, but also a time dimension and a direction. A causal effect of a variable x on a variable y implies that changing the value of x will produce another value of y after a (short or long) while. The concept of causality implies the concept of an *independent* variable and a *dependent* variable. A causal relationship is a unidirectional relationship ($x \rightarrow y$). Reciprocal causal relationships ($x \rightleftarrows y$) can be understood as two separate causal unidirectional relationships. A variable x is said to have an effect on a nominal variable y when changing x's value will, after a while, increase the chance that variable y will show a particular value. In the case of an ordinal, interval or ratio dependent variable y causality means that changing x's value increases the chance that y will increase (or decrease) after a while. A linear causal relationship exists when the ratio of the resulting change in the dependent variable to the preceding change in the independent variable is a given constant, regardless of the starting values of the dependent and the independent variable, or the precise history of the causal process. Linear causal relationships are assumed as the default in comparative political science.

6.1.1 Pure additivity, intervention, spurious correlation and interaction

This chapter deals with multivariate causal relationships. The relationships between a multitude of variables will be studied. As a first step towards the analysis of multivariate causal relationships we will consider the various ways in which a third variable *z* that is 'causally relevant' for the causal explanation of a dependent variable *y* might have an effect. A third variable might be causally relevant in four ways. Figure 6.1 summarizes these four ways.

Pure additivity. First, variable *z* may simply *add* to the explanation of *y*, without changing the effect of *x* on *y*. The effect of *z* on *y* does not affect the effect of *x* on *y*. The total effect on *y* is precisely the sum of the separate effects of variables *x* and *z* on *y*. Variables *x* and *z* are causally *independent* of each other.

Intervention. A variable *z* intervenes in the causal relationship between an independent variable *x* and a dependent variable *y* when *z* is influenced by *x*, and influences *y* in turn. The third variable *z* depends on *x* in the intervention model, whereas *x* and *z* were independent from each other in the additive model. If *z* is held constant – or 'controlled for' in the language of social science methodology – the association between *x* and *y* will cease to exist.

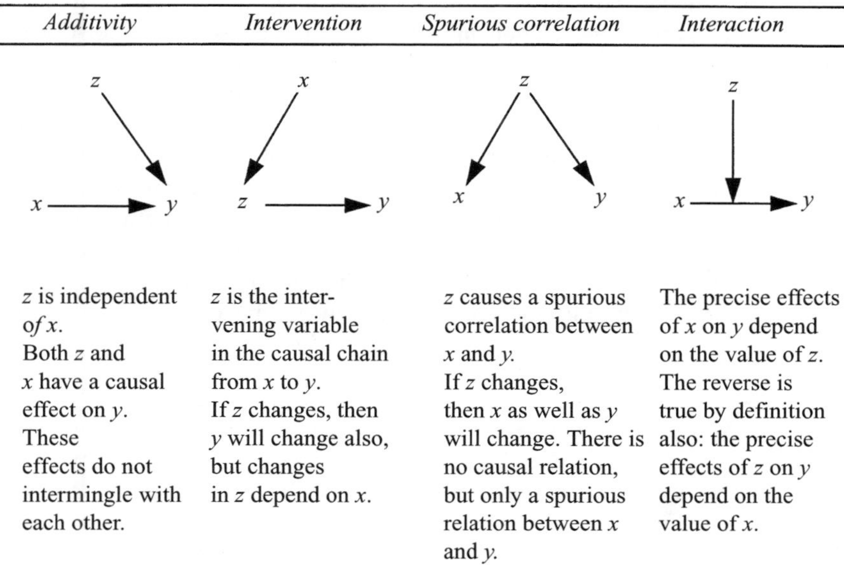

Figure 6.1 *Four types of multivariate relationships*

Spurious correlation. A variable z introduces a spurious correlation (spurious association) between x and y when it is the cause of y, as in the additive model, but also the cause of x. x and y will move in the same direction in response to their common cause. But their association is spurious: the association would vanish if z were held constant. One should note the similarity between the spurious correlation model and the intervention model at this point. Both models predict that the association between x and y will vanish when z is held constant.

Interaction. A variable z interacts with variable x when the effect of x on y depends on the level of the other variable. The magnitude or even the direction of the effect of x on y depends on z. Increase of social expenditures (y) may depend on the number of leftist seats in Parliament (x). A simple theory of leftist influence in multi-party systems is that leftist parties will especially succeed in increasing social expenditures when the coalition government includes leftist parties. In this example the inclusion of a leftist party in the coalition government is the interacting variable z.

The four models discussed here are only ideal type models. Usually political reality is something in between. Independent variables are often *collinear* instead of purely additive, for example. Collinear variables overlap each other. Therefore their joint influence is less than the sum of their separate influences, and disentangling their separate influence becomes nasty. Researchers do not test every conceivable model. They confine themselves to specific causal hypotheses which derive from a research question.

6.1.2 Association and causal effect

The discussion in the previous section of the additive model, the intervention model and the spurious correlation model allows us to discuss the relationship between association and causality more fully. Figure 6.2 shows a combination of the three models. The association between x and y is partially real and partially spurious due to the role of z. x is now an intervening variable in the relationship between z and y, but there remains a direct influence of x on y also. The causal effect of x on y is less than the association between x and y because the spurious association due to z adds to the association also. The direct causal effect of z on y is less than the association between z and y also because the indirect causal path z–x–y adds to the association also. Provided the causal relationship between x and y is a unidirectional one the relationship between bivariate association and

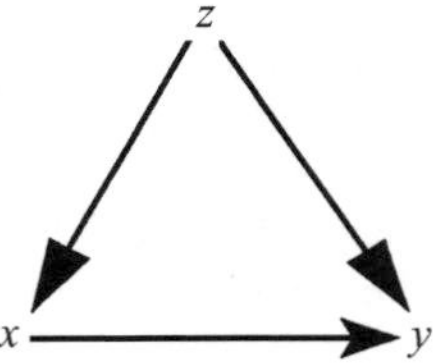

Figure 6.2 *Additivity, spurious correlation and intervention*

multivariate direct causal effects is represented in the decomposition formula below:

Bivariate association between x and y [on the basis of a sample]

= direct causal effect of x on y

+ indirect effects of x on y through intervening variables $z_1 \ldots z_k$

+ spurious correlation between x and y due to variables $u_1 \ldots u_k$

[+/− unreliability due to measurement errors]

[+/− unreliability due to sampling]

The formula elucidates that the direct causal effect is usually smaller than the bivariate association suggests. But the decomposition formula of the bivariate association also leaves open the possibility that x has a direct causal effect on y although there is no bivariate association between x and y. Direct and indirect effects may cancel each other out when their signs are opposite, for example. The *total effect* of a variable is defined as the sum of its direct and indirect effects.

The causal *effect* of a variable is an if–then construct. If the independent variable changes, then the dependent variable will change. The causal *impact*, defined as the degree to which a causal effect is realized, depends not only on the magnitude of the causal effect, but also on the magnitude of the changes in the independent variable, and on the amount of time elapsed since then. Small causal effects may correspond with a large impact when the independent variable moves in one direction for a considerable period of time. Huge causal effects have no causal impact at all when the independent variables are kept constant.

6.1.3 Endogeneous and exogeneous variables and the identification of causal models

In multivariate causal analysis a variable is called *exogeneous* when it is not influenced by other variables within the causal model. A variable is called *endogeneous* when it is influenced by other variables. An exogeneous variable is by definition an independent variable. An endogeneous variable is by definition a dependent variable with respect to at least one variable. Let's consider the models of Figure 6.1 as examples. In the additive model and in the interaction model, x and z are both exogeneous whereas y is endogeneous. In the intervention model x is the only exogeneous variable while z and y are endogeneous. In the spurious correlation model z is the only exogeneous variable while x and y are endogeneous.

Models without exogeneous variables can not be estimated with empirical data, because these models consist of endless cyclic causal paths. They are unsolvable 'chicken or egg' puzzles, known as *unidentified* models, regardless of the available empirical data. A model is identified when empirical data with respect to the variables in the model would allow for an estimation of the strength of the assumed causal effects. The presence of exogeneous variables does not completely guarantee that a model is identified, however. A more sophisticated rule of thumb is that a model is identified when at least one variable from each cyclic path is influenced directly by a unique exogeneous variable that does not influence other variables in the same cyclic path.

The concepts being discussed in this introductory section serve as the conceptual framework to discuss methods for causal analysis in the next sections.

6.2 AN OVERVIEW OF MULTIVARIATE DATA ANALYSIS TECHNIQUES

Table 6.1 gives an overview of frequently used methods for causal data analysis. Only two of the possible criteria to select a method of analysis are highlighted in Table 6.1: the number of cases and the level of measurement of the variables.

The first criterion is whether the number of cases considered is small or large compared with the number of variables being considered. If the number of cases is small, then researchers want to describe and to explain them as fully as possible. If the number of cases increases, a full, extensive description and explanation of each separate case tends to become rather cumbersome or even impossible. The researcher will attempt to explain most variation in all cases (or groups of cases) parsimoniously, albeit incompletely, by a few variables of theoretical interest only. We call this distinction the distinction between case-oriented and variable-oriented research, following Ragin (1987). Related, albeit not completely identical, distinctions are exploratory versus hypothesis-testing research and inductive research versus deductive research. *Case-oriented* research aims at a full understanding of a few cases using as many variables as necessary. Variable-oriented research aims at a full understanding of the role of a few variables in a multitude of cases.

Within the class of case-oriented methods, methods for pure case studies where one case is studied in depth and methods for a limited number of cases (typically

Table 6.1 *An overview of methods for causal data analysis*

Orientation	Measurement level of dependent variable	Measurement level of independent variable	Preferred method of data analysis
Case-oriented			Single case study (see Yin, 1996) Comparative Qualitative Analysis (*Section 6.3*)
Variable-oriented	Nominal	Nominal	Cross Table Elaboration (*Section 6.4*)
		Interval/ratio	Discriminant Analysis (*Section 6.5*)
	Interval/ratio	Nominal	Analysis of Variance (*Section 6.6*)
		Interval/ratio	Regression Analysis (*Section 6.7*)

less than 15) can be distinguished. Methods for the study of one case will not be treated here (but see Yin, 1996) because they serve as a first step for comparative research only. Methods for the study of a limited number of cases rely usually on John Stuart Mill's causal insights (see Chapter 3). Recently Charles Ragin (1987) has proposed a new approach known as Qualitative Case Analysis (QCA) to investigate a limited number of cases from a comparative point of view. This approach, which is restricted to dichotomous variables, will be discussed in Section 6.3.

In variable-oriented research the choice of the appropriate method depends on the levels of measurement of the dependent and independent variables. Elaborations of cross table analysis are appropriate when both the dependent and the independent variables are nominal variables (see Section 6.4). Discriminant analysis is appropriate when the dependent variable is nominal but the independent variables have a higher level of measurement (see Section 6.5). If the independent variables are nominal variables but the dependent variable has a higher level of measurement then analysis of variance can be recommended (see Section 6.6). If all variables are measured with interval or ratio precision then one of the many variants of regression analysis is possible (see Section 6.7).

6.3 THE CASE-ORIENTED APPROACH

If the occurrence of a phenomenon or an event is studied for a small number of cases then the aim of the investigation is to achieve a complete explanation. The aim is to identify precisely the conditions that led to the phenomenon or event, or at least to identify sets of conditions that might have led to it. A slightly more modest aim is to identify various sets of circumstances that preceded it or accompanied it. Ragin's *Qualitative Comparative Analysis* (QCA, Ragin, 1987; Berg-Schlosser and Quenter, 1996) has been developed as a method to formalize this approach.

The *variables* used to explain the occurrence of an effect are assumed to be dichotomous. Essentially the variables refer to the presence (1) or absence (0) of a condition or of an event. Whether the event of interest occurs or not is a dichotomous variable also. Each dichotomous variable can be represented as a letter of the alphabet. Capitals correspond with the value 1, lower-case letters with the value 0. We may ask ourselves, for example, why some democracies in inter-war Europe broke down (B) while others did not (b). Variables of interest might be the political role of the military (M is substantial, m is almost absent), the level of social unrest (U or u), the level of economic development (E or e), the level of integration into the world market (W or w), social homogeneity (H or h) and the domestic representation of commercial interests C or c). In this example a possible combination of variables might be listed as MuewHc → B: once upon a time a democracy broke down (B) when the political influence for the military was substantial (M), social unrest was low (u), economic development was slow (e), the integration into the world economy was poor (w), social homogeneity was high (H) and commercial interests were poorly represented (c). Suppose that democracy broke down in one other case only, namely when the combination MUEWhC $\rightarrow$ B occurred. Intuitively one would conclude that a breakdown of democracy (B) is associated with a political role for the military (M), but that the other factors are not important at all, since democracy collapsed both when they occurred and when they were absent. A political role for the military seems to be a necessary, albeit not necessarily sufficient, condition of the breakdown of democracy (M $\rightarrow$ B). If democracy never survives in cases where M is high, then M $\rightarrow$ B would be a completely satisfactory explanation. M would be QCA's explanation of B.

An explanation in QCA is technically just a parsimonious listing of the constellations which give rise to the presence (or absence) of the phenomenon of interest. Three types of explanation can be conceived: disjunctive explanations, conjunctive explanations and explanations with both disjunctive and conjunctive elements. A *disjunctive* explanation entails that circumstance A *or* circumstance B must have been present. A *conjunctive* explanation entails that both A *and* B must have been present. Disjunctive explanations are represented by the plus sign (+), whereas conjunctive explanations are represented by a multiplication sign (or no sign at all). One possible explanation of the collapse of democracy could for example be listed as:

$$\mathrm{C} = \mathrm{M} + \mathrm{hUw}.$$

This explanation entails that democracy will collapse (c) when the role of the military in politics is substantial, (M) or when three factors emerge simultaneously: poor social homogeneity (h), considerable social unrest (U), and a low integration into the world market (w).

To get a feeling for Qualitative Comparative Analysis a formal approach is helpful. With six explanatory variables, as in the previous example (M, U, E, W, H, C) the number of possible constellations amounts to $2^6 = 64$ (MUEWHC, MUEWHc, . . ., muewhc). In the case of k independent variables of interest, 2^k possible constellations can be listed. Depending on the empirical characteristics of the cases being studied, each of these 2^k constellations can be classified into one of four classes:

1 Only cases with high values on the dependent variable belong to the constellation (in our example, constellations characterized by B, the breakdown of democracy).
2 Only cases with low values on the dependent variable belong to the constellation (constellations characterized by b, the absence of a breakdown).
3 Contradictions: both cases with low and cases with high values on the dependent variable belong to the constellation.
4 Logical remainders, missing constellations: not a single case belongs to the constellation. All constellations that are not encountered in the empirical data are labelled as *logical remainder cases*.

Thus, the 2^k constellations can be divided into four groups. The constellations belonging to each group can be listed exhaustively. The idea of *Boolean minimiza-*

tion is simply that variables whose presence or absence apparently has no effect on the dependent variable can be neglected. Two complications render this task slightly less trivial than one might think at first. The first complication is that a parsimonious listing of the presence of the variable of interest (class 1) should not include constellations belonging to class 2. The second complication has to do with the logical remainders (class 4), thus with the class of conceivable constellations which are empty from an empirical point of view. Parsimonious explanations of the phenomenon of interest may include some but not all logical remainders. Suppose for example that the research question is to explain Z from the variables A, B and C. Suppose that empirically the constellations ABC → Z and Abc → Z are found, whereas constellations ABc and AbC are logical remainders, since they do not exist empirically, A parsimonious explanation of Z would be A → Z, since it seems irrelevant whether B and C are present. This explanation entails that the logical remainders are included in the set of constellations which would produce phenomenon Z.

Example: social welfare provisions in twelve nations in 1900

We will adopt a simple example from Berg-Schlosser and Quenter (1996), with three independent variables only. The dependent variable in the example is the development of social welfare provisions. The cases, or units of analysis, are twelve nations in 1900. Some of them have a low level of welfare provisions (italic font) whereas others have extended welfare provisions. The research question asks for an explanation of the development of social welfare provisions. Figure 6.3 gives an overview of the data on the available cases. Three independent variables are considered in the example. The curved *y*-axis represents the level of economic development. Values to the right of this axis represent a high economic development (D), whereas values to the left represent a poor development (d). Values above the curved *x*-axis represent that almost everybody is entitled to vote in national elections (E), whereas values beneath represent the absence of parliamentary democracy. The ellipse represents the strength of leftist parties. Outside (l) represents weak leftist parties, whereas inside (L) represents a strong leftist block. Three independent variables result in $2^3 = 8$ possible constellations.

As a first step each of the twelve countries are classified as belonging to one of the eight constellations. Consequently these constellations are classified into four classes of constellations:

1 Only cases with high values on the dependent variable belong to the constellation (the normal-font class, with 2 constellations: DeL + dEL).
2 Only cases with low values on the dependent variable belong to the constellation (the italics class, with 2 constellations: del + deL).
3 Or both cases with low and cases with high values on the dependent variable belong to the constellation (contradictions, with 3 constellations: dEl + Del + DEL).
4 Not a single case belongs to the constellation (logical remainders, with 1 constellation: DEl).

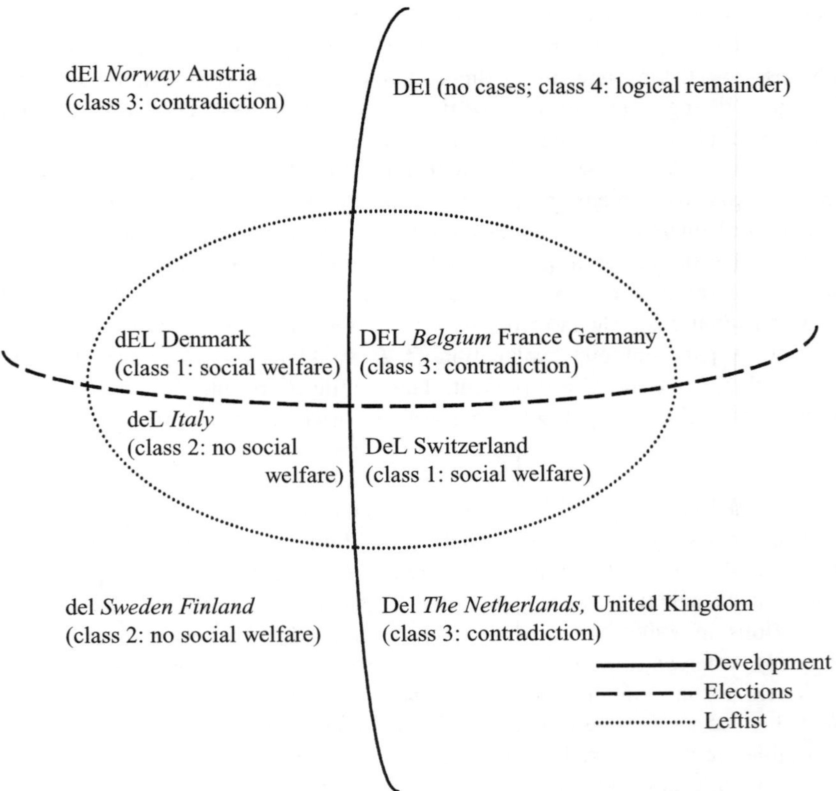

Figure 6.3 *Example of qualitative case analysis*

Each class of constellation consists of a list of constellations, either of zero, one or more constellations. The class of nations where social welfare provisions will surely come into being (class 1: DeL + dEL) can not be simplified to L(D + E), since the latter formula includes DEL, whereas the constellation DEL contains Belgium as an exception. Class 2 consists of del and deL which can be simplified to de. Apparently leftist parties cannot produce social welfare provisions when neither economic development nor parliamentary democracy helps. One could also ask of course in which nations social welfare provisions *can* emerge. Effectively this comes down to merging classes 1 and 3, thus to minimize DeL + dEL + dEl + Del + DEL. If the logical remainder class is added (DEl), then the list DEL + DEl + DeL + Del + dEL + dEl arises, from which it is clear that L(eftist party strength) is an irrelevant variable. These constellations can be simplified to D + E. Thus, either economic development or universal suffrage is enough to create the possibility of social welfare provisions. One can also ask which conditions can possibly result in a societal system without social welfare provisions. This comes down to merging classes 2 and 3. If once more the logical remainder is added,

1 + de + DE results. The first two terms are plausible, whereas the third one is not. It is plausible that social welfare provisions will sometimes not emerge when leftist parties are weak. It is also plausible that even when leftist parties are strong, social welfare provisions will not emerge when the economic development is slow and universal suffrage is absent. But why social welfare provisions did not emerge in Belgium is not easily explained. Actually one would have expected that the DEL constellation would have belonged entirely to the class of states with extended social welfare provisions. But Belgium is the exception. Variables should be discerned that may explain why in Belgium no social welfare provisions came into being.

The example shows clearly that Qualitative Case Analysis can offer intriguing, asymmetric insights. Strong leftist parties were irrelevant to explaining in which nations social welfare provisions *do* come about. But weak leftist parties were essential to explain why in some nations social welfare provisions *do not* come about.

The QCA-approach is useful when the number of cases is small compared with the number of variables. If the number of variables is small compared with the number of cases (e.g. less than a tenth) and the relationships between the variables are probabilistic to a certain degree, then almost all constellations tend to belong to the class of contradictions. There's little left to explain for binary deterministic data analysis models such as QCA.

6.4 NOMINAL DEPENDENT AND INDEPENDENT VARIABLES: CROSS TABLE ELABORATION

An introduction to cross tables was given in Section 5.3 using the relationship between the economy (before the oil crisis of 1973, before 1981, after 1981) on macro-economic-policy (restrictive, monetarist, austerity, or Keynesian) as an example. Here we will incorporate the electoral system of a nation as a third variable into this example to extend the use of cross tables from bivariate analysis to multivariate analysis.

The causal model to be tested

Electoral systems can be distinguished in proportional systems (e.g. the Scandinavian countries, Switzerland, Austria, Italy, the Netherlands, Belgium) on the one hand and majoritarian systems (e.g. Great Britain, USA, Canada, France) and semi-proportional systems (e.g. Australia, Ireland, Japan, Germany) on the other hand. Minorities in proportional systems have a good chance to be represented in parliament. Proportional electoral systems tend to lead to multi-party systems, whereas majoritarian systems and semi-proportional systems are often dominated by two or three parties. The dispersion of voters over parties is larger in proportional systems than in majoritarian and semi-proportional systems, as is indicated by the Herfindahl-index in number equivalents. For the period 1965–1990 this index amounts for the proportional electoral systems to 4.3 parties and for the other systems to 2.6 parties only ($n = 442$ nested country–year units). A proportional system favors consensus democracy, in which 'all significant political parties and representatives of the major groups in society share executive power' (Lijphart, 1984: 46).

The *hypothesis* to be tested here is that proportional electoral systems are conducive to Keynesian macro-economic policy, whereas majoritarian systems enhance a restrictive macro-economic policy. In proportional electoral systems, parties that promote the interests of a homogeneous segment of the population only in order to get some seats (rather than the majority of seats) can survive. Parties in proportional electoral systems can and will relatively often plead for public expenditures to favor their own group. The dominant parties in majoritarian systems will have to make broad appeals to a heterogeneous electorate with conflicting interests. They are therefore expected to favor broad tax cuts instead of public expenditures to help specific, homogeneous groups. In Figure 6.4. this hypothesis is depicted as a direct arrow from the electoral system towards the macro-economic policy.

Let's add a second hypothesis. In Section 5.3 the conclusion was that the economic crisis had opposing influences on macro-economic policy. Some countries shifted towards a more restrictive policy, others towards a Keynesian policy. This effect is visualized as a direct effect from the economy towards macro-economic policy in Figure 6.4. One expects that the type of reaction to a worsening economy is dependent on the electoral system. Or to put it differently, the economy determines also the *strength* of the effect of the electoral system on the type of

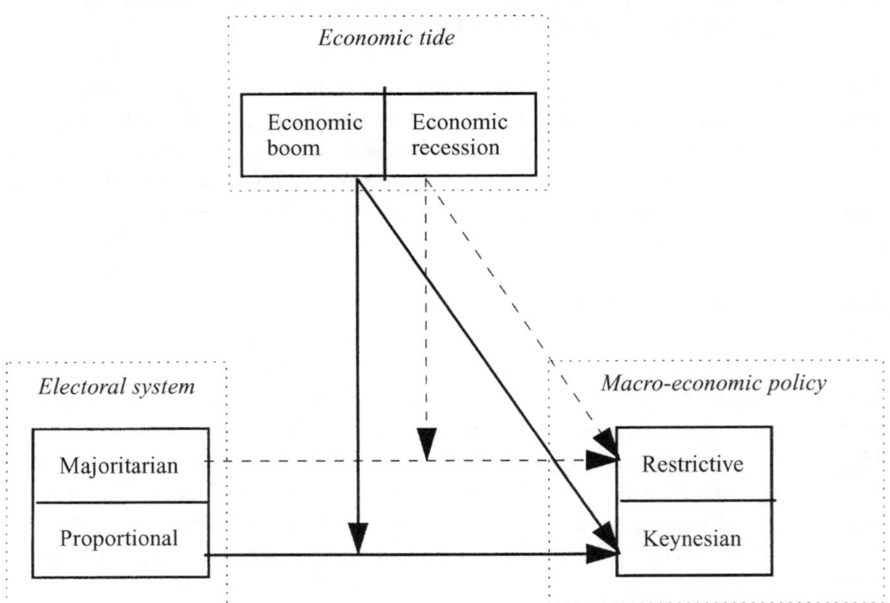

Figure 6.4 *Causal model of electoral system, economy and macro-economic policy*

macro-economic policy. In times of economic prosperity even politicians in majoritarian systems will often favor help for specific societal groups, since the electorate as a whole will not have to suffer because of it. This effect is visualized as the *interaction effect* from the economy on the direct effect from the electoral system on the type of macro-economic policy.

6.4.1 Cross table elaboration

The method of analyzing multivariate relationships with cross tables is called cross table elaboration. Here we will illustrate the method for three variables. The general idea is that the relationship between the two variables of primary interest x and y – in our example the relationship between the electoral system and the type of macro-economic policy – should be split up for each category of the remaining nominal variable z – in our example for each state of the economy. Thus, the dependence of macro-economic policy on the electoral system is depicted in partial tables for each value of the economy. In the jargon of cross table analysis the economy is held constant. Each partial table reflects only one particular state of the economy.

All partial tables will show an association of the same magnitude when the variable being controlled for is an additive variable that explains variance in the dependent variable, but is independent of the primary independent variable. The association in the uncontrolled cross table will have the same magnitude as the association in the partial tables.

When the variable being controlled for is either an intervening variable or an exogeneous variable responsible for spurious correlation then the associations in the partial tables will be small compared with the bivariate association. The column percentages in corresponding cells of the partial tables will be equal to each other.

When the variable being controlled for is an interacting variable the association should be strong in some partial tables but low in other ones.

First the overarching cross table between the electoral system and macro-economic policy will be inspected, regardless of the state of the economy (Table 6.2). Next, for each of the three values of the economy, the partial tables between these two variables could have been presented, but for simplicity's sake only the partial tables for the period before the oil crisis of 1973 and the crisis period of the

Table 6.2 *Cross-tabulation of Electoral system by macro-economic policy*

	Economic tide			
Macro-economic policy type	**1965–73**	**1974–80**	**1981–90**	**Total**
Restrictive	5.9%	23.5%	17.6%	15.2%
Monetarist	35.3%	23.5%	23.5%	27.6%
Austerity	41.2%	29.4%	29.4%	23.8%
Keynesian	17.6%	23.5%	29.4%	23.8%
Total	100%	100%	100%	100%
	(n = 153)	(n = 119)	(n = 170)	(n = 442)

1980s will be presented (Table 6.3). The actual relationship between the type of electoral system and the type of macro-economic policy is in line with the hypothesis. Keynesian policy is pursued in proportional election systems only ($\varepsilon = 44.9$ per cent). A restrictive macro-economic policy is pursued more often in majoritarian systems ($\varepsilon = 24.0$ per cent -7.3 per cent $= 16.7$ per cent).

The partial cross tables show clearly that the economy is neither an intervening variable nor an exogeneous variable causing spurious correlation, since the percentage differences in the partial tables do not vanish to near zero. The economy is an interacting variable, however. In the good old prosperous years before the oil crisis of 1973 the relationship between the electoral system and the pursued macro-economic policy is clearly extant, but relatively weak as compared to the years of crisis in the 1980s. Before the oil crisis Keynesian policy was pursued in proportional electoral systems only, whereas a restrictive policy was pursued in majoritarian electoral systems only. The percentage difference for Keynesian policy was 33.3 per cent, the percentage difference for restrictive policy 12.5 per cent. The years of crisis tightened up the differences between the electoral systems. In the 1980s the percentage differences had grown. They show an increase for Keynesian policy of 55.6 per cent and for restrictive policy of 25.0 – 11.1 per cent = 13.9 per cent. Before the oil crisis the association measure φ between the electoral system and the type of economic policy amounted to 0.49; in the 1980s it had increased to 0.62.

The partial cross tables are also consistent with an autonomous, additive effect of the economy on macro-economic policy. Restrictive policy became more popular in the early 1980s, as is indicated by an increase from 0 per cent to 11.1 per cent in proportional systems and from 12.5 per cent towards 25.0 per cent in majoritarian systems. The worse the economy, the more popular a restrictive macro-economic policy tends to become, regardless of the electoral system.

Table 6.3 *Electoral system by macro-economic policy elaborated for economy (period 1974–1979 not considered)*

		Electoral system[a]		
Economy	**Macro-economic policy type**	**Majoritarian or semi-proportional**	**Proportional**	**Total**
1965–73	Restrictive	12.5%	0	5.9%
(economy	Monetarist	37.5%	33.3%	35.3%
still	Austerity	50%	33.3%	35.3%
flourishes)	Keynesian	0%	33.3%	17.6%
Total		100% ($n = 72$)	100% ($n = 81$)	100% ($n = 153$)
1981–90	Restrictive	25.0%	11.1%	17.6%
(recession;	Monetarist	37.5%	11.1%	23.5%
economy	Austerity	37.5%	22.2%	29.4%
recovers slowly)	Keynesian	0%	55.6%	29.4%
Total		100% ($n = 80$)	100% ($n = 90$)	100% ($n = 170$)

[a]Source: Lijphart (1984).

6.5 NOMINAL DEPENDENT VARIABLE, INTERVAL DEPENDENT VARIABLES

If the variables have an interval level of measurement then they will have many values. Consequently the number of cases in each separate cell of the cross table analysis will be small, which will render percentage differences and association measures such as χ^2 shaky and therefore meaningless from a statistical point of view.

When the independent variables have a higher level of measurement, but the dependent variable is still nominal, the question becomes whether the value which the nominal dependent variable takes is predictable from the values on the independent variables. Discriminant analysis is the data analysis method to provide an answer to this type of question. Since each party can be considered as one value of the nominal variable party choice, discriminant analysis can be used to answer the question to what degree party choice in multi-party systems is dependent on various ideological and socio-economic variables with an interval level of measurement (education, income, sympathy ratings of electoral leaders, and so on).

Discriminant analysis will be discussed only cursorily here, because the combination of a dependent nominal variable and independent interval variables does not apply often. The mathematical and statistical properties will be left aside.

Discriminant analysis assumes a linear unidirectional model. The probability that a case has a given value on the nominal dependent variable is modeled as a linear function of the independent variables. Discriminant analysis assesses the direct effect of each separate variable controlled for the effects of the other variables. When the independent variables correlate with each other the direct effects of each separate variable may deviate strongly from what could have been expected on the basis of bivariate inspections of the data.

When the dependent variable is a dichotomous one, discriminant analysis is equivalent to multiple linear regression analysis with a dichotomous dependent variable (see van de Geer, 1986), but this equivalence is hidden by most statistical packages. The printed output for discriminant analysis will typically contain various overviews and details that are not printed in the case of regression analysis and vice versa. Even to sort out the exact correspondence of discriminant function coefficients with ordinary regression coefficients is non-trivial since regression coefficients and discriminant function coefficients tend to be standardized differently (even within the same statistical package). When the number of values of the dependent nominal variable is three or higher, the precise correspondence with multiple regression analysis is lost.

6.5.1 Discriminant analysis example: explaining the type of government

One of the nominal variables in the NIAS.SAV database is the Type of Government (TOGORI). This variable has four categories: single-party governments, minimal winning coalitions, surplus coalitions that rest on the official parliamentary support of more parties than strictly necessary for survival, and (various subtypes of) minority governments. Caretaker governments will be excluded from consideration here. A variety of explanations of the type of government has been offered (see de Swaan, 1973; Budge and Keman, 1990; Laver and Shepsle, 1996). Many theories emphasize aspects of coalition governments that are not captured by the single variable TOGORI (e.g. whether coalition partners occupy a smallest region in issue space, the distribution of cabinet portfolios among the coalition parties). The aim of the analysis presented here is simply to investigate whether a non-exhaustive number of selected variables with an interval level of measurement add to the explanation of the rough type of government. In the NIAS.SAV data base, data are available for 392 government–year combinations (sixteen OECD countries; period 1965–1990).

Once more the theory of the effects of the type of electoral system is useful. Majoritarian electoral systems will tend to produce two parties only. Single-party governments are likely. As compared with politicians in multi-party systems with the same ideology, party politicians in majoritarian systems will attempt to appease heterogeneous groups with low taxes and low social contributions. Thus, the existence of many parties (as measured by the index of Laakso and Taagepera) as well as high taxes and high social security contributions will decrease the likelihood of a single-party government. A surplus coalition will presumably result when party ideologies are deemed less important than national unity. One indicator of such a state of emergency is the number of *strikes*. Strikes increase the likelihood of a surplus government. Polarization between parties as measured by the *distance* between left-wing and right-wing parties (as measured by party manifestoes) on the other hand hampers government coalitions with centrist parties and will increase the likelihood of a minority coalition.

As a first step the plausibility of these hypotheses can be verified by the use of a bivariate analysis of variance. Table 6.4 depicts for each type of government the mean scores on the independent interval variables. The mean values per type of government are roughly in line with the expectations. The mean value of single-party governments on 'electoral system' of 1.2 as compared with 1.8 for other types of government indicates that majoritarian electoral systems do indeed

Table 6.4 *Mean values of independent variables per type of government*

	Type of government (TOGORI)			
	Single-party government	Minimal winning coalition	Surplus coalition	Minority government
	Mean	Mean	Mean	Mean
Electoral system (1 = majoritarian, 2 = proportional)	1.2	1.8	1.8	1.8
Effective number of parties (Laakso and Taagepera)	2.2	3.9	4.4	3.7
Taxes	33.5	37.5	34.3	42.2
Social security contributions	3.9	10.1	10	7.4
Left–right polarization	2.03	1.79	1.84	2.91
Number of strikes (ILO)	3571	1428	3387	2325

produce single-party governments. Remember that the variable 'electoral system' takes 1 as its value in the case of a majoritarian system and 2 in the case of a proportional system. Single party governments emerge when the effective number of parties is low (2.2 on the average), whereas surplus governments emerge when the number of parties is extremely high (4.4 on the average). Thus, fragmented societies with a proportional electoral system seem to produce political elites which tend to cooperate in large surplus coalitions. On average, low tax rates and low social security contributions do indeed correspond with single-party governments (33.5 and 3.9, respectively). Polarization favors minority governments indeed (mean polarization of 2.91). Surplus coalitions are indeed associated with a relatively high number of strikes, but the number of strikes is even higher when 'stubborn' single-party governments take office.

Discriminant analysis is the appropriate data analysis technique to assess to what degree the combination of these variables suffices to explain and to predict the type of government precisely. A central concept in discriminant analysis is the *(canonical) discriminant function*. A discriminant function is a *division function* which is construed to divide the cases which belong to two particular sets of categories of the dependent nominal variable on the basis of their values on the independent variables. The number of discriminant functions is one less than the number of categories of the dependent variable. In our example of four categories, three discriminant functions will be construed. Each of them adds statistically significantly to the explanation of the type of government. In Figure 6.5 the essentials of the SPSS-output concerning our application of discriminant analysis to our example is printed. The meaning of the discriminant functions should be retrieved by interpreting the 'rotated standardized discriminant function coefficients' of the dependent variables with regard to the three construed discriminant functions. The discriminant function coefficients of the independent variables on the discriminant functions in discriminant analysis are comparable to the factor loadings of variables on the factors in factor analysis. As a further means to clarify the meaning of the discriminant functions, a glance at the location of each of the group means (group centroids) with respect to these division lines is useful. Classification results can be trusted once the meaning of the discriminant functions is interpreted in the light of the available theory.

First the *division lines*, or in the jargon of discriminant analysis, the *canonical discriminant functions* that are construed by discriminant analysis to explain the type of government should be interpreted on the basis of the available theory. To get a feeling for these *discriminant functions*, a glance at the group centroids is useful.

The first discriminant function separates single-party governments (average position −1.53 with respect to first discriminant function) from the other types of governments, especially from surplus coalitions (position +1.32 with respect to first discriminant function). A look at the (rotated standardized) *discriminant function coefficients* shows that positive positions relative to the first discriminant function are associated with a proportional electoral system (+0.36), a high number of effective parties (+0.74) and high social security contributions (+0.55). Negative positions relative to the first division line are associated with low taxes

Rotated standardized discriminant function coefficients
Based on rotation of structure matrix

	Func 1	Func 2	Func 3	
ELSYS	.36258	.13412	.75953	Electoral System. Lijphart 1984
EFFNOP	.74963	−.03528	−.51300	Effective number of parties
TAX	−.49170	.65792	.50833	Taxes
SSC	.54635	−.91833	.03132	Social Security Contributions
POLAR	.24842	.58169	.31833	Polarization left-right
NRSTRIKE	.10818	.57047	−.32482	Number of Strikes (ILO)

Canonical discriminant functions evaluated at group means (group centroids)

Group	Func 1	Func 2	Func 3	
1	−1.53184	.33075	−.51097	Single Party Governm
2	.25861	−.48301	.21869	Minimal Winning Coal
3	1.32335	−.59363	−.35458	Surplus Coalition
4	.07335	1.13661	1.00438	Minority Gvt

Classification results -

Actual Group	No. of Cases	Predicted Group Membership 1	2	3	4
Group 1	105	91	12	0	2
Single Party Governm		86.7%	11.4%	.0%	1.9%
Group 2	114	21	41	32	20
Minimal Winning Coal		18.4%	36.0%	28.1%	17.5%
Group 3	103	0	25	71	7
Surplus Coalition		.0%	24.3%	68.9%	6.8%
Group 4	70	11	5	4	50
minority gvt		15.7%	7.1%	5.7%	71.4%
Ungrouped cases	24	2	2	7	13
		8.3%	8.3%	29.2%	54.2%

Per cent of 'grouped' cases correctly classified: 64.54%

Figure 6.5 *SPSS output of discriminant analysis to predict the type of government*

(−0.49). These results are pretty much in line with the basic theory. The first discriminant functions distinguishes between majoritarian electoral systems with a few parties only and low taxes and, on the other hand, proportional electoral systems with a great many parties and high social security contributions.

The second discriminant function separates the minority governments (average position +1.14) from the minimal winning coalitions and especially from the surplus coalitions (position −0.59). Positive positions with respect to the second discriminant function are associated with high taxes (+0.66), a high degree of polarization (+0.58) and strikes (+0.57). Negative positions are associated with low social security contributions (−0.91). The second division line has at its positive side the minority governments that arise when political agreements between coalition partners become impossible due to a high degree of possible polarization, societal tensions as indicated by strikes, and taxes that are already too high to increase them further so as to please everybody. Thus, the second discriminant function can be interpreted fairly easily also.

The third discriminant function is less easily interpreted on the basis of theory. Apparently the third function captures that surplus coalitions (average position −0.35) provide a political answer to labor unrest and strikes (−0.32) when the effective number of parties is high (−0.51). Note that the three minus signs merely indicate here that strikes, many parties and surplus coalitions are on the same side of the third discriminant function. In discriminant analysis, these signs are arbitrary (one may multiply them by −1). When the higher-order discriminant functions are completely random from the point of view of substantial theory, the number of discriminant functions should be reduced *a priori*, even when these higher-order functions are statistically significant.

To assess the quality of the overall explanation of the nominal dependent variable the *classification results table* is useful. Overall the type of government was predicted correctly for 91 + 41 + 71 + 50 = 253 cases, which amounts to 64.5 per cent of the 392 cases. This percentage is fairly impressive, since it is much higher than could be expected on the basis of the frequency of the modal type of government (the relative frequency of minimal winning coalitions amounts to 114/392 = 29.1 per cent).

The rows of the classification table should be inspected to get a feeling for the strengths and weaknesses of the explanation. Single-party governments are predicted quite well on the basis of the model (86.7 per cent correct). Surplus coalitions and minority governments are predicted correctly for roughly for two out of three cases. Surplus coalitions are often predicted when actually a minimal winning coalition came into being (24 per cent). The model provides poor predictions of the realization of minimal winning coalitions (36 per cent correct guesses). This poor prediction reflects that some minimal winning coalitions are politically attractive whereas others are absurd, depending on the policy distances between the parties within the minimal winning coalition (de Swaan, 1973).

It is worthwhile to examine the quality of predictions not only from a quantitative point of view but to examine precisely for which cases the model performs well or badly. For reasons of space we will not print casewise predictions here. It will be no surprise that the casewise predictions show that the model presented here has no difficulty in explaining the trivial facts that Great Britain has single-party governments whereas Switzerland has surplus coalitions. For some countries the model performs extremely poorly, however. Austria for example is predicted to always have minimal winning coalitions, but in reality Austria had all types of governments. Nevertheless the simple discriminant analysis model presented here predicts some shifts in the type of government remarkably accurately. For Belgium the model predicts correctly, for example, the succession in 1966 of a surplus coalition by a minimal winning coalition. For the Netherlands the succession in 1977 of a surplus coalition by a minimal winning coalition is predicted, whereas this shift came about in 1978 (at least according to the annual data). For Italy the succession in 1987 of a surplus government by a minority government is correctly predicted.

6.6 INTERVAL DEPENDENT VARIABLE, NOMINAL INDEPENDENT VARIABLES: ANALYSIS OF VARIANCE

Models for the analysis of variance (ANOVA) have a dependent variable with an interval level of measurement. In Section 5.2.2 an ANOVA-model with one independent nominal variable was presented. More complex ANOVA-models have been developed of course. First, *multiple* independent nominal variables can be entered. Next, models with *interactions* between the various nominal independent variables have been introduced. Third, *covariates* – variables with a higher level of measurement – can be introduced as additional independent variables to explain the value of the independent interval variable. Many other complications, such as repeated measurements or varying contrast groups, can be handled within the context of ANOVA-models also. Here we will not delve into the analysis of variance, since regression analysis can be used in many circumstances as an alternative.

The analysis of variance with one independent nominal variable with j categories is equivalent to regression analysis with $j-1$ dummy variables as independent variables. An obvious way to construe these dummy variables is to select one of the j groups as the reference category and to construct for each of the remaining groups a dummy variable that has the value +1 when a case belongs to that group and the value 0 otherwise. Let's use a simple example. Suppose one wishes to examine the effect of one's 'religion', conceived as a nominal variable with three values, namely 'Christian', 'none', and 'other (e.g. Islam)' on the interval variable 'Trust in government'. The regression approach to this problem would be to construe a variable 'Christianity' with value 1 when the nominal variable takes the value Christian and 0 otherwise. Furthermore a variable 'other religion' could be construed (1 = other religion, 0 = Christian or no religion). The regression equation to be estimated would be:

$$\text{'Trust} = b_1 \text{ Christianity} + b_2 \text{ Other Religion} + a\text{'}.$$

Instead of the binary 0–1 'contrast' to code a dummy variable, other numerical 'contrasts' can be used also. If not belonging to a specific group is considered not only as absence of group membership, but more strongly as group avoidance, then the value -1 is preferable to the value 0, for example. Many other contrasts have been used in the literature. One should keep in mind that the precise contrasts do have effects on the unstandardized regression coefficients, since the measurement scale of the independent variables is altered, but not on the explained variance, since the latter is independent of linear transformations in the independent variables.

An interaction effect of two nominal variables implies that each specific combination of the values of these two variables is associated with a particular level of the dependent variable. In regression analysis the (first order) interaction terms can be construed by multiplying each dummy that was used to represent the first variable with each of the dummies that were used to represent the second variable. If two variables have j and k values, respectively, then $j-1$ and $k-1$ dummies, respectively, should be created to deal with them in multiple regression analysis as independent variables, and $(j-1)(k-1)$ dummies should be construed to represent the interactions between the two nominal variables. To study the combined effect of religion and class – conceived of as a dichotomous nominal variable – on the trust in government, for example, one should first construct a binary variable 'class' with value 1 for the upper class and value 0 for the lower class. The regression model without interactions is:

$$\text{Trust} = \text{b}_1 \text{ Christianity} + \text{b}_2 \text{ Other Religion} + \text{b}_3 \text{ Class} + \text{a}.$$

A model with interactions allows for the fact that especially citizens from the higher class exhibit trust in government. In our example $(3-1)(2-1) = 2$ interaction variables should be created to enable a full regression analysis with interaction effects:

$$\text{Trust} = \text{b}_1 \text{ Christianity} + \text{b}_2 \text{ Other Religion} + \text{b}_3 \text{ Upper Class}$$

$$+ \text{b}_4 \text{ Christian Upper Class} + \text{b}_5 \text{ Other Religion Upper Class} + \text{a},$$

wherein Christian Upper Class $= 1$ if Christianity $= 1$ and Upper Class $= 1$; otherwise 0; and Other Religion Upper Class $= 1$ if Other Religion $= 1$ and Upper Class $= 1$; otherwise 0. The regression representation of analysis of variance allows easily for the possibility of including covariates, defined as other variables with a higher level of measurement, as independent variables in the regression equation. Interaction in regression models will be discussed in Subsection 6.7.4.

Thus, from a mathematical point of view, analysis of variance is equivalent to regression analysis. Nevertheless the required input and the printed output from both subroutines will be quite different in most statistical packages. The printed output of regression analysis concentrates upon regression parameters of separate (dummy) variables (that might or might not represent (interactions between) categories of nominal independent variables), whereas the printed output of the analysis of variance deals primarily with the statistical significance of complete nominal variables and their interactions. Thus, if one is interested in general questions such as whether nominal variables or their interactions have an effect on the dependent variable at all, ANOVA output should be requested. If one is interested in the precise effects of specific conditions, as most comparative political scientists are, then the regression approach is to be preferred. In this book we will concentrate on the regression approach.

6.7 INTERVAL DEPENDENT AND INDEPENDENT VARIABLES: REGRESSION ANALYSIS

Regression analysis is probably the most frequently used technique for data analysis in political science. Various extensions of bivariate regression analysis (Section 5.4) will be discussed in this section. Regression analysis is the appropriate technique whenever dependent and independent variables have an interval level of measurement.

In Subsection 6.7.1 the linear multiple regression model will be discussed. The precise assumptions of the linear multiple regression model are dealt with in 6.7.2. Subsections 6.7.3 and 6.7.4 serve to translate the general principles of testing causal theories, which were presented in Section 6.1, to variables with interval and ratio levels of measurement. The use of multiple regression analysis to deal with additive relationships, intervention and spurious correlation (see Section 6.1) is discussed in Subsection 6.7.3. Interactions in the framework of a multiple regression model will be discussed in Subsection 6.7.4.

A thorough discussion of the assumptions of regression analysis (Subsection 6.7.2) is required to prevent its unwarranted use. Moreover, knowledge of the assumptions of the technique is useful to understand the background of extensions of regression analysis. Almost without exception these extensions were developed to tackle violations of the assumptions of the pure linear regression model. In this book the focus will be on extensions of regression analysis to deal with time series (Subsection 6.7.5), pooled time series (Subsection 6.7.6), and reciprocal relations between variables (Subsection 6.7.7).

Time series data and pooled time series data (Subsections 6.7.5 and 6.7.6) are essential to test causal theories, since they give a clue to the temporal sequence of events. Nevertheless, time series data pose a serious problem to regression analysis, called *autocorrelation*. Autocorrelation signifies that the dependent variable displays a rigidness that is not accounted for by the independent variables. If autocorrelation exists, then a poor explanation at one point in time is predictably followed by a poor explanation at the next point in time. Prediction on the basis of a regression equation is tricky when autocorrelation exists. Various remedies to cure autocorrelation will be discussed in 6.7.5 and 6.7.6. These remedies either amount to more advanced estimation techniques or to an alternative specification of the regression model which allows for hypothesis testing nevertheless.

Reciprocal relationships constitute chicken or egg puzzles. Which party gets its way in a government coalition, for example? Who influences whom? A chicken or egg puzzle can only be solved when data on exogeneous variables are available. If one takes for granted that a party in government tries to implement their own party manifesto, then it is a good idea to find out which coalition partner wrote the party manifesto that resembles current government policy most closely. To put it in a more abstract form, if A and B reciprocally influence each other, then a third factor C that does directly influence A but does not directly influence B is required to estimate the strength of the reciprocal relationships between A and B. Models and estimation techniques for reciprocal relationships will be discussed in 6.7.7.

6.7.1 The multiple regression model

The linear multiple regression model is a straightforward generalization of the bivariate model. Instead of one independent variable, more than one independent variable is assumed to have an influence on the dependent variable. The value for case i on the dependent variable, Y_i, is assumed to be a linear combination of the values of case i on the independent variables X_{1i}, X_{2i}, ... X_{ki}, except for a *residual* ε_i, that is not accounted for by the independent variables. The residual for case i is the differences between the value of the dependent variable Y_i and the predicted value $\hat{Y}_i$:

$$Y_i = \mathrm{b}_0 + \mathrm{b}_1 X_{1i} + \mathrm{b}_2 X_{2i} + \ldots \mathrm{b}_k X_{ki} + \varepsilon_i$$

In the case of k independent variables X_1, X_2, ..., X_k the *predicted value* for case i, $\hat{Y}_i$, is a linear function of X_{1i}, X_{2i}, ..., X_{ki} multiplied with their respective regression slope coefficients b_1, b_2, ..., b_k and the regression constant b_0.

$$\hat{Y}_i = \mathrm{b}_0 + \mathrm{b}_1 X_{1i} + \mathrm{b}_2 X_{2i} + \ldots \mathrm{b}_k X_{ki}$$

The *Ordinary Least Squares* (OLS) procedure to estimate the *regression coefficients* b_0, b_1, b_2, ..., b_k prescribes that the *S*um of all *S*quared *R*esiduals, $\Sigma\varepsilon_i^2$, also denoted as *SSR*, should be minimized:

$$\text{Minimize } SSR, \text{ where } SSR = \textstyle\sum_i (Y_i - \hat{Y}_i)^2$$

The formulas for the regression coefficients b_0, b_1, b_2, ..., b_k which follow from this minimization procedure are rather cumbersome when k becomes large. Numerical procedures to minimize *SSR* are fairly efficient, however.

Dividing *SSR* by *SS*, the sum of squares of the values with respect to their mean $\overline{Y}$, gives the proportion of unexplained variance. The proportion of explained variance, R^2, is computed as one minus the proportion of unexplained variance.

$$R^2 = 1 - SSR/SS$$

$$\text{where } SS = \textstyle\sum_i (Y_i - \overline{Y})^2.$$

The nature of a regression coefficient in multivariate regression analysis

A regression coefficient in multivariate regression analysis reflects the influence of a variable X_k on Y when the other independent variables 'are *held constant*', or, 'are being *controlled for*'. To compute a single regression coefficient in multiple regression analysis, only those variations in X_k and Y are considered that do not depend on variations in the remaining independent variables. The disturbing influences of the remaining variables are filtered out by, first, computing the residuals in X_k that cannot be accounted for by the remaining independent variables from the original regression equation ($X_1 \ldots X_k$), by computing the residuals in Y. These residual variables will be denoted here as RX_k and RY. The regression coefficient b_k in the regression equation with Y as the dependent variable and the complete set of independent variables, $X_1, \ldots, X_{k-1}, X_k$, is identical to the *bivariate* regression coefficient of RY with RX_k.

Regression of Y dependent on $X_1 \ldots X_k$:

$$Y_i = \mathrm{b}_0 + \mathrm{b}_1 X_{1i} + \mathrm{b}_2 X_{2i} + \ldots \mathrm{b}_k X_{ki} + \varepsilon_i$$

Regression of Y on remaining $X_1 \ldots X_{k-1}$:

$$Y_i = \mathrm{c}_0 + \mathrm{c}_1 X_{1i} + \mathrm{c}_2 X_{2i} + \ldots \mathrm{c}_{k-1} X_{k-1,i} + RY_i$$

Regression of X_k on remaining $X_1 \ldots X_{k-1}$:

$$Xk_i = \mathrm{d}_0 + \mathrm{d}_1 X_{1i} + \mathrm{d}_2 X_{2i} + \ldots \mathrm{d}_{k-1} X_{k-1,i} + RX_{ki}$$

Bivariate regression of obtained residuals: $RY_i = e_0 + eRX_{ki} + \varepsilon_i$

$$\text{then } \mathrm{b}_k = e$$

A bivariate regression line is easily visualized in the flat plane. Predictions in multivariate regression do not amount to a straight line as in bivariate regression. In a regression analysis with two independent variables the predictions amount to a flat surface in the three-dimensional space. In a regression analysis with three independent variables the regression equation amounts to a three-dimensional object in an unintelligible four-dimensional space. It is impossible to visualize the regression coefficients in multiple regression analysis directly. But for each independent variable the *partial regression* with the dependent variable can be visualized. A partial regression plot of X_k with Y is a plot of RX_k as the independent and RY as the dependent variable. Instead of the original variables X_k and Y the residual variables RX_k and RY along the X-axis and the Y-axis, should be plotted respectively. RX_k represents only the variation in X_k that is not collinear with the other independent variables. RY represents only the variation in Y which could not be explained by the other independent variables.

Example: effects of an old population on public expenditures in addition to imports/exports

The responsiveness of the political system towards the growing share of elderly citizens poses a serious policy question in western democracies. Nations with an old population will tend to have high public expenditures since the elderly do not work anymore and consequently do not contribute to the gross domestic product. They are in need of health care and pensions instead. As an example, throughout this section the relationship between the percentage of the population older than 65 (AGE65 in NIAS.SAV) and public expenditures as a percentage of gross domestic product (PE) will be considered.

Since the influence of high imports and exports on public expenditures was discussed already in the introductory section on regression analysis (Section 5.4) the regression question to be answered here is whether an old population (AGE65) helps to explain high public expenditures (PE) in addition to imports and exports (IMEX2).

$$PE_i = \mathrm{b}_0 + \mathrm{b}_1\mathrm{IMEX2}_i + \mathrm{b}_2\mathrm{AGE65}_i + \varepsilon_i$$

As in Section 5.4 we will confine ourselves to data on the year 1988 for seventeen countries. But the precise percentage of people older than 65 for Japan in 1988 is missing in the data base. Therefore the regression model will be tested for sixteen countries only. Table 6.5 presents the regression coefficients as computed by SPSS. The table reveals that $\mathrm{b}_0 = 12.15$, $\mathrm{b}_1 = 0.28$ and $\mathrm{b}_2 = 1.83$, which gives rise to the regression equation:

$$PE = 12.15 + 0.283\,IMEX2 + 1.834\,AGE65$$

Thus, public expenditures (as a percentage of gross domestic product) tend to increase, on average, by 1.83 per cent when the percentage of elderly rises by one percentage point. This is what was to be expected: it is the elderly who boost public expenditures. When imports and exports increase by 1 per cent, then public expenditures tend to increase also, on average by 0.28 per cent. One should note that 0.28 is slightly less than 0.33, which was the regression coefficient found in the bivariate regression analysis of Section 5.4. Regression coefficients in multivariate regression analysis are lower than in bivariate regression analysis, when the additional variables are collinear to a certain degree, which is almost always the case. Multivariate regression coefficients will be precisely identical to bivariate regression coefficients when the independent variables show zero correlations among each other.

The *t*-coefficients in Table 6.5 indicate that both regression coefficients are significant when a one-sided test is applied, although not when a two-sided test is

Table 6.5 *Regression coefficients: an example*

	b (unstandardized coefficients)	Std error	beta (standardized coefficients)	*t*	Sig.
(Constant)	12.15	13.69	–	0.89	0.39
IMEX2[a]	0.28	0.13	0.48	2.26	0.04
AGE65[b]	1.83	0.94	0.41	1.95	0.07

[a] (imp/gnp + exp/gnp)/2.

[b] % population > 65.

applied (see Subsection 5.7.4; critical value at the 5 per cent significance level, $n = 16$, $df = 14$: $t = 1.746$). One-sided tests should be applied here since the hypotheses prescribed precisely the direction of effects (positive for both variables). The significance levels printed by SPSS refer to two-sided tests, which are applicable when no *a priori* assumptions with respect to the direction of a regression coefficient are made. The explained variance (not printed in Table 6.5) amounts to $R^2 = 0.41$.

To get a feeling for multivariate regression analysis it might be helpful to compare Figure 6.6, which represents the partial regression plot between IMEX2 and PE controlled for AGE65, with Figure 5.3, which represents the bivariate regression plot between IMEX2 and PE. Only small differences show up. Since the correlation between IMEX2 and AGE65 is almost absent ($r = +0.03$) only small differences are to be expected. The regression coefficient would have been hard to interpret had IMEX2 and AGE65 been highly correlated. The bivariate regression plot between IMEX2 and PE would have differed enormously from the partial regression plot between IMEX2 and PE controlled for AGE65 in the latter case. Multicollinearity is the technical name to label the problem of high correlations between independent variables (see 6.7.2.3).

6.7.2 Assumptions of the Ordinary Least Squares estimation method

Regression coefficients computed by the Ordinary Least Squares method (OLS) may give a false impression of precision.

Regression analysis assumes linear relationships. Regression coefficients are meaningless when relationships are *non-linear*. If relationships are heavily non-linear, then linear regression coefficients will tell a misleading story. The OLS

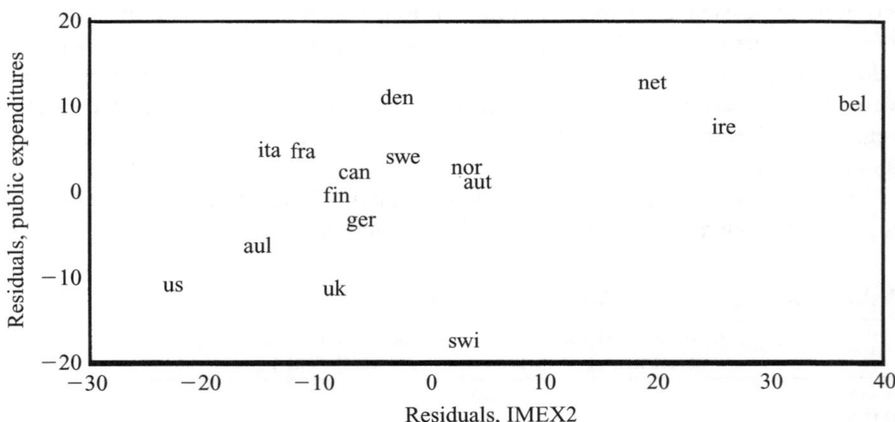

Figure 6.6 *Partial regression plot of openness of economy (IMEX2) and public expenditures (PE) controlled for the percentage of elderly (AGE65)*

method which is used to estimate regression coefficients may be inappropriate to estimate population regression coefficients when the data exhibit nasty properties. These nasty properties have received appealing names such as outliers, heteroscedasticity, multicollinearity and autocorrelation. OLS estimates will be biased, inefficient or non-robust in the presence of these data properties (see Subsection 5.6.2 for a discussion of unbiasedness, efficiency and robustness of estimators). The nature of these nasty properties will be discussed in this Subsection.

Non-linear relationships

Linear relationships are a basic assumption of multiple regression, but some theories give rise to non-linear relationships. Micro-economic models and game theory which have become popular in political science often give rise to non-linear relationships.

Sometimes a non-linear relationship between an independent variable and the dependent variable is still linear in the parameters to be estimated, however. The parabolic relationship $Y = \mathrm{b}_0 + \mathrm{b}_1 X + \mathrm{b}_2 X^2$, for example, can be estimated using linear multiple regression analysis. The construct X^2 might be treated as an ordinary variable. Parabolic and cubic relationships are often used to model apparently non-linear relationships, when no precise theory with respect to the nature of the non-linear relationship is available. However, parabolic and cubic relationships, and polynomial relationships in general, often give rise to absurd predictions for values of the independent variables that were not included in the sample.

Sometimes a non-linear relationship between an independent variable and the dependent variable can be changed into a linear relationship by a numerical transformation of the variables. Exponential relationships are quite common in rational theories of economic, political and social conduct (e.g. Coleman, 1991). The exponential relationship

$$Y = \mathrm{b}_0 X_1^{\mathrm{b}_1} X_2^{\mathrm{b}_2},$$

known as the Cobb–Douglas production function in economics, for example, can be turned into the linear relationship $\ln(Y) = \mathrm{b}_0 + \mathrm{b}_1 \ln(X_1) + \mathrm{b}_2 \ln(X_2)$ by taking logs of the separate variables. Taking logs is also a standard device in comparative political science when the original variables are expressed as quantities, whereas the theory deals with relationships between percentage changes.

Unfortunately, it is impossible to transform all non-linear relationships into linear ones. The logistic relationship (the S-curve)

$$Y = \frac{1}{1 + \mathrm{e}^{-\mathrm{b}_0 - \mathrm{b}_1 X}}$$

which is often used to model the probability of binary events, is an example of a pure non-linear relationship. The logistic function is often used when the dependent variable has a lower and an upper bound, for example when the dependent variable is a probability (which varies by definition between 0 and 1).

Most statistical packages have a separate procedure for *logistic regression analysis*. Moreover they have more or less flexible procedures to model other types of non-linear relationships. Non-linear regression will not be treated here any further.

Unbiasedness and efficiency of regression estimates

In the mathematical statistician's thought experiment of an infinite number of samples from the same population, an estimate is said to be unbiased when on the average it hits the mark precisely. Ideally an estimate should be efficient also (remember Sections 5.6 and 5.7). Fortunately, ordinary least squares (OLS) estimates are unbiased and efficient indeed when the variables involved in regression analysis are distributed normally, and relationships between them are linear. The (fairly simple) mathematical statistician's proof of this conjunction, based on the maximum likelihood procedure, is beyond the scope of this book. Many other assumptions also lead to the conclusion that OLS estimates are unbiased and efficient. The general claim is that OLS estimates are robust against violations of normality assumptions.

There are some noteworthy exceptions, however. Nasty properties of the data which will render OLS estimates dubious or even simply mistaken will be discussed in this subsection. Four aspects of the data which give rise to biased or inefficient regression estimates will be discussed: outliers, multicollinearity, heteroscedasticity and autocorrelation:

- *Outliers* are single cases which have a disproportionate attraction on the slope of the regression line. Generally these cases have extreme values on the dependent or on the independent variables in the regression model. In the presence of outliers a regression coefficient does not tell a story about the majority of cases, but a story about a few outliers.
- *Multicollinearity* means that two or more independent variables are almost inextricable. Disentangling almost inextricable variables will result in regression estimates that depend on small residual variations in the variables which may well be measurement errors.
- *Heteroscedasticity* means that the residual variance is much larger for some values of the independent variable (e.g. for cases with high values on the independent variable) than for other values of the independent variable (e.g. for cases with low values).
- *Autocorrelation* arises often in the context of regression analysis with time periods as units. Autocorrelation entails that a failure to explain the state of the dependent variable at one point in time carries over into subsequent time periods. The residual from the regression equation at one point in time depends upon the residual at the previous point in time. The number of independent observations is in fact smaller than the number of time periods.

In Subsections 6.7.2.1, 6.7.2.2, 6.7.2.3 and 6.7.5 the nature of the problem, the diagnosis, and the solution to outliers, multicollinearity, heteroscedasticity and autocorrelation will be sketched.

6.7.2.1 The outlier problem

Outliers are single cases with extreme values which have a fatal attraction upon the regression slope coefficient. An *outlier* is a single case which affects the slope of the complete regression line disproportionately. An example is given in Figure 6.7. Six data-points (P1–P6) are plotted in the $x-y$ plane. Without case P6 the slope of the regression coefficient would be negative ($y = -x$), but with case P6 included the slope coefficient will turn positive ($y = +x$).

The concept of an outlier should be clearly distinguished from the concept of a large residual. From Figure 5.3 it is apparent that public expenditures of the Swiss national government cannot be accounted for by imports and exports only. Switzerland has a large negative residual. But Switzerland is not an outlier, since the slope of the regression coefficient is not affected heavily by the precise size of Switzerland's residual. In Figure 5.3 the slope of the regression coefficient is not determined completely by a single outlier.

Two problems concerning outliers should be distinguished. The first problem is an interpretation problem *given* the sample data. The story of Figure 6.7 is not to be told with one regression slope coefficient. Figure 6.7 suggests one story about the cases P1 through P5 and another story about the outlier P6. The second problem has to do with the statistical properties of regression estimates on the basis of a sample when the population holds outliers. The regression slope coefficient on the basis of a sample for a given population depends critically on the accidental inclusion or exclusion of outliers in the sample. To put it otherwise, regression

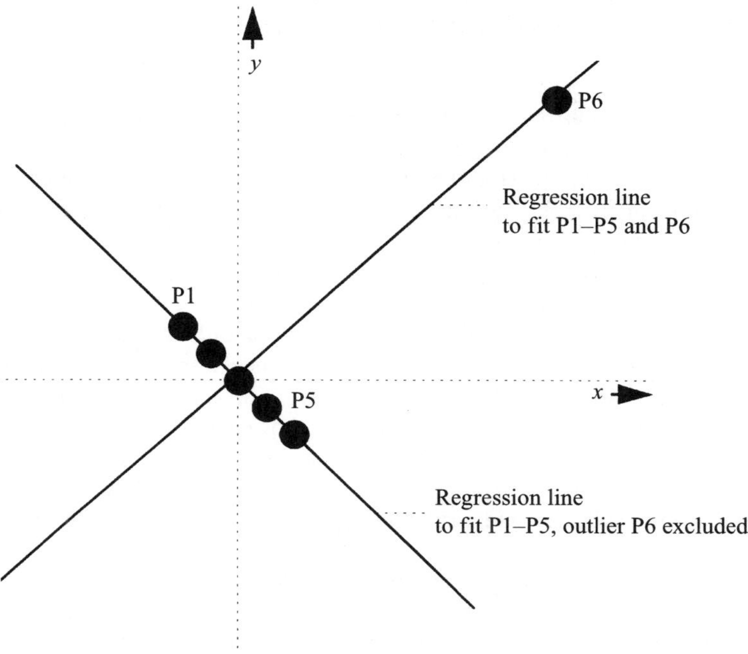

Figure 6.7 *Example of an outlier which changes the regression slope coefficient*

estimates on the basis of a sample will *not* be *robust* when extreme values both on the dependent and the independent variables are extant in the population. The choice of cases in a research design should warrant that the research results are not based on a few outliers.

Since outliers may influence regression coefficients enormously, the interpretation of regression parameters should be based on a careful analysis of outlier diagnostics. Especially in research based on small data bases, outliers are a potential source of serious misinterpretations. In larger data bases incidental outliers tend to cancel each other out.

DIAGNOSIS

With Figure 6.7 in mind as a typical example of an outlier, a visual inspection of bivariate and partial regression plots will give a first impression of whether outliers are present. Inspection of *partial* regression plots is necessary since, in multiple regression analysis, outliers can result from high correlations between the independent variables (*multicollinearity*, see 6.7.2.3).

Various measures have been suggested to quantify the influence of outliers on the regression slope coefficients. The simplest measure, DFBETA, is calculated for each case for each variable and for the constant in the regression equation as the difference between the regression prediction with and without the case included. Other measures such as Cook's distance are based on the DFBETA measure. The DFBETAs for the data from Figure 5.3 indicate that Belgium, Switzerland and Ireland have a disproportionate effect on the slope of the regression coefficient. Not a single case is strong enough to change the sign of the regression line, however.

SOLUTIONS

The therapy is less straightforward. One alternative is to develop an extended regression equation to model the outlier. Are the 'ordinary cases' and the 'outliers' both specimens of a more general theory when more variables are included? Inclusion of additional variables in regression models to increase model fit leads easily to fishing expeditions, however.

Dropping the outliers from the regression estimation is the appropriate solution when the aim of the regression analyst is to tell a story about the majority of cases and there is no plausible theory available to account for the outlier. Exclusion of an outlying case might also be a good solution when a closer inspection of the data with respect to that case suggests that measurement errors are at hand. The exclusion of outliers decreases the number of cases, however. The pretension that the ultimate story can be based on the remaining cases only may not be credible. The exclusion of outliers has to be accounted for in the research report, since research regression results depend critically on the inclusion or exclusion of outliers.

A technical alternative for dropping outliers completely is to create a dummy variable for each outlier with a 0 for all cases but a 1 for the outlier. The slope coefficient for such a dummy variable indicates the difference between the value of the outlier on the dependent variable and the prediction for the outlier produced by the regression equation based on the remaining cases. It indicates precisely how much the outlier is different from the remaining cases, but it does not provide an explanation of why this is the case. To fit the data from Figure 6.7, for example, one might create a dummy variable *DP6*. On this variable the value 0 is assigned to cases P1, P2, P3, P4 and P5, whereas the value 1 is assigned to case P6. The regression equation to produce a perfect fit would be $y = b_0 + b_1\ x + b_2\ DP6$. In comparative nation studies without a time dimension, a perfect fit can always be obtained by adding a separate dummy variable for all but one of the selected countries.

A rather different solution should be considered when one case or a few cases change the sign of the regression estimate. If this is the case then the relevant story to tell may be the story about the outliers as compared with the remaining cases, whose internal differences are uninteresting on further consideration. The argument for *maintaining the outliers* is that their story is theoretically interesting as compared with a story on the minor differences between the 'normal' cases.

6.7.2.2 Heteroscedasticity

Homoscedasticity and heteroscedasticity are antonyms that refer to the correspondence of the *spread* of residuals with the independent variables. If the residuals have a constant variance, regardless of the value of the independent variables, we call them homoscedastic; but if their variance is variable, we call them heteroscedastic. Dependence of the residual variance on the independent variables is termed *heteroscedasticity*. The type of heteroscedasticity depicted above occurs often when variables based on raw counts (e.g. receipts and expenditures; gross national product and military expenditures measured in dollars) are related to each other. Low corresponds always with low. But a high value on the independent variable is not sufficient, although necessary, to produce a high value on the dependent variable. Therefore the residual variance is low for low values of the independent variable, but high for high values. Heteroscedasticity impairs the efficiency of ordinary least squares estimators of the regression coefficients, but these coefficients are still unbiased.

DIAGNOSIS

A first means to trace heteroscedasticity is a visual inspection of bivariate and partial regression scatterplots. Most statistical packages offer the possibility to plot them. Heteroscedasticity is observed when the spread of the residuals increases or decreases with the values of the independent variables being plotted on the X-axis.

A generally accepted formal test is not available. When the residual variance is assumed to correspond linearly with an independent variable in the regression model, as in the examples given here, a split-half test on the basis of low and high values on this independent variable is often pursued. This popular split-half test is called the *Goldfield–Quandt* test. Two regression equations are estimated, one for values of X with a low residual variance and one for values of X with a high residual variance. Usually the group of cases with values beneath the median value of X is compared with cases having higher values on X. Heteroscedasticity is assumed when the two regression equations result in different explained variances according to the F-test to compare complete regression equations.

SOLUTIONS

What to do when heteroscedasticity is present? Often a necessary, but not a sufficient *cause* is at the heart of heteroscedasticity. The obvious solution would be to incorporate interaction terms in the regression equation to discriminate between cases in which the cause being considered thus far brings about the expected result and cases in which it is insufficient.

Transformations of the variables in the regression equation can reduce heteroscedasticity. Heteroscedasticity frequently occurs when the variables in the regression equation are based on counts (number of people, amount of money). Especially for high values of independent variables based on counts the residual variance of other variables based on counts tends to be high. Taking logs of the dependent and independent variables is an obvious device. Taking logs comes down theoretically to a substitution of a theory regarding relationships between pure counts by a theory regarding relationships between percentage changes. It is apparent from Figure 6.8 that taking logs will reduce heteroscedasticity. Another obvious means to avoid heteroscedasticity is to use *relative figures* instead of raw counts as variables. In the NIAS data base, for example, government expenditures are not expressed in US dollars, but as percentages of gross domestic product of a given nation in a given year. A disadvantage of the latter choice is that autonomous changes in the percentage base will affect the percentages. A sudden 'increase' in the percentage of public expenditures as a percentage of gross national product can be a result of a sudden economic recession which affects the economy negatively.

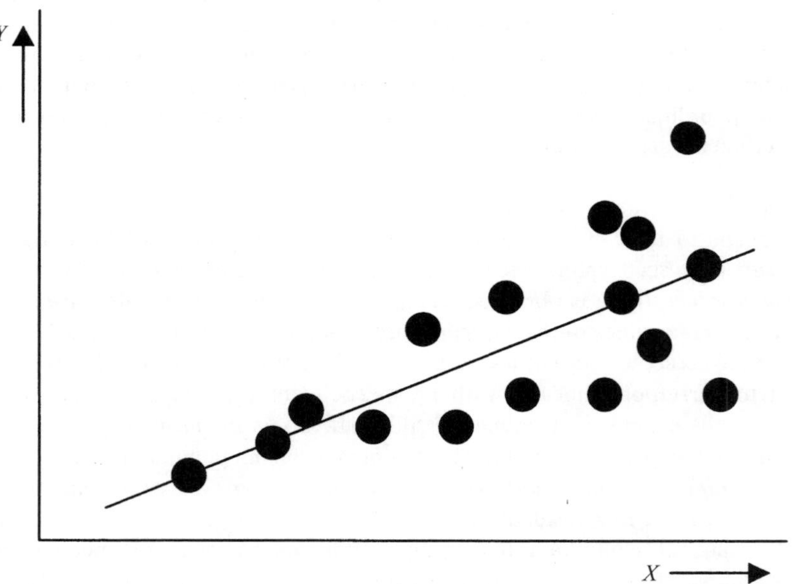

Figure 6.8 *Example of heteroscedasticity*

When theory-guided reduction of heteroscedasticity and even numerical transformations of the dependent variable do not work out, one of several advanced estimation techniques developed by econometricians to improve the efficiency of estimates might be applied. The most widely used technique is *Weighted Least Squares*. It is applicable when the residual variance is assumed to increase proportionally with the values of the independent variables in the regression equation. More advanced weighting procedures are available also (White, 1994: 209–217), but should be handled with care since these techniques are based on strong assumptions. They tend to produce quite chaotic results when regression analysis is based on a few cases only.

6.7.2.3 Multicollinearity

The aim of multiple regression analysis is precisely to unravel the effects of collinear variables. If the independent variables in a regression equation are completely independent of each other, then multiple regression analysis is redundant since it will show precisely the same regression coefficients as bivariate regression analysis. Multiple regression becomes worthwhile when the independent variables are collinear to a certain degree. Multicollinearity is the phenomenon of *highly* correlated independent variables. To understand why multicollinearity poses a problem, one should remember that a regression coefficient in multiple regression analysis is simply equal to the bivariate regression coefficient between the *residuals* from the dependent and the independent variable obtained by regressing the remaining independent variables on the dependent and the independent variable. If the independent variables in a regression equation correlate highly, then the variance of these residuals will become small compared with the variance of the original variables. Often the remaining residuals are simply a swarm of measurement errors. Modeling residuals which are really measurement errors will result in a chaotic pattern of regression coefficients. To put it differently, the standard errors of the estimates increase. They are *inefficient*, although still unbiased.

DIAGNOSIS

As a measure of dependence of one independent variable j on the remaining independent variables, R_j^2, the explained variance in the former due to the latter, can be computed. A widespread measure of multicollinearity is the tolerance. The *tolerance* is defined as one minus the explained variance in one independent variable j due to the other independent variables in the regression equation $(1 - R_j^2)$. If the tolerance of a variable amounts to 0.01, then the corresponding regression coefficient is based on only 1 per cent of the variance in the measured variable. Since most variables in political sciences have not been measured with such precision, regression coefficients based on such a low tolerance will usually be unacceptable. If measurement errors of 10 per cent or even 25 per cent are deemed possible, then variables in a regression equation with tolerances lower than 0.1 or 0.25, respectively, should be mistrusted. Table 6.6 can be used to interpret tolerance levels.

In economic research on stock quotations – which do not contain measurement

Table 6.6 *Diagnostics for multicollinearity*

Acceptable tolerance[a] (unexplained variance $1 - R_j^2$)	Corresponding variance due to remaining independent variables R_j^2	Acceptable correlation coefficient[b] among two independent variables r_{jk}
>0.50	<0.50	<0.71
>0.25	<0.75	<0.87
>0.10	<0.90	<0.95
>0.05	<0.95	<0.975
>0.01	<0.99	<0.995

[a]Rule of thumb: the accepted tolerance should be slightly larger than the proportion of the variance which is probably due to measurement errors.
[b]Upperbound of correlation coefficient corresponds only with bounds of other measures when only one pair of variables is highly correlated and the remaining independent variables are largely uncorrelated.

errors – multicollinearity poses no problem. In research based on data from official statistical agencies, tolerances below 0.05 or 0.10 may not be acceptable, since these data are not prone to measurement errors (although they may exhibit systematic biases). In survey research one would generally not accept tolerances below 0.25 or even 0.5, since respondents often interpret survey questions differently.

SOLUTIONS

Many remedies for unacceptably low tolerances can be considered. When two or more independent variables measure almost the same concept, then the least interesting variable from a theoretical point of view can be omitted. If the independent variables are actually indicators of one latent dimension, then one should construct one scale and enter this scale as the independent variable instead of the separate indicators.

But often the conclusion should be that the data at hand are simply insufficient to unravel the effects of the various independent variables. *Additional data* should be gathered (either cross-sectional, longitudinal or both) to ensure that the independent variables do not always coincide with each other. One may also gather more *refined data* with smaller measurement errors that will warrant the acceptance of lower tolerance levels.

6.7.3 Direct causes, intervening variables and antecedent variables

A political analyst using regression analysis for causal analysis may either assume that the interrelationships between the independent variables do not represent a causal ordering, or assume one specific causal order between the independent variables. One should realize that the technique does not assume by definition a causal order between the independent variables. In a causal diagram a curved, double-headed arrow is used to represent a non-causal relationship, whereas a straight single-headed arrow is used to represent a causal effect (see Figure 6.9). A variable has usually not only a direct effect but also *indirect* effects through

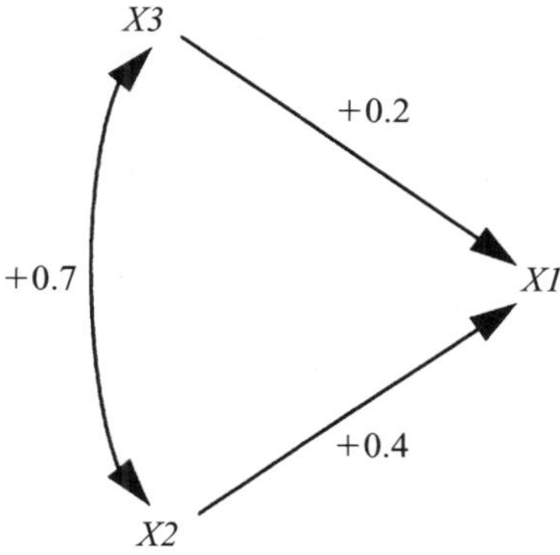

Curved arrow between *X3* and *X2*: impossible to compute indirect effect of *X3* on *X1*.

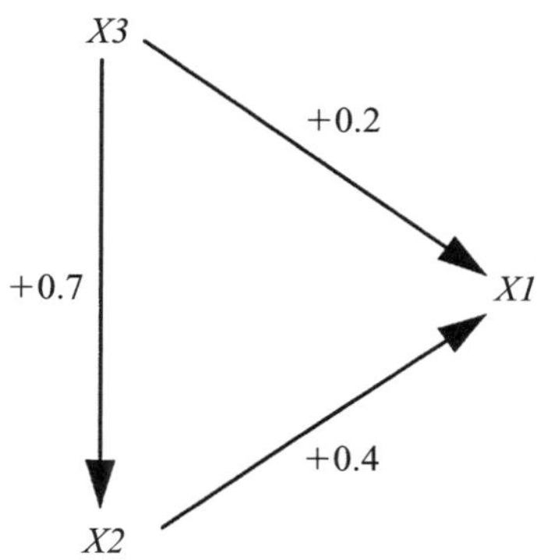

Straight arrow between *X3* and *X2*:
X3 is the antecedent variable,
X2 is the intervening variable.
Indirect effect of *X3* on *X1* amounts to +0.28;
total effect amounts to +0.20 + 0.28 = +0.48.

Figure 6.9 *Regression analysis and causal analysis*

intervening variables on the dependent variable. The size of an indirect effect is computed as the product of the regression coefficients belonging to the direct relationships which build up a causal path. The total effect is computed as the sum of all indirect effects and the direct effect. In Figure 6.9 this formula amounts to a total effect of *X3* on *X1* of $+0.2 + 0.4 \times 0.07 = 0.48$.

6.7.4 Interactions in the multivariate regression model: multicollinearity

An interaction refers to a conditional effect. The size of the effect of an independent variable *X1* on *Y* depends on the value of a third variable *X2*. To start the discussion we will first consider the case of a dichotomous interacting variable *X2* with values 0 and 1 (a binary, or dummy-variable).

As an example the relationship between the percentage of the population older than 65 (AGE65 in NIAS.SAV) and public expenditures as a percentage of gross domestic product (PE) is considered here. An ageing population will lead to high public expenditures since the elderly do not work anymore and consequently do not contribute to the gross domestic product. Moreover in welfare states the elderly are granted rights to receive pensions and health care, which require public expenditures. The precise relation may well depend on the electoral system. Party systems which are characterized by many different parties increase the chance that public expenditures are raised. Even the sheer existence of left-wing parties in these party systems will increase the chance that other parties will agree with higher public expenditures to accommodate low income groups. In proportional electoral systems at least one party will try to get the votes of the elderly. The sheer danger that such a party will become powerful will encourage other parties to accommodate the elderly also. In majoritarian electoral systems the chance that public expenditures are raised to meet the demands of the elderly is lower, since the two major parties will both have a strong incentive to promise lower taxes in order to accommodate a variety of electoral groups.

An interacting variable may influence the *slope* and/or the *intercept* of the regression line. If public expenditures in proportional systems are higher than those in majoritarian systems, regardless of the precise percentage of elderly, then only the intercept will be affected. If politicians are more sensitive to the percentage of elderly in proportional electoral systems, then the slope is affected.

Below, the general regression interaction model for two interacting independent variables is presented, together with the example discussed here.

$$Y = \mathrm{b}_0 + \mathrm{b}_1 X1 + \mathrm{b}_2 X2 + \mathrm{b}_3 X1X2 + \varepsilon$$

$$PE = \mathrm{b}_0 + \mathrm{b}_1 AGE65 + \mathrm{b}_2 PROP + \mathrm{b}_3 AGE65\ PROP + \varepsilon$$

In the case of a binary variable *X2* this regression equation is equivalent to two regression equations; one for cases with $X2 = 0$ and one for cases with $X2 = 1$. To obtain these two equations, one should fill in $X2 = 0$ and $X2 = 1$, respectively, in the equation presented above.

$$X2 = 0\colon\ Y = \mathrm{b}_0 + \mathrm{b}_1 X1 + \varepsilon$$

$$PE = \mathrm{b}_0 + \mathrm{b}_1 AGE65 + \varepsilon$$

$$X2 = 1\colon\ Y = (\mathrm{b}_0 + \mathrm{b}_2) + (\mathrm{b}_1 + \mathrm{b}_3) X1 + \varepsilon$$

$$PE = (\mathrm{b}_0 + \mathrm{b}_2) + (\mathrm{b}_1 + \mathrm{b}_3) AGE65 + \varepsilon$$

If coefficient b_2 is significant and positive, then a proportional electoral system (*X2*) has an effect on the intercept of the regression equation, indicating that politicians in proportional systems increase public expenditures more than do their colleagues in majoritarian systems. If b_3 is significant and positive, then a proportional electoral system (*X2*) has an effect on the slope. In proportional electoral systems politicians respond to an aging population with higher additional public expenditures than do their colleagues in majoritarian systems. First a binary variable *PROP* is to be computed. Semi-proportional electoral systems will be considered too as proportional ones in this subsection. The interaction term *PAGE65* is computed as the product of *PROP* and *AGE65*. This simplifies our equation to

$$PE = \mathrm{b}_0 + \mathrm{b}_1 AGE65 + \mathrm{b}_2 PROP + \mathrm{b}_3 PAGE65.$$

INTERACTION AND MULTICOLLINEARITY

The variables that are being multiplied to obtain an interaction term often correlate highly with the resulting interaction term. Multicollinearity easily comes in. In our example the correlation coefficient between *PAGE65* and *PROP* amounts to $r = +0.98$. Estimation of the regression equation above results in an unacceptably low tolerance of less than 0.05. The solution for the multicollinearity problem in regression analysis with interactive terms is to center the independent variables on zero before they are multiplied. The estimated regression coefficients will be based on the values of the transformed variables. They must be translated back to the values of the original variables to enable a substantive interpretation.

Let's continue our example. First the means of *PROP* and *AGE65* are computed (0.50 and 11.83, respectively). These means are subtracted from the original variables so as to obtain transformed variables *TPROP* and *TAGE65* with a zero mean. Next the interaction term *TPAGE65* is computed as their product, and the regression parameters are estimated.

$$PE = \mathrm{b}_0 + \mathrm{b}_1 TAGE65 + \mathrm{b}_2 TPROP + \mathrm{b}_3 TPAGE65$$

wherein: $TPROP = PROP - 0.50$; $TAGE65 = AGE65 - 11.63$; $TPAGE65 = TAGE65 \times TPROP$.

The test will be based on all country–year combinations in the NIAS data base with non-missing values for the variables ($n = 394$ nested country–year units of analysis). The regression equation expressed in the transformed variables now becomes:

$$PE = 40.72 + 2.24TAGE65 + 1.82TPROP + 0.77TPAGE65.$$

The correlation between *TPROP* and *TPAGE65* amounts to 0.42 only. The lowest tolerance is 0.70. Multicollinearity has vanished. By substituting $TAGE65 = AGE65 - 11.63$, $TPROP = PROP - 0.5$, and $TPAGE65 = (AGE65 - 11.63) \times (PROP - 0.5)$ the regression equation expressed in the original variables becomes:

$$PE = 20.05 + 1.86AGE65 + 10.78PROP + 0.77PAGE65.$$

The latter regression equation reduces to $PE = 20.05 + 1.86AGE65$ and to $PE = 30.83 + 2.63AGE65$ for non-proportional and proportional electoral systems, respectively. The intercept in proportional electoral systems is higher than in majoritarian systems, presumably since many minority groups are represented in parliament and compel higher public expenditures (10.78 per cent higher on the average). In non-proportional systems each percentage of elderly begets 1.86 per cent of the gross domestic product. In proportional electoral systems, where the minority of the elderly is more often represented, each percentage of the elderly begets 2.63 per cent. These percentages indicate that the electoral system determines to a large extent the degree to which public demands will be translated into public expenditures.

Thus, interaction in multiple regression analysis can be handled by entering the product of independent variables as an additional independent variable in the regression equation. To reduce the danger of multicollinearity the variables should be centered on zero. This procedure prevents us from underestimating the impact of interaction terms. The regression results must be translated back to the original variables to enable a meaningful interpretation. The procedure sketched here remains applicable when the interacting variable has an interval level of measurement. In the case of a dichotomous interacting variable, which was discussed here, the basic equation reduces to two regression equations, one for each value of the interacting variable. In the case of an interacting variable with interval level of measurement the original regression equation reduces to a multitude of regression equations, one for each value of the interacting variable.

6.7.5 Time series analysis: the autocorrelation problem

Time series analysis is ordinary regression analysis with points or periods in time as the units of analysis. The dependent variable y_t is measured at point t. Since it takes some time before effects come into place, the independent variables in time series analysis are often measured at earlier points in time than the dependent variable. Time series regression analysis is a powerful tool for causal analysis, since the temporal order of a cause and its consequence can be expressed with a time lag between the independent variables and the dependent variable. A typical regression equation for time series analysis would be:

$$y_t = \mathrm{b}_0 + \mathrm{b}_1 x_{t-1} + \mathrm{b}_2 z_{t-1} + \varepsilon_t$$

The availability of time series data allows one to construct an *autoregressive* model. The basic idea of an *autoregressive model* is that the current state of affairs y_t is dependent primarily on the state of affairs in the immediate past (y_{t-1}), although external influences (effects of x_t and z_t) and random shocks (ε_t) together with an autonomous trend (b_0) may sum up to a change.

$$y_t = \mathrm{b}_0 + \mathrm{b}_1 y_{t-1} + \mathrm{b}_2 x_t + \mathrm{b}_3 z_t + \varepsilon_t$$

The resulting R^2 from an autoregressive model is not to be compared with the R^2 in an 'ordinary' model. Especially when almost nothing changes compared with the previous point in time, the R^2 of an autoregressive model will be high, since a lack of changes (due to slowness of political changes and rigidities in political structures) will result by definition in a close correspondence between y_t and y_{t-1}. This contradicts the intuitive meaning of 'explained variance' of many political scientists.

Autocorrelation is defined as serial correlation between residuals. It occurs when the residuals in a given time period carry over into a later time period. First-order serial correlation is correlation between immediately successive points in time (between observations at time points t and $t-1$), e.g. when an overestimate in one year is likely to lead to an overestimate in the next year. False predictions for one point in time will result in false predictions for the next points in time. If autocorrelation is present, then it is misleading to think of the consecutive time points as *independent* observations. Autocorrelation implies that the number of independent observations is smaller than the number of time points. Whereas the computation of standard errors of regression estimates in OLS is based on the available number of time points, this computation should be based – less optimistically – on the (unknown) number of independent observations. In the presence of autocorrelation Ordinary Least Squares estimates of regression coefficients in non-autoregressive models are *inefficient*, although still *unbiased*. Autocorrelation in autoregressive models makes things even worse. Estimates will not only be inefficient but will be biased moreover.

Diagnosis

A straightforward diagnostic of first-order serial correlation would be the correlation coefficient $r_{t,t-1}$ between residuals in successive points in time. *Durbin–Watson's measure DW* is based on this serial correlation coefficient between residuals. It is roughly equal to $2 - 2r_{t,t-1}$. Since *DW* is roughly equal to $2 - 2r_{t,t-1}$ its value range is 0–4 instead of -1 to $+1$. $DW = 2$ corresponds with $r = 0$, $DW = 0$ with $r = +1$, and $DW = 4$ with $r = -1$. *DW* values in the neighborhood of 2 indicate the absence of autocorrelation. Durbin–Watson values are computed by most statistical packages, but usually it is still necessary to consult a table with *DW* values to find out whether a specific *DW* value indicates autocorrelation, no autocorrelation, or doubt given a specific number of time points as units of analysis and a given number of independent variables. Regrettably the *DW* tables have a region of doubt, in which it is undecided from a statistical point of view whether autocorrelation is present or not.

The formula of $r_{t,t-1}$ asks for separate standard deviations of ε_t and ε_{t-1}, however. In the *DW* formula ε_t is used as one single estimate of the standard deviation. The formula for Durbin–Watson's measure then reduces to:

$$DW = \frac{\sum_t (\varepsilon_t - \varepsilon_{t-1})^2}{\sum_t \varepsilon_t^2}$$

The Durbin–Watson DW test applies to non-autoregressive time series regression models, but should not be applied to autoregressive models. To indicate whether autocorrelation in the residuals from an autoregressive equation is absent, one should not use the ordinary Durbin–Watson test, but *Durbin's ħ-test*.

$$\text{Durbin's } \hbar = \left(1 - \frac{DW}{2}\right)\sqrt{\frac{n_t}{1 - n_t[\text{var}(\hat{\boldsymbol{\beta}}_{y_{t-1}})]}}$$

where

n_t = number of observations within the time series

DW = ordinary Durbin–Watson coefficient

$\text{var}(\hat{\boldsymbol{\beta}}_{y_{t-1}})$ = squared standard error of the OLS estimate of the regression coefficient of the lagged dependent variable

Some statistical packages, amongst others SPSS, will not report Durbin's $\hbar$, but these packages still have the facilities to compute the elements from which $\hbar$ can be computed according to its formula. To compute $\hbar$ one should first compute the ordinary Durbin–Watson *DW* and the (square of) the standard error of the OLS estimate of the regression coefficient of the lagged dependent variable. Durbin's $\hbar$ has a standard normal z-distribution. If the usual 5 per cent criterion is used, the assumption that serial autocorrelation is absent is tenable when $\hbar < 1.645$.

If Durbin's $\hbar$-test indicates that autocorrelation is present in an autoregressive regression equation estimated with Ordinary Least Squares, then the conclusion should be that Ordinary Least Squares should not have been used. One must resort to *generalized least squares* estimation procedures, which are beyond the scope of this book, but which are implemented in most statistical packages. Ordinary Least Squares estimates of regression coefficients can be used in autoregressive models, however, when Durbin's $\hbar$-test indicates the absence of autocorrelation.

Solutions: do not explain positions (states) but explain motions (changes) instead

An often-used, rather intuitive solution to obtain independent observations would be to diminish the number of time points in the regression analysis, for example by aggregating quarterly data to yearly data, or by aggregating yearly data to five years data, or by aggregating all time points before and after important historical events (e.g. Second World War, the 1973 oil crisis, the 1989 velvet revolution). Two procedures may be used: simply pick out one time point per period or smooth the data within each time period (for example by computing average values for each time period). This intuitive solution is flawed, however. Meaningful variation within the aggregated time spans is easily ignored. Moreover the periodization is often arbitrary, because each variable tends to have its own periodicity, its own rhythm of change. Here we will stick to solutions which retain all data points in the regression equation.

Let's first consider a non-autoregressive model which exhibits autocorrelation according to the DW test (*DW* far lower than 2). This indicates that the process being studied remains by and large in the same state as at the previous point in time. It may still be possible to explain changes, however. To explain changes relative to the status quo either a simple first-order-difference regression model or a more advanced autoregressive model should be used.

In the *first-order-difference model* the dependent variable is the change $Dy_t = y_t - y_{t-1}$ in y (the 'zero-order' dependent variable) compared with the preceding point in time. Regardless of the previous level y_{t-1}, Dy_t will become zero whenever

$y_t = y_{t-1}$. (The difference model $Dy_t = b_0 + b_2x_{t-1} + b_3z_{t-1} + \varepsilon_t$ is equivalent to a model $y_t = b_0 + b_1y_{t-1} + b_2x_{t-1} + b_3z_{t-1} + \varepsilon_t$ where b_1 is constrained to 1. In the latter formulation, y_t may be considered as the dependent variable, with y_{t-1} as an independent variable). A physical analogy may be helpful. In a first-order-difference model the motion of an object is the dependent variable, whereas in a zero-order model the position of an object is the dependent variable.

In an *autoregressive* model $y_t = b_0 + b_1y_{t-1} + b_2x_t + b_3z_t + \varepsilon_t$ the regression coefficient for the lagged dependent variable y_{t-1} is not constrained to 1, but empirically estimated. The autoregression coefficient b_1 gives information about what exactly is being influenced by the remaining independent variables. An empirical estimate of $b_1 = 0$ is equivalent to an ordinary regression model with y_t as the dependent variable. An estimate of $b_1 = 1$ is equivalent to the first-order-difference model. Empirical estimates of b_1 will often result in a value between 0 and 1. An estimate of $b_1 = \frac{1}{2}$ would indicate that the remaining independent variables in the model have an influence on $y_t - \frac{1}{2}y_{t-1}$.

To compare a non-autoregressive model ($b_1 = 0$), a first-difference model ($b_1 = 1$) and an autoregressive model (let's say with $b_1 = \frac{1}{2}$) it is helpful to think of the 'shocks' required from the remaining independent variables to keep y at an extreme high (or low) level. In a first-order-difference model a continuation of the shocks which brought about today's level of y_t is superfluous to preserve the status quo. For this reason a first-order-difference model is also known as a *random-walk* model. A random-walk process resembles a walker who time and again takes a step so as to keep a tail wind from the independent variables, regardless of where he came from or where he wants to go. He will stay where he is when it's dead calm. In a non-autoregressive model our walker will return home immediately once there's not a breath of wind. This property of a non-autoregressive model is known as regression towards the mean, which means that without continued external shocks the mean will be restored. An autoregressive model with an autoregressive parameter of 0.5 resembles a walker who returns half way home when the wind drops.

The solution for autocorrelation in an autoregressive regression equation (as indicated by Durbin's $\hbar$) or in a first-order difference model (as indicated by the ordinary DW-test) is subject to debate, both from a theoretical and from a statistical point of view. One solution would be to develop a second-order-difference model, which has as the dependent variable the rate of change of the change of the original dependent variable. A second-order model from physics would be a model with the *acceleration* of an object – rather than its position (zero order) or its motion (first order) – as the dependent variable. Second-order theories in political science are hardly available, however. A better alternative is possibly to use, instead of OLS, more advanced econometric estimation techniques which go beyond the scope of this book.

Example: public expenditures in France

A multiple regression analysis on the basis of cross-sectional data for 16 nations in 1988 revealed that public expenditures were dependent both on exports and imports and on the percentage of elderly. Here it will be tested whether time series data for France give rise to the same conclusion. Data on the relevant variables are available in the NIAS.SAV data base for the period 1965–1988 ($n = 24$ consecutive years). A preliminary question to be answered is how long it takes before changes in exports/imports and changes in the percentage of elderly amount to changes in public expenditures. What is the length of the time lags? Computation of the so-called *cross-correlation function* reveals for each lag of the independent variable what the correlation between the dependent and the independent variable is. Figure 6.10 exhibits a graphical representation of the cross-correlation function between openness of the economy on the one hand and public expenditures on the other. The horizontal axis displays a number of lags and leads of the independent variable IMEX2. The size of the correlation coefficient is plotted on the vertical axis. Figure 6.10 reveals that it takes the French government roughly two years to respond with public expenditures to the level of imports and exports. Correlation is highest when the independent variable IMEX2 is lagged with two years. The cross-correlation function between the percentage of elderly (65 years or older) and public expenditures (not displayed here) reveals that the French public expenditures respond to changes in the percentage of the population which is older than 65 years. To put it bluntly, it is not as much the people older than 65 years, but the people older than 70 years who are boosting public expenditures. The cross-correlation functions suggest that the following regression equation be tested:

$$PE_t = b_0 + b_1 IMEX2_{t-2} + b_2 AGE65_{t-5} + \varepsilon_t$$

The regression results are (t-values in brackets):

$$\underset{(-0.32)}{PE_t = -7.146} + \underset{(+1.96)}{0.818}\ IMEX2_{t-2} + \underset{(+1.24)}{2.812}\ AGE65_{t-5} + \varepsilon_t$$

$R^2 = 0.851$; $DW = 0.438$; $t = 1967–1988$ (1965 and 1966 missing due to lags)

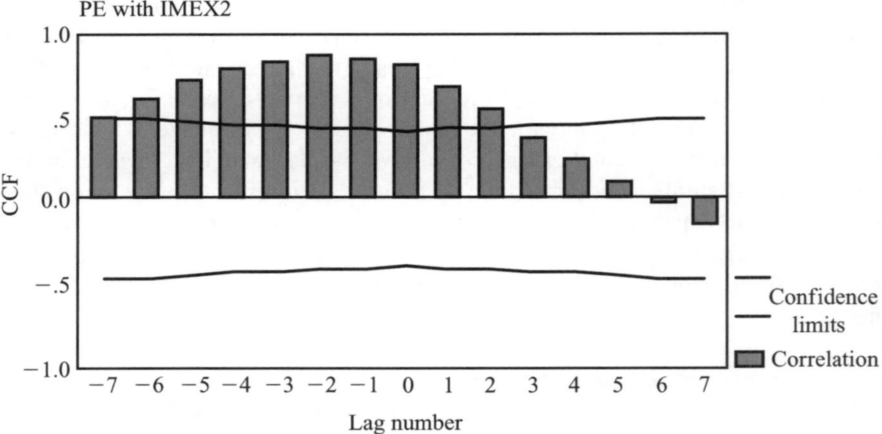

Figure 6.10 *Cross-correlation function for openness of economy (IMEX2) and public expenditure (PE)*

Table 6.7 shows the SPSS output with respect to the regression estimates. These results are confusing. On the one hand they seem to indicate that the theory is confirmed. The F-test for the regression equation as a whole (not printed here) reveals that a significant portion of public expenditures has been explained. The explained variance R^2 amounts to 0.851. The regression estimates suggest an even stronger relationship than the cross-sectional estimates (0.818 and 2.812 compared with 0.283 and 1.834, respectively).

The independent variables are fairly multicollinear in France, but since measurement errors in these macro-economic variables will be less than the tolerance (tolerance = 8.3 per cent), we will not concern ourselves with multicollinearity here. The regression coefficient for $IMEX_{t-2}$ is hardly significant (one-sided, $p_{H_0} \approx 0.064/2 = 0.032$) whereas the regression coefficient for $AGE65_{t-5}$ is insignificant ($p_{H_0} \approx 0.115$). Although the OLS regression estimates are still unbiased, the OLS standard errors, t-values and significance levels are completely meaningless, since the Durbin–Watson indicates serious autocorrelation ($DW = 0.438$; critical value $DW_{\text{Lowest}}(n = 24,\ k = 2) > 1.19$). It is misleading to think of the consecutive years as *independent* observations. The autocorrelation of the residuals implies that the observations are serially dependent.

A FIRST-ORDER-DIFFERENCE MODEL

An appealing procedure to get rid of most types of autocorrelation is to consider the first-order difference $dY_t = Y_t - Y_{t-1}$ as the dependent variable. A first-order-difference model is equivalent to an ordinary regression model with Y_t as the dependent variable and Y_{t-1} as an additional independent variable with a regression coefficient fixed to 1. One should realize that Y_{t-1} behaves as a pigeonhole for all structural long-term effects on Y_t. All effects on Y_t which were already incorporated in Y_{t-1} will be attributed to Y_{t-1}. Only effects which were not incorporated in Y_{t-1} will be attributed to exogeneous variables. A first-order-difference model is blind to cumulative long-term influences. It is not surprising therefore that the cross-correlation functions (CCFs) with the first-order difference dPE_t as the dependent variable reveal relatively short time lags. The CCFs suggest that yearly *changes* in public expenditures are primarily dependent on imports and exports in the preceding year and on the percentage of elderly two years before.

$$dPE_t = b_0 + b_1 IMEX2_{t-1} + b_2 AGE65_{t-2} + \varepsilon_t$$

The empirical results indicate that both regression coefficients are insignificant,

Table 6.7 *Public expenditures as a function of IMEX2 and AGE65 in France (OLS)*

	b (unstandardized)	Std error	beta (standardized)	t	Sig.	Tolerance
(Contstant)	−7.15	22.02	–	−0.32	7.49	–
IMEX2_2(2 lags)	0.82	0.42	0.57	1.96	0.06	0.08
AGE65_5(5 lags)	2.81	2.28	0.36	1.24	0.23	0.08

whereas the Durbin–Watson test still indicates autocorrelation. One simple reason is that short-term effects on public expenditures as a percentage of gross national product depend as much on public expenditures as on the development of gross national product. Economic growth (EG) will have a negative impact on public expenditures as a percentage of GNP when public expenditures remain constant. Therefore results will be discussed with respect to a regression equation with economic growth (EG) included. It is expected that the regression coefficient of economic growth is negative.

$$dPE_t = \mathrm{b}_0 + \mathrm{b}_1 IMEX2_{t-1} + \mathrm{b}_2 AGE65_{t-2} + \mathrm{b}_3 EG_t + \varepsilon_t$$

The regression estimates are presented below, with t-values in brackets.

$$\begin{aligned} dPE_t = {} & -5.91 - 0.394 IMEX2_{t-1} + 1.257 AGE65_{t-2} - 0.731 EG_t + \varepsilon_t \\ & (-0.81)(-3.04) \qquad (+1.82) \qquad (-4.90) \end{aligned}$$

$$R^2 = 0.599;\ DW = 1.73;\ t = 1966\text{–}1989\ (n = 24)$$

The Durbin–Watson test now indicates that autocorrelation is absent (critical value $DW_{\text{highest}}(n = 24,\ k = 3) > 1.66$). The regression coefficients of economic growth (negative) and the percentage of elderly (positive) are in the expected direction. The regression estimate of imports and exports is in the wrong direction, however. Whereas the correlation coefficient between $IMEX2_{t-1}$ and dPE_t amounted to $+0.29$, the regression coefficient is -0.394. Multicollinearity between imports and exports on the one hand and economic growth on the other ($r = -0.82$; tolerance $= 0.12$) is the technical reason for this negative regression coefficient. Doubt with respect to these results has the upper hand.

A FIRST-ORDER AUTOREGRESSIVE MODEL

An equivalent first-order autoregressive model (only the first-order lag of the dependent variable included as an independent variable) to the first-order difference model which was tested above is:

$$PE_t = \mathrm{b}_0 + \mathrm{b}_1 IMEX2_{t-1} + \mathrm{b}_2 AGE65_{t-2} + \mathrm{b}_3 EG_t + \mathrm{b}_4 PE_{t-1} + \varepsilon_t$$

The regression results indicate, however, that $IMEX2_{t-1}$ and $AGE65_{t-2}$ are insignificant. $IMEX2_{t-1}$ becomes significant only when EG_t is dropped, but even then $AGE65_{t-2}$ remains insignificant. After dropping the insignificant variables the following regression equation remains:

$$\begin{aligned} PE_t = {} & 4.01 \quad + 0.392 IMEX2_{t-1} + 0.748 PE_{t-1} + \varepsilon_t \\ & (+2.79) \qquad (+5.07) \qquad (+14.30) \end{aligned}$$

$$R^2 = 0.979;\ DW = 1.106;\ n = 24;$$

$$\text{standard error } PE_{t-1} = 0.0773;\ \text{thus Durbin's } \hbar = 1.051$$

The regression results indicate that two variables leave only 2 per cent of the variance in public expenditures unexplained. The regression coefficient of $IMEX2_{t-1}$ has the expected sign. Its magnitude exceeds the cross-sectional regression coefficient (0.283, Table 6.5). Public expenditures will increase by 0.39 per cent when imports and exports increase by 1 per cent. Durbin's $\hbar$ indicates that there is no significant autocorrelation left (since 1.051 is far less than the critical z-value 1.645). The ordinary DW-test is not appropriate in autoregressive models. The DW-test would have rendered a false conclusion! The main conclusion, however, remains that Katzenstein's hypothesis has survived another test. States increase public expenditures when exports and imports are increasing.

EPILOGUE

Time series data are a perfect means to assess the causal order, because of their temporal order. Therefore they are superior to cross-sectional models. The example discussed here is fairly typical of the difficulties one encounters when regression analysis is applied to the fairly short time series which are the rule rather than an exception in political science, however. The regression models based on the original variables typically suffer from the autocorrelation defect. Difference models and/or autoregressive models will usually cure the autocorrelation disease, but difference and autoregressive models are usually not robust. At least three origins of this lack of robustness can be mentioned.

Autoregressive models will usually leave only a small portion of the variance in the dependent variable unexplained. Exogeneous influences are hard to verify when the remaining unexplained variance is small, especially when measurement errors are present.

A second reason why autoregressive models and difference models often fail to retrieve the obvious is their fixation on short-term changes. Long-term shocks in exogeneous variables which have already influenced the lagged dependent variable will not be attributed to exogeneous variables but to the endogeneous lagged dependent variable. In the last decades *error correction models*, or *co-integration models*, have been developed to account for long-term effects of exogeneous variables, without introducing autocorrelation once more. These models will be left aside here.

The third, but primary reason, is simply the limited number of time points. Data on 25 consecutive years is almost nothing, especially when autocorrelation is present. Twenty-five years may shrink to 5 'independent' years when most years are almost perfect copies of their predecessors. Data on short time series cursed with autocorrelation are compatible with many simplistic rivaling theories, but they are simply insufficient to estimate the parameters of any complex theory. Data on post-war France, for example, are not only compatible with Katzenstein's simple theory on the crucial role of exports and imports; they are compatible with simple rivaling theories too. They are also compatible with the bivariate hypotheses that public expenditures rose due to demands of the working classes which were converted into strikes (variable NRSTRIKE), or due to demands for welfare expenditures in the party programs of the ruling party (GVT_WLF2), or due to the percentage of elderly (AGE65), or due to a disappointing economic growth (EG).

Time series data for post-war France are insufficient, however, to estimate with any precision which combination of variables was responsible for public expenditures. One way out of the data misery in time series analysis is to test elaborated theories for many time series simultaneously, which brings us to the topic of the next section.

6.7.6 Pooled time series analysis: autocorrelation and heteroscedasticity

The advantages of time series analysis for political science are its possibilities to assess the time dependency of causal relationships. Often the data available do mount up to short time series only (e.g. 40 points in time or even less). More often than not various plausible models will account for the data on such a short time series. One way out is to increase the quantity of the data used for testing.

Pooled time series analysis combines time series for several cross-sections. The data are stacked by cross-section and time points. The NIAS data base that is used in many examples in this book, for example, is a pooled time series data base of 828 units stacked by 18 countries over 46 years. Instead of studying the effects through time of various variables on public expenditures in each country, these effects may be studied for a number of countries simultaneously. Instead of testing a time series model for one country using time series data, or testing a cross-sectional model for all countries at one point in time, a pooled time series model is tested for all countries through time. Much more refined tests of theories will become possible, since the available units of analysis increase from T (number of time points) to NT (number of cross-sections times number of times points). Pooled time series analysis captures not only variation that emerges through time, but variation across different cross-sections as well.

Regrettably, pooled time series analysis has a serious drawback also. Since pooled time series analysis is still time series analysis, the problem of *autocorrelation* must still be dealt with. But in addition to autocorrelation per cross-section, heteroscedasticy between cross-sections comes in. Heteroscedasticity will usually arise because the appropriate models for the various cross-sections will not be precisely identical. Therefore a model to explain all cross-sections will usually do better for some than for others, which amounts to unequal variances of the residuals for the cross-sections (which is heteroscedasticity by definition). The tendencies which led to higher public expenditures in the 1970s manifested themselves in all capitalist countries. Nevertheless the precise effect of an increasing percentage of elderly on public expenditures may depend on polity variables such as the electoral system, and on policy and legislation with respect to health care technology, health care insurances and pensions for the elderly. If one model is tested for all cross-sections at all time points, then heteroscedasticity comes in, since the residuals for 'extreme' countries will be large compared with the residuals for mainstream countries.

The combination of autocorrelation and heteroscedasticity in sample data may result in extremely inefficient, although unbiased, estimates of the true population parameters.

Diagnosis of heteroscedasticity and autocorrelation in pooled time series data

The diagnosis of autocorrelation and heteroscedasticity in pooled time series analysis is fairly straightforward, although statistical software packages are usually not ideally suited for its implementation.

The degree of heteroscedasticity due to pooling, e.g. unequal residual variances per cross-section, is to be obtained by examining the residuals of the pooled model per cross-section. A sequence plot of the residuals for the various cross-sections (comparable to Figure 5.4) will give a first visual impression. Ideally the average of the residuals within each cross-section should be equal to zero. If an inspection of the sequence plot suggests that the mean residual varies from cross-section to cross-section then the conclusion should be that crucial variables that explain the differences between cross-sections (regardless of the precise time point being looked at) are still lacking.

A simple diagnostic test on the robustness of the pooled model is to run the same model on its residuals for each cross-section through time, and on its residuals for each time unit over cross-sections. If the same model holds for all cross-sections and all time points, then the pooled model will not be able to explain its own residuals split up by cross-section and time unit. Thus, for a regression model tested on 80 units stacked by 8 cross-sections over 10 years, $8 + 10$ regressions should be performed on the residuals from the pooled model. The model should not be able to explain significant proportions of the variance within its own residuals in more than 5 per cent of the cases. Thus, the pooled model from our example should not be able to produce significant regression estimates within its own residuals in more than four time units or cross-sections. If the model is able to explain additional variance in its own residuals for a large number of time units or cross-sections (more than four in our example) then the suspicion should be that the original model does not hold for all cross-sections and time-units equally well.

A proper diagnosis of autocorrelation in pooled time series analysis is cumbersome, because of its statistical relatedness with cross-sectional heteroscedasticity. If there is cross-sectional heteroscedasticity there will be autocorrelation almost by definition: if the prediction for the complete cross-section is wrong, then the mispredictions for each of its successive time points will be serially correlated. Model improvements to reduce the cross-sectional heteroscedasticity will therefore usually also diminish autocorrelation. Durbin–Watson's *DW* and Durbin's $\hbar$ can serve as diagnostics, when these measures are computed for all cross-sections simultaneously. One technical warning is probably not superfluous: the lag of the first time point for a specific cross-section is missing (and not equal to the last time point for the preceding cross-section in the data file). It is a pitfall to rely on autocorrelation diagnostics per time series. Precisely because the separate time series in pooled time series analysis are too short, Durbin–Watson tests per cross-section produce chaotic results.

Solutions

The solutions to the problems raised by pooled time series analysis might be divided into two groups. The first group of solutions is directed at the improvement of the models to fit pooled time series data. The second group of solutions is directed at the development of statistical estimation procedures to improve on OLS deficiencies when a combination of autocorrelation and heteroscedasticity is present.

Let's start with model improvements to get rid of heteroscedasticity between cross-sections. When the mean of the residuals for one or more specific cross-sections is unequal to zero, then one should add variables to the model so as better to explain these cross-sectional differences.

A non-theoretical model to get rid of heteroscedasticity between cross-sections completely would be to add one dummy variable to the model for each cross-section, except one. This model is called the Least Squares Fixed Dummy Variable Model in the jargon of pooled time series analysis. A more advanced variant would be to assume that each cross-section has a randomly distributed intercept associated with it (the Random Coefficients Model). We would advise against these non-theoretical solutions, since a-theoretical dummies and random intercepts that are added to a regression model will usually be collinear with some variables of theoretical interest. The explanatory power of the variables of theoretical interest will easily get obscured. It is far better to include a few variables which account for the major differences between the cross-sections, than to include every separate cross-section (except one) as a dummy-variable. The Least Squares Fixed Dummy Variable Model and the Random Coefficients model should be used only when the available theory gives no clues at all with respect to differences between processes in the cross-sections being studied.

To get rid of serial autocorrelation the same model ramifications (first-order-difference model, autoregressive model) should be considered as in ordinary time series analysis.

A rather different question is which estimation technique should be used when autocorrelation and heteroscedasticity have not been banned completely. How to deal with the fact that OLS estimates will be inefficient; that is to say, with the fact that they will usually underestimate the standard errors of the regression estimates? Econometricians have proposed various estimation techniques for this purpose. The most widely applied is the Parks–Kmenta method, a specimen of the Generalized Least Squares family of estimation techniques (White, 1994: 245–254). These estimation techniques guarantee that the estimates asymptotically hit the mark. They are unbiased when sample sizes draw near infinity. Recently Beck and Katz (1995) have shown that the Parks–Kmenta estimation technique produces quite chaotic results when time series are as short as in comparative political science (usually less than 50 years per cross-section). Katz and Beck showed also that Ordinary Least Squares estimates of regression coefficients are more robust than Parks–Kmenta estimates when sample sizes are small. Katz and Beck have developed a formula to compute *panel corrected standard errors* which encompass autocorrelation and heteroscedasticity in the computation of the standard errors of the OLS-regression estimates. An SPSS-macro using the matrix language of SPSS is available from the authors' website.

Example

In the epilogue from the section on time series analysis the conclusion was that time series data for France were insufficient to distinguish between rival theories. It was impossible to decide whether the level of public expenditures in France was due to the level of imports and exports, to the percentage of elderly in need of social support and health care, to economic decline, to the number of strikes, or to the emphasis on welfare provisions in the party programs of governing parties. The same research question can be asked for all countries. For twelve countries the NIAS.SAV data file contains data with respect to the variables mentioned above for the period 1971–1988 (18 years), namely for France, Sweden, Norway, Denmark, the Netherlands, Italy, Germany, Great Britain, Ireland, the USA, Canada and Australia. The number of units of analysis amounts to $12 \times 18 = 216$ units of years stacked within nations.

A preliminary analysis of lag structures using the CCF (cross-correlation function) procedure from SPSS reveals that the relationship between strikes and public expenditures is a complex one. Cross-correlations with various time lags for various countries amount to the conclusion that the hypothesis that strikes are a cause of higher public expenditure and not a consequence of lower public expenditure is not clearly supported. Therefore we will postpone the apparently reciprocal relationship between strikes and public expenditures until the next subsection and will not delve into it further here. The influence of strikes on public expenditures will not be included in the pooled time series model. The cross-correlations indicate also that the time lags involved for the other independent variables differ for the twelve countries being investigated. For the pool of twelve nations the best assumption to make seems to be that there are no time lags at all. On average the variables investigated here seem to have an immediate effect on public expenditures in these twelve nations.

The first model to be tested considers the level of public expenditures as the dependent variable. As a first model all the variables IMEX (imports and exports), AGE65 (percentage of the population older than 64 years), EG (economic growth) and GVT_WLF2 (percentage of party programs of governing parties devoted to welfare state provisions) are entered into the regression equation. By a 'backwards' procedure all variables not significant at the 5 per cent level are dropped from the equation, starting with the most insignificant one. The results of statistical testing based on the appropriate Panel Corrected Standard Errors (Beck and Katz, 1995) are compared with OLS Standard Errors in the output of the SPSS-macro PCSE (available from the authors' website) as shown in Figure 6.11. The results show that OLS Standard Errors and Panel Corrected Standard Errors amount to almost identical results. The dependence of public expenditures on each of the four variables examined is statistically significant at the 5 per cent level. Imports and exports, economic decline, the percentage of elderly and leftist party programs explain almost three quarters of the variance in the level of public expenditures in the twelve countries ($R^2_{adj} = 0.73$).

As was to be expected from the notion that the level of public expenditures is fairly rigid, a model with the level of public expenditures as the dependent variable gives rise to severe autocorrelation in the residuals. The DW and Durbin $\hbar$ statistics – which are computed by the PCSE-macro due to the RESID = 1 option – show autocorrelation in the residuals from the specified model ($DW < 1$;

OLS

	mse	R2	R2 adj	F	df1	df2	sig F
PE	4.4625	.7368	.7318	147.6470	4	211	.0000

	b	beta	se	T	sig T
IEØ	.1840	.5588	.0130	14.1229	.0000
AGØ	1.7485	.4641	.1450	12.0618	.0000
EGØ	−.6086	−.1571	.1394	−4.3666	.0000
GVT_WLF2	.1472	.0978	.0633	2.3255	.0210
const	12.8483	.0000	1.9582	6.5612	.0000

- - - - - - - - - - Panel Corrected Standard Errors

n total: 216
n cross: 12
n time: 18
n vars: 5

Dep: PE

PCSE

	mse	R2	R2 adj	F	df1	df2	sig F
PE	4.4625	.7368	.7318	147.6470	4	211	.0000

PC_SE

	b	beta	pc_se	T	sig T
IEØ	.1840	.5588	.0094	19.4796	.0000
AGØ	1.7485	.4641	.1264	13.8315	.0000
EGØ	−.6086	−.1571	.1555	−3.9136	.0001
GVT_WLF2	.1472	.0978	.0692	2.1284	.0345
const	12.8483	.0000	1.8576	6.9165	.0000

Figure 6.11 *SPSS-macro output for Panel Corrected Standard Errors, no autoregression*

Durbin's $\hbar > 1.645$). This raises some doubt about whether the independent variables tap only cross-sectional variation but do not explain also the changes in public expenditures as compared with the previous year. Therefore an autoregression model is tested with, as independent variables, the same variables plus the lagged dependent variable. Entering the lagged dependent variable as an independent variable in the regression model has the advantage that independent variables really have to explain short-term shifts in order to become significant. They will tend to reduce the autocorrelation within residuals. But one should keep in mind that the lagged dependent variable catches all the long-term effects of slowly operating variables, such as party programs and a growing percentage of the elderly also. Since autoregressive models will attribute long-term effects of exogeneous variables to the lagged dependent variable, they will underestimate long-term effects of exogeneous variables.

The results given in Figure 6.12 show that even an autoregressive model exhibits the influence of an economic decline on rising public expenditures. The influence of higher exports and imports and leftist party programs have borderline significance: the likelihood that they do not have an influence on changes in public expenditures is less than 7 per cent (two-sided test; less than 3.5 per cent in a one-sided test). The explained variance amounts to 97 per cent. This figure may seem impressive, but one should remember that for an autoregressive model a high explained variance merely indicates that the current public expenditures can be predicted fairly well on the basis of last year's public expenditures.

An inspection of Durbin's $\hbar$ statistics indicates that, for most countries, no significant autocorrelation in the residuals remains. But for Germany, Denmark and the United Kingdom the correlation between changes in public expenditures in successive years is still not accounted for completely by the twelve-countries model. One may wish to create additional country-specific models to explain the remaining 3 per cent residual variance for Germany, Denmark and the United Kingdom. Here we will not pursue such an analysis.

PCSE

	mse	R2	R2 adj	F	df1	df2	sig F
PE	1.5590	.9679	.9671	1265.3666	5	210	.0000

PC_SE

	b	beta	pc_se	T	sig T
LPE	.9072	.9099	.0221	41.1328	.0000
IEØ	.0140	.0426	.0072	1.9590	.0514
EGØ	−.4540	−.1172	.0547	−8.2966	.0000
GVT_WLF2	.0519	.0345	.0280	1.8509	.0656
const	4.5812	.0000	.8228	5.5681	.0000

Smalldw, for each time series: no_cross dw dh

11.00	1.56	.93	Sweden
12.00	1.31	1.47	Norway
13.00	1.03	2.06	Denmark
22.00	1.53	.99	the Netherlands
31.00	1.13	1.84	France
32.00	1.29	1.51	Italy
41.00	.56	3.07	Germany
51.00	.97	2.20	United Kingdom
53.00	1.32	1.45	Ireland
61.00	1.28	1.53	United States
62.00	1.41	1.25	Canada
63.00	1.32	1.45	Australia

Figure 6.12 *SPSS-macro output for Panel Corrected Standard Errors, autoregressive model*

6.7.7 Reciprocal causal relations: linear structural equation models

Thus far we have limited ourselves to unidirectional causal relations. Reciprocal relations might be expected, amongst others, when political actors interact with each other, and action–reaction spirals come into being. Two types of action–reaction spirals can be distinguished: the positive feedback loop and the negative feedback loop. An arms race is an example of a positive feedback loop. An increase in A's armaments will lead B to increase its armaments, which will evoke A to do the same, and so on. A *positive feedback loop* between A and B will result in a high correlation between A and B, which is easily misconceived as a strong unidirectional causal relationship.

Negative feedbacks underlie cybernetics. A negative feedback loop exists when a behavior of A will cause B to produce signals that reverse A's behavior which caused B's signals. As an example we have touched on the relationships between strikes of employees and government expenditures. Strikes of employees are often followed by higher public expenditures, which may appease employees and reduce strike activity. A *negative feedback loop* between A and B will result in a low correlation between A and B that is easily misconceived as the absence of a relationship between A and B.

Diagnosis

The first important thing to realize is that reciprocality within the relationship between two variables is not identifiable when the analysis is restricted to two variables. Additional data are required with respect to variables which influence one of these two reciprocally related variables, but not the other. The standard example comes from the field of political socialization. The two partners in a married couple may be assumed to influence each other reciprocally. It is impossible to decide who influences whom most strongly if we only know that both partners have identical political preferences at the present time. But if we know that the husband shares the political preferences of the parents of his wife, whereas his wife does not share the political preferences of the parents of the husband, then we may safely conclude that the husband did not influence his wife. It is more likely that the wife influenced the husband; at least, the data are compatible with the latter hypothesis. The presumptions of this reasoning are visualized in the path diagram of Figure 6.13. It is assumed that the convictions from one's parental home do not automatically dictate one's partner's current convictions. The only way to carry over one's tender sympathies onto the belief system of one's partner is through the direct exercise of influence during matrimony.

Ordinary regression analysis (OLS) is not suited to estimating the strength of reciprocal relationships. Since A influences B, which exerts again an influence on A, ad infinitum, the total influence of A on B in Figure 6.13 is not a, as in regression analysis, but $a + aba + ababa + abababa + \ldots$ which sums up to $a/(1 - ab)$ in the case of a negative feedback according to the high-school formula for the sum of an infinite geometrical row. Statistical packages such as LISREL, AMOS, EQN, GAUSS RATS, S PLUS or SHAZAM which implement more

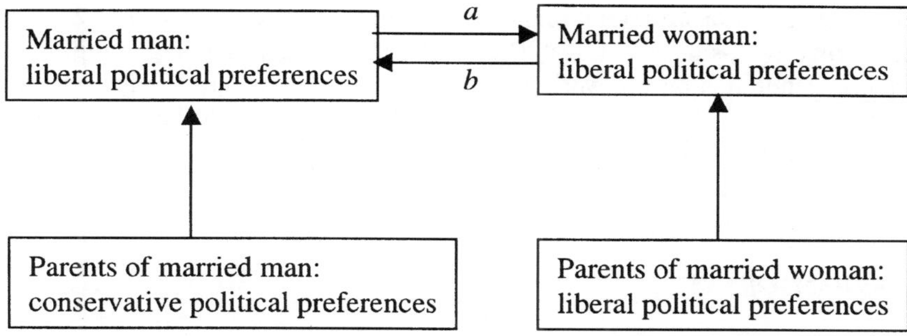

Compatible with hypothesis that $b > a$ (woman influences man).

Figure 6.13 *Tracing reciprocal influence*

general estimation techniques (generalized least squares, maximum likelihood based on normality assumptions) can be used to estimate such reciprocal relationships. These techniques are beyond the scope of this book.

Example

The causal relationship between strikes and public expenditures is probably not a unidirectional one. Strikes may lead to government expenditures (positive relationship), since the strikers will demand social services and provision that will amount to higher public expenditures. But higher public expenditures will probably appease the workers (negative feedback). No urgent necessity to strike will remain.

To assess the reciprocal relationship, equivalents of the political preferences of the parents of the man and woman in a married couple have to be found. Obvious candidates are the number of strikes at a previous point in time and the level of public expenditures at a previous point in time.

Figure 6.14 represents the LISREL-estimates of standardized effects. The

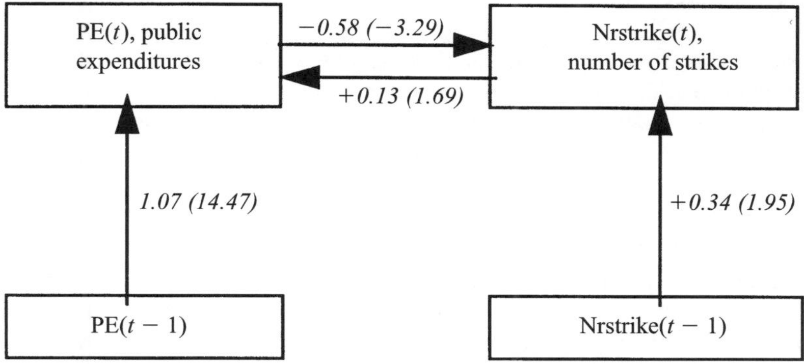

Figure 6.14 *Reciprocal effects of strikes and public expenditures in France ($n = 23$ years). Time-adjusted goodness-of-fit index = 0.88; $\chi^2 = 0.53$(df = 1, model probability = 0.47)*

numbers between brackets represent t-values ($n = 23$ years, $df = n - 2 = 21$, critical t-value (one-sided) $= 1.72$). The results indicate that the appeasing effect of public expenditures on the working class is the strongest effect. Rising public expenditures do result in a decrease of the number of strikes. Strikes have only a small, borderline insignificant effect on higher public expenditures ($t = 1.69$, critical value $t > 1.72$).

6.8 EPILOGUE

This chapter fits somewhere between the elementary, bivariate methods of data analysis that were discussed in Chapter 5, on the one hand, and the advanced methods of data analysis that dominate political science journals, on the other. The discussion aimed at an assessment of the applicability of intermediately advanced methods in comparative political science. Almost no attention has been given in this chapter to the statistical properties of the estimators used or to the mathematical background of the methods. No use was made of matrix algebra to set out the essentials of population parameters and their estimators concisely. The reader who uses this book as a stepping stone to read monographs and specialized research articles with respect to the methods discussed here will still face a hard task. But the reader should have acquired an overview of the type of methods available to analyze available data with respect to political systems from a comparative point of view. The next chapters will set these methods to work in comparative political science research.

6.9 ENDMATTER

Topics highlighted

- Causality: a likelihood above mere chance that a dependent variable will change in a specific direction when the independent variable changes in a certain direction.
- Case-oriented analysis: the analysis is aimed at a complete, non-statistical, description of relationships for a relatively limited number of cases.
- Variable-oriented analysis: the analysis is aimed at a summative, statistical description of the relationships among a relatively limited number of variables for a huge number of cases.
- Basic techniques of quantitative hypothesis testing: cross table analysis (dependent and independent variables have a nominal level of measurement), discriminant analysis (dependent variable nominal, independent variables interval or higher), analysis of variance (dependent variable has an interval level of measurement, independent variables interval or higher) and regression analysis (both dependent and independent variables have interval levels of measurement).
- Assumptions of regression analysis: linear relationships, no outliers, no multicollinearity, homoscedasticity, no autocorrelation of residuals.

Exercises

1. *Cross table elaboration*. The relationship between macro-economic policy (POP) and electoral system (ELSYS, recode semi-proportional systems to proportional ones first) depends partly on the economic tide. Does it depend also on the position of the parties in government on a left–right scale? If so, what is the nature of the dependency (intervention, exogeneous variable, interaction effect?). Use the NIAS.SAV data base to find an empirical answer. As a first step dichotomize the variable GVT_LR (or alternatively the variable GVT_WLF2) around its median.
2. *Discriminant analysis*. Perform an explorative discriminant analysis to find out which policy objectives of governments (as measured on the basis of the party manifestoes of the parties in government, variables GVT_LR, GVT_WLF2 and so on) are predictive of the type of macro-economic-policy (variable POP). As a first step select the years 1970 (before the oil crisis of 1973), 1977 (after the oil crisis) and 1984 (during the economic recession).
3. *Analysis of variance*. Perform an analysis of variance to find out how the level of public expenditures (PE) depends on the nominal variables 'electoral system' (ELSYS, recode semi-proportional systems to proportional ones first) and the type of government coalition (TOGORI), and on the interaction between these variables.
4. *Interaction in regression analysis*. Test whether the political color of the government (GVT_LR or GVT_WLF2) is an interacting variable in the apparent relationship between the percentage of imports and exports (variable IMEX) and public expenditures (PE). Do leftist governments respond more readily with higher expenditures to higher imports and exports. As a first step dichotomize the variable GVT_LR (or alternatively the variable GVT_WLF2) around its median.
5. *Time series analysis*. Test whether the conclusions for France in the subsection on autocorrelation (6.7.5) hold also for Germany and the USA. If not, how can one explain public expenditures in these two countries?
6. *Pooled time series*. Test whether government expenditures on social security as a percentage of public expenditures depend on the same variables as public expenditures according to Subsection 6.7.6.

Further Reading

- *General*: case study: Yin, 1996; case-oriented approach: Ragin, 1987; variable-oriented approach: Tacq, 1997.
- *Regression analysis, general*: Fox, 1997; Berndt, 1996; Greene, 1997.
- *Special issues in regression analysis*: regression assumptions: Berry, 1993; Fox, 1991; Interaction in regression: Jaccard et al., 1990; time series analysis: Greene, 1997; pooled time series analysis: Sayrs, 1989; Beck and Katz, 1995.

Part III

DOING POLITICAL RESEARCH

Introduction to Part III: Doing political research

This part focuses on the application of the methods and statistics that are discussed in the previous chapters: the '3 × P' designs (Chapter 1), the comparative methods (Chapter 2), the choices underlying Research Designs (Chapter 3) and, of course, the statistical techniques which are discussed in Chapters 4 to 6.

We do not pretend to cover the whole but a specific selection of central themes in political science. The themes are related to the politics of problem solving in post-war democracies. We focus on socio-economic problems as they are central in the concerns of the public, the parties and governments in modern democracies (see Keman, 1997).

The way problems tend to be solved is cyclic: problems get on the agenda, parties and governments present (partial) solutions, and the effectiveness of these solutions is again potentially relevant for the political agenda. Hence we follow the well-known Easton model; however, we attempt to fully specify it (see Figure III.1). We have divided this process into three parts that correspond to the input–throughput–output–outcomes mechanisms of the political systems, as follows.

Chapter 7 concentrates on input-related variables. *Problems arise* when there is a growing awareness of certain problems: the media are covering them, politicians are concerned about them, the public is alerted, interest groups are demonstrating. In sum, the problem is being put on the political agenda. The problem is now in the hands of politicians. Political parties are mandated by the voters to find solutions on the basis of their programmatic profiles (Klingemann et al., 1994).

Chapter 8 discusses research on the throughput side of the process. *Decisions are made* by political parties. The way parties handle problems is determined by their ideology but also by the institutional environment in which they are functioning. For example, the party system, federalism, presidentialism, corporatism are patterned institutions that shape the room for maneuver within which parties are operating and thus how politics is made.

Chapter 9 discusses the output side of the process. *The way problems are solved*, or the effectiveness of the solutions, is a complex mixture of actor-related and institutional factors. Problems are rarely completely solved, but there are variations in the degree to which problems are solved, or come back on the agenda. We will search for the factors that may explain these variations. In other words, the focus is on the material performance of political systems (Heywood, 1997).

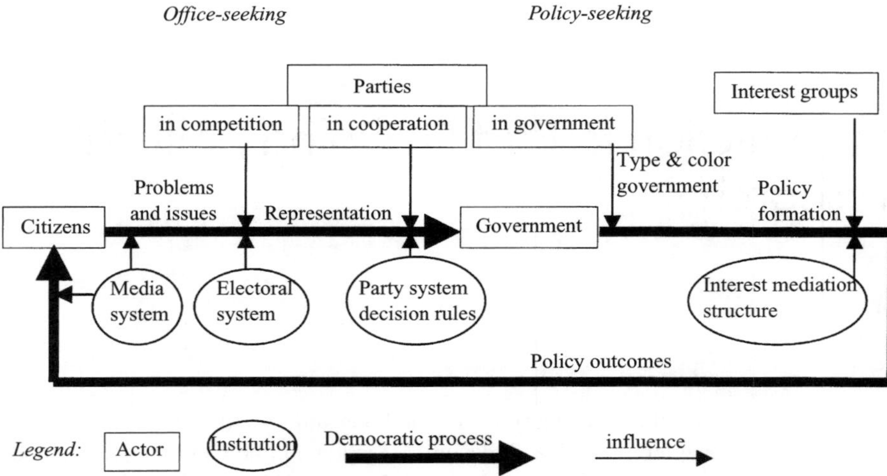

Figure III.1 *The chain of democratic control and command*

The cyclic process of the politics of problem solving can be understood with the help of the so-called 'Chain of Democratic Control and Command' (Chapters 1 and 2 in this book). This chain represents an overall schematic and descriptive overview of the role that political actors like parties play in the democratic process. This cyclic process is a 'bottom up' model. Research results suggest that problems on the political agenda have a profound influence on journalists, and problems discussed in the media have a major impact on the problem awareness of citizens. In the following chapters, however, we will not focus on these 'top down' influences.

Some basic assumptions on the role of parties in the democratic process are visualized in this scheme:

- Parties play *crucial* roles in the selection of problems that need to be solved and the transmission of preferences into decision making. Hence, they are what is commonly called gatekeepers.
- Parties play *institutionalized* roles: institutions provide the room to maneuver that parties can utilize in order to fulfill their democratic role. The type of electoral system and party system, for example, shapes the opportunities for policy formation.
- Parties play *differential* roles in the democratic process: these roles are competitive in relation to voters and cooperative in relation to government formation and functioning due to the institutional design within which parties operate – in particular in case of coalition government or of divided government (Weaver and Rockman, 1993).
- Parties play *reciprocal roles* in the democratic process, which is of a cyclic nature in the sense that the output/outcomes or material performance matter for the (re)newed inputs which in turn direct subsequent outputs/outcomes.

In sum, this part basically provides three things:

1 an overview of specific research methods and strategies that are relevant and basic for comparative political analysis;
2 a relatively easy access to data and techniques in this field to perform comparative political analysis and enable the student to do it on his or her own by developing a Research Question of his or her interest;
3 practical exercises and examples that stimulate the understanding of complex forms of analysis.

As our examples are a selection and presented in a summarized fashion, we provide additional references that may help students to get a deeper theoretical insight into the themes that are discussed. Generally speaking, we have tried to give a thorough overview of the theoretical background of the fields of research.
The techniques that are used in this part are more fully explained in Part II:

- factor analysis (Subsection 4.5.3)
- scalability analysis (Section 4.5)
- cross tabulation (Section 6.4)
- correlational analysis (Subsection 5.4.2)
- analysis of variance (Subsection 5.5.2)
- discriminant analysis (Subsection 6.5.1)
- multiple linear regression analysis (Section 6.7)
- time series analysis (Section 6.7)
- boolean analysis (Section 6.3)
- cluster analysis (Subsection 4.5.7)

These techniques are fairly representative of the techniques that are frequently used in quantitative political science.

Most of the data are made available so that students can replicate any (part of an) analysis and adjust elements of it (see the file methstat.zip that can be downloaded on http://welcome.to/PaulPennings). These data are related to a selection of modern classics in political science, among which are for example *An Economic Theory of Democracy* (Downs, 1957); *Parties and Party Systems* (Sartori, 1976); *The Rise and Decline of Nations* (Olson, 1982); *Democracies. Patterns of Majoritarian and Consensus Government in Twenty-One Countries* (Lijphart, 1984); *Ideology, Strategy and Party Change* (Budge et al., 1987); *Identity, Competition and Electoral Availability* (Bartolini and Mair, 1990); *Minority Government and Majority Rule* (Strom, 1990b); *The Comparative Political Economy of the Welfare State* (Janoski and Hicks, 1994).

In order to exemplify the working of the Chain of Political Control and Political Command we have decided to use socio-economic policy as the main field of policy. In addition, we also use electoral data, democracy scales, data on international conflicts and peace (COPDAB) and public opinion data. Exercises will stimulate and direct students to practice the techniques. The emphasis is really on *doing* political research in order to get a better understanding of the problem-solving capacities of political parties within the institutional context of modern democracies. We assume that the reader has read the preceding chapters before reading this part. Without doing so, this part is only accessible for advanced students in political science who have completed their basic courses on statistics.

Finally a few *practical hints* for the use of this part. In most cases the following steps can help students to get a practical understanding of the techniques that are involved.

1 Replicate the SPSS mode of analysis on the data presented in the chapter.
2 Study the SPSS output. Study the SPSS Manual in order to get additional information about the statistics in the output. This extra information is indispensable for a correct understanding of the often elaborate output that is not fully discussed in the following chapters.
3 Try to grasp the decisions that underlie the analysis that are presented in the book based on the nexus Research Design, Research Question, Research Answer as discussed in Part I.
4 Attempt to formulate at least one additional hypothesis which you wish to test.
5 Alter the presented analysis by adding, merging or recoding variables on the basis of the new hypotheses.
6 Check if the assumptions for the analysis are not violated.
7 Write a short paper in which the steps and results of the new analysis are presented in a correct way.
8 Let students present the results of their own analysis to the class, followed by a discussion.

One helpful key-text for the general conceptual background of the chapters is provided by *A New Handbook of Political Science* (Goodin and Klingemann, 1996). The methodological concerns are largely covered by *Comparative Policy Research: Learning from Experience* (Dierkes et al., 1987).

7 How problems arise

CONTENTS

7.1 PROCESSES OF ELECTORAL CHANGE

7.1.1 The problem of change

This chapter examines the trends in voting behavior and preferences and shifts in party priorities and subsequent consequences for the political agenda. The shifting preferences of voters and parties are important for a correct understanding of why and how certain problems get on the political agenda and other problems do not, i.e. how societal problems become political ones. Both descriptive and explanatory research strategies will be utilized in this chapter by means of time series data on the preferences of voters (electoral data) and the preferences of parties (manifesto data based on the coding of the main party manifestoes of post-war democracies).

Electoral change affects the relationships between the three main actors in the democratic process: voters, parties and governments. In this chapter we will focus on voters and parties. Chapter 8 will also include governments. Countries in a given time period serve as the units of analysis since ultimately it is countries that are being compared. Parties are often the unit of measurement, as the data on seats and votes are linked to political parties.

Several forms of change are to be distinguished that stress different dimensions of changing relationships between parties and voters and among parties. We distinguish several types of indicators that can be used to measure, model and classify electoral change (see Chapters 1 and 4) – in most cases countries are the units of analysis and parties are the units of observation:

- party system indicators, e.g. the number of (effective) parties according to the Herfindahl index (see Subsection 5.1.2); this indicator distinguishes between types of party systems, such as two- and multi-party systems;
- electoral system indicators such as the fragmentation of seats and votes that distinguish between systems that are more or less proportional;
- volatility indicators, such as the *block volatility* (measuring electoral gains or losses of party blocks and families within a system) and *total volatility* (the net electoral change between consecutive elections); these are commonly used indicators to distinguish between more and less stable systems;
- party organizational indicators (e.g. the number of party members, party finance) and party–voter indicators (such as party identification); these are often used to distinguish between systems with a high and low potential for change.

These different types of electoral change are caused by sudden events (regime collapse, earthquake elections) and also by more enduring factors like dissolving cleavage structures, such as the waning of religion or the emergence of post-materialism (Inglehart, 1990). Electoral change can be limited to one party system

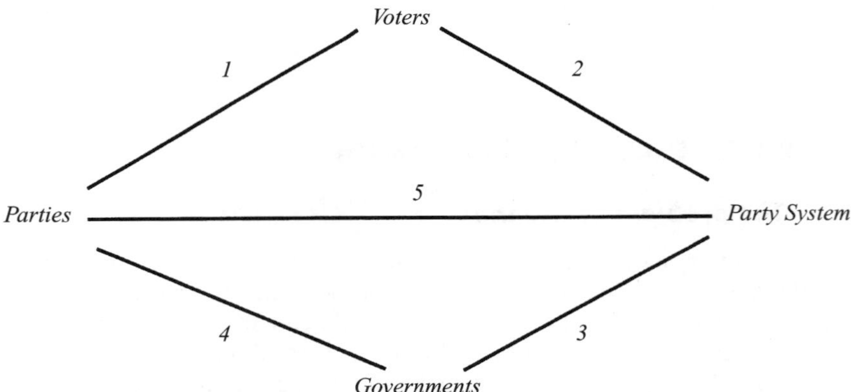

Figure 7.1 *Party systems and electoral change: 1, voter–party relationship (changing voter preferences evoke electoral change); 2, voter–party-system relationship (mediated by the electoral system); 3, party-system–government relationship (affects type and color of government); 4, party–government relationship (parties are in or out of government); 5, party–party-system relationship (affects party competition)*

component (the so-called restricted party system change) or can have a more enduring impact on all party system components (the so-called party system transformation). Figure 7.1 shows how party systems and electoral change are interrelated.

Figure 7.1 shows that electoral change does not only affect the party–voter relationship, but has also potential consequences for the type and composition of government and the functioning of the party system. The indicators of electoral change that are mentioned above are devised to analyze the (inter)relationships which are shown in Figure 7.1.

In this chapter we will discuss examples of the measurement of electoral change (especially volatility) (7.1.2.), the regression modeling of electoral change (7.1.3), the comparison of the expert and Manifesto left–right scales plus scalability analysis (7.2.2), factor analysis and regression analysis on party emphasis and the calculation of median voter positions (7.2.3 and 7.2.4). These sections will introduce the main aspects of contemporary empirical research on processes of electoral and party change. The accompanying exercises will deepen these insights and encourage reporting of this type of empirical research in a paper.

7.1.2 Measuring electoral change

In Chapter 4 we discussed the problems that are involved with measuring. This section focuses on one specific measurement problem, namely how to measure the degree and nature of electoral change. In *Identity, Competition and Electoral Availability* Stefano Bartolini and Peter Mair analyze the levels of electoral stability in western Europe. Their ultimate concern is to account for variance in electoral stability/instability (the dependent variable) which is defined as the degree of electoral change between elections. Among the independent variables are electoral disproportionality (how votes are translated into seats), voter turnout, the number of parties contesting election, policy distance between parties and their ideological difference, societal segmentation, issue saliency, cleavages, party membership rates and trade union density (Bartolini and Mair, 1990: Part IV).

Most prominent in the study of Bartolini and Mair is the total volatility (or system volatility): that is, volatility measured at the level of the individual party and summed up for the party system as a whole (the so-called 'total net electoral interchange'). The volatility measures are suited to comparative political analysis because they enable us to analyze electoral change in any selection of time points and countries and also to link the empirical analysis to the theory on party systems and cleavage structures. Although there are more indicators of electoral change, such as those based on election surveys, these alternative indicators are only available for a limited number of time points and countries.

The formula for total volatility is:

$$TV = \frac{|PiV| + |PjV| + |PkV| + \cdots |PnV|}{2}$$

where TV = total volatility; $|PiV|$ = the absolute vote share of party i.

The formula divides the sum of the individual *party volatilities* by 2 in order to avoid a double counting of the same electoral shifts: if one party loses 5 per cent of the votes and the other parties win 5 per cent in total, the net volatility is 5 per cent and not 10 per cent. The theoretical range of values runs from 0 (no change) to 100 (maximum change). The empirical (or actual) range is in reality much smaller and varies per political system (or 'polity') and per period. This is clearly shown by Figure 7.2, which presents the mean volatility rates in thirteen western European democracies. The graph indicates that the 1950s and the 1970s are (in total) characterized by a more volatile trend and the 1960s and the 1980s by a less volatile trend. This confirms the hypothesized cyclical nature of electoral change. The graph also shows that there are significant country differences: some countries are consistently unstable (i.e. a high level) (France), others are consistently stable (i.e. a low level) (Austria and Switzerland), whereas other countries vary in stability over time (Norway and Sweden). The differences can also be shown by using a descriptive statistics module.

The same index of total volatility can also be based on change at the level of blocks of parties – what Bartolini and Mair call the *block volatility*. A 'block' of parties can be a party family, or it can refer to other distinctive groups of parties such as left and right, new and old, opposition and government parties etc. Block volatility is more directly linked to the policy-making process than is total volatility: when the vote share of the liberal or conservative block goes up significantly we expect a more restrictive type of policy making. Such a hypothesis could not be

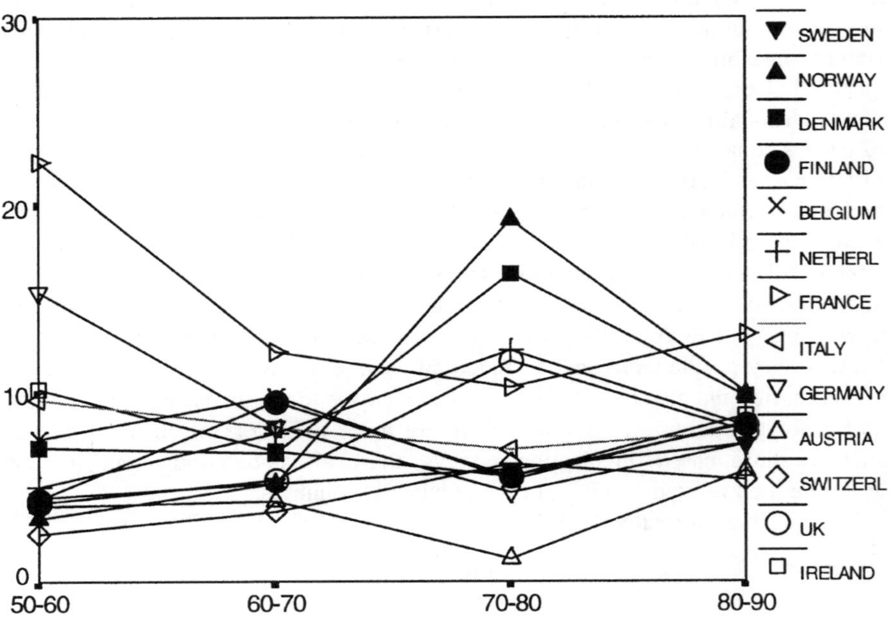

Figure 7.2 *Total volatility in Europe (trends)*

made solely on the basis of a rise (or decline) of total volatility. Block volatility is formalized as follows:

$$BV = \frac{|P(iV + jV + kV)| + |P(lV + mV + nV)|}{2}$$

where BV = block volatility, Pi = party i, V = votes.

Figure 7.3 shows the development of the block volatility of social democrats and Christian democrats compared with liberals and protest parties in the post-war period ($n = 13$ European countries). Figure 7.3 clearly demonstrates that block volatility is mostly cyclical in nature: no relevant party group is only winning or losing in all the subsequent election years. In most cases parties are moving to or from a winning or losing position. The winning of one party group always involves the electoral backlash of one or more other groups. In this particular case we see that the winning blocks of parties share a common property. If this property is ideology we speak of *party families*. Whereas the block volatility measures the electoral interchange between blocks of parties, the *within-block volatility* (WBV) measures the interchange within blocks. The WBV formula sums up the total of party net changes which have an algebraic sign contrary to that of the block as a whole. The total volatility is in fact the additive index of both scores. Concrete examples of how the measures are calculated are given in Figure 7.4. The figure shows the situation of two party blocks (e.g. a left and a right block), each with three parties (A, B, C and D, E, F). On the basis of the party volatility scores it is possible to compute the block volatility (BV), the total volatility (TV) and the within-block volatility (WBV).

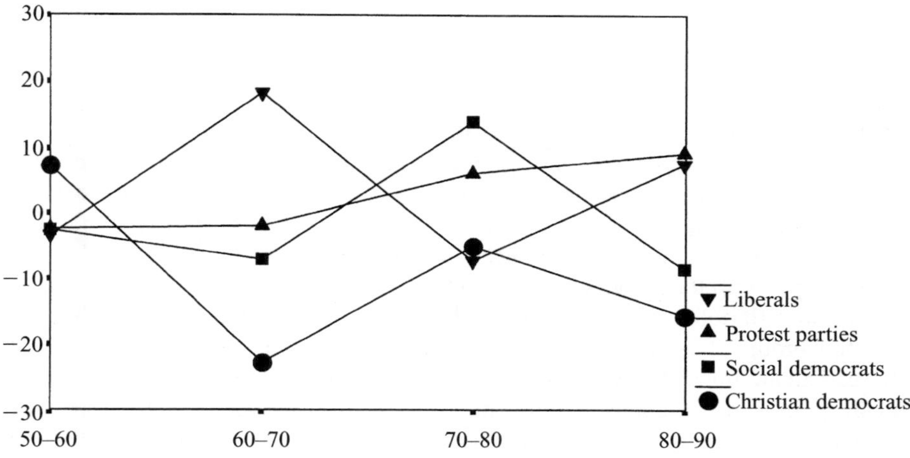

Note: n = 151 election years in 13 European countries

Figure 7.3 *Block volatility in Europe*

$$
\begin{array}{l}
Blocks = \underbrace{A \quad B \quad C}_{1} \qquad \underbrace{D \quad E \quad F}_{2} \\
PV = +6 \;\; -2 \;\; -1 \qquad -5 \;\; -2 \;\; +4 \\
BV = \dfrac{|(+6-2-1)| + |(-5-2+4)|}{2} = 3 \\
TV = \dfrac{|+6| + |-2| + |-1| + |-5| + |-2| + |+4|}{2} = 10 \\
WBV = |-2| + |-1| + |+4| = 7 \quad (10-3)
\end{array}
$$

Total volatility=Block Volatility + Within-Block Volatility
Legend: PV=Party Volatility, BV=Block Volatility, TV=Total Volatility, WBV=Within Block Volatility.

Figure 7.4 *Examples of the calculation of volatility scores (Bartolini and Mair, 1990: 24)*

In this section we have focused on total and block volatility. It has been shown that it is important to decompose overall trends into periods and categories and not to trust averages that may well hide relevant variations. Total volatility and block volatility are crucial measures for the study of party behavior. Total volatility is an indicator of the degree of electoral instability of party systems. Block volatility indicates the electoral strength of blocks, which has implications for the office- and policy-related room to maneuver of political parties. There are, of course, more indicators of electoral change. Some of these other indicators, like the effective number of parties, disproportionality, convergence etc. will be discussed in Chapter 8. In general, these indicators may help us to spot variations in electoral and party behavior and also help to dispel certain generalizations or even certain myths on supposedly universal trends in party behavior, such as overall convergence or catch-all-ism (i.e. the attempts to transgress the socio-economic and cultural cleavages among the electorate in order to attract a broader audience; see: Krouwel, 1998).

7.1.3 Modeling change

In Chapter 4 the processes of measuring and modeling were presented as two complementary research activities. The modeling of electoral change appears as a necessary and logical step after we have measured electoral change by means of various volatility indicators. We again follow the arguments of Bartolini and Mair who apply the multiple regression technique that is explained in Section 6.7. In its most simple form the model looks like Figure 7.5.

The way Bartolini and Mair model electoral change is linked to the 'theory–method problem' as discussed in Chapter 1 and can be seen as theory-guided Research Questions. As we are basically interested in the system level, the conceptualizations and operationalizations are directed to this level. In some cases the operationalizations of systemic variables (meaning: part of a system) are based upon individual behavior, which clearly confronts us with the problem of data aggregation as explained in Chapter 3.

The variables shown in Figure 7.5 are related to actors (such as electoral participation), institutions (such as change in electoral institutions) and the

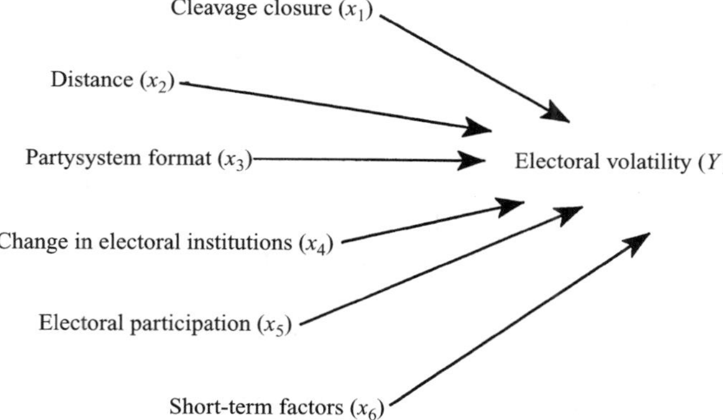

Figure 7.5 *Determinants of electoral instability: x_1 to x_6 are the independent variables selected by Bartolini and Mair (1990)*

systemic features of democratic polities (such as cleavage closure) and they are all potential sources of aggregate volatility. Bartolini and Mair describe these as (1990: 37–40):

- *Cleavage-closure*: cleavages are enduring dividing lines in a society based on socio-economic or socio-cultural divisions like class, religion, language or ethnical differences. Societies with a distinct cleavage structure are called plural or fragmented. In systems where cleavages do not produce a full closure of relationships, there is a higher chance of electoral mobility. Bartolini and Mair restrict their analysis to one important cleavage in mass politics: namely the class cleavage, more specifically the class-left block volatility, being the aggregate block volatility of left parties. This measure is used to test the Lipset–Rokkan 'freezing hypothesis' which states that the cleavage structure did not fundamentally change (remained 'frozen') since it came into existence in the 19th and the beginning of the 20th century (Lipset and Rokkan, 1967).
- *Policy distance*: in case of small distances between parties we expect more electoral volatility as party switches by voters are made easier. These distances are measured in several ways which will be shown in Subsection 7.2.2.
- *Party system format* is operationalized as the number of effective parties. The more options are offered to the voter, the more voters will change their vote from election to election.
- *Change in electoral institutions* affects the structure of opportunities for the electorate at large and modifies the preference rankings of individual voters. These changes have a legal-institutional origin. Bartolini and Mair refer to the enfranchisement of new sectors of the population, a new electoral law, the introduction or abandonment of compulsory voting, and variations in the disproportionality potential (meaning the disproportionality between votes and seats) in different systems.

- *Electoral participation*: changes in the level of electoral participation (rather than the levels as such) are assumed to increase electoral volatility, especially in cases where former non-voters add substantially to the pre-existing active electorate.
- *Short-term factors* refer to contingent factors like specific salient issues, the appeal of individual candidates and exceptional and unforeseen events, e.g. scandals during the political campaign. These factors do change from election to election, and their occurrence and impact are highly unpredictable.

The basic underlying assumption of the model (as in all models) is that the variance in total volatility will be significant to the extent that it is possible to disentangle the *relative* weight of the different components indicated in Figure 7.5. The assumption is justified only if the model is well specified, meaning that it is neither underspecified (i.e. missing significant relationships that are commonly assumed in the literature) nor overspecified (i.e. including too many relationships and that the model becomes too detailed and descriptive). The inclusion of the actor-related, institutional and systemic variables into the model indicates that it presents an encompassing schematic overview of relevant independent variables.

Table 7.1 is an initial scheme based on theoretical considerations and it is not yet quite suited for regression analysis. In a step-by-step analysis the factors are analyzed and sometimes abandoned if their effect can be largely attributed to the mediating effects of other variables (Bartolini and Mair, 1990: 279). The remaining independent variables are then combined into a set of more general indices. The regression analysis is based on a simplified (parsimonious) model of the determinants of electoral instability which incorporates the individual variables into the broader socio-political phenomena of which they are part.

Figure 7.6 shows the results of the regression analysis that are reported by Bartolini and Mair ($n = 231$ election years in 13 European democracies in the period 1918–1985). The explained variance is 44.6 per cent. Apart from the short-term factors they find moderate betas (lower than 0.35) in case of the direct effects of the institutional incentives (i.e. the party system format and institutional change) and socio-organizational bonds (i.e. cultural segmentation plus organizational density). The amount of variation which is not explained by the model is assigned to the short-term factors. These factors turn out to be potentially crucial for the explanation of electoral instability.

Table 7.1 *Aggregated categories in the Bartolini and Mair model*

Determinant	Variables
Institutional change	Occurrences of franchise elections plus occurrences of changes in the electoral system
Cultural segmentation	Ethno-linguistic plus religious heterogeneity
Organizational density	Party-membership rate plus trade union density
Party-system format	Number of political parties

Source: Bartolini and Mair, 1990: 280.

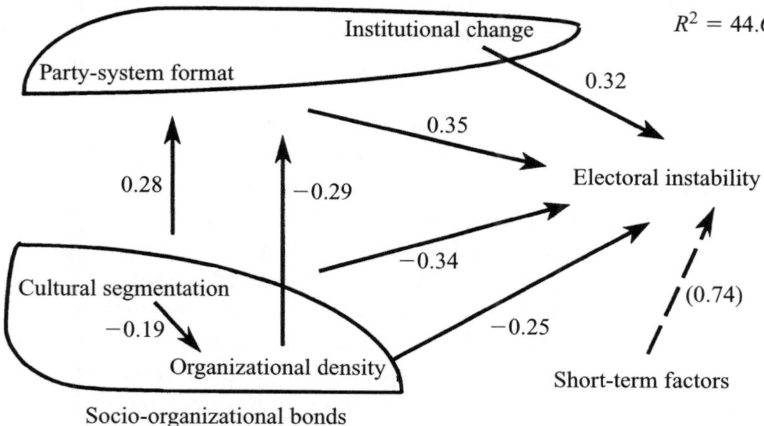

Figure 7.6 *Bartolini and Mair's final causal model. Source: Bartolini and Mair (1990: 282); n = 231 election years in 13 European democracies in the period 1918–1985*

The black-box character of the Bartolini and Mair model is invoked by the relatively strong effects of the unknown short-term factors. Although Bartolini and Mair are correct in stating that an exact measurement and modeling of short-term factors is difficult, it is nevertheless possible to select variables that represent short-term developments which vary from election to election.

We have constructed a new regression equation that includes (proxies for) short-term factors on the basis of the hypotheses shown in Box 7.1. These hypotheses

Box 7.1 Hypotheses that underly our model of the short-term factors in the Bartolini and Mair model

We assume that the total volatility is higher in situations where:

1 the bond between voters and parties is weak (a low party membership rate represented by the variable 'gemmem');
2 the economic situation is weakening (variable 'misery');
3 the electoral support for left parties is weakening (variable 'leftv': the vote share of the left parties; if this share is high, then the impact of the overall decline of left parties on volatility is also higher);
4 the established parties are converging on the socio-economic left–right scale (variable 'partysys');
5 the economy is vulnerable because of its openness (variable 'imex');
6 the working population is dissatisfied with the working conditions (variable 'nrstrik').

have in common that they refer to socio-economic conditions and party–voter relationships that change from election to election. As such they differ from structural features like institutional incentives and socio-organizational bonds that are not likely to change over short time periods.

Note that the variables are not based on an exact measurement of short-term trends as we *assume* that a relatively low average score of, for example, misery indicates that there is a gradual decrease in misery. Figure 7.7 presents the model graphically. Step by step those variables are omitted that appear to be insignificant: strikes and misery. The remaining variables do present a model with an adjusted R^2 of 0.68 (n = 13 European countries). The results are presented in Table 7.2. All our hypotheses are confirmed, except one: the high level of convergence relates negatively to the degree of total volatility. Note that our model is not wholly comparable with Bartolini and Mair's model. Not only are our variables proxies (being 'stand ins' for variables that are difficult to operationalize), but the units of

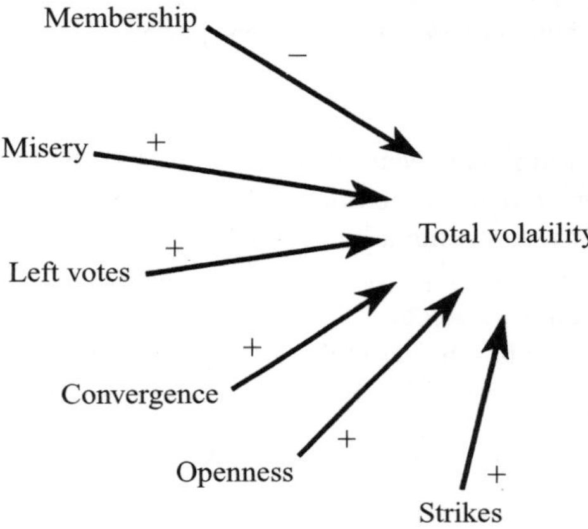

Figure 7.7 *Expected causal effects of the short-term factors*

Table 7.2 *Regression results of two models which seek to explain total volatility with solely short-term factors*

	OLS regression results on the basis of aggregated data[a] (R^2_{adj} = 0.68)			PCSE regression results on the basis of pooled time series data[b] (R^2_{adj} = 0.28)		
Proxies:	**beta**	***t***	**Sig. *t***	**beta**	***t***	**Sig. *t***
Membership	−0.67	−3.5	0.0078	−0.47	−8.65	0.00
Left votes	0.76	3.3	0.0106	0.40	4.4	0.00
Convergence	−0.62	−3.8	0.0054	−0.35	−8.3	0.00
Openness	0.44	2.1	0.0701	0.27	4.4	0.00
Constant	–	0.81	0.4402		3.7	0.00

[a] n = 13 European countries.
[b] n = 299 (13 European countries × 23 years).

analysis are also quite different (the regression is based on 13 cases as compared with $n = 231$ in the Bartolini and Mair analysis). The small number of cases renders our model vulnerable to small changes (see Subsection 5.6.2 for an elaboration on robustness). Adding or leaving out one variable destroys the promising relationships we have found. It makes sense, therefore, to apply the model to time series data. That can only be done properly by correcting for errors that are related to autocorrelation. One modern technique to do this is the Panel Corrected Standard Errors (PCSE) method, which is explained in Section 6.7. The results of the PCSE regression analysis show that our suspicion toward the 13-cases model was justified. The betas and the adjusted R^2 in the PCSE model are much lower. The signs of the betas are identical in both types of regression analyses (two variables in the short-term factors model are not significant at the 0.05 level).

Recent instances of electoral instability, such as earthquake elections and heavy electoral losses of pivot parties, cast some doubt on the overall validity of the Bartolini–Mair model. First of all, electoral volatility is only one way of looking at party system change. There are more detailed ways of looking at recent forms of party system change in a comparative manner, such as examining the effects of regime breaks or processes of redemocratization (Pennings and Lane, 1998). Secondly, Bartolini and Mair examine electoral change at the aggregate level. Looking at the individual level might reveal more change. This is shown by Ersson and Lane who examined volatility at the individual level (Ersson and Lane, 1998). It is well known that the bonds between voters and parties are becoming weaker (Katz and Mair, 1992). Other forms of political participation and new potentials are arising (Kriesi and Koopmans, 1995) which have, for instance, led to the rise of protest parties.

The conclusion is as follows. In this section we have examined processes of electoral change along two lines: the type and degree of variation and the explanation of these variations with the help of causal modeling. The two subsequent steps of finding and explaining variations are crucial to comparative research. Without variations we cannot compare, and without explanation the art and craft of comparing loses most of its scientific significance. The problem is, however, that there is mostly more than one way to find and explain variations. One way to cope with this problem is to relate the Research Question to earlier research on the topic. This is, in fact, also what Bartolini and Mair did, as their research builds on the work of Lipset and Rokkan. This type of theoretical basis has a structuring impact on the Research Question and the Research Design to be developed by students in comparative political science.

7.2 PROCESSES OF PARTY CHANGE

7.2.1 The role of parties

Parties have different functions and roles and related dilemmas (Strom, 1990a): seeking for votes, office and policy simultaneously.

- Parties that are solely vote-seeking are vote maximizers. It was Anthony Downs who proposed this vote-maximizing model of party behavior (Downs, 1957).
- Office-seeking parties seek to maximize, not their votes, but their control over political office. Office mainly refers to cabinet portfolios (Riker, 1962).
- The policy-seeking party seeks to maximize its effect on public policy. Policy-based coalition theory assumes that coalitions will be formed by parties that are 'connected' (Axelrod, 1970) or at least close to each other in policy space (we will come back to that in Section 8.4).

Strom criticizes the three models on their static and non-institutional character. He proposes a unified model of party behavior that focuses on the interrelations and trade-offs between the three party goals. Strom argues that pure vote seekers, office seekers, or policy-seekers are unlikely to exist. Party objectives are mostly mixed.

Figure 7.8 represents a three-dimensional space where each party goal is represented by one dimension. Strom suggests that each case of party behavior is a linear additive function of the three party goals:

$$B = w_1 V + w_2 O + w_3 P$$

where B is position in behavioral space, V is vote-seeking behavior, O is office-seeking behavior, P is policy-seeking behavior, and w_1 through w_3 are coefficients

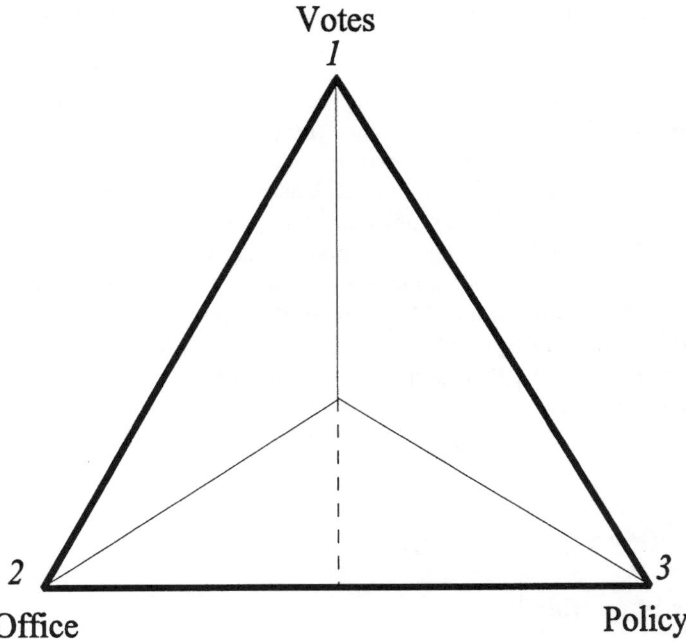

Figure 7.8 *Strom's range of feasible party behaviors (Strom, 1990a)*

representing the weights of each type of behavior. The weights w_1, w_2 and w_3 signify the relative importance of different types of party behavior, identical to the beta weights in regression analysis. The weights are constrained to sum up to 1, so that all feasible forms of party behavior fall in the triangle in Figure 7.8. A pure vote-seeking party would be located at point 1, a pure office-seeker at point 2, and a pure policy-seeker at 3. Parties that pursue all three objectives fall somewhere in the interior of the triangle. A party that places some value on votes and more on policy than on office, will fall inside the right-hand area of the triangle. Although there are no data available that can be used to test this specific model, the idea of party goals has proved to be useful. This book shows several examples of it (like the 'Chain of Democratic Control and Command' and Robertson's 'two-stages factor analysis' (Subsection 7.2.3)).

Strom distinguishes between two sets of factors that systematically affect the trade-offs between votes, office and policy. One set of factors is to be found in the organizational properties of parties (such as the constraints on party leaders). The second set of variables is constituted by the electoral, legislative, and governmental institutions. There is always a potential conflict between the different objectives, which often boils down to a trade-off between short-term and longer-term benefits. For example, a party may benefit from the decision to join a government, in terms of office, but suffer from it in terms of future votes. Given these conflicting aims, parties have to make choices and formulate priorities. How these choices are made depends on the functioning of the party as an organization (the internal affairs) and on the impact of electoral, legislative and governmental institutions (external environment). These institutions determine how votes are translated into seats, bargaining power into government status, and government status into office and policy benefits. In Chapter 8 we will examine several examples of the impact of institutions which can be seen as the 'rules of the game' determining the constrained opportunities for each party to achieve its goals (or not).

7.2.2 Parties and ideology scales

One main aspect of party change is the ideological change. In this section we will demonstrate how this can be measured. According to Lipset and Rokkan, different ideologies stem from cleavage systems and result in different party families. Party families are groups of parties with a similar ideological background or roots. One important cleavage in most parliamentary democracies is the class cleavage which is strongly linked to the left–right division in politics. Three kinds of scales are developed to measure left–right positions of parties: expert-scales, voter-scales and manifesto-scales. The expert-scales are based on the positions of parties on the basis of a selection of expert opinions. Three prominent expert-scales are those of Castles and Mair (1984), Laver and Hunt (1992) and Huber and Inglehart (1995). An extensive summary of expert scales is presented in Laver and Schofield (1990: Appendix B). An example is presented in Figure 7.9.

The manifesto scales are based on the emphasis that parties put in their manifestoes on left and right issues. The party manifestoes (see Section 4.5) are coded for the relevant parties in most democracies for the post-war period (these are the

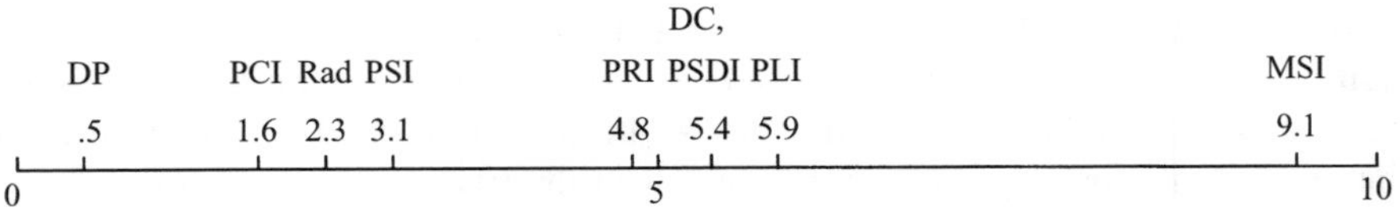

DC,
DP PCI Rad PSI PRI PSDI PLI MSI
.5 1.6 2.3 3.1 4.8 5.4 5.9 9.1
0 5 10

Figure 7.9 *The position of Italian parties on the Castles and Mair expert-scale (1984): DC, Christian Democrats; DP, Proletarian Democrats; MSI, Nationalists; PCI, Communists; PRI, Republicans; PLI, Liberals; PSDI, Social Democrats; PSI, Socialists; Rad, Radicals*

parties gaining more than 5 per cent of the vote at any post-war election, together with all which were potentially pivotal in coalition bargaining (Laver and Budge, 1992: 17). Each sentence is assigned to one of the 54 coding categories. In the end of the coding process all sentences per category are summed up and taken as a percentage of the total number of coded sentences. A recent example is a left–right scale that is constructed by summing up 13 left and 13 right items; and the latter are subtracted from the former. The result is an interval score for each party in each election (Klingemann et al., 1994: 40). Another example stems from Laver and Budge, who made the selection of left and right variables on the basis of factor analysis. This enables them to combine the original 54 policy-coding categories into 20 in order to diminish the overlap between these categories (Laver and Budge, 1992: 24).

It is possible to compare both types of scales once they are put into the same format, notably the 10-point scale. Figure 7.10 gives the example of the Italian parties in 1992.

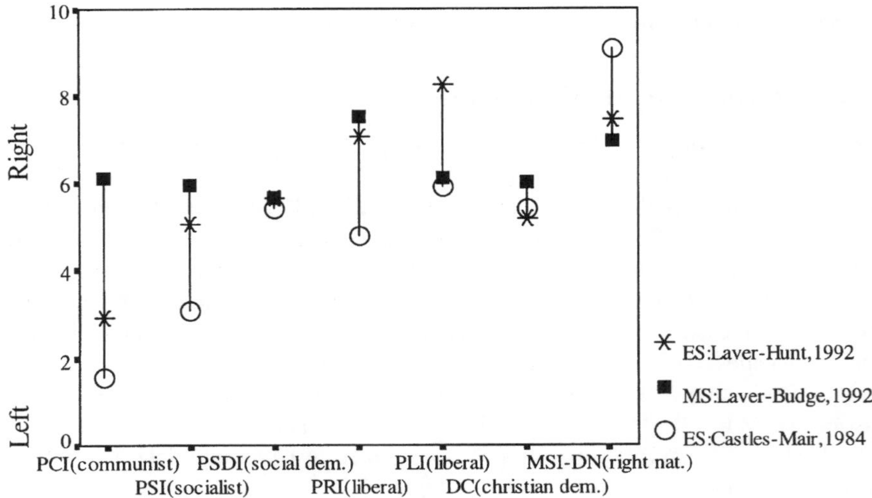

Figure 7.10 *Position of Italian parties on expert-scales (ES) and manifesto scale (MS). Source: Laver and Schofield, 1990, p. 260*

The manifesto-scales tend to assign moderate scores to all parties, even if these parties are distinctive left or right parties. The expert-scales, on the other hand, make sharper distinctions between the parties. A comparison of three scales in Figure 7.10 illustrates this point clearly. You can use the same setup in Chapter7.sps to make a similar drop-line chart for any country or election year that is included in the party manifesto data set.

Another important difference is the dynamics of the scales. The expert-scales are static. Apparently, they do not measure the positioning of parties at many points in time (mostly only at one). As a consequence there is not much variation between the expert-scales in time. Most expert-research in 1995 still produces more or less the same results as it did in 1984! The Castles and Mair and the Huber and Inglehart scales differ in 23 cases (being parties), meaning that the positions of the parties differ by more than 1 point (Castles and Mair regard a difference of 0.5 significant!). It is striking that these differences in nearly half of the cases apply to social-democratic parties. The Huber–Inglehart scale places these parties more to the right than the Castles–Mair scale. This might imply that there is a bias in these scales but it also means that there has been a movement to the right of social democratic parties. The Laver–Hunt and the Huber–Inglehart scales differ in the case of 22 parties. This time there is no 'bias' towards one particular party family, but there appears to be a more 'nationalistic' bias as the differences apply to many Belgian parties. Laver applies the Laver–Hunt expert-scale (1992) also to the Dutch elections in 1994 (Laver, 1995). Inglehart's analysis originates from the end of 1994, which is approximately the same point in time as Laver used. It is striking that Huber and Inglehart place all parties more to the left than Laver does.

We conclude that there are remarkable differences between the ranges of the expert-scales and the manifesto-scales. Between the expert-scales are more differences in the scaling of parties than is generally assumed. The (dynamic) manifesto-scales have a centripetal bias, whereas the (static) expert-scales are more centrifugally oriented. The fact that both types of scales have pros and cons does not imply that either scale will do for any research. In case of doubt, it is always better to compare several scales in order to grasp the degree of consistency between the scales. The analytical comparison of two or more scales is to be based on the reliability of the scale (as demonstrated in Section 4.5), on the number of parties that is included and on the external validity of these scales (this is, do the scales produce roughly the same results?).

Another topic that needs attention is the scalability of the manifesto-scales. Most of the scales are constructed on theoretical grounds and not on empirical grounds. This implies that these scales – as they are used and applied in the publications of the Manifesto Research Group – do contain items that do not fit into the scale very well. We will present an example here of the construction of a left–right scale (with the help of the SPSS procedure Reliability) that results in a Likert scale (see Subsection 4.5.1). We limit the analysis to the Labour Party and the Conservative Party in the UK. We select the economic variables in the Manifesto data set (the so-called 'domain 4').

The first step in the analysis is to recode the scores on the items into the same direction. In the original data set all scores are positive. The construction of a left–

right Likert-scale is only possible if contrary signs are assigned to the left and the right issues (here we assigned negative signs to the left items). The main criterion is Cronbach's α: one by one we delete those items with the highest score on 'Alpha if item deleted' when this additional alpha exceeds alpha for all items. In our example we start with a selection of 13 items and end up with a selection of 10 items with an alpha-score of 0.8001 and a standardized item alpha of 0.8065.

The final left–right scale is an additive index of these ten variables (this index is presented in the file Chapter7.sps). The procedure descriptives reveals that the scale ranges from −23 (left) to +26 (right). By computing the additive index we have created a score on the left–right scale for both parties for all election years. These scores are plotted in Figure 7.11. The figure shows that the two parties consistently move in their own side of the party system and that there is a cyclical movement toward both convergence (1945–70) and divergence (1970–92). Both conclusions have far-reaching consequences for our thinking on parties. The results are not so obvious as they seem. This can be illustrated by comparing these empirical results (which are not unique to the UK! – see also the two-stage factor analysis on the US data in the next section) with the theoretical assumptions and predictions of Anthony Downs (Figure 7.12).

Electoral volatility is the change of vote between parties and thus must be explained within the context of choices offered by parties. Especially on the basis of the Bartolini–Mair discussion (see Section 7.1), emphasizing movement between left–right party blocks, it is useful to define choice in left–right terms. This also gives us the opportunity to present a spatial representation of such movements. One of the most widely discussed hypotheses on vote-seeking party behavior was formulated by Anthony Downs in *An Economic Theory of Democracy*. Downs'

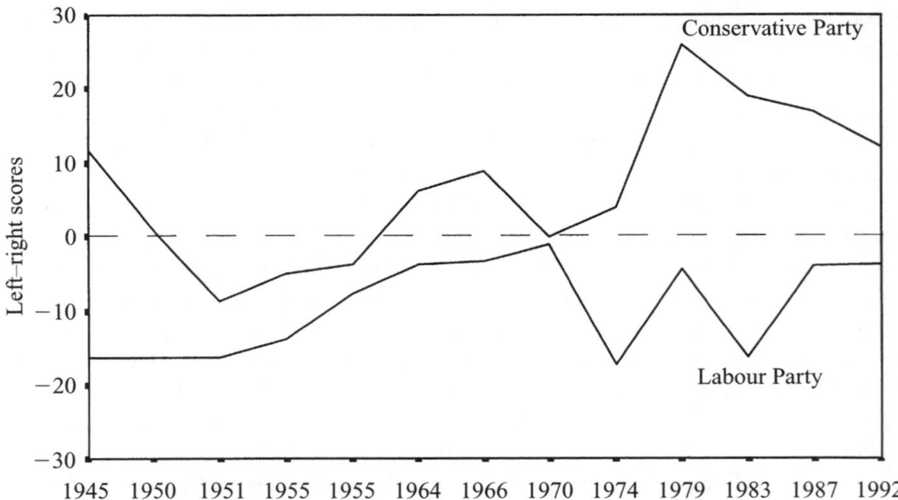

Figure 7.11 *Movement of British parties on the left–right scale, based on the SPSS procedure Reliability. Source: Comparative Manifestoes Project (Volkens, 1994)*

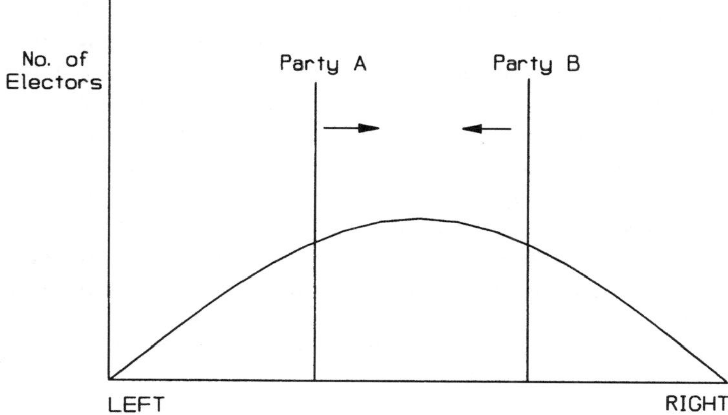

Figure 7.12 *Downs' model for two-party competition (Downs, 1957)*

main assumption is that parties are moving, and that the electoral preferences are more or less fixed. On the basis of the party manifestoes it is possible to confront Downs' long-term expectation of party convergence, as represented in Figure 7.13, with actual party movement. This is done with the left–right scales that are discussed in the previous section. Most of the graphical presentations which have been made on the basis of the Manifesto-scales show that parties are for instance not 'leapfrogging', as they stay in their own ideological segment and are thus ideologically fixed (Laver and Budge, 1992).

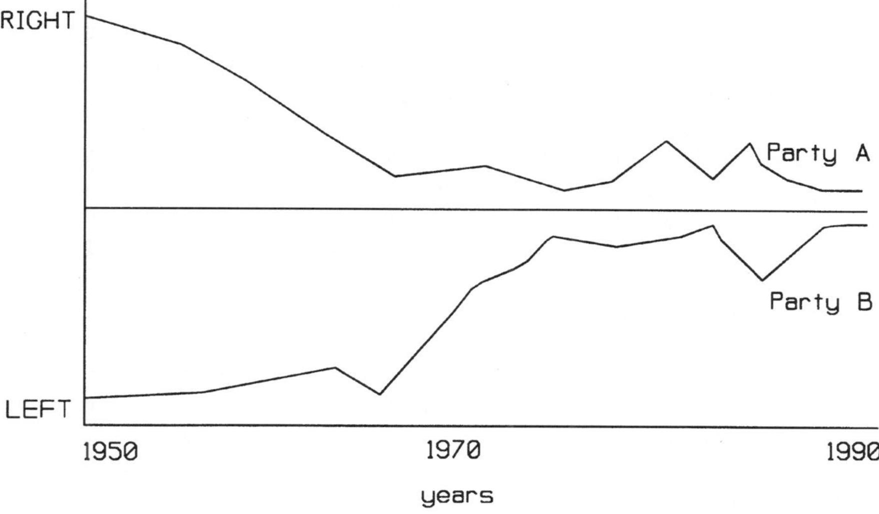

Figure 7.13 *Downs' single election model leads to the expectation of convergent party positions over time (Downs, 1957)*

How can we explain these characteristics of party behavior? One explanation lies in the information shortage of parties. Parties do not know exactly where the voters stand. Consequently, parties rely on their own ideology. If parties don't move, volatility must be explained by voters moving or by the rise of new cohorts of voters. However, note that volatility is limited. The best predictor of the next election result is the previous result. Sometimes enough electors get concerned about a problem which is 'owned by' one party other than the one they have been voting for. This may cause enough imbalanced movement at the aggregate level to change the election result. The saliency theory of party competition (nowadays often labeled as the 'issue ownership theory', see Petrocik, 1996) is designed to allow understanding of the impact of issues 'owned by' parties. When the saliency of issues changes, this gives an electoral advantage to those parties which 'own' the salient issues (Budge and Farlie, 1983).

7.2.3 Parties and issues

Issues refer to societal problems that are to be solved, although not necessarily by means of government policy. They play an important role in the competition between parties. Parties seek to present themselves to the voters by means of specific issues that enable voters to identify themselves with these parties. The way parties select issues is clearly patterned. This pattern is linked to the party family concept. In this chapter we will use factor analysis to illustrate the paradoxical relationship between parties and issues: many parties 'own' specific issues in the sense that they are the natural bearers of this ideology, but at the same time, parties are also inclined to change and modernize their ideology and presentation of issues in order to stay attractive to the voters. It is clear, for example, that the Christian ideology is very much at the heart of what Christian Democratic parties stand for, but if these parties were not to adapt this ideology to modern circumstances, they could not survive. The same goes for the socialist and the liberal party ideologies, which need constant adaptation to modern conditions and preferences.

One seminal study in this field is the edited volume of the British political scientists Ian Budge, David Robertson and Derek Hearl under the title *Ideology, Strategy and Party Change: Spatial Analysis of Post-war Election Programmes in 19 Democracies* (1987). Their approach is spatial, i.e. dimensional. On the basis of positive and negative associations between percentage scores they have identified sets of related policy areas. Each set can be represented spatially by a line, thus becoming a dimension of some space (Budge et al., 1987: 29). This only holds when there are not more than three clusters of dimensions.

Each manifesto is located on each dimension by the percentage of references made to the issue-areas associated with it, multiplied by the 'loading' of these areas on the dimension (factor loadings higher than 0.30 are considered by these authors as an indication that a policy area is indeed important). The factor analysis brings to the fore the paradoxical relationship between parties and issues:

1 Parties compete on the basis of a fixed set of issues that belong to dimensions of conflict. The *first stage* of the factor analysis examines these cleavages.

2 Parties move their party positions over time, meaning that the relative position of election programs within the multi-dimensional space is not stable. The *second stage* of the factor analysis examines the movements of parties within the substantive domains.

Although factor analysis is primarily a data-summarizing technique, one still needs some theoretical assumptions that structure the data. An analysis of 54 issue categories would produce blurred results, difficult to interpret and statistically dubious as the number of variables would outnumber the number of cases (as the analysis is performed on the country level). For this reason Budge et al. use the two leading factors in each of the seven domains as new variables for the second-stage factor analysis in order to get a simple description of the over-arching structure of party competition.

Table 7.3 is an example of the first-stage factor analysis. The table shows a summary of the results of factor analysis in the economic domain. In technical terms it is based on Principal Axis Factoring (PAF) with communality estimates in the main diagonal, followed by Varimax rotation. The setup for this analysis is included in the file Chapter7.sps.

Table 7.3 shows the following results:

1 the two factors for four countries: these are the two dimensions that represent the variables in the economic domain;
2 The factor loadings of the variables on these factors;
3 The explained variance of the two factors;
4 The eigenvalues: they represent the degree of association between the factors and the variables that they represent.

Table 7.3 *Results of the factor analysis in the economic domain*

	US		UK		NZ		Australia	
Factor:	**1**	**2**	**1**	**2**	**1**	**2**	**1**	**2**
Eigenvalue:	3.3	2.4	2.7	1.3	1.9	1.7	1.3	1
% of variance explained:	30%	22%	27%	13%	21%	19%	14%	11%
Variable								
401 Free enterprise	−0.89	−0.07	0.69	0.53	−0.23	−0.63	−0.28	0.28
402 Incentives	0.19	−0.21	0.34	0.89	0.93	−0.21	0.39	0.09
403 Regulation of capitalism	0.69	−0.07	−0.39	−0.22	−0.01	0.63	0.38	−0.30
404 Economic planning	0.46	0.48	−0.52	0.02	−0.09	0.87	0.31	−0.04
406 Protectionism	−0.46	−0.10			−0.06	0.37	−0.02	0.10
408 Specific economic goals	0.59	−0.39	0.03	−0.41	0.15	−0.16	0.51	−0.11
410 Productivity	0.29	−0.45	0.04	0.27	−0.27	0.07	0.22	0.89
411 Technology and infrastructure	0.65	−0.07	0.42	−0.48	−0.66	−0.14	−0.04	0.02
412 Controlled economy	0.17	0.94	−0.44	−0.26				
413 Nationalization	0.07	0.92	−0.61	0.10				
414 Economic orthodoxy	−0.85	0.01	0.80	0.01	0.59	0.11	−0.69	−0.06

Source: Budge et al., 1987: 55. A blank means that a variable is omitted from the analysis.

The results indicate that the structure of party competition on economic issues differs per country but also that, despite these differences, the left–right dimension is clearly present in all four countries. The American parties compete along two dimensions, the first being *laissez-faire* versus regulation of capitalism, which accounts for 30 per cent of the variance. The second dimension contrasts controlled economy and nationalization on the one hand with productivity on the other hand. In case of the UK the first factor is a classic left–right clash. Within the second factor a stress on economic goal attainment is contrasted to economic ideology *per se* (incentives and nationalization). For New Zealand the first factor contrasts two classic 'right-wing' economic symbols (namely incentives and economic orthodoxy versus technology and infrastructure and productivity). The second factor shows the contrasts between conservative and socialist economic issues (free enterprise versus planning and regulation). The first Australian dimension is a left–right clash and the second is a unipolar and single-category stress on productivity.[1]

In the first stage of the analysis the seven domains are split into two factors that represent what parties are competing for (the policy-seeking goals of these parties). In this way the 54 categories in the party manifestoes are reduced to 14 variables (an exception is domain two of which the original scores are used). In the second stage of the factor analysis these 14 variables are fed in. The setup that does this job for the USA is included in file Chapter7.sps.

In Figure 7.14 the means that result from the second stage analysis are presented in a two-dimensional space. The figure confirms the basic hypotheses on how party competition works: the movement of parties is restricted, but at the same time this rigidity does not mean that parties do not change. They are constantly adapting their party goals and this is done in a more or less cyclical movement as shown in Figure 7.14. In terms of Strom's division into three party goals, we have been mainly looking at the changes in the policy-seeking related goals of parties. These

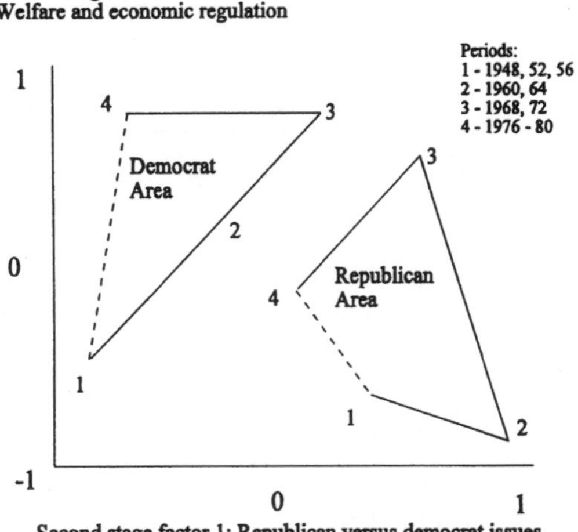

Figure 7.14 *US party positions, 1948–1980. Source: Budge et al., 1987*

changes indirectly also affect the vote and office-seeking goals of parties. The degree to which this is the case depends on the electoral system and the party system. In the case of the USA, the room to maneuver of parties is affected by the characteristics of the two-party system. If, for example, a third relevant party were to be introduced into the American party system it would certainly affect the policy positions and the movements of the established parties.

Although the results of the two-stage factor analysis appear convincing for the USA, it is not the technique as such that invokes these kinds of results, it is the ideas, theories and assumptions of the researchers. Even the smallest changes in the selection of years or variables would produce different results (you can test this statement by adapting the setup slightly and rerunning the factor analysis for the period 1948–1992). David Robertson (Budge et al., 1987) not only used factor analysis as a data-reducing technique, but also as a theoretically guided (and manipulated) tool in order to corroborate the hypothesis that the division in left and right matters in the USA. This particular use of factor analysis requires an experienced outlook on the subject in order to be useful and reliable. Simpler examples of factor analysis will be given in Sections 8.2 and 9.4.

7.2.4 Public opinion and party responsiveness

Until now we have mainly concentrated on party positions as such. A relatively new topic in party literature is the so-called party responsiveness: the degree to which parties are responsive to external factors like voter opinions and shifting problem intensities.

The saliency theory of party competition, or issue ownership theory, claims that parties are mainly ideologically driven (ideology refers here to left–right positions) and not very responsive to sudden shifts in problems and public opinion. This challenging hypothesis is tested by confronting the salience theory with alternative explanations of party behavior. In this way we can determine to what extent the saliency model is the best-fitting model of party emphasis.

Basically, there are three competing models:

- The Downsian model predicts that parties are not ideologically driven nor problem driven. Instead, parties are following public opinion and voter preferences in order to maximize their votes. Parties are very responsive to voter preferences ('competition-driven').
- The saliency issue model (Budge et al. 1987) predicts that parties are ideologically driven. The implication of this is that parties are characterized by ideological rigidity and are not responsive to voters or problems ('cartellization-driven').
- The combined model predicts that parties will be driven by both ideology and public opinion. This model is based on the hypothesis that most parties base their choices on both ideological and electoral considerations.

These three models are tested by means of regression equations on the basis of pooled time series data. As the Research Question focuses on trends and variations in party behavior we obviously have to adopt a cross-national and cross-time perspective. The first step is to define the dependent variables. We haven chosen the emphasis of political parties on economic restrictiveness (*market*) versus economic interventionism (*planning*), as this juxtaposition is fundamental for party competition, which has been revealed by the factor analysis of Robertson et al. in Subsection 7.2.3. The operationalization of these variables is explained in Box 7.2.

One independent variable is the so-called median voter position on the planning and market variables that are defined above. The median voter position is a measure of the ideological position of a particular electorate that is comparable across countries and across time. It is the central ideological tendency among voters. If parties are following voter preferences, then we expect them to move towards the median voter positions, especially when they are (potential) cabinet parties. The calculation of the median voter position is based on a well-known formula that incorporates the policy positions and the votes shares for the relevant political parties (Bohrnstedt and Knoke, 1982: 52; Kim and Fording, 1998: 79). For each party the midpoint is calculated between the one immediately left of it and the one immediately right of it. It is assumed that voters on the left side of this interval will vote for the party on the left and the ones on the right side will vote for the party on the right of it:

$$M = L + \{(50 - C)/F\} \times \mathrm{W}$$

where M is median voter position (ideological score), L is the lower end (ideological score) of the interval containing the median, C is the cumulative frequency

Box 7.2 The operationalization of the planning and the market scores that are used as dependent variables in three competing models on issue saliency

The *planning score* adds up the three variables:

- controlled economy: general need for direct government control of economy; control over prices, wages, rents etc.;
- economic planning: favorable mentions of long-standing economic planning of a consultative or indicative nature, need for government to make such a plan;
- market regulation: need for regulations designed to make private enterprises work better.

The *market score* adds up the two variables:

- free enterprise: favorable mentions of free enterprise capitalism; superiority of individual enterprise over state and control systems;
- economic orthodoxy: need for economic orthodoxy, e.g. reduction of budget deficits, retrenchment in crisis.

(vote share) up to but not including the interval containing the median, F is the frequency (vote share) in the interval containing the median, and W is the width of the interval containing the median (ideological score).

The three elements needed to perform the calculations are:

1 the mean scale positions of the parties;
2 the vote percentages of the parties;
3 the scale positions of each party.

Here follows a short example of how this formula works for a country with a left party (A), a center party (B) and a right party (C). The ideological score refers to either the left–right scale, the planning positions or the market positions. Suppose that the median voter in this country in a particular election year is in party B, because by the time we move through party B, we have covered more than 50 per cent of all voters. Having identified party B we can figure out that L, the lower ideological score of B, is the midpoint between party A and B. The value of W equals L minus the midpoint of the ideological scores of B and C. The value of C is the sum of all votes to the left of party B. The value of F is the vote percentage of party B.

We will also give a more empirical example of the calculation of the median voter position of the left–right scale for a multi-party system: Sweden. We use the file that is extracted from the *International Almanac of Electoral History* (Mackie and Rose, 1991). The rows comprise the parties. The columns comprise the (interpolated) vote percentages of the election years and the in-between years.

Firstly, we line up the parties from low to high on the scale of interest. This is done by means of the command ‘sort cases’ which orders the parties from a high score to a low score. As the parties do not sum up 100 per cent of the votes, we also calculate the adjusted vote shares by recomputing the vote percentage by dividing each by the sum and multiplying by 100. The next step, which is also taken in the case of a two-party system, is to determine which party has more than 50 per cent of the votes: the median party. After these steps have been taken we are ready to calculate L, C, F and W. This is done by means of the steps given in the file Chapter7.sps. The main results for Sweden (1945–1990) are reported below as an example:

1945	12.54	1956	12.08	1967	12.28	1979	11.15
1946	12.54	1957	11.98	1968	12.28	1980	11.73
1947	12.54	1958	11.95	1969	12.33	1981	11.73
1948	12.54	1959	11.95	1970	12.33	1982	11.73
1949	12.22	1960	11.95	1971	12.07	1983	12.25
1950	12.22	1961	12.20	1972	12.07	1984	12.25
1951	12.22	1962	12.20	1973	12.07	1985	12.25
1952	12.22	1963	12.20	1974	11.66	1986	12.18
1953	12.08	1964	12.20	1975	11.66	1987	12.18
1954	12.08	1965	12.28	1976	11.66	1988	12.18
1955	12.08	1966	12.28	1977	11.15	1989	12.41
				1978	11.15	1990	12.41

Note that these computations have to be adapted for each particular party system and each different policy scale (Y) in order to correct for different numbers and positions of parties on the policy scale. Assuming that the given example in the file Chapter7.sps gives an impression of how the median voter position is computed, we continue with the data analysis on the determinants of party responsiveness.

The second independent variable is the left–right ideology scale in Klingemann et al. (1994). Exercise 7.3 gives detailed information on the calculation of this particular scale. As indicated above, the three models that represent the main theoretical positions in the debate on party responsiveness are (Y = the party emphasis on planning or market):

- the Downsian model: $Y = a + (b \times \text{median voter position}) + e$;
- the Salience model: $Y = a + (b \times \text{ideology}) + e$;
- the Combined model: $Y = a + (b \times \text{ideology}) + \text{median voter position} + e$.

The Downsian and Salience models are quite unequivocal. The combined model combines the other two models by predicting that the emphasis on planning and market is a function of both ideology and public opinion. Table 7.4 shows the results of a regression analysis on the three models. The results on the basis of these computations do provide more support for the saliency model than for the Downsian model. Parties are to a large extent ideologically driven. There is no

Table 7.4 *Regression analysis on models that predict the party emphasis on market and planning (n = 803).*

Model	*Y*	*X*	beta	*t*	Sig. *t*	Adj. R^2
Downs	Market	Median voter emphasis on market	0.17	4.88	0.00	0.03
	Planning	Median voter emphasis on planning	0.15	4.26	0.00	0.02
Salience	Market	Left–right	−0.52	−17.3	0.00	0.27
	Planning	Left–right	0.41	12.7	0.00	0.17
Combined	Parties' emphasis on market	Median voter emphasis on market	0.13	4.19	0.00	0.29
		Parties' emphasis on left–right	−0.51	−17.08	0.00	
	Parties' emphasis on planning	Median voter emphasis on planning	0.13	4.0	0.00	0.18
		Parties' emphasis on left–right	0.40	12.56	0.00	

Market = the additive index of the programmatic emphasis on the Manifesto categories: free enterprise plus economic orthodoxy. Planning = *idem* for control of the economy plus planning plus market regulation. Left–right = the Klingemann et al. (1994) scale. $n = 803$ election years in 17 OECD countries.

consistent and far-reaching party responsiveness to shifting problem intensities or voter preferences, at least not the type of responsiveness predicted by the Downsian median voter theorem.[2] When parties are responsive to the public or to problems, these reactions are limited to particular issues and policy areas.

We conclude that voter preferences do not affect party priorities (in general) to a high extent. In this sense parties are myopic. This may not come as a big surprise, because the role of parties is considered more encompassing than just to reflect what the voters want. The saliency theory of issues gives an additional explanation of this by arguing that non-responsiveness is electorally more rewarding than responsiveness, as rigidity makes parties reliable and credible in the eyes of the voters. Other theories, like the cartel theory, explain non-responsiveness out of the integration of the party elites within the state so that parties have lost their feeling for society. The welfare state regime explanation explains it by picturing parties as bounded actors operating within the historical boundaries of welfare state regimes. So, we conclude that what various theories on party behavior have predicted has been empirically confirmed in the regression analysis, although it is not possible to conclude solely on the basis of the regression analysis whether or not these theories provide empirically sound and plausible alternative explanations.

7.3 CONCLUSIONS

In this chapter we have discussed aspects of the 'input-side' of the chain of democratic control and command, with an emphasis on electoral change and party change. We have shown that in order to be able to analyze electoral change we need a range of indicators that capture the phenomena under study. As the comparative method aims at explaining cross-national variations, we need a comparative Research Question and Research Design in order to be able to come up with plausible explanations. Table 7.5 gives an overview of the main Research Questions, Research Designs and Research Answers that are discussed in this chapter.

Chapters 1 to 6 have focused on the theoretical, methodological and technical aspects of comparative research, of which several are summarized by the first two columns of Table 7.5. In this chapter we have applied comparative methods and statistics to Research Questions which relate to changes in the preferences and behavior of voters and parties. In doing so, we have illustrated that the quality of the research answer highly depends on the preceding steps in the research: the Research Question, the hypotheses, the operationalizations, the specification of the model, the interpretation of the results. The most important guide in this process is theory, i.e. a clear and consistent set of hypotheses that guides the researcher through all the necessary steps. These steps are part of an iterative process of choice (how to operationalize and analyze) and interpretation (how to make sense of the results by relating them to existing knowledge). Starting from one and the same Research Question there is more than one road to a plausible answer. This gives the researcher the freedom to explore but it also necessitates a full and detailed elaboration on all the steps taken. A short check list which examines whether these steps are correctly taken includes:

Table 7.5 *Overview and examples of the main stages in comparative research on the preferences and behavior of parties and voters*

Research question	Research design	Research answer
§7.1.2. What variations in electoral volatility are there?	Operationalization of *Y*; indicators of change; examination of trends by means of descriptive techniques such as graphical presentations	The aggregated, country-specific and party family-specific results show cross-national and cross-time variations which can only be explained by means of theory
§7.1.3. How do we explain variations in electoral volatility?	Operationalization and modeling of *X* and *Y*; time series and regression analysis	Variations in electoral change are partly explained by institutional and socio-organizational factors. The plausibility of this answer depends on the specification of the model that is used to analyze the data
§7.2.3. What are the underlying dimensions of party competition?	Conceptualization and operationalization of issues that belong to dimensions of political conflict, and application of factor analysis on them	The left–right dimension is one of the most prominent conflict dimensions. This answer is based on the interpretation of factor scores
§7.2.4. What drives parties: voter preferences or ideology?	Operationalization of median voter positions and party emphasis on dimensions of party competition (left versus right, market versus planning) plus the modeling of *X* and *Y*	Ideology seems to be the most important drive for parties. Parties are rigid and not very responsive. There is more than one theory to interpret this result

1 The Research Question: does it refer to variations in a dependent variable and to possible explanations of these variations, e.g. by means of hypotheses or assumptions?
2 The Research Design: are the cases properly selected, the variables clearly operationalized and integrated in a well-specified model? Is the choice of the technique related to the levels of measurement and the type of Research Question?
3 The Research Answer: do the interpretations and conclusions give a direct answer to the Research Question and are they related to the findings of similar research projects?

7.4 ENDMATTER

Exercises

The exercises cover some of the main subjects in this chapter. The formulated Research Questions in the exercises are suited to the writing of a short research note. Exercise 7.1 focuses on the problem of the Research Answer. The other exercises focus on statistical and methodological aspects of the Research Design.

EXERCISE 7.1: MEASURING ELECTORAL CHANGE

Files: bartmair.sav, nias.sav, pol4.sav.

How correct is Bartolini's and Mair's finding that there is not much change in Western European party systems? Answer this question by means of an extensive descriptive analysis (by examining the trends and variations of crucial party system variables).

Suggested steps: 1. Select several indicators of electoral change. 2. Examine the trends of these indicators by means of 'plot' or 'graph'. 3. Examine the country-specific trends by comparing the period before and after 1970, with the help of the command 'aggregate'.

Background reading: Bartolini and Mair (1990); Pennings (1998b).

EXERCISE 7.2: MODELING ELECTORAL CHANGE

Files: Pol4.sav and Nias.sav.

Construct a multivariate regression equation that explains the variation of the block volatility of left parties. One assumption behind this equation is that the vote share of left parties is more stable when their rank-and-file is well organized (and when these organizations are incorporated in cooperative forms of decision-making). Test your model by means of multiple regression. Integrate the relevant scores of the regression analysis into a table that is understandable for outsiders. Extend your model by introducing an interaction term into the equation. Examine whether the assumptions for regression are violated. Concentrate on linearity and multicollinearity (see Chapter 6 for those tests).

Perform also a second analysis, this time for total volatility as the dependent variable. Integrate one interaction term into your model. Study the residuals of the total volatility model. Are there significant outliers?

Suggested steps: 1. Formulate several hypotheses that can be modeled and that explain either left volatility or total volatility. 2. Add an interaction effect to the hypotheses. 3. Test the models (check the violation of assumptions, especially tolerance).

Background reading: Bartolini and Mair (1990).

EXERCISE 7.3: THE KLINGEMANN ET AL. LEFT–RIGHT SCALE

Perform a reliability test on the Klingemann et al. scale (1994). This scale was originally computed as:

```
compute leftklin
    = per103+per105+per106+per107+per202+per403+
      per404+per406+per412+per413+per504+per506+per701.
compute rigtklin
    = per104+per201+per203+per303+per401+per402+
      per407+per414+per505+per601+per603+per605+per606.
compute scalekli = leftklin-rigtklin.
variable label SCALEKLI 'left-right scale Klingemann et al.
1994'
```

If you have no access to the data set (which is accessible via the Essex Archive) you can use the Dutch data in the file 'nethman.sav'.

Suggested steps: 1. Recode the issues into the same direction (namely either left or right). 2. Perform the reliability analysis by dropping variables with the highest score on 'Alpha if Item Deleted'.

Background reading: Klingemann et al. (1994).

EXERCISE 7.4: THE MEDIAN VOTER POSITION

Compute the median voter position on the left–right scale position for at least one election year in both a multi-party system and a two-party system. You can compute the median voter positions manually or with the help of SPSS. Take, for example, the data shown in Table 7.6.

Suggested steps: 1. Determine which party is the median party. 2. Calculate L (the lower ideological score), C (the cumulative frequency), F (vote share of the interval containing median), W (width of this interval). 3. Insert the numbers into the formula.

Background reading: Klingemann et al. (1994); Pennings (1998a).

Topics highlighted

- The problem of electoral change: how to measure and model it with the help of regression analysis:
  - What variations in electoral volatility are there?
  - How do we explain variations in electoral volatility?
- The problem of party change: how to measure and model it with the help of factor and scalability analysis:
  - What are the underlying dimensions of party competition?
  - What drives parties: voter preferences or ideology?

Further reading

- *General*: Bartolini and Mair, 1990.
- *Specific*: Budge et al., 1987; Klingemann et al., 1994; Laver and Budge, 1992.

Table 7.6 *Data for the calculation of the median voter positions in Sweden (1970) and the USA (1972) on the basis of the Klingemann et al. left–right scale*

Party[a]	Left–right position[b]	Vote share	Adj. vote share
Sweden: SLP	42.3	4.76	4.87
Sweden: SDA	14.9	45.34	46.38
Sweden: FP	9.2	16.21	16.58
Sweden: CP	6.2	19.92	20.38
Sweden: MUP	−35.2	11.53	11.79
USA: Democrats	14.2	37.53	38.21
USA: Republicans	−13.6	60.69	61.79

[a]The parties are ordered from left to right.

[b]A high score denotes a leftist position.

Box 7.3 Glossary of basic terms

- *Electoral system*: the set of rules that determines how votes are translated into seats.
- *Issue ownership*: the ownership (i.e. monopolization) of certain issues or policy areas by parties.
- *Left–right scales*: the positioning of parties between two poles that represent left and right on the basis of expert opinions or party manifestoes.
- *Median voter position*: the policy preferences of the voters, which are derived from the preferences of the parties they are voting for.
- *Median Voter Theorem for two-party systems* (Downs): Parties are assumed to move towards the median voter position and will thus converge to the middle of the distribution.
- *Party competition*: the moulding or profiling of parties in order to keep or achieve votes, policy goals and office.
- *Party system*: the cooperation and competition between political parties which is influenced by the number of parties and their ideological distance.
- *Volatility*: how many parties win or lose per election (this includes all parties).

Notes

1 This use of factor analysis is only sound when there are no issues involved that are typical for parties in the middle of the party system. If this is the case, factor analysis will produce two related left–right dimensions whereas only one is present. Therefore, one has to delete the issues in the middle before one starts this type of analysis.

2 Other models have been recently proposed, e.g. the directional model of G. Rabinowitz and S. E. Macdonald (1989). See for a recent discussion: J. Krämer and H. Rattinger (1997). Also note the discussion about the applicability of the Downsian median voter theorem in the case of multi-party systems (see Barry, 1978; Budge, 1993).

8
How decisions are made

CONTENTS

8.1 INTRODUCTION

Chapter 7 indicated that the behavior of voters and parties should be understood within their institutional context. In this chapter several of these contexts (and relations between them) will be explored. As institutions shape the behavior of actors, these institutions are decisive for the decision-making process. Like all the chapters in this part of the book, this chapter aims to improve the understanding and the accessibility of data and the techniques. We will not discuss all the details and backgrounds of the techniques (this has already been done in Chapters 4–6) but focus on how to use and apply them within cross-national Research Designs that aim at answering substantial Research Questions.

We focus on the institutional and constitutional foundations of modern democracies. These foundations are summarized by Lijphart in his seminal text *Democracies* (1984). This chapter starts with an overview of Lijphart's operationalization of the main characteristics and variations of political institutions in modern democracies (Section 8.2). Special attention will be given to the factor analysis that Lijphart uses and that leads to the division between consensus and majoritarian democracies. This division is crucial – in his ideas – for understanding variations in political behavior and the functioning of democracy.

In the following sections we will explore the working, trends and effects of several institutions that are central to the functioning of democracies. A proper overview of the main concepts from a comparative perspective can be found in Gallagher et al. (1995). See also our definitions of the basic terms in Box 8.1. First, we will discuss the party system typologies and ways to study party system change (Section 8.3). Party systems can be seen as the main institutional environment of party competition and cooperation. We will compare the party system typologies of Lijphart and Sartori which originate from the same period but are also very different in their assumptions. Sartori assumes that sooner or later pluralism inevitably leads to instability. Lijphart emphasizes the possibility that elites may handle conflicts properly so that plural societies remain nevertheless stable (Sartori, 1976; Lijphart, 1977).

Box 8.1 Glossary of basic terms

- *Consensus democracy*: the whole of intertwined institutional arrangements that enhance elite cooperation and coalition building in the parliamentary arena.
- *Minimal winning cabinets* (MWC): cabinets that are based on more than 50% of the parliamentary seats ('winning') and that are devoid of unnecessary partners ('minimal').
- *Median legislator*: this median position is found by adding up the number of seats that each party controls from the left to the right.
- *Distributional coalitions*: the alignment of pressure groups at various levels of government in ways that are Pareto suboptimal (i.e. at the expense of collective welfare).
- *Corporatism*: institutionalized cooperation ('concertation') of trade union federations, employers' organizations and the state by means of non-parliamentary consultation in order to avoid or reduce suboptimal (zero-sum) outcomes of policy formation.
- *Federalism* is a state structure with a high degree of geographical autonomy *vis-à-vis* the political center, which is expressed by means of constitutionally sharing power between the federal state and its parts.
- *Centralism* is the degree to which aspects of policy-making are directed from the central political institutions.
- *Institutional autonomy* (or devolution-index): the degree to which decentralized governing units, like local communities, have powers to control policy-making independently from the center (i.e. forms of self-regulation).

How do party systems matter? They have an enduring impact on party behavior, both during and after elections, which leads to different types of interaction between parties. In Section 8.4 we will therefore discuss the different forms of cabinet formation and functioning of government with reference to coalition theories that make predictions on the composition of governments given the vote shares of parties and/or their policy stance. Special attention will be given to the central role of the party that controls the median legislator, often being the core party in the political system. This party is decisive in any democracy regarding both government and policy formation. Finally, we will apply regression analysis (both linear and logistic) on the possibility that minority governments are formed as well as on the duration of governments in general.

As political parties are not the sole (albeit a crucial) actor in modern societies, we also focus on other actors that may affect the 'democratic performance' (i.e. the effects of democratic practices and institutions on the quality of life) and their level of affluence in a society. Important in this respect are the governmental institutions and personnel: the bureaucracy. Several theories are designed to explain the relationships between these institutional aspects of government functioning and economic growth. One of the best-known theories originates from Mancur Olson (1982). His theory will be discussed and tested in Section 8.5 with the help of regression analysis. Additionally, the size and growth of the public sector will be explained by means of regression analysis, as this technique is suited to the analysis of causal models.

A related topic is the degree and nature of interest intermediation. In Section 8.6 the focus will be on the concept of corporatism (i.e. the structure of interest intermediation), its operationalization and its relationship with consensus democracy. It will be shown that both concepts should be distinguished because they are too different to be amalgamated into one score, like the one that was proposed by Lijphart and Crepaz (1991).

There are more institutions which affect the nature and degree of state intervention and policy formation. The degree and nature of regional and institutional autonomy is indicated by the federal or unitary state structure since in particular the implementation is differently organized. In Section 8.7 the variations and policy effects of federalism, centralism and autonomy will be discussed and analyzed with the help of regression analysis. The executive–legislative relations are also crucial determinants of decision-making because the separation of powers is differently organized. Two major institutional variants of these relationships are presidentialism and parliamentarism. Section 8.8 analyzes the variations of presidentialism and its effects on democratic performance. This is done by applying the most different design (comparing the democratic performance of all systems in the world), the most similar design (comparing the effects of presidentialism in the OECD, which holds systems with a similar economic development) and the comparative case study (explaining the special character of American presidentialism).

This chapter ends with a set of exercises that relates to the subsequent paragraphs. These exercises may help students to assess the ins and outs of the application of statistical techniques to the working, effects and change of political and socio-economic institutions.

8.2 TYPES OF DEMOCRACIES

This section focuses on the main features of democratic political systems in the OECD world, especially on the quantitative and statistical aspects of identifying system properties. The basic institutional framework that structures the decision-making process is the type of the democratic system. In his book *Democracies* (1984) Lijphart describes two extremes – majoritarian democracies versus consensus democracies – which are presented as 'ideal types' (i.e. sketched in their archetypal or perfect form). These types are compared on the basis of a range of variables. A selection of eight of these variables seems to be crucial for a correct understanding of the differences between these two types of democracies. Here follows a critical overview of the conceptualization and operationalization of the five most relevant variables.

1 *Minimal Winning Cabinets* (minwin): Power concentration versus power-sharing: the percentage of time that a country was governed by minimal winning coalitions instead of oversized cabinets (see table 4.2 in *Democracies*). A high percentage of minimal winning coalitions indicates a low degree of consensus democracy. In consensus democracies the oversized cabinets, consisting of more parties than strictly necessary for the parliamentary vote of confidence, should predominate, according to Lijphart's reasoning (this assumption neglects the possibility that minority cabinets can also be based on a broad parliamentary support: see Section 8.4).

2 *Executive Dominance* (cabdur) versus executive-legislative balance: the average durability of cabinets (see table 5.3 in *Democracies*). A government may be defined as an administration that is formed after an election and continues in the absence of a change of Prime Minister, a change of the party composition and the resignation during an inter-election period followed by a reformulation of government (Woldendorp et al., 1993: 5). Lijphart operationalizes the duration in terms of days instead of months (the former being more accurate). According to Lijphart, stable systems are characterized by a relatively long duration of cabinets. As consensus democracies are relatively stable systems, due to the accommodating behavior of the political elites, the durability of cabinets is assumed to be high. On the other hand, since coalescent strategies are not always effective, the consensus democracies are potentially unstable: all depends on the effectiveness of the coalescent strategies. The overall conclusion about the durability of cabinets in consensus democracies is therefore not uncontested (Warwick, 1994).

3 *Effective Number of Parties* (nrpties): this number is computed with the help of the Laakso–Taagepera index (see Figure 8.1) which resembles the Herfindahl index as explained in Chapter 5 (see also Lijphart, 1984: 120 and his table 8.1) on the basis of the *Electoral Almanac* (Mackie and Rose, 1991).

According to Lijphart, most consensus democracies are characterized by a high number of effective parties because of the high plurality of these systems. The high number of effective parties implies that the formation of coalitions is a standard practice in consensus democracies as no party is able to reach a

$$\frac{1}{\sum_{i=1}^{n} Pi^2} \quad (P = \%\ \text{seats})$$

Example (three parties):

$$0.45^2 = 0.20$$
$$0.42^2 = 0.20$$
$$0.10^2 = 0.01$$
$$= 0.41$$
$$1{:}0.41 = 2.4$$

Figure 8.1 *Laakso and Taagepera's index of the effective number of parties*

Table 8.1 *Lijphart's concepts and operationalizations in* Democracies *(1984)*

Majoritarian democracy	Consensus democracy	Operationalization	Variable
Concentration of executive power	Executive power-sharing	The percentage of the time that minimal winning cabinets were in power	Minwin
Cabinet dominance	Separation of powers	Average cabinet stability	Cabdur
Asymmetric bicameralism	Balanced bicameralism and minority representation	A quantitative index with the range: 0 (bicameral) to 4 (unicameral)	Unicam
Two-party system	Multi-party system	The number of effective parties (Laakso & Taagepera)	Nrpties
One-dimensional party system	Multi-dimensional party system	The number of issue dimensions (range: 1–4.5)	Issuedim
Plurality system of elections	Proportional representation	Index of disproportionality (votes minus seats shares)	Elecdis
Unitary and centralized government	Territorial and non-territorial federalism and decentralization	Central governments's shares of tax receipts	Govtax
Unwritten constitution and parliamentary sovereignty	Written constitution and minority veto	Index of constitutional lexibility: range 1–3	Conflex

majority position. Although this assumption looks plausible, it is not the whole story. In many party systems it is not the number of parties as such that invokes consensual practices, but the presence and size of center parties, on the one hand, and the representation of social cleavages by parties, on the other (Gallagher et al., 1995).

4 *Number of Issue Dimensions* (issuedim): This number is based on interpretative evaluations of qualitative sources on issue dimensions and cleavage structures. In Lijphart's operationalization there are strong relationships between the number of issue dimensions and the party system and the number of cleavages (see Table 8.1). According to Lijphart's theory, a high number of issue dimensions

indicates a high level of consensus democracy, as societal cleavages in plural societies are apt to produce many corresponding issue dimensions. Lijphart assumes that two-party systems are characterized by 1 or 1.5 issue dimensions (a half means a medium-salience dimension), whereas most of the multi-party systems are characterized by two or more dimensions. The correlation between the number of issue dimensions and the number of effective parties is 0.70. This strong relationship is not so obvious as Lijphart implicitly assumes. The number of issues operationalized by Budge and Farlie (1983: 35) hardly correlates with the effective number of parties ($r = 0.08$) ($n = 21$ OECD countries that are included in Lijphart, 1984). Hence, the caveat is that this type of variable strongly relies on subjective interpretations.

5 *Plurality vs Proportional Representation* (elecdis), i.e. the difference between a society-based type of representation and one based on geographic distribution. Here the average deviation between the vote and seat shares of the two largest parties in each election (electoral disproportionality or 'wasted votes') is the indicator (see table 9.1 in *Democracies*). Lijphart assumes that a high degree of proportionality also indicates a high degree of consensus democracy, as these democracies are mostly dominated by proportional representation (PR systems). The majoritarian systems are mostly characterized by first-past-the-post systems. The problem with this indicator is that the proportional electoral system is more often than not historically given as a result of the endeavors of the political elites to invoke consensus democracy when general suffrage was introduced (Rokkan, 1970). Hence, elite behavior has led to the adoption of an electoral system suitable for plural societies. As a consequence, the electoral system does not presently appear to be a very valid indicator of consensus democracy.

The factor analysis on Lijphart's data (Table 8.2) is the 'proof of the pudding': is there really *one* underlying dimension, emerging from the eight variables, which distinguishes consensus and majoritarian democracies? This particular application of factor analysis differs from the one applied in Subsection 7.2.3. In this section we apply a confirmative factor analysis which is meant to test whether a set of indicators correlates with one underlying dimension. The factor analysis in Subsection 7.2.3 was more explorative than confirmative because there was no pre-given assumption on the number and nature of dimensions.

The emergence of two factors shows that there are three variables which are more strongly related to another dimension: constitutional flexibility, centralization and unicameralism. Lijphart labels the first factor as 'the executives–parties dimension' and the second factor as 'the federal–unitary dimension' (Lijphart, 1984).

It is possible to cluster the countries on the basis of the two factor scores that are saved into the file. Table 8.3 is nothing more than a listing of the two factor scores per country. The results are based on Manfred Schmidt's re-analysis of Lijphart's data and based on 18 instead of 22 countries. For this reason the results are not wholly identical to Lijphart's results. It is remarkable, for example, that Switzerland, Norway and Sweden end up in the same cluster of consensual countries

Table 8.2 *Lijphart's basic dataset in* Democracies *(1984) (lijpdat.wpd)*

Country	minwin	cabdur	unicam	nrpties	issuedim	elecdis	govtax	conflex
Australia	86	102	0	2.5	2.5	6	80	0
Austria	86	100	3	2.2	2	2	70	0
Belgium	76	26	1	3.7	3	2	93	1
Canada	87	104	2	2.4	1.5	8	50	0
Denmark	66	34	4	4.3	2.5	1	71	1
Finland	38	30	4	5	3.5	2	70	1
France	37	60	2	3.3	3.5	12	88	1
FRG	78	47	0	2.6	2	2	51	0
Ireland	89	70	3	2.8	1	2	92	1
Italy	35	17	1	3.5	3	2	96	1
Japan	81	58	1	3.1	3	4	65	0
Netherlands	27	34	1	4.9	3	1	98	1
New Zealand	100	64	4	2	1	6	93	3
Norway	83	55	4	3.2	3.5	3	70	0
Sweden	66	74	3	3.2	2.5	1	62	1
Switzerland	0	30	0	5	3	2	41	1
UK	95	81	2	2.1	1.5	6	87	3
USA	100	30	0	1.9	1	6	57	0

Source: Adapted and provided by M.G. Schmidt (1995).

Table 8.3 *Factor scores of Lijphart's two basic dimensions of consensus democracy*

Country	Factor 1	Factor 2
Majoritarian		
New Zealand	1.22	2.16
UK	1.16	1.47
Ireland	0.72	0.82
Majoritarian-federal		
Canada	1.37	−1.08
USA	0.99	−1.26
Austria	0.87	−0.41
Australia	0.83	−0.86
FRG	0.26	−1.5
Japan	0.04	−0.91
Consensual-unitary		
France	−0.18	0.48
Belgium	−0.64	0.41
Denmark	−0.73	0.6
Italy	−1.06	0.2
Netherlands	−1.47	0.55
Finland	−1.49	0.57
Consensual		
Sweden	−0.02	−0.01
Norway	−0.21	−0.08
Switzerland	−1.67	−1.14

Notes: The table is based on the data that are presented in Table 8.2. A positive score indicates majoritarianism and a negative score consensualism. When both columns hold positive scores, countries are grouped into the majoritarian category. In the case of negative scores, the group is consensual. Otherwise, in the case of positive and negative signs, the groups are in-between.

(although Switzerland clearly fits best into this cluster). We can learn from this that factors should be evaluated in relation to each other and that the clustering of cases on the basis of factors is rather arbitrary and should therefore be treated with care. The technique of cluster analysis, as explained in Subsection 4.5 (and also applied in Section 8.4), would be more suited to cluster the 18 countries, because the criticism of an arbitrary division into clusters would not apply in the same manner to the clustering technique.

Lijphart's juxtaposition of majoritarian and consensual systems is one of the most influential empirical studies on the functioning of democracies recently made. A study of his conceptualization, operationalization and factor analysis shows that his interpretation is based on assumptions which are not necessarily adequate, nor are they the only ones that are plausible. One might also wonder if his polar approach to democracies is becoming (partly) outdated as most systems nowadays are (becoming) mixed systems (Dunleavy and Margetts, 1995). These mixed systems might not function according to most of Lijphart's descriptions.

This confronts us with the problem of changing conditions of consensus and majoritarian democracy. How these conditions are changing can be examined by selecting the theoretically most convincing institutional variables and studying the developments over time. It can be argued that three factors are inextricably linked to the division between consensus and majoritarian democracy:

1 the degree of disproportionality;
2 the effective number of parties;
3 the type of government.

These three indicators have in common that they are related to the functioning of electoral systems. In proportional systems, we expect a high degree of proportionality, which enhances a high number of effective parties and thus (indirectly) the formation of coalition governments. In majority systems, on the other hand, we expect the opposite: a low degree of proportionality, a low number of parties, and majority governments.

Factor analysis can be used to combine these conditions for consensus and majoritarian democracy into one single factor score. First, the nominal variable type of government has to be recoded into a dichotomous (interval) variable. The next step is to perform the factor analysis on the NIAS data (1950–1990, $n = 738$) which throws up one factor with an explained variance of 51.7. The factor loadings are for the type of government, 0.44, for the effective number of parties, −0.88 and for the electoral disproportionality, 0.78. These scores are in line with our expectations. A high factor score indicates favorable conditions for consensus democracy. On the basis of the constructed factor it is possible to examine trends per country or clusters of countries. We refer to Exercise 8.1 for further details on this longitudinal approach (see also Pennings, 1997). By restricting the factor analysis to the three crucial indicators of consensus democracy, the outcomes of this analysis are easier to interpret since one factor is extracted instead of two.

In this section we have questioned aspects of the operationalization and analysis of the conditions for consensus democracy. The questions raised are not meant to downgrade Lijphart's work. We think that the analysis of his data, as they are presented here, is still an effective way to get acquainted with the main characteristics of modern democracies. This section has also shown that it is worthwhile to improve existing knowledge by applying the 'check list' at the end of Chapter 7 to the research on which this knowledge is based.

8.3 PARTY SYSTEMS

Party systems comprise different kinds of relationships between parties in terms of competition, coalitions and ideology which lead to patterned interactions. A party system has certain properties that distinguishes it from other party systems, e.g. the number of parties, electoral disproportionality, fragmentation, centripetal (towards the center) or centrifugal (towards the extremes) party competition (Gallagher et al., 1995). Party systems structure the type of competition and representation on the one hand and the consensus-building and mode of governance on the other hand.

Three main questions have dominated party system literature: what party systems are there?, what countries are characterized by what systems?, and how do party systems change over time? Party system typologies seek to answer the first two questions. We will concentrate here on two well-known typologies of Lijphart and Sartori (see Tables 8.4 and 8.5). For the use and limitations of typologies, we refer to Chapter 3.

In Sartori's typology the two dimensions are ideological distance between political parties and party system fragmentation (indicated by the number of 'relevant parties': those are parties with either coalition potential or blackmail potential; see Sartori, 1976: 121–3). These dimensions are dependent as they co-vary directly: the higher the number of parties, the larger the mean ideological distance (i.e. the range of the party system) is assumed to be (Sartori, 1976: 291). The number of parties and the ideological distance are positively correlated: Sartori expects more polarization in countries with a high number of parties. This linear correspondence between these two dimensions enables us to reformat Sartori's typology into a one-dimensional scale that combines the two original dimensions. In this new dimension, the predominant type (low number of parties and ideological

Table 8.4 *Lijphart's typology of democratic systems*

Elite behavior	Structure of society: Homogeneous	Structure of society: Plural
Coalescent	*Depoliticized* Austria (1966–)	*Consociational* Belgium, The Netherlands, Switzerland, Austria (1945–66)
Adversarial	*Centripetal* Finland, Denmark, UK, USA, Norway, Sweden, FRG	*Centrifugal* France, Italy, Canada

Source: Lijphart (1977).

Table 8.5 *Sartori's typology of party systems*

Ideological distance	Party system fragmentation	
	Low	**High**
Low	*Two-party* Canada, USA, Austria, UK	FRG, Switzerland, The Netherlands, Denmark, Belgium, France V
High	*Predominant* Norway, Sweden	*Extreme and polarized* Finland, Italy, France IV

Source: Sartori (1976: 314).

distance) is the opposite of the polarized type (high number of parties and ideological distance).[1] This particular type of one-dimensional scale is also applied by Sartori himself (Sartori, 1976: 283). The resulting one-dimensional scale is incorporated into Table 8.6.

Lijphart's typology of democratic systems represents perhaps the most important alternative to Sartori's typology of party systems. Although Lijphart's typology is strictly speaking a classification of *democratic* systems, it has far-reaching implications for the ways in which party systems are assumed to function. Recall that Lijphart's main hypothesis is that segmental cleavages at the mass level can be overcome by elite cooperation (Lijphart, 1977). Lijphart proposed a typology that is based on the structure of society (homogeneous versus plural) and the behavior of elites (coalescent versus adversarial). The elites behave in a cooperative and stabilizing manner by means of four practices: grand coalition, segmental autonomy, proportionality, and mutual veto. In Lijphart's typology the key category is the consociational type, as this type entails the cooperation by segmental elites in spite of the deep cleavages separating the segments (Lijphart, 1977: 53).

The Sartori and the Lijphart typologies seem to be quite the opposite: in several instances where Lijphart predicts stability, Sartori predicts instability and vice versa. One example is provided by the countries that fall into the category of

Table 8.6 *Typologies of party systems*

Sartori	Lijphart
Predominant: Norway, Sweden	*Centrifugal*: France, Italy
Two-party: Austria, UK	*Centripetal*: Finland, Denmark, Norway, Sweden, UK, Germany, Ireland
Moderate multipartism: Germany, Switzerland, The Netherlands, Denmark, Belgium, France V, Ireland	*Consociational*: Austria, Belgium, The Netherlands, Switzerland
Polarized: Finland, Italy, France IV	

Adapted from: Von Beyme (1985), Lange and Meadwell (1991), Keman (1995).

'moderate multipartism'. According to Sartori these countries are likely to be politically unstable because of their fragmented party systems. Lijphart, however, asserts that these countries may be stable democracies if, and only if, the elites are cooperative. As both typologies can hardly (in their original format) be equally valid at the same time, it is interesting to test their predictive and explanatory capacity just by comparing them in this respect.

There are several tests that could be imagined in order to test the validity of both typologies, i.e. the degree to which the theoretical assumptions underlying the typologies match the empirical characteristics of countries. We use regression analysis to study the interrelation between the party system scales of Lijphart and Sartori on the one hand and a variety of dependent variables that are related to the votes, office and policy-seeking behavior of political parties and to characteristics of party systems on the other hand. On doing so, we extend the use of typologies from solely explaining stability to a wider range of party system characteristics.

The first step is to change the nominal party system scores into ordinal ones. Ordinal scoring implies that the two-dimensional typologies are reformatted into a one-dimensional rank ordering of countries. Sartori's rank orders become an indicator of 'multi-partism' (corresponding to the degree of polarization) and Lijphart's dimension can be interpreted as 'degree of coalescent elite-behavior' (that also – at least in theory – should linearly correspond to stability). The analysis is based on the Multiple R scores (the roots of the R^2) on the basis of regressions of the party system scales (in dummy format) on variables that are related to votes, policy and office. The highest rank order scores serve as the reference group in the regression analysis, which can be omitted and to which the other groups are compared. These dependent variables figure prominently in the literature as characteristics related to the functioning of party systems.

In total, 17 hypotheses are tested. For every variable a hypothesis has been formulated on the basis of Lijphart's and Sartori's assumptions. These hypotheses simply express whether we expect no relation or a positive or negative relation between the independent and dependent variables. This is done for both the 1960s and the 1980s, because the predictions may better hold for the 1960s than for the 1980s. The results are reported in Table 8.7. The selected variables cover the features of party-government (e.g. color, duration, reason of termination), of party systems (e.g. the type of leadership, the number of parties), the electoral system (e.g. disproportionality), interest group intermediation (e.g. organizational unity) and voter–party relationships (e.g. membership rates). When the real-world relations that are expressed by means of the Multiple R scores match the hypotheses, then we may conclude that the typologies generate reliable predictions. The results are quite promising for both typologies. Three hypotheses that are related to the theory of Sartori are not confirmed (namely Cpgdef, Polarsys and Elsys). In the case of Lijphart's theory, one or two hypotheses are not confirmed (Cpgdef and Nrpties). These results imply that both typologies, although they were devised in the mid-1970s, are still useful tools to designate relevant party system properties and formulate relevant consequences. Sartori's typology has the disadvantage that the basic hypothesis on polarization ('Polarsys') is not confirmed. Thus, Lijphart's theory is more fully confirmed by the data.

Table 8.7 *A test of Sartori's and Lijphart's predictions of party system properties on the basis of their typologies (Multiple R)*

Typology	Sartori hypothesis	1960s	1980s	Lijphart hypothesis	1960s	1980s
Color of party government (CPGDEF)	$R = 0$	−0.50	−0.33	$R = 0$	0.35	0.23
Cabinet duration (DUR)	$R < 0$	−0.32	−0.35	$R > 0$	0.28	0.33
Reason of termination (dummy) (RFT_REC)	$R > 0$	0.15	0.35	$R < 0$	−0.20	−0.29
Type of government (TOGORI)	$R > 0$	0.48	0.54	$R > 0$	0.56	0.39
Polarization (POLARSYS)	$R > 0$	−0.41	−0.25	$R < 0$	−0.11	−0.42
Type of leadership (LEADERSH)	$R < 0$	−0.50	−0.50	$R > 0$	0.72	0.72
Number of issue dimensions (ISSUEDIM)	$R > 0$	0.50	0.50	$R > 0$	−0.42	−0.42
Number of parties (NRPTIES)	$R > 0$	0.70	0.49	$R > 0$	−0.43	−0.35
Effective number of parties (EFFNOP)	$R > 0$	0.62	0.55	$R > 0$	0.26	0.38
Fragmentation of votes (FRAGVOT)	$R > 0$	0.70	0.55	$R > 0$	0.17	0.25
Organizational unity (UNITY)	$R < 0$	−0.39	−0.39	$R > 0$	0.73	0.73
Union density (DENSITY)	$R < 0$	−0.60	−0.39	$R > 0$	0.58	0.57
Electoral system (ELSYS)	$R > 0$	0.37	0.37	$R > 0$	0.46	0.46
Total volatility (TOTVOL)	$R > 0$	0.45	0.22	$R < 0$	−0.47	−0.28
Disproportionality (DISPRDEF)	$R < 0$	−0.20	−0.42	$R < 0$	−0.33	−0.35
% Party membership (PERCMEM)	$R < 0$	−0.46	−0.50	$R > 0$	0.21	0.22
% No attachment (NOATTCH)	$R < 0$		−0.36	$R < 0$		−0.31

The scores are Multiple *R* scores based on regression analysis on the country-by-year data set. The dependent variables are listed in the left column of the table. The independent variables are dummy variables that assign a 0 or a 1 to the countries for each category of the typologies. The sign is added on the basis of separate correlations. $N = 598$: country-by-year format (western Europe). The sources and operationalizations are explained in Appendix 8.1. The hypotheses are implicated (not given!) by Sartori's and Lijphart's typologies and assume either no relationship ($R = 0$), or a positive relationship ($R > 0$) or a negative relationship ($R < 0$). Adapted from: Pennings (1998b).

This section focused on the Research Question of whether the theoretical assumptions underlying party system typologies match the empirical characteristics of countries. The answer to this question resulted from several steps. First, we made the theoretical assumptions explicit and operationalized the relevant empirical characteristics of party systems. Second, we used regression analysis in order to examine to what extent the observed features of party systems correspond with the hypothesized traits. In doing so, this section has illustrated the central importance of hypotheses for doing comparative political research. Without these hypotheses it would be impossible to explain or even examine variations and trends in party system characteristics.

8.4 CABINET FORMATION AND DURATION

Coalition theories try to predict what governments will be formed if and when the vote shares of parties and/or their policy stances are known. What coalitions are formed is not totally accidental, as many coalition theories have shown (Laver and Schofield, 1990). Most of these theories are one-dimensional (left–right). Only recently have multi-dimensional theories been tested (Austen-Smith and Banks, 1988; Laver and Budge, 1992; Laver and Shepsle, 1996). Five different types of coalitions are predicted by different one-dimensional theories on the basis of three criteria: the number of parliamentary seats, the policy preferences and the number of (potential) cabinet parties. The combinations among A, B, C, D, E refer to the example in Table 8.8.

- *Minimal winning coalitions* (MWC) or bare-majority cabinets are coalitions of two or more parties that are winning and minimal, namely: ABC, ADE, BCD, BE, CE (these combinations are explained in Table 8.8). The term 'minimal' means here that only those parties are included that are necessary to form a majority government. 'Winning' means that the coalition must be based on more than 50 per cent of the parliamentary seats. The underlying assumption of the MWC theory, as first proposed by Riker in 1962, is that political parties are power-maximizers and solely office-seeking. Power refers here to participation in government with as many portfolios or ministries as possible. One shortcoming of Riker's theory is that his predictions are not very precise, as they predict several simultaneous outcomes.
- *Minimum size coalitions* resemble Riker's definition, but this type of coalition is more precise, as the cabinet should be based on the narrowest possible parliamentary majority, namely: ADE. Parties would prefer this specific type of coalition, as costs of sharing portfolios are minimized.
- *Coalitions with the smallest number of parties* ('bargaining proposition'): this prediction assumes that a coalition is more easily formed with the smallest number of parties bargaining, namely: BE, CE.
- *Minimal range coalitions*: coalitions will form among parties with similar policy preferences, namely: ABC, BCD, CE. This type of coalition differs fundamentally from the first three coalitions in that the element of policy preferences is introduced. The 'range' refers here to the policy distance between parties. A smaller range increases the possibilities to cooperate and to form a government.
- *Minimal connected winning coalitions* are introduced by Axelrod: coalitions are formed that are connected (adjacent on the policy scale) and devoid of unnecessary partners, namely: ABC, BCD, CDE. The theory is a combination of the minimal range assumption and the Riker principle.

The best predictions are made by the 'policy-based theories' (about 50 per cent of the coalitions are correctly predicted; see Lijphart, 1984). This empirical advantage is also theoretically understandable. The utility-maximizing principle of Riker ignores the possibility of minority governments and also the possibility that parties might prefer to join the opposition as this may be electorally more profitable. Hence we see a trade-off between parsimony and plausibility here: the Riker model is too parsimonious to be plausible.

However, the predictive capabilities of the policy-based theories are also modest. One weakness is the uni-dimensionality of the left–right scale that is used to determine the policy distances between parties. Additionally, most policy-based theories also handle the size principle, but this principle is not always valid. Some

Table 8.8 *Overview of the 25 possible coalitions in a situation with five parties*

	Party:	**A**	**B**	**C**	**D**	**E**	
		Left					**Right**
	Seats:	**8**	**21**	**26**	**12**	**33**	
	Party	**Seats**					**Total seats**
1	A, D	8	12				20
2	A, B	8	21				29
3	B, D	21	12				33
4	A, C	8	26				34
5	C, D	26	12				38
6	A, E	8	33				41
7	A, B, D	8	21	12			41
8	D, E	12	33				45
9	A, C, D	8	26	12			46
10	C, B	26	21				47
11	A, D, E	8	12	33			53
12	B, E	21	33				54
13	A, B, C	8	21	26			55
14	B, C, D	21	26	12			59
15	C, E	26	33				59
16	A, B, E	8	21	33			62
17	B, D, E	21	12	33			66
18	A, C, E	8	26	33			67
19	A, B, C, D	8	21	26	12		67
20	C, D, E	26	12	33			71
21	B, D, E, A	21	12	33	8		74
22	B, C, E	21	26	33			80
23	A, B, C, E	8	21	26	33		88
24	B, C, D, E	21	26	12	33		92
25	A, B, C, D, E	8	21	26	12	33	100

Adapted from Lijphart, 1984: 48.

pivot parties, for example, which play a crucial role in coalition building, may prefer to form larger coalitions as this increases their potential to impose their preferences on their coalition partners because they are able to govern without one of the partners.

Empirically, minimal winning cabinets (that are based on the size principle) are dominant in: New Zealand, Luxembourg, UK, Ireland, Iceland, Canada, Austria, Australia, Norway, Japan, Germany, Belgium, Denmark, Sweden. Oversized cabinets (that include more parties than necessary for a bare majority) are dominant in: Switzerland, Israel, France, the Netherlands, Italy and Finland. Of course, these are only major trends as both types may be present in particular countries.

Why does this pattern occur? According to Lijphart there is a strong relationship with the degree of organized pluralism: the number of cleavages in a country. Minimal winning cabinets are a characteristic of the Westminster model of democracy; oversized cabinets are more typical of the consensus model. But, as indicated before, there are exceptions.

Table 8.9 presents an alternative view on coalition theory by showing the 'prediction sets' of two alternative criteria. One is the viability criterion that drops the traditional assumption that cabinet parties need to be represented by at least 50 per cent of the parties in parliament. Instead, the viability criterion depicts cabinets as viable that will survive a vote of confidence. Thus, also minority cabinets may be viable. The other criterion is that the party that controls the median legislator is expected to be a crucial party in the process of cabinet formation. Thus, the assumption is that only cabinets will be formed that include this party. In Table 8.9 the parties are aligned on a left–right dimension in the order of A (most to the left) to E (most to the right). Four different assumptions are compared:

1 Riker's criterion: only those cabinets are formed that are based on more than 50 per cent of the parliamentary seats ('winning') and that are devoid of unneces-

Table 8.9 *Prediction set with different assumptions: a hypothetical example*

	Government composition	Seats	Riker	Axelrod	Viability	Median legislator
1	A	20			*	
2	B	20			*	
3	C	20			*	*
4	D	20			*	
5	E	20			*	
6	A, B	40			*	
7	A, C	40				
8	A, D	40				
9	A, E	40				
10	B, C	40			*	*
11	B, D	40				
12	B, E	40				
13	C, D	40			*	*
14	C, E	40				
15	D, E	40			*	
16	A, B, C	60	*	*	*	*
17	A, B, D	60	*			
18	A, B, E	60	*			
19	B, C, D	60	*	*	*	*
20	B, C, E	60	*			
21	C, D, E	60	*	*	*	*
22	C, D, A	60	*			
23	D, E, A	60	*			
24	D, E, B	60	*			
25	E, A, C	60	*			
26	A, B, C, D	80				
27	A, B, C, E	80				
28	B, C, D, E	80				
29	C, D, E, A	80				
30	D, E, A, B	80				
31	A, B, C, D, E	100				
Predicted coalitions			10	3	12	6

Source: Bergman (1995). The criteria of Riker, Axelrod, viability and the median legislator are explained in the text. An asterisk indicates that such a criterion is met.

sary partners ('minimal') ($n = 10$). One-third of all possible government combinations are included in the prediction set. Fifteen combinations are excluded because they do not form a majority. Another six coalitions are excluded because they are 'oversized'.

2 Axelrod's criterion: coalitions are formed that are connected and devoid of unnecessary partners ($n = 3$).
3 Viability criterion: selects cabinets with adjacent positions on the left–right scales, including the single parties that are capable of running a cabinet ($n = 12$).
4 The median legislator criterion selects the party that controls the median legislator and also all cabinets that includes this party, provided that the coalition partners are adjacent on the left–right scale ($n = 6$).

It seems from Table 8.9 that there is a difference between the traditional criteria and the criteria that put the majority threshold aside. When the traditional criterion of winning size is dropped, the prediction set becomes huge. In its original formulation, the viability criterion assumed that a new government must have at least plurality support in the parliament. More recently this criterion was reformulated to one of being able to survive a vote of confidence in the parliament (Laver and Schofield, 1990: 66; Budge and Keman, 1990: 34). The viability criterion drops the 'must contain an absolute majority' while keeping the assumptions that we should normally not expect oversized coalitions and that we should expect parties who are adjacent in policy space to form coalitions. The phenomenon that parties sometimes form minority governments can be explained by the 'party goals theory' of Kaare Strom (see Chapter 7). If a party believes that its voters are going to disapprove of a particular coalition and there are possibilities of influencing policy from its position in parliament, this diminishes the party's desire to get into government. Predictive theories should be as precise as possible. As the viability criterion selects twelve possible coalitions, it is vital to find a way to narrow this prediction set. Bergman suggests one way to do this, namely by predicting that the party that is in control of the median legislator will be decisive for the outcome of the government formation process. The median legislator is found by adding the number of seats that each party controls from the left to the right (or in the reverse order). In the example of Table 8.10 the Social Democrats hold the median

Table 8.10 *One-dimensional view of the Danish party system, 1966*

Left–right	Party	No. of seats
L	Socialist People's Party (SFP)	20
	Social Democrats (SD)	69
	Radical Liberals (RV)	13
	Liberals (V)	34
R	Christian People's Party (KPF)	35
	Others	8
Total		179

Source: Laver and Schofield (1990: 112).

legislator after the Danish elections of 1966. In the hypothetical example of Table 8.9 it is assumed that only coalitions will form that include party C (which controls the median legislator) which seems a plausible assumption (Laver and Budge, 1992).

How plausible this really is can be tested with the help of a data file that is an amalgamation of three types of data:

1 data on the characteristics of governments (composition, duration, reason for termination) (Woldendorp et al., 1993);
2 data on left–right positions (several left–right scales) (Volkens, 1994);
3 data on the distributions of seats and votes (Mackie and Rose, 1991).

This file (empol966.sav) holds information on 135 parties that participate in post-war governments (1945–1990) in 16 OECD countries (the USA and Japan are excluded). With the help of these combined data it is possible to test nearly all hypotheses and predictions included in the established coalition theories. We will demonstrate one example of this that relates to the parties that control the median legislator. Are these parties actually included in most of the governments? The party that controls the median legislator is defined as the party that is nearest to the 50 per cent border of legislator control.

Table 8.11 is based on a cross tabulation that determines for every country which percentage of the post-war cabinets controls the median legislator. The following conclusions can be drawn on the basis of this table. First of all, the two left–right

Table 8.11 *The percentage of each cabinet which controls the median legislator*

Country	Median legislator 1	Median legislator 2
Australia	42.1	43.8
Austria	53.8	61.5
Belgium	42.9	33.3
Canada	0	0
Denmark	23.8	29.4
Finland	53.8	40
France	14.3	18.2
Germany	45.5	71.4
Great Britain	41.7	45.5
Ireland	28.6	30
Italy	18.2	0
Netherlands	64.3	57.1
New Zealand	35.7	28.6
Norway	42.9	50
Sweden	78.6	81.8
Switzerland	100	100

Median legislator 1 is based on the Laver–Budge scale (1992). Median legislator 2 is based on the Pennings–Keman (1994) scale. A score of 0 means that the party that controls the median legislator did not participate in any post-war cabinet. A score of 100 means that this party participated in all (1950–1990) post-war cabinets.

scales produce similar but not identical results. The main reason for this is that these scales sum up different sets of left and right issues. Secondly, the control of the median legislator is an important determinant of government participation, but it is certainly not the only or the most influential factor (given the low percentages in several countries). Thirdly, there are significant differences between the countries. In Sweden, for example, we see that the median party is nearly always in government. In Italy and Canada this is rarely (or never) the case. These results suggest that there are more factors that have an impact on the coalition potential of parties or else that parsimonious explanations do not result in complete explanations (Bartolini, 1998).

One of the weakest aspects of traditional coalition theories is the (implicit) assumption of the majority threshold, namely that governments are only viable if they control more than 50 per cent of the seats. This assumption does not match with the frequency of minority cabinets. When one wants to drop the 50 per cent threshold for viability, one consequently has to formulate a new conceptualization of what viability means. This is done by Kaare Strom who formulated a *rational choice* theory on the phenomenon of minority governments. One of his hypotheses is that political parties are constantly weighting the costs and benefits of being in government. In cases where the costs of governing are higher than the costs of being an opposition party, it is expected that the rise of a minority government is more likely than in other cases. In this way, viability is disconnected from the number of seats and connected to a larger range of factors that relates to the costs and benefits of governing. Strom selects ten variables that in particular might influence the rise of minority governments (Strom, 1990b: Chapter 3):

- *Opposition influence*: a five-point index based on the properties of parliamentary committees. Hypothesis: the greater the potential influence of the opposition, the lower the relative benefits of governing and the higher the probability of minority governments.
- *Electoral salience*: the identifiability of viable government alternatives and the proximity of the formed governments to general elections. Hypothesis: the higher the electoral salience, the better the chance for minority governments.
- *Volatility*: the electoral volatility between successive elections, measured by the Pedersen formula which is similar to Bartolini and Mair's measure of total volatility which is discussed in Chapter 7. Hypothesis: the more volatility, the higher the costs and the greater the chance that minority governments will be formed.
- *Responsiveness*: the proportion of electoral gainers among its constituent parties. Hypothesis: the higher this proportion, the higher the chance of minority governments.
- *Crisis duration*: the duration of the cabinet crises in days. Hypothesis (based on conventional wisdom): minority governments should be associated with particularly long cabinet crises. (Strom expects no relationship. Note that it may be theoretically fruitful to incorporate relationships in the model in order to show that they are *not* as important as often thought).
- *Formation attempts*: the total number of the formation attempts of every

government. Hypothesis: minority governments should be associated with numerous formation attempts (again, this hypothesis is based on conventional wisdom: Strom expects no relationship).

- *Fractionalization*: measured by Rae's index (which subtracts the sum of the squared seats percentages from 1). Hypothesis: the more fractionalized the parliamentary system, the more difficult the formation of a winning coalition and the greater the likelihood of an undersized solution.
- *Polarization*: the proportion of all parliamentary seats held by extremist parties. Hypothesis: polarized parliaments should experience frequent minority governments.
- *Government extremism*: the proportional distribution of the opposition along the left–right dimension. Hypothesis: the bargaining advantage of centrist parties makes it easier for them to form minority governments.
- *Investiture*: a dummy variable for constitutional requirements of parliamentary investiture at the time of government formation (1 = existent). Hypothesis: minority governments are more difficult to form if a new government needs an immediate vote of confidence in its first encounter with the national assembly.

The occurrence of minority cabinets may be analyzed by both linear and logistic regression. In the case of the latter technique the dependent variable is a dummy variable: either there is a minority cabinet (1) or not (0). In the case of linear regression, the dependent variable is continuous and comprises the percentage of seats. By constructing two different dependent variables we are able to answer the Research Question by means of two different (but related) techniques. We do this in order to illustrate the differences and similarities between OLS and logistic regression. We hypothesize that the empirical results of these techniques are more or less similar. If so, we would ultimately prefer the logistic regression because it is theoretically directly linked to the question: what is the chance of finding minority cabinets given the circumstances which are defined by Strom's rational choice theory?

The results of both analyses are compared by listing the partial correlation of the linear regression and the R of the logistics regression because these two coefficients can be interpreted in the same way (Table 8.12). Both types of regressions support *all* hypotheses. In both cases the electoral salience is a relatively important factor. The OLS regression also designates the degree of polarization as a meaningful factor. The major theoretical significance of these models is that they confirm the basic predictions based on choice theory. At the same time, it is clear that some (unknown) theoretical factors are missing, as the explained variance of the model is poor. Thus, we have corroborated a rational choice theory on government formation by means of two related statistical techniques. The application of OLS and logistics regression was possible because the dependent variable can be measured with an interval score (i.e. the percentage of cabinet seats needed for OLS regression) and with a dichotomous score (the presence or absence of a minority cabinet) which is needed for logistic regression. Of these two techniques, logistic regression should be preferred because it is most directly linked to the research question: when do minority cabinets occur?

Table 8.12 *OLS and logistic regression on cabinet formation, based on Strom's data*

		Partial correlation	log *R*
V34	Opposition influence	−0.11	−0.07
V50	Electoral salience	−0.29	−0.18
V27	Decade volatility seats	−0.07	−0.05
V21	Responsiveness	−0.11	0
V05	Crisis	0.13	0.11
V10	Formation attempts	−0.07	−0.06
V25	Fractionalization	−0.09	−0.11
V29	Polarization	−0.23	−0.06
V51	Opposition unipolarity	0.1	0.04
V52	Investiture	0.06	0
	Explained/predicted	0.14	0.706

Source: Strom (1990b: 77, 83) and Strom's data file 'clean87.sav'. The operationalization of the variables is explained in the file documentation. ($N = 326$ governments in 15 European countries in the period 1945–1985).

Until now we have discussed the *one*-dimensional approach to cabinet formation: the policy distances are solely defined by the left–right differences between parties. Michael Laver and Ian Budge proposed an innovative multi-dimensional approach to cabinet formation by applying *cluster analysis* to the Party Manifesto data which is discussed in Section 4.5 (Laver and Budge, 1992). By means of exploratory factor analysis the 54 original issues are rearranged and fused into 20 issue dimensions. These new dimensions represent the main sources of party competition and are therefore more encompassing than merely the left–right distinction.

Laver and Budge's 'modeling of coalition formation in high-dimensional policy spaces' (as they describe it) is based on an inductive kind of modeling, derived from Grofman (1982). Grofman's model assumes that coalitions are formed in a series of stages, in which parties first combine into *protocoalitions*. In the following stages, these protocoalitions combine into larger coalitions (i.e. a protocoalition merges with another protocoalition) until some threshold is reached which makes the coalition large enough to take office (Laver and Budge, 1992: 30). Whether or not the combination is large enough depends on the viability of a government, and not necessarily on its majority. It is assumed that each stage of the government formation process is driven by the desire of political parties to form coalitions with a minimum of ideological diversity, similar to Axelrod's theorem.

Laver and Budge apply *cluster analysis* in order to be able to combine parties into protocoalitions. Cluster analysis approaches coalitions as clusters of parties by taking a set of points (i.e. the 20 dimensional policy positions) and combining them into a cluster. This process of combining continues until there is one single cluster (a grand coalition that comprises all parties). The cluster analysis is based on the matrix of policy distances between all pairs of parties, the so-called *city-block distance matrix* where city-block refers to the metric that measures the policy distance (namely, the distance between two points or parties is the sum of the policy distances between them on each of the 20 issue dimensions). We give an arbitrary example of the Swedish formation process in 1988 in Table 8.13 (Laver and Budge, 1992: 128).

The clustering technique will group parties on the basis of the distances. The formation of protocoalitions may be visualized by means of a so-called *dendrogram* that indicates not only which clusters are joined but also the distance at which they are joined. We show, again, the dendrogram based on the distance matrix for Sweden, 1988 (Figure 8.2).

The cluster analysis, as it is applied here, is solely based on programmatic differences and it totally ignores the institutional settings of party behavior. Therefore, the aim of cluster analysis is not so much to forecast a coalition, but to examine the institutional conditions that are at work. When 'obvious' coalitions are not formed, then there must have been additional, often institutional, factors which explain the formation of that particular coalition. In the example of Sweden, we need Strom's rational choice theory on minority coalitions to understand why the Social Democrats (SSA) are able to form a single party government in 1988 whereas a coalition government was more probable.

Table 8.13 *City-block dissimilarity coefficient matrix, Sweden 1988*

	Ecology	VK	SSA	FP	MS
VK	50				
SSA	68	72.6			
FP	68	59.8	83		
MS	102.9	101.5	105.7	66.9	
CP	59.8	77.8	65.6	71.6	86.7

Ecology = The Greens; VK = Communist Party; SSA = Social Democrats; FP = People's Party of the liberals; MS = Moderate Unity Party; CP = Center Party. The coefficients are based on the city-block measure (see Subsection 4.5.6). Source: Laver and Budge (1992: 141).

```
                          Rescaled Distance Cluster Combine

   C A S E      0         5        10        15        20        25
 Label     Num  +---------+---------+---------+---------+---------+

 Ecology     1   -+---------------+
 VK Commu    2   -+               +-------+
 FP Peopl    4   -----------------+       +-----------------------+
 SSA Soci    3   -------------------+-----+                       |
 CP Centr    6   -------------------+                             |
 MS Moder    5   -------------------------------------------------+
```

Figure 8.2 *Dendrogram using average linkage (between groups) for Sweden, 1988. The dendrogram is based on the distances that are reported in Table 8.13. One looks for the solution (combination of clusters) just before the distances at which the clusters are combined become too large. In this case, one would expect an Ecology–VK–FP coalition or a SSA–CP coalition. In reality a SSA-minority cabinet was formed. Source: Laver and Budge (1992)*

Until now we have discussed some aspects of cabinet formation. Another widely studied topic is cabinet functioning or cabinet performance (i.e. what cabinets do or produce). There are several ways to measure this, e.g. by means of cabinet duration or socio-economic performance. Here we concentrate on the factors that influence the duration of cabinets.

In the recent literature on cabinet stability there is a discussion about the relative merits of the attributes and the events approach toward cabinet duration. Strom's model concentrates on the attributes, being systemic features of countries that influence the cabinet duration (Strom, 1985). Frendries et al. (1986) focus on the so-called events, being unforeseen and unpredictable incidents that lead to the end of cabinets King et al. (1990) try to combine these two approaches in a so-called unified model.

Let's first start with an attributes model and thereafter discuss the pros and cons of such a model. Strom proposed a model that explains cabinet duration with the help of a set of attributes-variables that overlap with the previous selection of ten variables that was used to explain government formation (Strom, 1985). The determinants of cabinet duration may be divided into country attributes, party structure attributes and coalition attributes:

1 country attributes: electoral salience (the salience of general elections for government), opposition influence (a five-point scale based on characteristics of the legislative committee systems), investiture (the (non)existence of legislative investiture requirements), volatility (electoral volatility for parliamentary seats), responsiveness (of government formation to electoral verdicts);
2 party system attributes: fractionalization (Rae's index: 1 − the sum of the squared percentages of the seats per party), polarization (extremist party support: Powell's index, 1982: 95).
3 coalition attributes: parliamentary status (the percentage of parliamentary seats held by the governing parties), crisis duration (preceding each government duration), formation attempts (during these crises), opposition concentration (measured as the number of seats held by parties on the numerically largest opposition side as a proportion of all opposition seats).

Note that this combination of variables into one model is the result of a multi-level conceptualization of factors relating to systems, parties and governments. Such a multi-level structure is linked to potential methodological problems, like the ecological fallacy and problems of inference.

Strom has applied regression analysis in order to determine the relative causal effects of the three types of attributes. The regression results are visualized by means of a causal path model (Figure 8.3). Strom's model has an explained variance of 0.29, being the R^2 of the 'main model' (namely: cabinet duration with parliamentary basis, electoral salience and crisis duration). The strongest beta value is electoral salience, and the positive sign is no surprise: the more salient elections are for government formation, the longer governments endure. Electoral salience has also several (weak) indirect effects on government durability: through crisis duration, formation attempts and parliamentary basis.

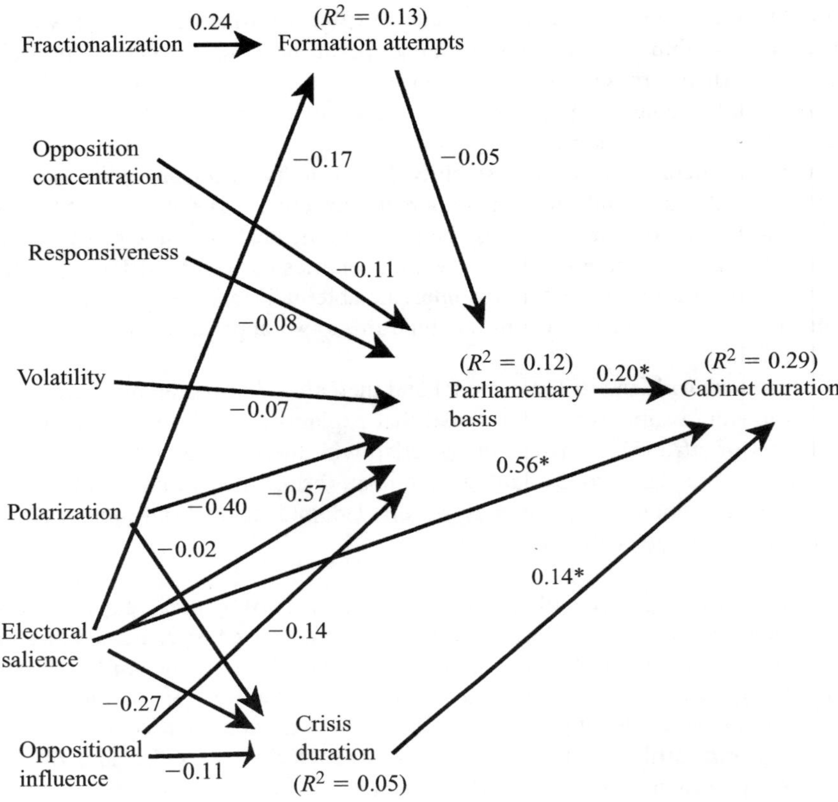

Figure 8.3 *Strom's causal path model of cabinet duration, 1946–1987. DW = 2.3; n = 313. An asterisk implies significance at the 0.01 level. Source: Strom (1985: 748). Data: Strom's data file on minority governments 'clean87.sav'*

The low explained variance asks for more (and other) factors than the attributes. Whereas the attributes theorists (like Kaare Strom) seek to explain cabinet duration as a fixed function of measured explanatory variables, the events process theorists model cabinet duration as a product of purely stochastic processes, i.e. generated by a particular 'critical' or 'terminal' event (Browne et al., 1988).[2]

8.5 INSTITUTIONS, ECONOMIC GROWTH AND THE PUBLIC SECTOR

In this section we will examine the determinants of economic growth and public sector growth. Several influential theories in political science have been formulated to explain both phenomena. However, these theories are mostly difficult to test because of a lack of adequate data or operationalizations. This section is intended to give two examples of how to handle such a situation. It will be argued and illustrated that it is sometimes possible to test or adjust existing theories by asking the question: 'What may be reasonably expected if the theory is correct?'. This gives the researcher room for maneuver for an indirect testing and elaboration of existing models. At the same time, we must be aware that this type of theory testing has some serious drawbacks because it is often too indirect to be a valid test of the original theoretical assumptions.

In Section 8.4 we referred to the rational choice theory of cabinet formation. One difference with the theory on minority cabinets is that most theories of economic growth and public sector growth are too complex or encompassing to be tested by one single model. We will therefore start with one particular model that has the advantage that it has been empirically tested, namely that of Mancur Olson (Mueller, 1983; Lane and Ersson, 1986).

In the *Rise and Decline of Nations* (1982) (often abbreviated as RADON) Olson argues that a crucial factor in explaining the rise and decline of nations is the structure of pressure groups at various levels of government. These so-called distributional coalitions reduce economic growth by pushing for their special interests. The wealth of nations is not only a function of economic variables but also of the political authority structure (Lane and Ersson, 1986: 19). The more segmented the political structure in terms of the size and strength of distributional coalitions, the less is the economic advancement. Olson's theory comprises nine hypotheses that focus on the conflict between overall economic efficiency and growth on the one hand and the interests of distributional coalitions on the other.

Lane and Ersson have, among others, tested the Olson model (Lane and Ersson, 1986; see also Choi, 1983; Czada, 1987). Lane and Ersson admit that there is no straightforward way of testing the nine hypotheses comprising the core of the argument. Firstly, the operationalization of concepts as distributional coalitions appears somewhat problematic (Czada, 1987: 22–3). Secondly, how can we measure the true *partial* impact of the distributional coalitions in relation to other factors that influence the economic development? Lane and Ersson approach this problem by asking: 'What could be reasonably expected if the RADON argument is true?'. First, they expect that the country variations in GDP growth rates are larger than the variation across time. In order to test this assumption, they apply two separate ANOVA analyses (see Subsection 5.5.2). Both have economic growth as dependent variable. One model has country ($n = 18$) as independent variable and the other year (1965–1995) (see the file Chapter8.sps for the SPSS setup).

The results are reported in Table 8.14. The η^2 value indicates the explained variance in economic growth. The ANOVA analysis shows that the cross-time

Table 8.14 *Analysis of variance of GDP growth rates by country and time (1965–1995)*

	η^2	F	Sign. of F
Country ($n = 18$)	0.09	3.1	0.00
Year ($n = 30$)	0.38	10.8	0.00

variation ($\eta^2 = 0.38$) is much more pronounced than the between-nation differences ($\eta^2 = 0.09$). The assumption that country variations in GDP growth rates are larger than the variations across time is not supported by the ANOVA test. Lane and Ersson's conclusion is that, as the structure of political institutions does not change radically from one year to another, the implication of this finding is that the RADON argument cannot explain the short-run variation in economic growth. The question remains, then, whether political institutions have an impact on the average (long-run) growth levels in advanced democracies. For this purpose Lane and Ersson select variables that may be suited to test the general hypothesis that 'politics matters for long-run economic growth'. The following variables of this selection are especially relevant given their impact on economic growth, which is the dependent variable (the real gross domestic product: year to year changes (Source: OECD, 1995)).[3] Box 8.2 gives an overview of the independent variables, their operationalization and the underlying hypotheses (as formulated by Lane and Ersson, 1986: 24–5).

The test of Olson's model has been performed by means of OLS regression on

Box 8.2 Overview of the independent variables in Lane and Ersson's test of Olson's model

- *GDP65*: the GDP per capita in 1965. *Hypothesis*: a negative relationship is expected: OECD countries with a relatively low level of performance in 1965 grow relatively fast.
- *TOTCIV*: total civilian employment × 1000. *Hypothesis*: the growth of the tertiary sector would imply a slowdown in economic growth because this sector has a lower potential for productivity.
- *Choi*: the index of institutionalization or institutional sclerosis as developed by Choi (1983). *Hypothesis*: a negative relationship is expected, as a high level of institutionalization will generate a low rate of economic growth.
- *Corporms*: corporatist interest intermediation as operationalized by Schmidt (1982: 245). (The higher the score, the higher the degree of corporatism). *Hypothesis*: corporatist avenues to national decision-making may result in encompassing decision-making and therefore enhance economic growth.
- *Consoc*: the degree of consociationalism based on annualized scores of Lijphart's index (1984). (A high score indicates a high degree of consociationalism.) *Hypothesis*: identical to corporatism: broad social decision-making would be conducive to encompassing social solutions.
- *CPG*: Colour of Party Government as operationalized by Schmidt (1992) (a high score denotes a leftist government). *Hypothesis*: a socialist government favors redistribution whereas non-socialist governments emphasize economic growth.
- *Trans*: social transfers as a percentage of GDP (Source: OECD, Historical Statistics). *Hypothesis*: an increase in transfer payments would have a negative impact favoring distribution over growth.

Source: Lane and Ersson (1986: 24–5).

Table 8.15 *OLS and PCSE regressions on Olson's model, 1965–1990*

	OLS regression (n = 17)		PCSE regression (n = 442)	
Variable	**beta**	t	**beta**	t
GDP65	−0.15	−0.72	−0.10	−1.90
Totciv	−0.01	−0.05	0.00	0.04
Choi	−0.69	−3.49	−0.20	−4.47
Corporms	0.26	1.48	0.08	2.78
Consoc	−0.45	−2.50	−0.12	−2.40
CPG	−0.37	−2.12	−0.06	−1.48
Trans	−0.17	−1.13	−0.31	−4.13
Constant		9.43		
R^2	0.84		0.18	
R^2_{adj}	0.72		0.17	

The variables are explained in Box 8.2. The dependent variable is economic growth. New Zealand is excluded because of missing data on transfers. The PCSE regression corrects for both heteroscedasticity and serial autocorrelation, which explains the differences in the results of the PCSE and OLS regressions. However, PCSE does not, of course, compensate for erroneous model specifications!

17 cases and PCSE regression on 442 cases (17 countries and 26 years). Both techniques produce quite similar results. The main difference is that the OLS regression leads to an explained variance of 0.72 whereas the PCSE regression technique throws up the much lower number of 0.17. The latter is probably more reliable as it is based on more cases. The results of the PCSE regression (which was explained in Section 6.7) indicate that all hypotheses are confirmed, except the hypothesis on consensus democracy. Relatively important variables are transfers and Choi's index of institutionalization. However, we must be cautious when drawing conclusions. The low explained variance indicates that we are missing additional variables that might explain economic growth. However, here it was not our aim to explain as much in the variation in economic growth as possible. The aim was to relate economic growth to a selection of variables that are more or less typical for Olson's theory. The low explained variance does not mean that Olson's theory is incorrect, because it is questionable whether the selection of variables in Box 8.2 really fully represents Olson's theory.

Another debated topic is the explanation of the continuous growth of the public sector in the post-war period. Several rational-choice and new-institutionalism theories seek to explain public sector growth. For example, North has formulated a theory that states that the transaction costs are an important determinant of public sector growth (North, 1990). Niskanen's theory claims that the bureaucracy tries to maximize the budget which steers the public economy (Dunleavy, 1991). We will not try to test these (and other public sector) theories here. Instead, we will simply present a model that integrates the role of actors and institutions regarding the public sector in ways that are related to, but not identical to, existing theories. This approach enables us to determine which actor-related and institutional determinants of public sector growth are important. This is an indirect way to test existing theories. First, we start with the ANOVA test on the cross-time variation and between-nation differences regarding public sector growth. This analysis shows us that the country variations on public sector growth (operationalized as government employment) are more important than the yearly variations (the η scores are 0.85 and 0.33, respectively). These results run contrary to the previous ANOVA test on economic growth. Second, we have designed a model that holds the main explanatory variables. This model includes both institutional variables and actor-related variables because these are the principal factors in the 'Chain of Democratic Control and Command' that has been visualized and explained at the beginning of Part III. These variables are:

- *The style of political leadership*, as operationalized by Peters et al. (1977). We expect that coalescent systems have a larger public sector than competitive systems.
- *Presidentialism*, as operationalized by Lijphart (1984: 88). It is assumed that presidentialism hampers government employment.
- *Consensus democracy*, as operationalized by Pennings (1997). The hypothesis here is that consensual systems stir government employment.
- *Federalism*, as operationalized by Lane et al. (1997). It is expected that federalism hampers government employment.
- *Left votes*, as operationalized by Keman (1988). We expect that the electoral strength of left parties correlates positively with government employment.

The outcomes of the PCSE regression indicate that the style of political leadership seems relatively important (beta = 0.47). It is remarkable that consensus democracy throws up a negative beta whereas a positive sign was expected. The variables Presidentialism and Left Votes confirm the hypothesis, be it that these causal effects are very moderate. The regression outcomes suggest that both actor-related and institutional variables are important for the understanding of cross-sectional and cross-time variations in government employment, but also that we need additional variables. In this sense, the conclusions regarding the economic growth and the government growth models are similar, be it that the latter model generates a higher explained variance.

One way to examine the possibilities for the inclusion of alternative and

Table 8.16 *PCSE regression on government employment (1965–1990)*

Variable	beta	t
Leadership	0.47	10.59
Presidentialism	−0.15	−5.1
Federalism	0.05	2.15
Left votes	0.26	6.38
Consociationalism	−0.33	−8.03
Constant	0	7.66

The variables are explained in the text. $N = 468$ (18 countries; 26 years). All scores are significant at the 0.05 level. $R^2 = 0.36$; $R^2_{adj} = 0.36$. Government employment is an indicator of the size of the public sector.

additional determinants in the model is to study the residuals of this regression on the country level. These scores indicate whether countries have more or less government employment than may be expected on the basis of the scores of the independent variables. When the residual analysis shows that one or more countries are outliers, then it makes sense to include variables that represent additional explanations for these outliers.

8.6 INTEREST INTERMEDIATION

Corporatism has been much debated since Philippe Schmitter's article 'Still the century of corporatism?' (1974). Since that time many corporatism scales have been developed. Most of them are based on different conceptualizations and operationalizations, so that they are hard to compare. In this section we will compare some of these scales with the help of correlation and regression analysis. These two techniques serve our aim of comparing the degree of correspondence between several scales. The background is set by a discussion between Crepaz/ Lijphart and the authors of this book. The following examples relate to this discussion (Keman and Pennings, 1995).

Various similar corporatism scales have been developed in order to capture the nature and degree of socio-economic interest intermediation (see Table 8.17). One of the potential problems behind these scales is that their similarity may be highly misleading. Corporatism scales may have strongly similar scores for each of the countries, but more often than not they have a different meaning. Thus, and this is the main lesson of this section, dissimilar indicators sometimes yield the same results! Let's have a look at the following examples of dissimilar corporatism scales:

1 Schmitter, Crouch and Cameron regard the *organizational features* of the actors involved and their *threat potential* (e.g. strike-activities) as vital to their conceptualization.
2 Schmidt and Czada emphasize in their definition of corporatism *social partnership* with state involvement in the bargaining process.
3 Paloheimo and Lehner emphasize 'concertation' i.e. *a general economic consensus* among the main participants which induces a 'logic of accommodation'.

These various definitions indicate that the underlying meaning of the term corporatism is not equivalent. The three groups of indices mentioned here as examples will thus have a different theoretical impact: the scores may more or less match, but that does not imply that they mean the same thing in the different countries! It is striking to observe, for instance, that the indexes of Schmidt and Paloheimo statistically almost completely overlap (Tables 8.17 and 8.18), but are at the same time conceptualized quite differently. Although the various indices broadly correspond, quite a few do not show strong inter-correlations. The reason for this is simple: there are some countries that are scored in an opposite fashion. This neatly illustrates the general point made above.

Table 8.17 *A selection of influential corporatism scales*

Country	Crouch	Schmitter	Schmidt	Czada (1983)	Czada (1987)	Paloheimo	Lehner	Cameron	Keman	Lehmbruch	Corp. AL	Cons. AL
Australia	0		2	1	2	2	3	40	2	1	−1	−0.9
Austria	1	1	3	3	5	3	4	100	5	4	1.6	−0.4
Belgium	0	7	2	2	4	2	3	77	2	3	0.3	0.6
Canada	0	11	1	1	2	1	1	21.6	1	1	−1.4	−1.5
Denmark	1	4	2	2	4	2	3	91.8	3	3	0.5	0.8
Finland	1	4	2	2	4	2	3	84.6	3	3	0.4	1.5
France	0	13	1	2	1	1	1	16.8	2		−0.7	−0.2
FRG	1	8	2	2	1	2	3	44.8	3	3	0.5	−0.1
Ireland	0	11	1	2	3	1	3	41.6	1	3	−0.5	−0.7
Italy	0	15	1	2	2	1	2	32.8	2	2	−0.9	1
Japan	0		2	1	1	3	5	6.4	3		0.1	0
Netherlands	1	6	3	3	3	2	4	39.2	4	4	1	1.4
New Zealand	0		2	1	3		3		2	1	−1.1	−1.3
Norway	1	2	3	3	5	3	4	117	5	4	1.5	0.2
Sweden	1	4	3	3	5	3	4	126	5	4	1.4	0.1
Switzerland	1	9	3	2	3	3	5	33.6	4	3	0.5	1.7
UK	0	14	1	2	2	1	2	45	2	2	−0.9	−1.3
USA	0	11	1	1	1	1	1	18.9	1	1	−1.3	−1.3

Sources: Crouch (1985); Schmitter (1981); Schmidt (1982); Czada (1983, 1987); Paloheimo (1984); Lehner (1988); Cameron (1984); Keman (1988); Lehmbruch (1984); Lijphart and Crepaz (1991).

Table 8.18 *Spearman's rho correlations of corporatism indices (n = 18)*

	Crouch	Schmitter	Schmidt	Czada (1983)	Paloheimo
Schmitter	−0.81 $n = 15$ Sig 0.00				
Schmidt	−.78 $n = 18$ Sig 0.00	−0.83 $n = 15$ Sig 0.00			
Czada (1983)	0.70 $n = 18$ Sig 0.00	−0.64 $n = 15$ Sig 0.01	0.58 $n = 18$ Sig 0.01		
Paloheimo	0.66 $n = 17$ Sig 0.00	−0.84 $n = 15$ Sig 0.00	0.92 $n = 17$ Sig 0.00	0.43 $n = 17$ Sig 0.09	
Lehner	0.59 $n = 18$ Sig 0.01	−0.71 $n = 15$ Sig 0.00	0.87 $n = 18$ Sig 0.00	0.43 $n = 18$ Sig 0.07	0.91 $n = 17$ Sig 0.00

Source: see Table 8.17. Schmitter's scores are inversed, which explains the negative relations with other indices.

In sum, both the conceptualization and the operationalization of corporatism is strikingly divergent so that the correlations have a very limited value here. It is doubtful whether the method advocated by Lijphart and Crepaz of combining a number of corporatism indices yields either valid or reliable results (Lijphart and Crepaz, 1991). It would have been better if they had selected one (or two) of the existing indices for the analysis on the basis of their own arguments put forward. The communality is derived from a crucial feature underlying both concepts, namely collective decision-making by means of compromise and cooperation between the relevant actors involved (i.e. political parties in a consensus democracy; socio-economic actors in corporatist arrangements). The assumption is that all actors involved know that if another strategy is pursued the resulting decision-making will more often than not be *sub*-optimal. However, and this is an *essential* difference between the concepts, consensus democracy represents a mode of institutionalization of political actors by referring to aspects of parliamentary democracy, whereas corporatist interest intermediation represents the incorporation of societal actors typically by means of non-parliamentary consultation in order to avoid zero-sum outcomes of policy formation.

If our line of reasoning is correct, then it follows that both measures are based on the 'logic of accommodation' and may empirically co-vary, but at the same time it does not imply that consensus democracy and corporatism have the same effect on the results of the decision-making process. Hence there appears to be a structural affinity, but the concepts are not identical nor can one category be considered as a superordinate or subordinate category of the other. Assuming a proper measurement of both concepts as comparative variables, we should be able to assess to what extent both dimensions of political decision-making in democracies occur together in reality. To this end we have correlated (using Spearman's rho because we are relating ordinal scales) the various measures of corporatism employed by Lijphart and Crepaz to construct their index of corporatism with the index of consensus democracy (see their table 1, p. 239). From this exercise it appears that the composite index of corporatism developed by Lijphart and Crepaz (the 'lump sum' measure) is among those that correlate most strongly with their own index of consensus democracy ($r_s = 0.569$). Only Crouch ($r_s = 0.589$), Lehmbruch ($r_s = 0.577$) and Schott ($r_s = 0.527$) come close to this degree of association. These results demonstrate that the various indices of corporatism differ among each other in at least two respects: firstly, the extent to which countries are considered as being corporatist, and secondly the way the various authors have placed countries on their respective scales. We must conclude therefore, given the variation in conceptualization, that the index developed by the authors is meaningless in terms of validity and is dubious in terms of reliability. In other words, regardless of the structural affinity between consensus democracy and corporatism, it appears that the empirical relationship is by and large identical. Hence, the lesson here is that additive indexes should be based on a univocal conceptualization and operationalization of the constituent elements.

Corporatism and consensus democracy are different concepts as there seems neither a theoretical nor an empirical reason to subsume corporatism under the characteristics of consensus democracy. We can determine the relative weight of corporatism in explaining the variance of consensus democracy by looking at the regression of the nine features of consensus democracies plus the composite scale of corporatism (Table 8.19). Although the bivariate relationship between consensus democracy and corporatism is moderately strong ($r_s = 0.64$), the *relative* weight of corporatism is so small that it does not fit into the model. If compared with other factors, corporatism explains a negligible part in the variance of the features of consensus democracy as defined by Lijphart. Both concepts should be analyzed independently, together with other political variables, in order to assess the extent to which each does indeed influence democratic decision-making.

Table 8.19 *Regression of the nine characteristics plus corporatism on consensus democracy ($R^2_{adj} = 0.99$)*

Variable	beta	t	Sig. t
Minwin	−0.34	−5.61	0.00
Elecdis	−0.27	−5.23	0.00
Cabdur	−0.24	−6.71	0.00
Issuedim	−0.22	−4.08	0.00
Npties	−0.17	−2.25	0.06
Corporal	0.07	1.41	0.20
Conflex	−0.03	−0.86	0.42
Govtax	0.02	0.68	0.52
Referend	0.1	0.19	0.85
Unicam	0.1	0.38	0.72
(Constant)		1.13	0.29

See, for an explanation, Table 8.1.

Additional variables are Corporal (Corporatism scale Lijphart/Crepaz) and Referend (frequency of referenda). Sources: Lijphart (1984); Lijphart and Crepaz (1991). $n = 18$.

We have demonstrated that both concepts are strongly intertwined with the type and the organization of the political system and also strongly related to the complexion of government and parliament. Although both concepts are apparently similar, they do not have the same meaning and can empirically be distinguished in relation to features of liberal democratic decision-making. In general, it makes sense to inspect the underlying dimensions of a concept and to confront various measures with each other in order to be assured that the chosen indicator is valid and reliable and adds to a substantially plausible explanation of the dependent variable. Correlation and regression analysis provide the necessary tools to do so.

8.7 FEDERALISM, CENTRALISM AND INSTITUTIONAL AUTONOMY

The constitutional design of the democratic state is a defining element of the room for maneuver of government (Lijphart, 1984; Lane and Ersson, 1994). Three variables that are important for the cross-national variation in policy-making are (Keman and McDonald, 1996):

- *Federalism versus the unitary state*: the degree of geographical autonomy *vis-à-vis* the political center that often manifests itself, among other things, in the level of taxation. In unitary states we expect a stronger impact of governments on policy-making.
- *Centralized versus decentralized governance*: the degree to which aspects of policy-making are directed from the central political institutions. Some federal states are centralized in some respects and some unitary states have decentralized features, either functionally or geographically.
- *Institutional autonomy*, or devolution-index: the degree to which decentralized governing units, like local communities, have powers to control policy-making independently of the center (i.e. forms of self-regulation).

These distinctions are necessary in order to understand the high degree of variation in forms of institutional autonomy. A unitary state with a high degree of institutional autonomy (like the Netherlands during the period of 'Verzuiling') may well exert more influence independently than sub-national units in a more or less federalized polity.

Table 8.20 indicates that most federalist countries are characterized by a high degree of institutional autonomy. Countries with a low degree of federalism are not automatically centralistic. Examples of non-federalist and decentralized countries are Sweden, Denmark and Finland.

Figure 8.4 is a scatterplot of the data presented in Table 8.20 (see chapter8.sps for the SPSS syntax). Federalism is responsible for the vertical spread of the cases, centralism and autonomy for the horizontal spread. This figure shows, more clearly than the table does, that there are three groups of low, medium and high levels of federalism. The more a country is removed from the origin, the more it is characterized by federalism, decentralism and institutional autonomy. The figure shows

Table 8.20 *Scales of federalism, autonomy and centralism*

Country	Federalism	Autonomy	Centralism
Ireland	1	0	1
France	1	0	2
The Netherlands	1	2	1
New Zealand	1	2	2
UK	1	3	3
Norway	1	4	3
Denmark	1	4	4
Finland	1	4	4
Sweden	1	4	5
Japan	1	4	5
Italy	2	3	1
Austria	2	4	3
Belgium	2	5	2
Australia	3	6	3
Germany	3	6	4
Switzerland	3	7	5
USA	3	7	5
Canada	3	8	6

Federalism: the degree of federalism: 1 = unitary, 2 = quasi-unitary (with regional and community levels of government), 3 = federal. Source: Lane et al. 1997.
Autonomy: index of devolution; adds up the scores for five dimensions: federalism, special territory autonomy, regional and financial autonomy, local government discretion and functional autonomy, which are all explained in Lane and Ersson, 1994, Ch. 6.
Centralism: the degree of centralism; index based on tax-income of central state relative to total revenues in rank orders: high = 1; low = 6. Source: OECD, Revenue Statistics.

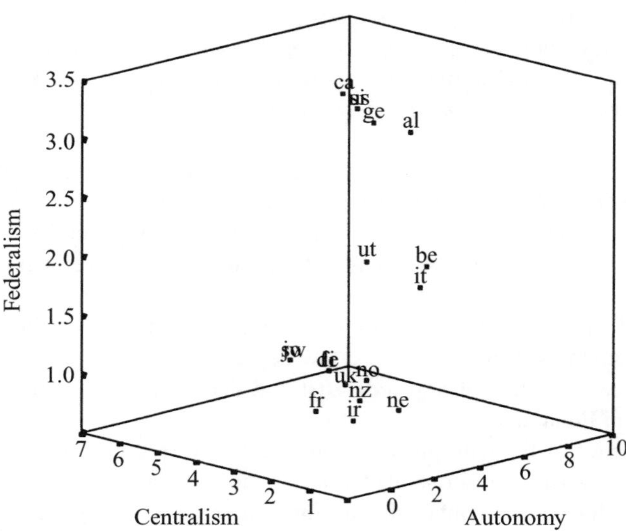

Figure 8.4 *A three-dimensional scatterplot of federalism, centralism and autonomy*

that these three institutional structures are interrelated, although they are not identical (because in that case the distances between the countries would be smaller or even absent). This type of plot is also useful for the study of other relationships, like those between corporatism, consensus democracy and world market integration at the country level (Section 8.6) or those between office-seeking, vote-seeking and policy-seeking behavior at the party level (Subsection 7.2.1).

The variations in the degree of federalism, centralization and institutional autonomy do relate to variations in public policy-making. This can be examined by means of separate bivariate regression analyses in which federalism, centralism and autonomy are the independent variables and several policy indicators the dependent variables. Table 8.21 shows that federal states are characterized by lower levels of welfare state provision than unitary states. This is shown by the negative relationships with the total government expenditures (public economy), and the expenditures on education, health and transfers as percentages of GDP. Additionally there is a very consistent pattern related to the four economic policy scales (Keman, 1993a): fiscalism, monetarism, economic interventionism and social interventionism (see for the operationalization the notes in Table 8.21). Federalist, centralist and autonomist nations are hardly inclined toward socio-economic interventionism. Federal systems are mostly decentralized with a public economy under one-third of GDP.

The moderately high beta-weights suggest that several countries form an exception to the 'rule' that unitarism and centralism are favorable for welfare state provision. This may be illustrated by means of residual analysis. Table 8.22 shows that the residual scores are quite stable. This indicates that federalism, centralism

Table 8.21 *Policy-formation and constitutional design (1970–1990)*

	Policy outcomes		Beta-weights (= X)		
Policy area (= Y**)**	**Real**	**Est'd Federalism**	**Federalism**	**Centralism**	**Autonomy**
Public economy	44.7%	54.9%	−0.53	−0.36	−0.43
Education	5.9%	6.5%	−0.2	(−0.04)	−0.03
Transfers	14.9%	18.0%	−0.32	−0.51	−0.46
Health	5.6%	6.7%	−0.38	(−0.10)	−0.33
Fiscalism			0.42	0.56	0.5
Monetarism			0.46	0.35	0.43
Economic interventionism			−0.47	−0.43	−0.46
Social interventionism			−0.32	−0.44	−0.42

Public Economy = total expenditures as % GDP; Education = education expenditures as % GDP; Transfers = transfers to households as % GDP; Health = health expenditures as % GDP; Fiscalism (relates to the outlays) = factor analysis (first principal component scores) on the variables autonomy of the central bank ('AUTOBANK', see Busch, 1995), public economy ('PE') and budget deficits ('DEF'); Monetarism (relates to the circulation of money) = factor analysis on the variables Money Supply ('MS'), Discount Rate ('DR') and Government Consumption ('GC'); Economic interventionism = the TEDC factor scores (see Section 9.2); Social Interventionism = the WEDC factor scores in parentheses (see Section 9.2).

All regressions are bivariate and OLS. Beta-weights are not significant (>0.05). $N = 288$.

Source: Keman (1993); Keman and McDonald (1996).

Table 8.22 *Residual scores of the regression of federalism, autonomy and centralism on public economy (PE)*

Country	Federalism	Autonomy	Centralization
Japan	−17.2	−14.34	−10.85
Switzerland	−10.43	−11.4	−12.22
New Zealand	−9.5	−9.51	−9.09
Australia	−4.86	−7.26	−10.61
USA	−4.76	−5.73	−6.56
Finland	−4.75	−1.89	−0.38
UK	−3.24	−1.82	−0.85
Ireland	−1.09	−3.98	−2.65
France	0.74	−2.15	1.15
Norway	2.79	5.65	5.18
Italy	3.04	0.39	−2.59
Canada	3.64	4.11	3.82
Austria	5.36	4.15	3.68
Denmark	5.81	8.67	10.17
The Netherlands	7.67	7.65	6.11
Germany	7.79	5.38	4.02
Belgium	8.84	9.06	5.18
Sweden	10.14	13	16.48

$N = 18$; period = 1965–1990. See for explanation Table 8.20. A negative score means that the level of public economy is lower than would be expected on the basis of the degree of federalism, autonomy or centralization, a positive score that this level is higher. A score near zero means that the observed and expected levels are nearly identical.

and institutional autonomy are strongly interrelated. It appears that Switzerland's public sector is *not* small because of its federalism or lack of centralism: the negative residuals indicate that there are additional country-specific factors that may account for this. The same goes for Sweden, which has a larger public sector than is expected on the basis of its degree of federalism, etc. Again, we need additional factors to account for this, such as its social democratic dominance. This reciprocal relationship between generalizing models and country-specific information is characteristic of small-n comparative analysis (see also Part I).

8.8 PRESIDENTIALISM

The distinction between parliamentarism and presidentialism clearly matters for the democratic process and the policy process (Sartori, 1994). In this section we will study presidentialism from three comparative perspectives:

- The *most different approach*: are worldwide presidential systems less democratic than parliamentary systems? (Note that the most different approach is only partly applicable, because this question is not based on the causal logic behind this approach: we are only asking for variations and not for explanations.)

- The *most similar approach*: do presidential systems in OECD countries lead to different socio-economic performance?
- The *comparative case study approach*: how can we account for the exceptionally high democratic and socio-economic performance of the US presidential system?

The third Research Design is a logical continuation of the first two designs. This design confronts the empirical findings of comparative research with one challenging case that does not fit. This case derives its more or less deviant status from the comparative research, but its existence can at the same time not be explained by this type of research. For that we need the comparative case study.

In the most different design we may distinguish between several types of executive systems: Parliamentary, Limited Presidential, Dual systems, Unlimited Presidential, Communist, Military and Absolute (Derbyshire and Derbyshire, 1990). The results of this analysis are quite univocal: parliamentary systems are more democratic than other systems. The limited presidential systems are clearly less democratic, as is shown by the one-way analysis of variance on the Gastil index (Table 8.23). The unlimited presidential systems are the least democratic systems, even less than the military and the absolute executive systems.

Another way of looking at the democratic character of the various executive systems is to look at the frequency and character of political protest and violence. Here we limit the data analysis of the Parliamentary systems ($n = 33$) and Limited ($n = 53$) and Unlimited Presidentialism ($n = 7$). Analysis of variance is applied in order to determine to what extent these systems differ in their degree of democracy. For this purpose we utilize the Yearly Political Events Data of the *World Handbook of Political and Social Indicators* (Taylor and Jodice, 1977) for 93 countries in the period 1948–1982 (although first published in 1977, the period was later extended to 1982). These events were coded on the basis of the New York Times Index and numerous national newspapers. Table 8.24 shows that there are significant differences between the executive systems. The most important differences are distinguished by the (significant) relevant high F-scores: executive renewal, adjustments and transfers and political execution.

Table 8.23 *One-way analysis of variance of the Gastil democracy index per regime type, 1972–1989*

Group	n	Mean	Standard deviation	Standard error	Minimum	Maximum	95% conf. int. for mean
Parliamentary	468	12.18	2.53	0.12	4	14	11.95–12.41
Limited Presidential	648	6.94	3.46	0.14	2	14	6.68–7.21
Dual	90	10.31	2.88	0.3	5	14	9.71–10.91
Unlimited Presidential	90	2.81	1.13	0.12	2	6	2.57–3.05
Communist	342	4.22	1.78	0.1	2	9	4.03–4.41
Military	198	4.05	1.86	0.13	2	11	3.79–4.31
Absolute	90	5.42	1.45	0.15	3	9	5.12–5.73
Total	1926	7.33	4.14	0.09	2	14	7.14–7.51

Summary statistics: F-ratio = 461.15; F prob. = 0.0000.

Table 8.24 *Analysis of variance of political events per regime type, 1948–1982*

Event Type	Parliamentary	Limited presidential	Unlimited presidential	Mean	*F*	Sign. *F*
Protest demonstrations	−0.06	0.16	−0.89	3.51	0.447	0.639
Regime supportive demonstrations	−0.21	0.04	0.73	0.57	13.312	0
Riots	0.16	0.05	−0.12	2.79	2.093	0.124
Armed attack	6.49	−4.94	6.81	17.1	4.528	0.011
Assassination ⟨success⟩	−0.04	0.02	0.04	0.23	0.612	0.542
Political strikes	0.72	−0.31	−0.104	0.124	16.01	0
Executive renewal	0.24	−0.13	−0.16	0.41	36.673	0
Executive adjustments	−0.3	0.08	0.81	1.17	36.674	0
Unsuc. reg. executive transfer	0.07	−0.04	0.07	0.12	7.107	0.001
Reg. executive transfers	0.02	−0.02	0.02	0.41	1.11	0.329
Unsuc. irreg. executive transfers	−55.97	26.9	60.17	66.36	21.045	0
Irreg. executive transfers	−34.69	16.15	41.26	48.54	15.646	0
Election	59.4	−20.08	−127.98	319.82	13.265	0
Imposition of political sanctions	−1462.2	288.96	4702.63	8732.62	7.66	0
Political execution	−2828.99	−813.13	19540	3357.6	49.654	0
Relaxation of sanction	−411.04	136.55	903.85	1602.65	14.438	0
Death from violence	−6.21	−1.16	38.09	29.81	14.438	0

$N = 3255$ (35 years for 93 countries). Source: Taylor and Jodice (1977) [Data file ICPSR I7761].

Until now we have approached presidentialism starting from the most different method. It is also possible to apply the most similar method, but then we have to reformulate the Research Question by restricting presidentialism to similar cases, such as liberal democracies that are part of the OECD. We may hypothesize that in most democratic polities presidentialism *as such* is not the main determinant of policy-formation and that its significance depends on its interaction with other, mostly institutional, factors.

The occurrence and effects of presidentialism must be examined in combination with other institutional structures. Our approach here has been inspired by a comparative study on the policy effects of presidential and parliamentary decision-making structures (Weaver and Rockman, 1993). The institutional environment does not only shape the room for maneuver of presidents, but also of other important actors like political parties, organized interest groups and the bureaucracy. *Boolean analysis* is one way to examine these institutional combinations and their policy effects. This technique has already been explained and applied to several data sets in this book.

It is not feasible to measure the exact room for maneuver of different actors within various institutional environments. We have to hypothesize what the institutional impact on actors might be. This is done in Table 8.25. The room for maneuver and influence of these actors is operationalized by multiplying their presence (0,1) by the occurrence of three institutions: federalism, centralization and majoritarianism (Sections 8.2 and 8.7). Federalism is supposed to restrict the room to maneuver of actors (they cannot impose their will on others), but organized interest groups are an exception to this 'rule'. Centralized state structures are supposed to be conducive to the room to maneuver of all actors. The same effect is expected in case of majoritarianism (but the interest groups are, again, an exception). Another matter is how the varying room to maneuver matters for the outcomes of the decision-making process. We have selected three indicators that represent these policy effects: the size of the public economy (measured as the total expenditures of the general government as a percentage of GDP), the economic performance (computed as: inflation + unemployment − economic growth). We do not expect overall strong relationships between the policy outcomes and the room to maneuver of actors, because of a third unknown factor, namely how actors use their room to maneuver. For example, parties with a relatively large room to maneuver might use this either to enlarge or to restrict the public sector. Without

Table 8.25 *The hypothesized room for maneuver of actors given the institutional environment (Boolean scores)*

	Federal	Unitary	Centralized	Decentralized	Majoritarian	Consensus
President	0	1	1	0	1	0
Government	0	1	1	0	1	0
Parties in Parliament	0	1	1	0	1	0
Organized interests	1	0	1	1	0	1

The Boolean scores indicate whether the room for maneuver is large or small. For example, it is hypothesized that a President's room for maneuver is severely restricted (score = 0) in a federal system.

additional data on the behavior and ideology of actors it is hard to make any specific predictions on the policy effects of the institutional room for maneuver of actors like presidents, parties, interest groups and governments. Here we can only analyze the *conditions* for actors to influence the decision-making process. Note that this was also the case when we operationalized the conditions for consensus democracy and not the actual degree of consensus democracy.

The conditions for having a say in (or even dominating) decision-making is calculated by computing the interaction terms of actors and institutions on the basis of Boolean scores that are derived from Table 8.25. The results are presented in Table 8.26. The table shows that from the four countries with more or less 'strong Presidents' (Finland, France, Switzerland and the USA) only the French president is confronted with favorable conditions for a final say on decision-making. The reason for this is that the institutional environments of the other presidents appear to limit their influence. This will be explained below in greater detail with the help of a case study on the USA. Political parties are present in all democracies, but the conditions for influence are only favorable in 10 of the 18 democracies (mostly characterized by centralized and/or majoritarian institutions). Organized interest groups (operationalized as the degree of corporatist interest intermediation (Keman, 1988) meet better conditions for influence in 5 of the 18 countries. The conditions for an influential bureaucracy are better in 9 of the 18 cases.

The effects of these varying conditions on the outcomes of the policy-making process are quite diffuse. This can both be examined 'at first sight' and also explored more systematically by means of a QCA analysis (see Section 6.3). The QCA analysis throws up a considerable number of 'contradictory configurations'

Table 8.26 *The institutionally determined influence of four actors on decision-making plus three outcome indicators (Boolean scores)*

	Influence of actors				Outcome indicators		
Country	President	Parties	Interest groups	Government	Public economy	Economic performance	Government employment
Sweden	0	1	1	1	1	1	1
Norway	0	1	1	1	1	1	1
Denmark	0	0	0	0	1	0	1
Finland	0	0	0	0	0	0	0
Belgium	0	1	0	1	1	0	1
Netherlands	0	1	1	1	1	1	0
France	1	1	0	0	1	0	1
Italy	0	1	0	1	0	0	0
Germany	0	0	0	0	1	1	0
Austria	0	1	1	1	1	1	0
Switzerland	0	0	1	0	0	1	0
UK	0	1	0	1	0	0	1
Ireland	0	1	0	1	0	0	0
US	0	0	0	0	0	1	0
Canada	0	0	0	0	0	0	1
Australia	0	0	0	0	0	1	1
New Zealand	0	1	0	1	0	0	1
Japan	0	0	0	0	0	1	0

(different institutional environments lead to the same policy effects). For example, the USA and Australia have the same independent Boolean scores and yet different scores on the dependent variable. This illustrates our earlier statement that the actual influence of actors is not a direct reflection of the institutional room for maneuver, but of the way this room is utilized.

The third approach is *the comparative case study approach*. A comparative case study examines one case in relation to other cases in order to test a series of theoretical assumptions (see also Chapter 3). For example, one might ask the question why presidentialism in the USA is a highly democratic institution whereas presidential systems in general are not that democratic (i.e. executive powers dominate parliamentary rule, which may frustrate the democratic process). This case study has actually been done by Riggs (1994), and we will follow his reasoning here.

Presidentialism is based on the separation of powers between executive (President) and legislative institutions (Congress) that stems from the fixed term of the President. In parliamentary systems the head of state and the head of government are two different persons with different roles, whereas in presidential regimes the elected head of government always serves concurrently as head of state. Thus, presidentialism is defined by Riggs as representative government in which the head of government is elected for a fixed term of office; that is, he or she cannot be discharged by a no-confidence vote. The fixed term assures continuity of leadership, but at the same time presidents are hampered in their leadership roles. Their inability to fulfill, popular expectations often leads to crises and regime breakdowns (Riggs, 1994: 81). Because of the fixed term, presidential regimes lack the basic motor of parliamentarism which promotes party discipline.

Riggs argues that the survival of presidentialism in the USA hinges on, among various factors, the responsiveness of its political parties and the semi-disciplined voting patterns which this engenders (p. 95). 'Responsive' is defined by Riggs as a balanced intra-party distribution of power that combines local autonomy with headquarters guidance. Intra-party groups are permitted to organize informally but not to become oppressively prominent. Because of the 'responsive' two-party system and federalism, the President cannot command the loyalty nor control the actions of local politicians (p. 107). The separation of powers in the Federal government also means that presidential power is shared with Congress and a powerful judicial system. Compared with the presidential systems, the governmental powers in the USA are not very extensive. Due to the centripetal (non-ideological) two-party system the actual programs of the government are never radically reformed (p. 109).

The case study of Riggs clearly shows how features of presidentialism, federalism, (non-)corporatism and the party system interact with each other. The functioning and policy effects of one institution can therefore not be seen as independent from the impact of other institutions. In the USA the institution of presidentialism is democratic because it is counterbalanced by other institutions and decision-making structures, which leads to enduring forms of 'power sharing'. As a consequence, the American President is not the 'winner-who-takes-all' but 'the winner-who-shares-all' (p. 109).

To conclude: the most different, the most similar and the case study approach are different, but related, ways to cope with comparative Research Questions. Presidential systems are generally less democratic systems than parliamentary systems, but there are presidential systems with a high democratic performance. We have illustrated in this section that presidentialism *varies* and clearly *matters* (under certain conditions) for 'how decisions are made'. We have also illustrated in this section that there are several comparative Research Designs that may be used to study one phenomenon. Which Research Design is used depends on the Research Question. In this section the US presidential system has more or less served as an example of both a *contrasting case* (presidential systems versus parliamentary systems), a *similar case* (part of a group of liberal democracies), a *crucial case* (the American system combines institutional arrangements that make it typical) and a *deviant case* (it does not share the presidential dominance of most presidential systems). In all these different cases the US presidential system is looked upon from a specific comparative perspective. Consequently, given this variety of comparative approaches and options, comparing as such is not 'one' way to look at things but it embodies a whole range of different methodologies. What makes a Research Design comparable is that it relates cases to each other in a specific manner. The proper way to come to plausible conclusions is to follow the 'comparative logic' by logically integrating the Research Question, the Research Design and the Research Answer.

8.9 CONCLUSIONS

The 'chain of democratic control and command' shows how actors and institutions interact in the iterative process of democratic decision-making. In this chapter a selection of significant institutions of liberal democracies have been discussed: types of democracies and their characteristics, party systems, the formation and duration of governments, the institutional determinants of economic growth and public sector growth, structures of intermediation, forms of institutional autonomy and presidentialism. In most sections the discussion focuses on the policy effects of these institutions in a way that is similar to 'the chain'. All sections also embody (preliminary) Research Questions, Research Designs and Research Answers. These are summarized in Table 8.27.

Table 8.27 and this chapter do not present, of course, a complete overview of all types of comparative research on institutions. This chapter presents a selection of institutions that is more or less derived from or complementary to Lijphart's systematic study of institutional variations in *Democracies* (1984). Furthermore, there are other ways to formulate Research Questions, Research Designs and Research Answers. This is illustrated by the discussion between Keman/Pennings and Lijphart/Crepaz on the use of corporatism scales (Keman and Pennings, 1995; Crepaz and Lijphart, 1995). The most important thing, however, is that the arts and crafts of doing political research on institutions are laid down in the sections and the exercises in an accessible and informative way.

One 'unresolved' problem is that the operationalization of institutional variables

Table 8.27 *Overview and examples of the main stages in comparative research on political and socio-economic institutions*

Research Question	Research Design	Research Answer
§8.2. What types of democracies are there?	Conceptualization and operationalization of democratic institutions and the detection of the underlying dimensions by means of factor analysis	Factor analysis suggests two underlying dimensions, albeit that the clustering of the countries on the basis of factor scores do not wholly match with juxtaposition of majoritarian and consensus democracies
§8.3. Do the theoretical assumptions underlying party system typologies match the empirical characteristics of countries?	Identification of the theoretical assumptions; operationalization of the empirical characteristics; regression analysis of these characteristics on the main party system dimension	There is a fair match between what the typologies predict and the actual characteristics of countries
§8.4. What factors determine the formation and duration of governments?	The operationalization and modeling of the determinants of government formation and duration. Test of the models by means of regression	The models confirm the direction of the relationships but the explained variance is low: the models are missing crucial attributes or events
§8.5. What factors determine economic growth and public sector growth?	The operationalization and modeling of the determinants of economic growth and public sector growth	The models confirm the direction of a few variables. The public sector model has more explanatory power than the economic growth model
§8.6. How similar are corporatism scales and can they be merged as part of a consensus democracy scale?	The comparison of the conceptualization and operationalization of corporatism scales and the analysis of these scales in relation to consensus democracy	Many corporatism scales are highly related but still very different. They can not be merged into a consensus democracy scale
§8.7. How does the geographical autonomy of state units affect the policy-making process?	Operationalization of federalism, autonomy and centralism and policy variables; regression and residual analysis	Federal and decentralized states are characterized by lower levels of welfare state provision
§8.8. How democratic is presidentialism and how does it matter for the policy-making process?	The question is answered by means of a most different, a most similar and a case study design which are logically related to each other	In general, presidential systems are less democratic (but this need not be the case) and there is no *direct* relationship with the policy-making process

is still strongly based on non-dynamic scores. For example, all corporatism scales just present one figure per country to cover the whole of the post-war period, whereas we know that the degree and type of corporatism has changed in most liberal democracies. This poses a problem for the statistical research, as it implies that the theoretical variance (how we conceptualize institutional variations) and the empirical variance (how we measure institutional variations) do not match. For this reason the previous sections and also the exercises that follow include the analysis of institutional change, such as party system change and change in the conditions of consensus democracy.

8.10 ENDMATTER

Exercises

The exercises aim at:

1 examining how the functioning of institutions varies cross-sectionally and through time;
2 examining how institutions and institutional change affect the room to maneuver of actors and the process of policy-making.

EXERCISE 8.1: TYPES OF DEMOCRACIES

File: Nias.sav.

Lijphart distinguishes eight features of consensus democracy on the basis of factor analysis. Apply factor analysis to construct a time series variable of the conditions for consensus democracy on the basis of three variables: disproportionality, effective number of parties and the type of government. Also apply regression analysis to the resulting factor score in order to analyze the consequences of these changes.

Suggested steps: 1. Check whether the three selected variables are suited for factor analyses (examine the positive and negative signs, missing values and operationalization). 2. Accomplish the changes that are necessary in order to decrease the number of missing values and to make the variables interpretable (by means of 'recode' and the if-statement). 3. After that the factor analysis may be completed. 4. After these procedures, we are able to establish the degree and nature of change in the conditions for consensus democracy per country (by means of 'select if').

Background reading: Lijphart (1984); Pennings (1997).

EXERCISE 8.2: PARTY SYSTEMS

File: Nias.sav.

Select two crucial party system characteristics and determine their development in time and in relation to each other: for example 'the effective number of parties' and 'the dynamics of centrifugalism'.

Suggested steps: 1. Select the main party system variables. 2. Formulate the underlying hypotheses (e.g. we expect that the effective number of parties is increasing since the rise of protest parties). 3. Operationalize the key variables (e.g.

the Taakso and Taagepera measure for the effective number of parties). 4. Reveal some trends by means of the procedure graph.

Background reading: Lane and Ersson (1994); Pennings and Lane (1998).

EXERCISE 8.3: CABINET FORMATION AND FUNCTIONING

Files: empol966.sav, medlegis.sav.

Examine those governments which do not include the party which controls the median legislator. Do these governments distinguish themselves from governments which do hold this median party?

Suggested steps: 1. The first step is to determine which parties control the median legislator (see Section 8.4). 2. The second step is to formulate some hypotheses (for example, governments that do not hold the median party are relatively unstable). 3. The next step is to test these hypotheses by means of, for example, ANOVA.

Background reading: Laver and Schofield (1990); Laver and Budge (1992).

EXERCISE 8.4: INSTITUTIONS, ECONOMIC GROWTH AND THE PUBLIC SECTOR

File: nias.sav.

Some rational-choice approaches aim at explaining the continuous growth of the public sector. Design a model that holds institutional and actor-related variables and that explains the recent *decline* of the public sector (the politics of retrenchment).

Suggested steps: 1. The first step is to design a causal model: what is Y and what is X and how does the institutional context matter? Formulate the underlying hypotheses. 2. Apply regression analysis. 3. Report on the results.

Background reading: Esping-Andersen (1996).

EXERCISE 8.5: INTEREST INTERMEDIATION

File: corpor.sav.

Examine how corporatism relates to the eight features of consensus democracy. Do the results suggest that corporatism is very much like consensus democracy? Examine the residual scores of the countries. What cross-sectional variations are there?

Suggested steps: 1. Select the relevant variables. 2. Perform a regression analysis that includes the residuals. 3. Examine the residuals. 4. Construct a scatterplot with corporal and consens. 5. Formulate your conclusions.

Background reading: Lijphart and Crepaz (1991); Keman and Pennings (1995); Crepaz and Lijphart (1995).

EXERCISE 8.6: FEDERALISM

File: Nias.sav.

Examine the degree to which federalism, decentralization, divided government and institutional autonomy are interrelated.

Suggested steps: 1. Aggregate the data to the country level. 2. Construct two scatterplots (autonomy with federalism and centralism with federalism). 3. Interpret the results.

Background reading: Lane and Ersson (1994: Ch. 7).

EXERCISE 8.7: PRESIDENTIALISM

Files: polsoc.sav, gastil.sav.

Why are some presidential systems more democratic than others? Distinguish between democratic and non-democratic presidential systems and examine their features.

Suggested steps: 1. Distinguish within the group of restricted presidential systems between more and less democratic systems (apply the 'if-statement'). 2. Determine on theoretical grounds which factor is likely to affect the degree of democracy (e.g. the more economic welfare the higher the level of democracy). 3. Apply ANOVA in order to test this hypothesis.

Background reading: Riggs (1994); Derbyshire and Derbyshire (1990).

Topics highlighted

The working, trends and effects of several institutions that are central in the functioning of democracies are comparatively analyzed by means of statistical techniques (i.e. regression and factor analysis). The focus is on the following Research Questions (see also Table 8.27):

1 What types of democracies are there?
2 Do the theoretical assumptions underlying party system typologies match the empirical characteristics of countries?
3 What factors determine the formation and duration of governments?
4 What factors determine economic growth and public sector growth?
5 How similar are corporatism scales and can they be merged as part of a consensus democracy scale?
6 How does the geographical autonomy of state units affect the policy-making process?
7 How democratic is presidentialism and how does it matter for the policy-making process?

Further reading

- *General*: Lijphart, 1984; Weaver and Rockman, 1993.
- *Specific*: Laver and Schofield, 1990; Lane and Ersson, 1994; Keman and Pennings, 1995; Pennings and Lane, 1998.

Appendix 8.1: Overview of the indicators used to test the underlying assumptions of Sartori's and Lijphart's party system typologies (as reported in Table 8.7)

- CPG = Color of Party Government (range 1–5; high score = left) (Source: Woldendorp et al., 1993).
- DUR = Duration of Government measured in days (Source: Woldendorp et al., 1993).
- RFT = Reason of Termination of Government (range 0–1; high score = discordant ending) (Source: Woldendorp et al., 1993).
- TOG = Type of Government (Range: 0–1; high score = multi-party government) (Source: Woldendorp et al., 1993).

- POLARSYS = The degree of Polarization measured with the Sigelman and Yough formula (1978).
- LEADERSHIP = The type of political leadership (Range: 1–5; high score = coalescent leadership) (Source: Keman, 1988).
- ISSUEDIM = The number of issue dimensions (Source: Lijphart, 1984).
- NRPTIES = The total number of parties (Source: Bartolini and Mair, 1990).
- EFFNOP = The number of effective parties on the basis of the Laakso and Taagepera index (Source: Mackie and Rose, 1991).
- FRAGVOT = The fragmentation of the votes based on Rae's index of fractionalization (Source: Mackie and Rose, 1991).
- UNITY = The degree of organizational unity of trade unions (Range: 0–1; a high score means a high degree of unity) (Source: Cameron, 1984).
- DENSITY = Trade union density (% of non-agrarian employees) (Source: Visser, 1989).
- ELSYS = The type of Electoral System (Range: 1–2; a high scores means a PR-like system) (Source: Lijphart, 1984).
- TOTVOL = Total volatility (Source: Bartolini and Mair, 1990).
- DISPRDEF = The disproportionality of seats and votes (Source: Mackie and Rose, 1991).
- PERCMEM = Percentage of adults that are members of a political party (Source: Katz and Mair, 1992).
- NOATTCH = Percentage of voters without attachment to party for which they voted (Source: Cumulative file Eurobarometers, 1970–1990).

Notes

1 One problem with Sartori's typology is that the predominant system, where one party has an enduring winning majority of parliamentary seats, fits rather uneasily with Sartori's framework, as this type is not exclusive (since any other type may become predominant) (Mair, 1996a).

2 Cases for which the event does not occur during the period of observation are called censored cases. Cox regression models, also known as proportional hazards models, can be used when there are censored observations, namely those cabinets that ended solely because of the end of the so-called 'Constitutional Interelection Period' (CIEP), which is mostly fixed to three, four or five years. Censored governments would probably have lasted longer without a CIEP. For a further discussion we refer to King et al. (1990) and Warwick (1994).

3 Note that our operationalization of the variables is not fully identical to that employed by Lane and Ersson.

9
How problems are solved

CONTENTS

9.1 INTRODUCTION

This chapter deals with the output and performance side of the so-called 'Chain of Democratic Control and Command' which was introduced at the beginning of Part III. This chain represents the stages in the democratic decision-making process and focuses on the interactions between political institutions and actors with regard to socio-economic policy formation. The dependent variables are variations in output and performance. Output refers mainly to the decisions that governments make. The main indicator for output is public expenditures as there is precious little policy-making without any costs. Performance refers to the effects that the implementations of decisions have. The distinction between output and performance (or outcomes) is crucial. The output only reflects some of the intentions that policy-makers have. Whether they achieve their goal is a totally different question and is measured by performance. We limit ourselves in this chapter mainly (but not exclusively) to the socio-economic realm, as this is a central concern to any government in the OECD world. A glossary of basic terms is given in Box 9.1.

Socio-economic performance refers to the levels of social and economic welfare. In this chapter we link the variations in democratic and socio-economic performance of welfare states to cross-national and institutional contexts (Almond et al., 1993; Keman, 1993a). We examine the role of actors, institutions and the way actors and institutions interact. In most applications we are comparing similar countries which are facing similar problems. And we ask the question why some countries perform better than others and why the types of policy-making differ.

We work with both aggregated files ($n = 18$ OECD countries) and (pooled) time series data in order to be able to illustrate the pros and cons of both 'large-n' and 'small-n' in most-similar Research Designs.[1] Sections 9.3 and 9.4 cover the impact of central actors (parties and unions) and crucial institutions (corporatism, style of leadership, consociationalism) on policy-formation and socio-economic problem-solving. The data are aggregated on the level of national systems, and the analysis integrates the results of Boolean analysis, regression analysis, factor analysis and analysis of variance in order to be able to show how these different techniques complement each other.

Box 9.1 Glossary of basic terms

- *Output*: decision of governments, known as regulation and expenditures.
- *Performance or outcomes*: the effects or results of the governmental decisions and interventions.
- *The style of political leadership*: the way in which conflicts are resolved by political elites (being either more competitive or coalescent, which is expressed on a 4-point scale).
- *Political business cycle*: the cyclical trend in socio-economic state intervention that is caused by governments which attempt to influence their re-election prospects by manipulating the state of the economy in ways that are (in the short run) electorally rewarding.
- *The social democratic model*: the assumption that the parliamentary social democratic policy strategies will produce higher levels of welfare state development and full employment than non-social democratic strategies, especially when it is accompanied by trade union power.
- *Gastil democracy index*: the ranking of each nation of separate 7-point scales for 'political rights' and 'civil liberties'.
- *Mandate model* (or theory): the assumption that the democratic process is based on a mandate of voters to political parties on the basis of their manifestoes.
- *Dyadic analysis*: time series analysis based on dyads: relations between states at given points of time.

The second part of this chapter is less aggregated in measurement (and more complicated) than the first part, yet it also relates to the 'Chain of Democratic Control and Command'. It covers time series analysis on output and performance variables that relate to the so-called Political Business Cycle (meaning that governments may attempt to influence the re-election prospects – Section 9.5). In Section 9.7 the mandate model of party accountability (i.e. parties carry out pledges once in government) is tested on data that cover the USA, the UK (representing two-party systems) and the Netherlands (representing a multi-party system). This combination of topics enables us not only to describe variations in policy types and policy regimes (in terms of more or less restrictive policy-making) but also to explain the outcomes in effectiveness of these policy types and regimes.

Finally, the chapter also includes some non-economic issues. The democratic performance, meaning the quality of democracy, and the output and performance in the international arena (i.e. the degree of cooperation between the Soviet Union and the USA) are also important aspects of policy making that have received considerable attention in comparative analysis (Sections 9.6 and 9.8).

Finally, the exercises focus on the empirical validation and explanation of variations in types of policy performance. The main determinants of these variations relate to actors (Chapter 7) and institutions (Chapter 8).

9.2 WELFARE-RELATED OUTPUTS AND PERFORMANCE

The aim of this section is to introduce the main indicators of social and economic welfare. These indicators are linked to the output or the outcomes in the socio-economic realm, although it is sometimes hard to distinguish between these. Output refers to all the decisions and interventions in the economy. Performance refers to the intended or unintended effects of these decisions and interventions.

Social welfare means the regulation and provision of social security (i.e. income maintenance), health care, education, etc. Economic welfare means the increase of the national or the public income (redistributive justice) and the regulation of the private economy (the enhancement of public welfare). Both components of the welfare state are highly interdependent and they can and should not be seen separately but as interdependent (Keman, 1988).

Many indicators are developed in order to measure the socio-economic performance. For the sake of clarity we distinguish between three types of indicators:

- social indicators, which refer to levels of social welfare (education, health, transfers, etc.);
- economic indicators, which refer to levels of economic welfare (unemployment, employment, inflation, economic growth);
- indicators that reflect the relationship between social and economic indicators (e.g. when one goal is accomplished at the cost of another goal, which is called trade-off).

Sometimes the distinction between the social and economic indicators is difficult to make. Unemployment, for example, has both a social and economic side, as it affects and is affected by the level of social and economic welfare in a country. Below, a selection of indicators is shown that are frequently used in comparative socio-economic research.

Examples of the *economic performance* measures are (we are only discussing a small selection of all existing measures):

- unemployment rates: unemployment as a percentage of the total labor force (Source: OECD);
- employment: the percentage change as compared with the previous period of the total number of employed as a percentage of the total population (Source: OECD);
- inflation: private consumption deflator, percentage change from previous period (Source: OECD);
- the misery index (percentage unemployed plus inflation divided by two).

A useful *economic output* measure is the TEDC-scale. TEDC stands for the 'Tax-related Extraction–Distribution Cycle' (Keman, 1993a), meaning that it measures the degree to which governments extract money from society and redistribute it to society in order to (re)direct the economic welfare of a country. The scale therefore represents the degree of economic interventionism. This scale is based on factor analysis on a selection of variables. Factor analysis is used (instead of scalability analysis) because we want to extract one dimension from a variety of indicators:

- deficit spending (variable name def): general government financial balances: surplus (+) or deficit (−) as a percentage of nominal GDP;
- total taxation (variable name tax): total tax receipts as a percentage of GDP;
- public economy (variable name pe): general government total outlays as percentage of GDP;
- the total of social security contributions as a percentage of GDP (variable name ssc).

Examples of the *social performance* measures are (and again we select a few measures) infant mortality, school enrollment, income inequality and poverty (Ravallion, 1994). The social performance clearly is the most difficult to measure because these measures are heavily based on individual circumstances and are therefore based on survey research, such as employed by the Luxembourg Income Study (Atkinson et al., 1995). These measures are examples of bottom-up aggregates: the data are country means of scores on individuals (persons or families).

The *social output* measures are easier to construct than social performance measures because the former are based on official data, mostly on public expenditures, such as social expenditures on health, education and transfers. One summarizing measure is complementary to the TEDC scale, namely the WEDC-scale, which stands for the 'Welfare-related Extraction Distribution Cycle' (Keman, 1993a). This scale measures the degree of social state intervention. It is based on factor analysis on the variables direction taxation (variable name dtax), social security contributions by employers (variable name sscap), social security contributions by employees (variable name sscwo), education expenditures (variable name ed), health care expenditures (variable name he) and transfer payments to households (variable name trans). All expenditures data are taken as a percentage of GDP as this is the standard measure of the OECD and enhances the comparability of the data.

All the variables underlying the TEDC and WEDC indicators are derived from OECD data (see the list of references). Most of the mentioned social and economic indicators will be discussed and applied further in the following sections when they are related to Research Questions and Research Designs. Let us summarize the rationale underlying the Research Design on the basis of the information in Chapters 1 to 3. The basic steps are as follows. First we explain *what*, *how* and *why* we are comparing:

1 *What* we compare are systemic variations in the 'Chain of Democratic Control and Command': this chain designates what kind of variations in actors and institutions are important in relation to policy making. Hence the main Research Question is how different democratic institutional environments affect the socio-economic policy formation.
2 *How* we compare is defined by the Research Question, which relates the relevant independent variables (i.e. political institutions and actors) to the dependent variable which is often one of the output and performance indicators that are discussed in this section.
3 *Why* we are comparing originates from the need to explain variations in policy output and policy performance cross-time and cross-nationally. It is impossible to explain without comparing variations in the dependent and independent variables.

Hence, the Research Design results from a series of explicit choices on:

1 the choice of cases and periods, being the 'universe of discourse';
2 the choice of data and transformations, being the operationalizations on the dependent and independent variables;
3 the choice of statistical techniques that enables the analysis of the relationships between the dependent and independent variables in such a way that we can detect patterned variations and causal relationships.

In short, the Research Question defines *what* we want to know, and the Research Design expresses *how* we want to produce this knowledge. By following all the necessary steps in the right order (e.g. first the question, then the hypotheses, then the analyses) we can draw sound, plausible and well-founded conclusions about reality (= positive science) or to refute existing knowledge or dispel existing myths. The following sections will present examples of this scientific approach.

9.3 ACTORS AND SOCIO-ECONOMIC PROBLEM-SOLVING

In this section we shall analyze the role of actors *vis-à-vis* socio-economic policy outputs and outcomes, in particular those of social democratic parties (Pennings, 1995). We will apply three techniques – namely regression, discriminant analysis and Boolean analysis – in order to analyze the relationships between the dependent and independent variables. These techniques are chosen because they are part of the examples that are derived from two well-known explanations of variations in welfare state development:

1 the development of social insurance schemes around 1900 (Alber, 1982);
2 the so-called social democratic model (Korpi, 1983).

The first investigation relates variations in the degree and extension of social insurance to systemic features of (pre-)democratic polities in their earliest phase of development. Some important determinants are the degree of industrialization, urbanization, the level of socio-economic development, the level of enfranchisement, the share of votes of labor parties ('left votes'), the degree of unionization, the degree and type of religousness and the regime type. Alber has chosen to keep the data analysis descriptive, so he did not apply advanced statistics to analyze the relationships between the dependent and independent variables.

Dirk Berg-Schlosser and Sven Quenter have used Alber's data and operationalizations in order to discuss the application of several statistical techniques (see Table 9.1). They have applied macro-quantitative and macro-qualitative methods to Jens Alber's data on the variation and development of social insurance schemes (Alber, 1982; Berg-Schlosser and Quenter, 1996). They argue that these two different methodological outlooks are complementary, as the quantitative techniques are designed to analyze relationships between *variables* whereas the qualitative techniques are better equipped to study variations between *cases* (see also the discussion of Ragin's comparative methodology in Section 6.3).

The quantitative approach (represented by regression and discriminant analysis) and the qualitative approach (represented by Boolean analysis) are applied on one single data set which is partly shown in Table 9.1.

When examining relationships between the dependent and independent variables it is crucial to be critical about the results because of excluded exogeneous factors that are influencing the results. This is demonstrated by the first part of Berg-Schlosser and Quenter's analysis, which is macro-quantitative. Bivariate regression analysis is used to examine the relationship between the share of left votes (X) and extension of social insurance (Y). The scatterplot of the relationship shows that the (moderately strong) explained variance ($R^2 = 0.4$) is mainly caused by the outlier Germany, which has relatively high scores on both variables (see also Section 6.7). After deleting this case, the explained variance reduces to near zero!

Table 9.1 *A selection of Jens Alber's data on (determinants of) social welfare around 1900*

	Socio-economic development[a]		Share of enfranchized men		Share of votes for Labor parties		The reach of social insurance schemes[b]	
Country	Real figure	Boolean score	Real figure	Boolean score	Real figure	Boolean score	Real figure	Boolean score
Austria	38	0	85	1	0	0	9	1
Belgium	70	1	90	1	21	1	3.8	0
Denmark	49	0	87	1	14.3	1	10.5	1
Germany	69	1	94	1	27.2	1	40.8	1
Finland	18	0	19	0	0	0	1.8	0
France	54	1	88	1	11.3	1	6.8	1
Italy	48	0	25	0	13	1	2.8	0
The Netherlands	68	1	51	0	3	0	0	0
Norway	45	0	90	1	3	0	3.3	0
Sweden	41	0	25	0	0.4	0	3.3	0
Switzerland	65	1	79	0	9.7	1	4	1
UK	111	1	62	0	1.3	0	9.8	1
Median	51.5	–	82	–	6.4	–	3.9	–

If the 'real figures' are higher than the median score the Boolean score is 1. Otherwise the Boolean score is 0. Thus the Boolean score is to be interpreted as high/low or present/absent.

[a]The socio-economic development in 1900 is the sum of the share of the working population in the industrial sector plus the urban population.

[b]The reach of social insurance schemes is operationalized as the share of the working population that is included in these schemes (accidents, sickness, rent and unemployment insurances).

Source: Berg-Schlosser and Quenter, 1996: 107 as adapted from Alber, 1982.

In this sense, regression analysis is more or less 'case-blind', and a proper use of it assumes that the assumptions on the distribution of cases are not violated (see Chapter 6).

A different quantitative technique is discriminant analysis, which groups the cases around the two poles of the dichotomized dependent variable. The dichotomization is based on the median because this measure of central tendency is not influenced by cases with extreme values. The aim of discriminant analysis is to predict whether the cases belong to the group with a high level of social insurance or to the group with a low level. The independent variables are interval variables, whereas the dependent variable is dichotomous. In Section 6.5 is has been explained that the distance between the poles should be as large as possible and the distances between the cases and the poles should be as small as possible. The simultaneous inclusion of the most important variables (industrialization, urbanization, enfranchisement and left votes) has led to a correct grouping of 9 of the 12 cases. Only Belgium, Norway and the Netherlands were not grouped correctly: they were predicted to be in the group with a high level, whereas the observed level was low. Chapter9.sps gives all the technical details of this analysis.

It is argued by Berg-Schlosser and Quenter that discriminant analysis as a quantitative technique differs from regression in that it is more case-oriented, but it is in their view still not as well equipped to discriminate between groups of cases as Boolean analysis (or qualitative comparative analysis: QCA).[2] Quantitative comparative analysis is highly (but not exclusively) variable oriented, whereas qualitative comparative analysis is more oriented towards the analysis of cases (Ragin, 1987). This difference is illustrated by applying Boolean analysis to Alber's data. An initial simple QCA analysis is based on three of the most significant variables of Jens Alber's work on the historical development of social insurance schemes (the dependent variable) in western Europe (Alber, 1982):

- socio-economic development (E);
- mass enfranchisement of new voters (W);
- the left votes as a percentage of all votes (L).

These three Boolean variables make $2^3 = 8$ possible combinations, namely from not present (000) to all conditions available: 000, 100, 110, 010, 011, 001, 101, 111 (111). The QCA analysis suggests the following minimization for situations where the dependent variable = 0:

$$0 = E + W + L$$

Table 9.2 shows the minimized functions that summarize the six cases with a low social insurance level into one single function:

$$0 = w \cdot e$$

meaning a low degree of enfranchisement and a low level of socio-economic development (the lowercase indicates the low level). This function is only valid for three of the six cases: Finland and Sweden (0,0,0) and Italy (0,0,1). (Table 9.3).

The two positive outcome cases Denmark (0,1,1) and Switzerland (1,0,1) are indicated by the formula:

$$1 = e \cdot W \cdot L + E \cdot w \cdot l$$

The character '·' stands for 'and', and the plus sign stands for 'or'. The formula signifies that a highly developed social insurance scheme is prevalent in the case of *either* low socio-economic development (e) and mass enfranchisement (W) and a

Table 9.2 *The QCA minimized function summary for the model: Social Insurance (0) = E + W + L*

	0 Configs		Cases		1 Configs		Cases	
	n	%	*n*	%	*n*	%	*n*	%
ew–[a]	2	40	3	50	0	0	0	0
Checked	2	40	3	50	0	0	0	0
Total	5	100	6	100	5	100	0	0

The table is derived from the QCA output. E = socio-economic development; W = enfranchisement; L = left votes.

[a]ew– refers to countries with a low score on socio-economic development and enfranchisement.

Table 9.3 *The QCA minimized function summary for the model: Social Insurance (1) = E + W + L*

	0 Configs		Cases		1 Configs		Cases	
	n	%	*n*	%	*n*	%	*n*	%
eWL[a]	0	0	0	0	1	20	1	17
Ewl[b]	0	0	0	0	1	20	1	17
Checked	0	0	0	0	2	40	2	33
Total	5	100	6	100	5	100	6	100

The table is derived from the QCA output. E = socio-economic development; W = enfranchisement; L = left votes.

[a]eWL refers to a low score on socio-economic development, a high score on enfranchisement and a high score of left votes.

[b]Ewl refers to a high score on socio-economic development, a low score on enfranchisement and a low score of left votes.

high share of the left votes (L) *or* a high level of socio-economic development (E) and a low level of enfranchisement (w) and a low share of left votes (l).

The seven 'unexplained' cases are so-called contradictory cases that cannot be explained by the three selected independent variables. Note that these kinds of and/or statements are also part of regression analyses except that they figure at the basis of the analysis (all regression starts with conjunctive and disjunctive modeling) whereas the reported statements emerge as the *results* of Boolean analysis.

The statement of Berg-Schlosser and Quenter that quantitative and qualitative comparative methods are complementary is certainly true. The quantitative method requires a theoretical insight into the (assumed) interrelationships between variables, whereas the qualitative approach requires insights into the peculiarities and characteristics of particular cases. The less well QCA is able to minimize functions, the more important the role of theory and interpretation becomes. For example, if QCA does not minimize a set of constellations at all (meaning that there are as many functions as cases), then theory (i.e. hypotheses that discriminate between cases) is the only device left to group the functions into additive formulas. When there are many cases, this grouping on the basis of theoretical considerations becomes nearly impossible. Another problem of Boolean analysis is the data reduction. The dichotomization places quite different cases in the same categories. As a consequence, because quite different situations lead to the same results, the explanatory capacities of QCA are often limited. See for a further overview and evaluation of the method Ragin et al. (1996).

Until now we have focused on one particular actor (i.e. the electoral strength of left parties) in relation to socio-economic policy-making regarding welfare state regimes. We continue doing this, but now we will focus on the post-war period again. One influential theory that seeks to explain variations in welfare state development is the so-called 'social democratic model' (Korpi, 1983). This model assumes that there is a causal effect of social democracy on welfare state outcomes. It predicts that the parliamentary socialist strategy will produce higher levels of welfare state development and full-employment than non-socialist strategies, especially when the electoral strength of the party is accompanied by trade union power.

Esping-Andersen and Van Kersbergen have identified a variety of *Research Designs* based on different (comparative) methodologies (Esping-Andersen and Van Kersbergen, 1992: 190–1). The two main types are comparative case studies and cross-sectional studies. Some comparative case-studies emphasize the Scandinavian experience of social democratic dominance, but the problem with them is often that it is hard to assume that left party cum trade unionism will bring similar results outside Scandinavia (p. 203). More valid comparisons may result from case-studies which employ matched comparisons between 'failed' and 'successful' cases in order to identify the conditions under which social democratic movements are capable of introducing change. The cross-sectional studies test the social democratic thesis on the basis of 16–20 advanced nations. The problem here is often over-determination, meaning that it is difficult to determine the causal connection between social democratic power on the one hand and policy performance on the other. This problem is partly solved by the pooled time series analyses of both social democratic strength and policy outcomes. But here the problem lies in the restricted variance over time which makes it hard to get proper data, or to put it otherwise, the extremely high autocorrelation (see Section 6.7).

Studies departing from the social democratic model are often based on the power resources argument that states that the social democratization of capitalist societies depends on the degree to which the balance of power favors labor. Two factors are considered to be of a special importance here: the strength of trade unionism and the degree of neocorporatism. At the moment that the causal impact of the social democratic actors depends on the strength of other actors and institutions, we are confronted with the possibility of *spurious relationships* (the effect of social democracy may be spurious when other factors have as well an explanatory power) and *over-determination* (it is difficult to separate the neocorporatist argument and the social democratic thesis).

We will apply a simple OLS regression on 18 countries in order to test the social democratic model. As independent variables we select left votes (representing the strength of labor parties), trade union density (percentage of the non-agrarian labor force) and unity of confederations (two measures of trade union strength as constructed in Cameron, 1984). The dependent variables of the subsequent regression models are unemployment, employment and economic growth. The underlying hypothesis is that social democratic dominance will lead to less unemployment, more employment and less economic growth (due to the growth of an ineffective welfare-consuming public sector). These hypotheses are based on the general findings of existing theories of social democratic influence that are reported by Esping-Andersen and Van Kersbergen. We focus on the specific relationship of the mentioned variables in periods of economic growth (1965–1973), economic deterioration (1974–1980) and gradual economic recovery (1981–1988). Table 9.4 reports the basic empirical results of this test.

The analysis is extended by residual analysis in order to examine the cases that do more or less confirm the general pattern. Table 9.4 confirms several of the

Table 9.4 *Cross-sectional test of the Social Democratic model for four periods (OLS regression; betas reported)*

	1965–1973			1974–1981			1982–1992			1965–1992		
	unem	**em**	**eg**	**unem**	**em**	**eg**	**unem**	**em**	**eg**	**unem**	**em**	**eg**
Left votes	−0.62**	0	0.25	−0.55**	0	0.2	−0.18	0	−0.25	−0.42	−0.3	0.1
Trade union density	0.79**	0	−0.2	0.64**	0.2	0	0.43	−0.44	0	0.60*	−0.2	0
Unity of trade union confederation	−0.77**	0	−0.4	−0.66**	0	0	−0.62*	−0.11	−0.28	−0.69*	0	−0.4
Interaction term LV × Unity	−0.52*	0	−0.3	−0.57**	0	0	−0.44	−0.34	−0.39	−0.52*	−0.4	−0.3
R^2	0.52	0	0.1	0.5	0	–	0.14	0.12	0.04	0.36	0	–

LV = left votes (Mackie and Rose, 1991); Den = Union Density (Armingeon, 1989); Unity = organizational unity of federations (Cameron, 1984); LV × Unity = interaction term that is only used in bivariate regressions; ** = significant at 0.01 level; * = significant at 0.05 level. $N = 18$.

conclusions and methodological problems that are discussed by Esping-Andersen and van Kersbergen. The main conclusions on the basis of the regression analysis are as follows.

- There is a positive relationship with unemployment and not with employment. This indicates that there is redistribution within a fixed sum and not enhancing welfare.
- The influence of social democracy is a phenomenon of the 1960s ($R^2 = 0.52$) and 1970s ($R^2 = 0.50$) and it vanishes in the 1980s ($R^2 = 0.14$). The overall result for the period 1965–1992 is therefore misleading. It suggests that social democracy is the omnipresent causal factor, whereas in reality a wider range of indistinguishable factors is working, of which social democracy is only prominent in particular time periods.
- Density has not the same effects as left votes, but unity (and the interaction term) have. A possible explanation is that high levels of density do not indicate strength but weakness (i.e. union membership may be seen as a way to cope with the problem of unemployment). The identical effects of unity and left votes is an illustration of the over-determination problem.

This section has focused on three types of problems:

1 *theoretical problems* related to the Research Question and variables: how to define the relationships between the dependent and independent variables;
2 *methodological problems* related to the Research Design and the selection of cases;
3 *statistical problems:* the validation of the statistical results to make sure that they are not distorted due to problems related to the operationalization of variables and the selection of cases.

It has become clear that the actor model in its simplest form is too one-dimensional, as it assumes univocal effects on welfare state development from the presence or absence of one dominant actor. Modern research on welfare states has moved in the direction of studying the institutional properties of welfare states and has moved away from the linear social democratization concept. The chain of democratic control and command is, as a theoretical model, an example of this new approach. In the next section we will look at some ways to study socio-economic problem-solving in relation to both actors and institutions.

9.4 INSTITUTIONS AND SOCIO-ECONOMIC PROBLEM-SOLVING

In order to examine how the institutional environment matters for the type and degree of social and economic problem-solving (and management) it is important to define the institutional impact in *relative* terms: that is, in relation to actors and economic conditions. Institutions do not take decisions by themselves, of course, but they do shape the conditions under which actors are involved in decision-making. That's why it makes sense to study institutions within a wider (relational, interactive) context of reference. That is done in this section.

Our starting point is, again, the most-similar Research Design. During the 1970s and 1980s the OECD world was confronted with severe economic crises (the oil shocks in 1973 and 1979). The reactions of the OECD countries to these crises differed significantly. Our purpose here is to explain these different ways of reacting and problem solving with a special reference to the political-institutional environment in which actors operate (and make decisions).

We have already stressed the importance of the difference between the concepts of output and outcomes. Here we have opted for two *ordinal* scales (contrary to the *interval* scales WEDC and TEDC). One of these scales, namely the ordinal variable 'pop', has already been introduced in Section 5.1.[3]

Insert of Table 9.5 Overview of socio-economic policy types.

- *The policy output* (pop) refers to the governmental policies and is measured by (various categories of) expenditures and regulation. Table 9.5 presents an overview of the main socio-economic policy types. Our ordinal score has a range of 1 (meaning restrictive policy making) to 4 (meaning interventionist policy making) as has been explained in Section 5.1. In sum, the higher the score is, the more governments are inclined towards interventionist policy making (Keman, 1993a).
- *The policy outcomes* (poc) are the effects of the governmental policy making (equivalent to performance). This time we use an additive index that includes both indicators of economic performance (unemployment and economic growth) and social performance (income inequality, infant mortality and the participation rate in education) (Keman, 1993a).

Given the dual nature of the welfare state, it is understandable that policy decisions have consequences for the relationship between the two basic components of the welfare state: *economic welfare* (unemployment, inflation, growth) and *social welfare* (education, health and transfers). Basically we may distinguish between four socio-economic policy types (= output) that refer to the distinguishable ways in which governments react to economic crises. These policy types affect the relationship between social and economic welfare directly. Pay-off and

Table 9.5 *Overview of socio-economic policy types (pop)*

Types	Social welfare	Economic welfare
Restrictive	−	−
Monetaristic	−	+
Supermarket	+	−
Interventionistic	+	+

Source: Keman (1988).

trade-off situations may occur that affect the balance between social and economic welfare (see Table 9.6). We distinguish between situations of positive and negative pay-off and trade-off. Chapter 5 discussed the switches in policy types from the period before the oil crisis to that after it. These switches are summarized in Table 9.7. The cases on the diagonal line are without a policy shift. These countries stuck to their policies. The countries above the diagonal moved their policies in a more interventionist direction. Most countries moved towards a more restrictive stance. These cases are positioned below the diagonal line.

Thus far we have been describing variations: exploring the *Y*-variable. This is a necessary step in most quantitative research. Before the stage of explaining is reached, one has to be aware of the type and degree of variation of the dependent variable. During the explanatory stage of the research the variations in the dependent variable are to be explained by independent variables which are selected on the basis of theoretical assumptions. This selection is directed by the Research Design. In the case of a most-similar design, countries are selected that are most alike so that the number of explanatory variables is and should be by definition limited.

Given what we have said about the interactive institutional approach (meaning that institutions have an interactive relationship with actors) it makes sense to select three types of factors:

In the case of an exclusive saliency of the economic factors ('economics matters') we would expect a high explained variance. If such a strong relationship

Table 9.6 *Pay-off and trade-off*

		Change in social welfare	
		Positive or none	**Negative**
Change in economic welfare	Positive or none	+ pay-off	– trade-off
	Negative	+ trade-off	– pay-off

The division and interpretation of the four categories is based on the definition that social welfare ranks higher than economic welfare, because the origin of this particular typology lies in research in social welfare statism. Source: Keman, 1988.

Table 9.7 *Change in policy types after the first oil crisis*

		After 1973									
		Restrictive		**Monetarist**		**Supermarket**		**Interventionist**		**Row total**	
(before 1973)	Restrictive					100%	(1)			5.6%	(1)
	Monetarist	50%	(3)	16.7%	(1)	33.3%	(2)			33.3%	(6)
	Supermarket	12.5%	(1)	37.5%	(3)	25.0%	(2)	25.0%	(2)	44.4%	(8)
	Interventionist					33.3%	(1)	66.7%	(2)	16.7%	(3)
	Column total	27.8%	(5)	22.2%	(4)	27.8%	(5)	22.2%	(4)	100%	(18)

The diagonal line contains cases which did not change their policy after the oil crisis. The cases above this line did change their policy in an interventionist direction. The cases under the line did change their policy in a more restrictive direction.

is found, we can subsequently forget about other factors. This is the main reason why the first step in the analysis starts with the economic factors. The division into three periods corresponds to the phases of affluence, crisis and recovery.

1 Economic factors
   - economic growth
   - world market dependency
2 Structural factors (institutions)
   - consensus-generating traditions
   - left–right omplexion of government
3 Actors
   - political parties
   - voters
   - employers and employees.

Note that the construction of Table 9.8 is done in several steps and not in one single step. The table justifies the following observations:

- The economic factors are not decisive (the Pearson's *r* scores show no association).
- It makes sense to distinguish between national factors (e.g. EG) and international factors (e.g. WM), as their influence is different.
- When the economic conditions deteriorate, it can be suggested that mainly the international dimension remains important.

The table also illustrates the relevance of the distinction between output and outcomes. This is apparent in the case of the variable world market dependance, being the additive index of imports and exports as a percentage of GDP. In all periods the world market dependance strongly relates to interventionistic policy making. This is understandable, as open economies with high scores on world market dependance are vulnerable to outside influences (i.e. fluctuations on the world market). These countries need an extensive social infrastructure in order to guarantee everybody's material well-being in case (parts of) the economy is negatively affected by fluctuations on the world market. At the same time the world market dependance only has a moderate impact on the policy outcomes. This is

Table 9.8 *The relationships between economic factors and policy types and policy outcomes (Pearson's r)*

	1965–1973		1974–1980		1981–1988		1965–1988	
	POP	POC	POP	POC	POP	POC	POP	POC
WM	0.49	0.30	0.54	0.12	0.59	0.07	0.61	0.22
EG	−0.48	0.34	0.21	−0.08	−0.11	−0.04	−0.23	0.06

POP = Policy Output, POC = Policy Outcomes, WM = world market dependence, EG = economic growth.

also understandable, as there is no reason why open economies should have a better or worse economic performance than closed economies.

The low correlations between the economic variables and the policy variables enable us to introduce the institutional factors and the role of actors, as mentioned above. Two institutional structures may influence the way political and socio-economic actors handle conflicting views on socio-economic policy making. Remember that in particular the socio-economic area is often one of the most crucial battlefields in politics and in particular in times of recession. Chapter 7 illustrated this point by showing that the left–right division is one of the most important structuring forces of political systems and the relationships between parties.

We distinguish between two arenas of conflict-solution: those in the political and in the socio-economic realm.

- In the political arena the style of leadership refers to the way conflicts are resolved by the political elites (namely either more competitive or more coalescent, which is measured on a 4-point scale: 1 = most competitive; 4 = most coalescent). See Peters et al. (1977).
- In the socio-economic arena the degree of corporatism refers to modes of conflict resolution by means of frequent interactions between governments and the main economic organized groups (also called tripartism or interest intermediation or industrial relation systems). This variable is measured on a 5-point scale: 5 = cooperative and 1 = cooperation is absent (see Keman, 1988).

Both the concepts 'style of leadership' and 'corporatism' have been discussed in the previous chapter and we shall therefore not go into further detail. Table 9.9 shows two interesting results:

- The style of leadership often coincides with state intervention.
- Corporatism affects the policy performance.

As a general result, these conclusions are correct. But as the relationships are far from perfect, there must be exceptions, meaning countries where these institutional structures do not coincide with the expected outcomes. Hence, regression analysis can be used as a tool to determine to what degree this is the case or whether or not there is a causal mechanism present. (See Table 9.10).

Residual analysis tells you whether countries have a higher (positive residual) or

Table 9.9 *The relationships between institutions, output and outcomes (Spearman's rho)*

	1965–1973		1974–1980		1981–1988		1965–1988	
	POP	POC	POP	POC	POP	POC	POP	POC
Leadership	0.6	0.18	0.43	0.36	0.55	0.6	0.6	0.43
Corporatism	0.2	0.56	0.4	0.84	0.40	0.8	0.3	0.88

POP = Policy Output; POC = Policy Outcomes.

Table 9.10 *Residual scores of the regression of policy types (Y) on the style of leadership (X)*

Switzerland	−2.05
Australia	−1.46
Canada	−0.94
Japan	−0.86
Norway	−0.43
Finland	−0.43
UK	−0.35
USA	−0.35
New Zealand	−0.35
Austria	0.17
Italy	0.25
Sweden	0.68
Denmark	0.68
Germany	0.76
Ireland	0.76
Belgium	1.28
Netherlands	1.28
France	1.36

Note that a regression on ordinal variables with a few categories is strictly not correct and is only justified when the purpose is to produce a simple descriptive graphical plot of the residuals.

a lower (negative residual) Y-score than you would expect on the basis of the independent variable(s). One problem with residual analysis is how to determine the adequate threshold for residual scores: what score makes an outlier? There are no general rules to answer this question. As in our analysis the distribution of cases is not too dispersed and, consequently, the outlier scores are moderate, we have chosen a not too high threshold, namely a standardized residual score of ± 1. Given this threshold, Switzerland is a clear example of an outlier. This country combines a restrictive style of policy making with a *coalescent leadership*. The graphical juxtaposition of France and Switzerland makes clear what the positive and negative residual scores mean: these outliers indicate that cooperation in politics (coalescence) is not always a necessary nor a sufficient condition for active state intervention.

Factor analysis can be used in order to see whether the variables – the degree of coalescent leadership, corporatism, world market integration and interventionistic policy types – can be summarized by one dimension. Factor analysis means in this case the amalgamation of four variables into one new variable, as has been done before in the case of the factors TEDC and WEDC. This is done in Table 9.11.

The countries are ordered on the factor scores, which leads to an interesting result. It seems that the size of the country dominates the results. Small countries are characterized by a relatively high degree of coalescent leadership, corporatism, and interventionism in the economy. One major cause for this can be found in the high degree of world market integration of small countries, which is assumed to

Table 9.11 *Factor analysis on four variables*[a]

Japan	−1.44
US	−1.27
Australia	−1.20
Italy	−1.09
France	−0.80
UK	−0.65
New Zealand	−0.59
Canada	−0.54
Germany	−0.14
Switzerland	−0.03
Ireland	0.06
Finland	0.60
Austria	0.84
Denmark	1.04
Belgium	1.14
Netherlands	1.33
Sweden	1.37
Norway	1.37

[a]These variables are: the style of leadership, corporatism, world market dependance and policy types. Positive factor scores are most likely in the case of small countries with coalescent styles of leadership. High factor scores are more likely with larger countries with competitive cultures. Eigenvalue = 2.379; explained variance = 59.5%.

increase their vulnerability or need to adapt to fluctuations in the world market. Corporatism and coalescent leadership can be seen as institutional devices to cope with this problem. These institutions direct the negotiating process towards *pay-off* (the equal distribution of economic distress) and avoid a *zero sum* outcome (that one actor absorbs the welfare of another).

Leadership and corporatism are institutions with a more or less constant or structural impact on the policy-making process. The behavior of actors has a more conjunctural character. The latter is measured by:

- complexion of government and parliament (CPG): a 5-point scale constructed by Schmidt (1992) in which 5 = left wing, 3 = balance, 1 = right wing;
- strike-activity (socio-economic unrest): an interval variable on the basis of ILO-data;
- electoral strength of left parties (LEFTV): an interval variable based on electoral data (Mackie and Rose, 1991).

Correlating these conjunctural variables – which may change from election to election – with more structural variables may shed some light on the interactive relationship between actors and institutions.

Table 9.12 shows one crucial aspect of the interrelationships between institutions

Table 9.12 *The relationship between the behavior of actors and the political-institutional room to maneuver (Pearson product-moment correlations)*

	1965–1973		1974–1980		1981–1988		1965–1988	
	LS	CO	LS	CO	LS	CO	LS	CO
CPG	0.49	0.45	0.33	0.29	0.21	0.45	0.46	0.55
Strikes	−0.69	−0.49	−0.62	−0.55	−0.22	−0.33	−0.64	−0.55
Leftv	0.21	0.57	0.17	0.63	0.16	0.55	0.18	0.59

LS = leadership, CO = corporatism, CPG = political complexion of government and parliament, strikes = working days lost, leftv = left votes.

and actors. The institutions (corporatism and the style of political leadership) shape the *room to maneuver* of political and socio-economic actors. The stability of the relationship is an indicator of this working of institutions. The stable negative signs indicate that corporatism has a tempering effect on strike activities.

The interrelationships between actors and institutions do not mean that there is no direct relationship between actors and policy-making. This is shown by Table 9.13. The table indicates that there is a significant direct effect of actors and socio-economic policy-making. This effect is not the same in all time periods. These relationships need further examination, for example by means of analysis of the residuals (as has been demonstrated before).

Do all four policy types lead to similar outcomes? This question refers to the degree of correspondence between POP and POC. Analysis of variance is used to examine the variations of performance per policy type (see Section 6.6). This is done in Table 9.14. The table shows that only the monetarist policy type has a

Table 9.13 *The relationship between the behavior of actors and socio-economic policy-making in three post-war periods (Pearson product-moment correlations)*

	1965–1973		1974–1980		1981–1988		1965–1988	
	POP	POC	POP	POC	POP	POC	POP	POC
CPG	0.37	0.25	0.26	0.37	0.09	0.24	0.42	0.50
Worklos	−0.60	−0.50	−0.40	−0.54	−0.20	−0.09	−0.44	−0.59
Leftv	0.25	0.59	0.45	0.57	0.28	0.25	0.26	0.60

POP = Policy Output, POC = Policy Outcomes, CPG = political complexion, Worklos = working days lost.

Table 9.14 *The performance per policy type (one-way analysis of variance)*

Policy type	Mean	SD	*n*
Restrictive	0.49	0.21	84
Monetarist	0.38	0.19	122
Austerity	0.53	0.18	156
Keynesian	0.53	0.15	104

F-ratio = 18.3 *F*-Prob. = 0.0000.

relatively lower performance. The between-group variance is rather weak: the various policy types do not lead to fundamentally different results ($\eta^2 = 0.11$).

A simple listing could also show us another aspect of the degree of correspondence: namely the equi- and pluri-functionality. These phenomena can be summarized as:

- *equi-functionality*: different policy types lead to the same results (e.g. Japan and Sweden);
- *pluri-functionality*: similar policy types lead to different results (Australia and Ireland).

We will not elaborate on this further here, but it is clear from the above analysis that we should be very careful to avoid too deterministic reasoning or jumping to causal conclusions. Additionally, it is also clear now how 'critical cases' are selected (see also Part I). They emerge as particular cases from the analysis because of their specific combination of values which turns them into non-representative exceptional cases that do not corroborate the theory. Comparative cases, on the other hand, emerge as common and therefore representative cases.

Path analysis helps to summarize the main conclusions by means of regression analysis (see Figure 9.1). The distance between the left and the center is computed as the average position of the center parties on the left–right scale *minus* the average position of the left parties. The explanatory power of this model is rather poor compared with the explained variance of the socio-economic model, which is summarized in Figure 9.2.

In general we may draw several conclusions from the above exercises:

1 The degree to which the models are to be generalized is limited given the moderate relationships and explained variances – we must be aware of outliers and the statistical complications that emerge from a small *n*.
2 'Politics does matter', especially in relation to the output.
3 'Corporatism' does matter, especially in relation to the outcomes.

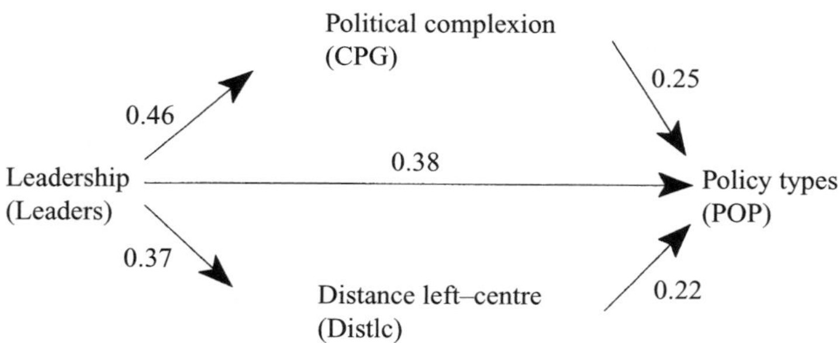

Figure 9.1 *The main political determinants of Policy Types ($R^2_{adj} = 0.19$)*

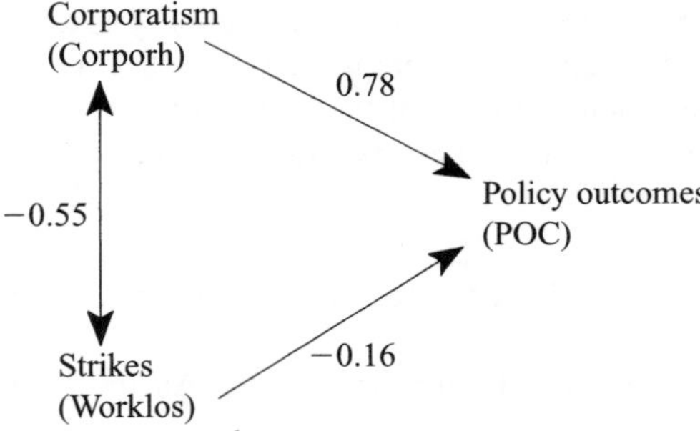

Figure 9.2 *The main socio-economic determinants of policy outcomes (beta-weights) (R^2_{adj} = 0.74; n = 17)*

The importance of both types of institutional factors is based on their enduring relevance over time. Most importantly, we may conclude that causality is first and for all a theoretical assumption that we try to make plausible, but it will be difficult (or even impossible) to prove empirically. Thus, the plausibility of an assumed causal relationship depends on the adequacy of the steps taken in the Research Design. Here we see the interaction between method (the way to approach a Research Question) and statistics (the devices used to answer the Research Question in quantitative terms). This interaction must be seen in relation to the cyclical character of the research process: theory is often needed to approach reality in a comparative manner and the results of this research often lead to adapted theories, which are again the basis for new Research Designs.

9.5 ELECTORAL CYCLES AND MACRO-ECONOMIC POLICY

Politico-economic models of the macro economy and political process can be developed by assuming that the government maximizes its own utility subject to various constraints (Schneider and Frey, 1988: 240). The most important constraint is political: a government only stays in power when it is re-elected. For that it needs the electoral support of voters. The electorate's voting decision is supposed to depend on the state of the economy, and the government may attempt to influence its re-election prospects by altering the state of the economy. This is one of the basic assumptions of the so-called '*Political Business Cycle*'.

Schneider and Frey's overview of empirical studies which have tested for systematic business fluctuations coinciding with election periods has found mixed results at best. In this section we will focus on the empirical study of Sabine Lessmann (1987) because it presents an interesting integration of three techniques that are used to test the Political Business Cycle: regression analysis, discriminant analysis and analysis of variance. Lessmann has chosen these three statistical techniques for the identification and specification of the assumed synchronization of expenditure in electorally appealing areas with the timing of general elections.

The focus here is primarily on the Research Design: assuming that the political business cycle exists, how can we determine how it works? It is clear from the beginning that the Research Design must meet specific characteristics in order to enable a fruitful analysis. Most importantly, the data must have a time series format in order to be able to detect the pattern that suggests a business cycle, since it is change that matters.

In Lessmann's analysis, a regression analysis is run with three dummy variables as independent variables, denoting the pre-election, election and first post-election year. The expenditure variables are then regressed on the different years. The intercept or constant is in this case equal to the mean of the second post-election years which are assigned 0s throughout. The *a* and *b* values will tell us which independent variable leads to what kind of allocation. The R^2 quantifies the proportion of variance in the expenditure data, accounted for by the different years of the election period. The *F* ratio associated with the R^2 determines whether the groups differ significantly. The results of the regression analysis will tell us whether the different years of the election period can account for much of the variance encountered in the expenditure series. Secondly, the results will indicate if it is the pre-election year or the election year which is actually more important as an explanatory factor; thirdly; and most importantly, we will see if there is any systematic synchronization at all.

In order to determine which groups of years actually differ from each other, Lessmann took one of the 'multiple comparisons between means' approaches in the frame of an analysis of variance (ANOVA) (see Section 6.6). Important comparisons are the allocations in pre-election and election years versus post-election allocations. Other values like the sum of squares, the mean squares and *F* are the same as those obtained with regression analysis.

Finally, discriminant analysis is also a regression technique which aims at statistically distinguishing between two or more groups of cases on the basis of a number of interval variables. This enables us to compare, for example, expenditures in election years with expenditures in the first post-election year in order to see whether they are statistically different or not. If they are different, there is some empirical ground for a Political Business Cycle.

Lessmann's various analyses are carried out as follows: firstly, the expenditures in election years were statistically compared with the expenditures in the first post-election year. According to the literature on Political Business Cycles, the two groups should be different, and the expenditures in the election year group should be systematically higher than those in the post-election year group. Secondly, the expenditures in election years were compared with the second post-election years. Thirdly, the two analyzed groups consisted of the pre-election and the election year itself. According to some suggestions in the literature, the expenditures of the election years should be statistically different but also higher. Fourthly and finally, the expenditures of the pre-election year were tested against the expenditures of the first post-election year. In this case the pre-election years were assumed to be higher. In its most simple form this can be visualized as in Figure 9.3.

Lessmann's analysis is limited to Germany. A similar Research Design can also be applied to our selection of 18 OECD countries with the help of the country–

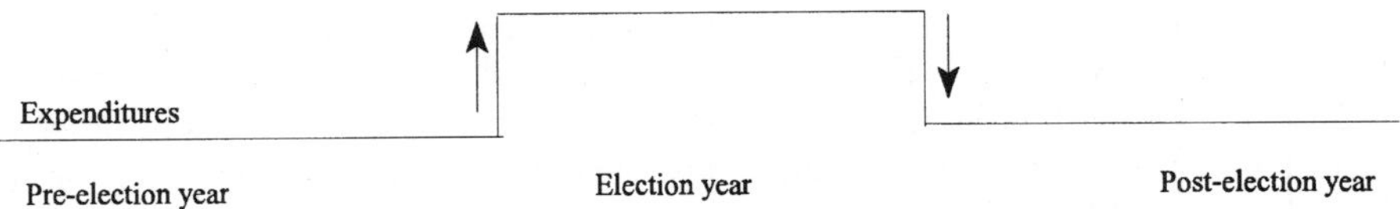

Figure 9.3 *Schematic example of a Political Business Cycle*

year data set (1965–1990). We can test the assumption that parties will lower the taxes in the year before an election year in order to gain votes. In addition we add two extra variables into the models – social transfers and the complexion of government and parliament – which offer the *alternative hypotheses* that the level of taxes relates more to the type of welfare state and/or the government complexion than to the occurrence of election years.

First of all we have to distinguish between three types of years: pre-election (variable 'preelyr'), election year (variable 'elyr') and post-election years (variable 'postelyr'). Next we construct a dummy variable that divides the years into election and non-election years (variable 'prior'). The three statistical techniques are applied in order to test the initial hypothesis. These steps are taken in the file Chapter9.sps, under section 9.5. The results of the analysis are presented in Table 9.15.

In the ANOVA and regression analysis the relative weight of Trans, Prior and CPG are measured. The results of both analyses show that the dummy variable Prior is not able to explain variation in the dependent variable taxes (given the low F and beta scores which are also not significant). The discriminant analysis tests if the level of the taxes and transfers corresponds to two groups: the pre-election years and the non-pre-election years. The discriminant analysis clearly shows that such a grouping cannot be made on the basis of these variables. The values of the eigenvalue, canonical correlation and the Chi-squares are very low, and the overall model is not significant (see Section 6.5 for an explanation of these terms). The overall conclusions confirm the results of Lessmann and many others, namely that the evidence for a political business cycle is extremely poor. Other factors, such as

Table 9.15 *The application of three statistical techniques on Political Business Cycles*

	ANOVA		**Regression**		**Discriminant functions**[a]	
	F	**Sign.** *F*	**beta**	**Sign.** *t*	**Wilk's Lambda**	**Sign.**
Transfers	480.6	0.0	0.71	0.0	0.9996	0.7249
Prior	0.010	0.919	0.0	0.97	0.9994	0.9168
CPG	23.5	0.0	0.23	0.0	0.9994	0.9817
Explained/predicted	57.8		0.56		51.04	
n	335		335		444	

[a]The variables in the discriminant function do not add significantly to the distinction between the categories of the dependent variable.

the type of the welfare state (see taxes) and the color of government appear to be more important.

9.6 DEMOCRATIC PERFORMANCE

The term democratic performance refers to the quality of democracy as indicated by, for example, freedom, equality, rates of participation and political stability (see e.g. Lane and Ersson, 1994). If we are looking for variations in the degree of democracy we can mostly not apply the most-similar Research Design, since the similarity of, for example, OECD countries is partly derived from the fact that these countries have the same level of democracy (but not equality). Hence, the first half of this section demonstrates a *most different* Research Design which is based on a comparison of the research of Burkhart and Lewis-Beck on the relationship between democracy and economic welfare and the research of Vanhanen on democratization (Vanhanen, 1990; Burkhart and Lewis-Beck, 1994).

The Burkhart–Lewis-Beck data set is an adapted and extended version of the well-known Gastil/Freedom House democracy indicators (see, for an overview, Lane and Ersson, 1997: 93). Gastil ranks each nation on separate 7-point scales for 'political rights' and 'civil liberties'. Burkhart and Lewis-Beck added to this data dummies for the position of countries c = core, m = semiperiphery, p = periphery). They also employ the energy consumption per capita (logged) as an economic development measure (which correlates 0.9 with gross national product per capita). Burkhart and Lewis-Beck test the 'economic development thesis' with the following model:

$$D_t = \mathrm{a} + \mathrm{b}D_t - 1 + \mathrm{c}E_t + \mathrm{d}(M \times E_t) + \mathrm{e}(P \times E_t) + \mathrm{u}$$

where: D_t is the democracy index at time t; $D_t - 1$ is the democracy index from the year before; E_t is energy consumption per capita (logged to the base 10) at time t; $(M \times E_t)$ is the dummy variable for semiperiphery status multiplied by E_t; P is a dummy for periphery status.

The Burkhart and Lewis-Beck model is an autoregressive model having the lagged dependent variable at the right-hand sight of the equation (as in: $Y_t = Y_{t-1} + X_t$). This type of modeling is not without complications as it may well boost the R^2 and beta-weight. $D_t - 1$ acts to control for omitted independent variables: as the other forces acting on democracy are uncertain, they will be essentially summarized in the democratic performance of the nation during its previous year. Their estimation procedure is GLS-ARMA, as this procedure avoids first-order autocorrelation and cross-sectional heteroscedasticity. Their model throws up a pseudo-R^2 of 0.71 and the b-scores are 2.49 (for E_t), -1.33 (for $M \times E_t$) and -1.54 (for $P \times E_t$). Their conclusion is that economic development matters most for nations in the core; it still matters, but about half as much, in the semiperiphery. For nations in the periphery, the economic effect is just a bit less. Taken together, economic factors, both international and domestic, appear decisive in shaping a nation's democratic future.

Table 9.16 *Two models on democratization (1988)*

	The Burkhart and Lewis-Beck model (1994), $n = 131$			The Vanhanen model (1990), $n = 147$	
Variable	**beta**	**Sign. t**		**beta**	**Sign. t**
LG10ecpc	0.57	0	IPR	0.84	0.00
Met	−0.52	0			
Pet	−0.43	0			
Constant		0.06			
R^2_{Adj}	0.36			0.71	

LG10ecpc = energy consumption per capita (logged to the base 10); Met = the dummy variable for semiperiphery status multiplied by Et; Pet = the dummy variable for periphery status multiplied by Et; IPR = Index of Power Resources.
Sources: Burkhart and Lewis-Beck, 1994; Vanhanen, 1990.

We will replicate the analysis in a more simple format, with OLS regression on a 1988 cross-section (Table 9.16). The results of our analysis match with that of Burkhart and Lewis-Beck, albeit that our estimates indicate moderate effects (see the SPSS setup Chapter9.sps). This outcome confirms our suspicion that the autoregressive model might not throw up a reliable R^2. A theoretical, instead of statistical, explanation of the moderate performance of the Burkhart and Lewis-Beck model is provided by Vanhanen (1990). He proposed an alternative for the socio-economic hypothesis of democratization, by hypothesizing that 'democratization takes place under conditions in which power resources have become so widely distributed that no group is any longer able to suppress its competitors or to maintain its hegemony' (Vanhanen, 1990: 66). Vanhanen's dependent variable is an Index of Democratization (ID) which multiplies the following two variables and divides the outcome by 100:

1 The degree of legal competition (in a democracy there will be at least two equal groups which are free to compete for power) which is operationalized as 100 minus the percentage of the votes won by the largest party (a high score indicates a high degree of competition).
2 The degree of participation, which is operationalized as the number of voters as a percentage of the total population (a high score indicates a high degree of participation).

Vanhanen's independent variable is the Index of Power Resources (IPR) which is operationalized by means of six indicators:

- (1) Urban and (2) non-agricultural population indicate the degree of occupational diversification and the level of socioeconomic development.
- (3) Students and (4) literates indicate the distribution of knowledge and intellectual power resources.
- (5) Family farms and (6) the degree of decentralization of non-agricultural economic resources are intended to measure the degree of resource distribution.

The main difference with Burkhart and Lewis-Beck is that Vanhanen not only looks at the level of welfare but also, and more importantly, at the distribution of a wider range of power resources. Vanhanen's conceptualization and operationalization of the Index of Power Resources indeed results in a much higher explained variance of 0.709.

This example shows us that a high explained variance is only to be trusted when *both* the theoretical and statistical specifications of the model are correct. The Burkhart and Lewis-Beck model is far more complicated than our replication. But by reducing its complexity and by comparing its results with other research outcomes, it becomes clear what the weaknesses of this model are.

Until now, we have mainly focused on the bivariate relationship between democracy and economic development. But there is also a large body of literature discussing a variety of possible determinants of democratization. Historically, democracy arose along with capitalism, and this suggests a causal relationship. Flourishing liberties are a prerequisite for capitalism, and capitalism itself gives power to the bourgeoisie which has an interest in liberties. The rise of capitalism will normally be accompanied by the growth of the middle class and a greater need for education. Both are often considered as moderating factors. Education, according to Seymour Martin Lipset, makes people less apt to adopt extreme doctrines and more able to make rational choices. Education also gives power to the middle class. The interest in liberties is shared with the bourgeoisie, as is the need for rationalization of government in the increasingly complex society. Increased wealth moderates the lower classes as well, and together this paves the road for democracy. But which multivariate relationships between democracy and a range of other variables are there? This question is both relevant in relation to Part I (i.e. Galton's problem) and Part II (i.e. causality and regression) of this book.

The analysis of the determinants of democratization is based on a file ('widlak. sav') which holds a representative sample of the countries of the world.[4] From every continent a country is included. From every group in the world system, as seen by the qualitative researchers, at least one country is included. There are five observations for 62 countries for all variables but dependency. After performing a lag on the X-variables, three observations remain, being a combination of the values of the Y-variables and the values of the X-variables five years before. So the data set has a multilevel structure and this has consequences. For example, the level of democracy of Sweden in 1970 is not independent of the level of democracy in Sweden in 1980. But independence of Y-values is assumed when using OLS-regression; therefore we apply PCSE-analysis which corrects for this violation of assumptions. The values of the independent variables ought to be measured independently of each other – in this case economic development and dependency. If this is not the case we speak of multicollinearity: an independent variable is almost a linear function of a combination of the other independent variables.

We will discuss the variables most often used in this stream of research. First of all democracy. Democracy can be analytically separated in civil liberties and political liberties. However, this distinction is not very useful, since these dimensions are not empirically distinguishable. The variable Democracy is based on several indicators (derived from the Polity III data set): competitiveness of political participation, the openness of and competitiveness of executive recruitment and the level of constraints on the chief executive. The dependent variable ranges from 0 to 10; 0 meaning no institutional democracy at all, and 10, full institutional democracy.

Income inequality is the other dependent variable. The GINI measure is developed in order to assess the degree to which a population shares the national income inequality. Its values range from 0 (total equality) to 100 (one person having everything).

The most important independent variable, economic development, is measured as the GNP per capita. Since the relationship between democracy and economic development is slightly curvilinear, usually the natural logarithm of this score is taken to correct for this. Economic development is also used as proxy for literacy or education since they correlate almost perfectly. Using both would result in problems of multicollinearity (as discussed in Section 6.7).

Another independent variable is dependency. Although dependency is not important for the timing of development, it does have a negative impact on the level of democracy and a positive relationship with income inequality. The score was developed by Smith and White (1992) and resulted from a quantitative network analysis of international commodity trade flows. The measure ranges from 1 to 5, representing respectively core and periphery. An important intervening variable, the size of the middle class, is not used in the example below, because of the small number of countries for which a score is available.

There are a range of methodological problems to be handled here. The autocorrelation problem stems from the use of aggregated values for several succeeding years. The level of democracy of 1965 obviously had an impact on the level of democracy of 1970. Whereas autocorrelation is the dependence of the values of the dependent variable, multicollinearity is the dependence of the values of the independent variables. Multicollinearity is the problem where one independent

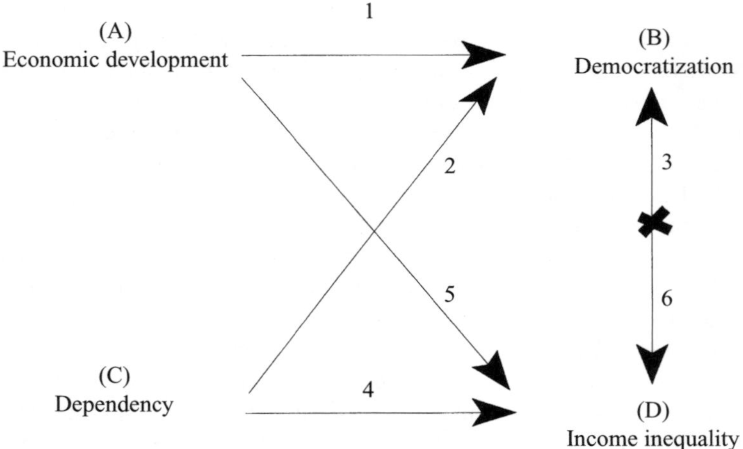

Figure 9.4 *A hypothetical model of the main determinants of democratization*

variable is almost a linear function of a combination of other different independent variables.

Galton's problem is a typical problem of cross-national and cross-temporal research. Can a phenomenon such as the level of democracy of a country better be explained by its history and the diffusion of ideas during its history or by a macro-economic determinant such as GNP per capita? Is it reasonable to expect that a country becomes less democratic when its GNP per capita goes down? Perhaps we can better predict the level of democracy in a country by the level of democracy of its neighboring countries than we can by its economic development. Is democracy a characteristic of Britain or any other individual country or of western Europe as a whole? In general it is advisable to combine a structural view of properties with a diffusional view. In our investigation of the relationship between economic development and democratization we have used the dependency variable as a control variable for Galton's problem. The dependency variable divides the world, economically and geographically, into a core and a periphery. Both variables are incorporated into the regression analysis and there is still a relationship between economic development and democratization; therefore it is plausible to assume there is a structural part besides the diffusional explanation.

We will try to put some of these findings together and test the model displayed in Figure 9.4. The hypotheses are as follows:

1 The more economic development, the higher the level of democracy.
2 The stronger the dependency, the lower the level of democracy.
3 Increase in the level of income inequality does not result in a lower level of democracy.
4 The stronger the dependency, the more income inequality.
5 The more economic development, the less income inequality.
6 The level of democracy does not affect income inequality.

Table 9.17 lists the results of the PCSE regression. The relationship between economic development and democratization is confirmed once again. This structural relationship is found after taking the dependency variable into account. So in a

Table 9.17 *PCSE regression on the relationships in Figure 9.4*

Relationship in model	beta
AB	0.39*
CB	−0.37*
DB	−0.07
AD	0.05
CD	0.48*
BD	−0.12
R^2 B	0.59*
R^2 D	0.28*

* = significant at 0.05 level. $n = 62$.

way we have controlled for the historic-diffusionistic explanation of democracy, and still find a strong positive correlation between economic development and democratization. There is also a strong negative relationship between dependency and democratization. So the qualitative researchers' hypothesis is confirmed since we find a significant β of -0.37. Hypothesis 3 seems also correct since we find almost no effect of income inequality on democratization. The test for linearity is significant, so we should not expect to find an inverted U-curve as Muller (1995) expected. The finding of Bollen and Jackman (1985) and Doorenspleet (1997) – that there is no relationship to be found between income inequality and democratization when dependency and economic development is taken into account – is confirmed. On the relationship between economic development and income inequality on the one hand and the relationship between dependency and income inequality on the other, the authors seem to contradict each other. Bollen and Jackman find that the relationship between dependency and democracy vanishes when economic development is taken into account. Doorenspleet on the contrary finds that the relationship between economic development and income inequality vanishes when dependency is taken into account. On the basis of our findings we would expect the level of income inequality only to be determined by the position of the country in the world system and not at all by the level of economic development. The world system position explains about 30 per cent of the level of income inequality. The sixth hypothesis is also confirmed. Democratization has no significant impact on the level of income inequality and vice versa.

We can conclude that the hypothesized relationships are almost completely confirmed. The only eye-catching finding is that there seems to be no relationship between economic development and income inequality. We found a significant outcome when performing a linearity test on this relationship, but the tiny effect of economic development is not significant at all. The theoretically expected U-shaped relationship is not confirmed. In contrast with democracy, the variance of income inequality can be explained for less than a third. Moreover, income inequality seems to be dependent only on historic and geographically diffusionistic factors and not on economic development and the level of democracy. This implies, for example, that for the idea of fighting a class war through democracy is without foundation. Here also, new thinking has to be done.

We started this section with the remark that the most-similar design is not suited for research on democratic performance when the universe of discourse holds countries with a similar *degree* of democracy. But, it should be added that a most-similar design is certainly suitable if not the degree but the *type* of democracy is the object of study. This is what is done by Arend Lijphart in a recent article on democratic performance in 18 well-established democracies (Lijphart, 1994, 1997). In Lijphart's study the type of democracy is the independent instead of the dependent variable. The conventional wisdom is that consensus democracies are good at representation, whereas the majoritarian democracies provide a more effective government. Lijphart uses a data set comprising several performance indicators to show that majoritarian systems do not perform better in maintaining public order and managing the economy. He even claims that the overall performance of consensus democracy is superior.

Table 9.18 *Lijphart's bivariate regression analyses of the effect of consensus democracy on ten performance variables*

	Estimated regression coefficient	Standardized regression coefficient[a]	*t*-values	*n*
Women's representation (1980–1982)	5.292	0.61	3.06	18
Family policy (1976–1982)	1.56[b]	0.44	1.95	18
Voting turnout (1971–1980)	1.26	0.1	0.4	18
Income top 20% (1985)	−1.64[b]	−0.52	2.37	17
Dahl rating (1969)	−1.37[b]	−0.71	4.02	18
Riots (1948–1977)	−0.14	−0.06	0.24	18
Political deaths (1948–1977)	−2.18	−0.31	1.31	18
Economic growth (1961–1988)	−0.02	−0.02	0.08	18
Inflation (1961–1988)	−0.47	−0.26	1.01	18
Unemployment (1965–1988)	−0.6	−0.32	1.1	13

$n = 18$ OECD countries.

[a]This coefficient equals the coefficient of covariation.

[b]Statistically significant at the 1 per cent level (one-tailed test). The other values are not significant.

Source: Lijphart (1994: 10).

Table 9.18 shows that women's parliamentary representation and family policy are strongly correlated with the degree of consensus democracy; voting turnout is not, probably because of the relatively low turnout in Switzerland and the USA. Income inequality and democratic quality (the Dahl rating: 1 is the highest and 6 the lowest point on this scale) are also significantly correlated with consensus democracy. The other variables are either not significant or the causal relationship is very weak. Lijphart recognizes that the favorable findings concerning consensus democracy may be due to usual Nordic cultural factors or to a potential disturbing influence of population size. After controlling for these factors (e.g. by comparing the results of the designs in which they are included with those in which they are excluded), Lijphart concludes that they do not distort the results.

Some problems with Lijphart's analysis of the performance of consensus democracies are that it is based on a few cases, that it is rather aggregated and that the number of significant relationships is small. Furthermore, majoritarian and consensus democracies are not homogeneous blocks as most democracies are more or less 'mixed' types. For example, as has been shown in Section 8.8, there is also extensive 'power sharing' in the majoritarian system of the USA! Consequently, given this diversity rather than a dichotomy, it is not wholly correct to generalize on either consensus or majoritarian democracies. In the next section we will give an example of this diversity by discussing the degree to which the majoritarian systems of the UK and the USA are uniform in their policy effectiveness.

9.7 PARTIES AND ACCOUNTABILITY

Responsiveness and accountability are two important aspects of the process of democratic decision making and therefore central mechanisms in the chain of democratic control and command. In Chapter 7 we discussed and analyzed party responsiveness in relation to the median voter. In this section we will focus on party accountability, which is strongly linked to *the mandate theory*. This theory states that voters mandate parties to fulfill their promises once they are in office. The way parties use this mandate depends on the type of party system (two-party system vs multi-party system) and the constitutional features of the system (presidentialism or not). This section applies the mandate theory to a multi-party system (the Netherlands) and two-party systems (the USA and Britain).

Budge and Hofferbert have presented a range of regression equations that model the linkages between party program emphases on the one hand and expenditures in several policy areas on the other hand for the American political parties. These models are based on different hypotheses about factors that might influence the impact of parties. In general we distinguish between three types of modeling:

- additive of conjunctive modeling (for 'and–and' relationships)
- multiplicative modeling (for 'or–or' relationships)
- a combinations of the above types (for more complex and elaborate models).

Table 9.19 summarizes the models.

The Budge and Hofferbert models can be applied to any category of expenditures and corresponding program emphases. Here we will not replicate their analysis, but ask the question to what extent their models are applicable to other political systems. Here we take the example of the Dutch system, but any other multi-party system could have been chosen. We limit the analysis to the three main Dutch parties: the CDA (Christian Democrats), the PvdA (Labor Party) and the VVD (Liberals).

Following van Wijck's operationalization, the degree of income inequality is measured as the proportion of the Old Age Pension (in Dutch: AOW) as a share of the average monthly income (van Wijck, 1991). We also followed van Wijck's method of how to cope with two major adjustments on the AOW in 1965 and 1985. To be sure that these policy shifts do not influence the results, two dummies are added to all regression equations (named D65 and D85). We refer to the file Chapter9.sps for all the details.

Table 9.20 gives an overview of the mandate models applied to the Netherlands. These models are adjusted to the multi-party system by assuming that the three parties CDA, PvdA and VVD are the three major parties (either in the role of cabinet party or opposition party). The results show that the Christian democratic party CDA plays an important role as a 'pivot party'. In the competitive model the CDA appears to be the only party that matters. This pivotal role can be explained by the fact that this party was present in all post-war cabinets (until 1994). As a consequence, it did not matter much for policy outcomes whether either the PvdA or the VVD joined the CDA-dominated cabinet. The two dummy variables D65 and D85, both representing policy shifts, have stronger causal effects than the party variables.

The Budge and Hofferbert test of the mandate theory has recently been compared with other approaches of the mandate theory. The American political

Table 9.19 *Regression equations that model the impact of American parties on the level of social expenditures*

Label	Equation	Type	Hypothesis
Competitive model	$y = \alpha + \beta R + \beta D$	Additive	The expenditures will rise if the Democrats or the Republicans focus on it, and they will rise even more if both parties emphasize it
Complementary model	$y = \alpha + \beta(R + D)$	Additive	The Democrats and Republicans have an equal influence on the level of expenditures
Consensus model	$y = \alpha + \beta(R \times D)$	Multiplicative	The expenditures will only rise when there is consensus (or when $R \times D > 0$)
Control model	$y = \alpha + \beta(R \times P_R) + \beta(D \times P_D)$	Both additive and multiplicative	Both the Republicans and the Democrats may have influence as long as they have the President ($P =$ the Presidency)
General program model	$y = \alpha - \beta R - \beta D + \beta(R \times P_R) + \beta(D \times P_D)$	Both additive and multiplicative	When in office, both parties take the opposite position to that of the parties not in office (thereby undoing each others' influence)
General partisan influence model	$y = \alpha - \beta R - \beta D + \beta(R \times P_R) + \beta(D \times P_D) + R$	Both additive and multiplicative	The same as the general program model, but this time a constant extra influence is given to the Republicans

Source: Budge and Hofferbert (1990).

scientist Terry J. Royed has made an overview of the major tests of mandate models (Royed, 1996). He criticizes the Budge and Hofferbert approach by stating that the relationship between policy statements and spending is not direct, that the percentage of sentences is a very imprecise indicator of party intentions and that the spending categories are too broad and aggregated. Given these limitations, the results of the Budge–Hofferbert approach is at best a very rough estimate of the relationship between party programmatic commitments and policy actions due to a trade-off between a large cross-sectional comparability and a low degree of specificity of the dependent and independent variables. Hence, Royed reverses this trade-off by making the dependent and independent variables more specific and by consequently reducing the universe of discourse.

In doing so, Royed is seeking an alternative to the mechanical relationships that are assumed by Budge and Hofferbert. He focuses more on 'real' specific promises that are made and compares them with the 'real' accomplishments related to that specific pledge. Royed compares the effectiveness of the 'Conservative revolutions'

Table 9.20 *The mandate models applied to the Netherlands, 1948–1991 (n = 40)*

Label	Hypothesis	Equation	Result	R^2_{adj}	*DW*	Interpretation
Competitive model	The sum of all parties' emphases is positive ($\beta_1 + \beta_2 + \beta_3 > 0$)	$Dvt = \alpha + \beta_1 D65_t + \beta_2 D85_t + \beta_3 CDAP_t + \beta_4 VVDP_t + \beta_5 PVDAP_t + e_t$	Dvt = −0.011 + 0.081 D65t − 0.122 d85t + 0.003 CDAPt + e	0.6	2.9	The CDA-party beta is the only one that is significant. The other parties do not matter
Complementary model	The total positive emphases of all parties leads to less income inequality ($\beta_3 > 0$)	$Dvt = \alpha + \beta_1 D65_t + \beta_2 D85_t + \beta_3 tot_t + e_t$	Dvt = −0.008 + −0.081 D65t + −0.111D85$_t$ + 0.001TOTt	0.6	2.8	Both governmental and opposition favored income equality
Consensus model	Only when there is a consensus between government and opposition do we expect an increase in income equality ($\beta_3 > 0$)	$Dvt = \alpha + \beta_1 D65_t + \beta_2 D85_t + \beta_3 con_t + e_t$	Dvt = −0.005 + 0.081 D65t + −0.115 D85t + 0.00002 CONt + e	0.6	2.8	The degree of consensus is very moderate
Control model	Only parties in government matter	$Dvt = \alpha + \beta_1 D65_t + \beta_2 D85_t + \beta_3 gvt_t + e_t$	Dvt = −0.003 + 0.086 D65 + −0.111 D85 + 0.002 gvt + e	0.6	2.9	Only the ideology of the government has a significant beta score
General program model	The objectives of government and opposition parties are opposed	$Dvt = \alpha + \beta_1 D65_t + \beta_2 D85_t + \beta_3 gvt_t + \beta_4 opp_t + e_t$	Idem	0.6	2.9	Idem

Dvt = the degree of income inequality; TOT_t = Sum of positive and negative emphases of the parties in year *t*; CON = the multiplication of the party emphases; GVT = positive minus negative emphases of the government; OPP = same for opposition parties.

Sources: CBS (1994), *Vijfennegentig jaren statistiek in tijdreeksen*. 's Gravenhage: SDU en CBS; Volkens (1994).

in the USA (Reagan) and the UK (Thatcher). Royed's primary finding is that more Conservative party pledges were fulfilled, compared to those of the Republican and Democratic parties in the USA. Royed's basic data are summarized in Table 9.21. Whereas Budge and Hofferbert find that both the USA and the UK confirm the mandate model equally, Royed argues that the institutional differences between the two countries make the UK more effective (i.e. the mandate model is more fully confirmed) than the USA. The most basic difference is the presidential/parliamentary distinction. The USA is characterized by a system with separation of powers, low party cohesion and multiple centers of power – a combination that may invoke *deadlock*. In both countries the decision-making environment may vary. In the USA there may be *divided or united government*, and the UK may have a large, small or even no majority. Even when there is united government in the USA (meaning that the President is of the same party that 'controls' both houses), there are still incohesive parties, and an independent legislature and a strong committee system.

Royed opts for a firmer connection between party programmatic commitments ('pledge') and policy action ('pledge fulfillment') by examining, for different policy areas, to what degree *specific* pledges are fulfilled. The results in Table 9.21 show that indeed the Thatcher administration is more effective in achieving its goals than the Reagan administration. Royed argues that the high performance in the Thatcher era is *not* borne out by leadership qualities or economic circumstances (these factors were similar in both countries) but out of the decision-making environment.

The fact that Royed reaches a different conclusion from Budge and Hofferbert is based on their different conceptualization, operationalization, theoretical assumptions and data gathering. Although their Research Questions are the same, the differences in Research Design result in a different Research Answer. Instead of correlating platform pledges to spending data (as Budge and Hofferbert did) Royed examines relationships between 'real' pledges and 'real' fulfillments. This

Table 9.21 *Rate of fulfillment of party pledges by policy area in the USA and Britain under the Reagan and Thatcher administrations*

	USA: Republicans				UK: Conservatives			
	1980		1984		1979		1983	
	Perc. Fulfilled %	*n*	Perc. Fulfilled %	*n*	Perc. Fulfilled %	*n*	Perc. Fulfilled %	*n*
Social welfare	66.7	30	53.8	13	88.2	17	84.2	19
Economic	64.6	48	55.9	34	84.4	32	86.1	36
Civil rights/liberties	36.4	11	63.6	11	50	8	100	1
Natural resources	55	20	70	10	57.1	7	88.9	9
Education	33.3	6	16.7	6	100	4	66.6	3
Crime	50	4	77.8	9	83.3	6	100	6
Other	90	10	66.7	6	100	4	100	7
Total	61.2	129	58.4	89	80.8	78	87.6	81

Source: T.R. Royed (1996). *n* = the total number of pledges.

alternative approach leads to the plausible outcome that the effectiveness of the decision-making system is higher in the UK than in the USA.

9.8 OUTPUTS AND OUTCOMES IN THE INTERNATIONAL ARENA

Until now the focus has been on the output and performance of national governments. Also important are, of course, the output and performance in the international arena, being the results of the interactions between national governments. Output refers here to the steps taken by actors (e.g. greater or lesser cooperative actions) and outcomes refer to the effects of these steps (i.e. greater or lesser international tensions).

There are different types of interactions between actors in the international arena. Here we focus on the bilateral relations between actors (the so-called dyads) within a multilateral network. The simple fact that two actors operate within a network shapes their bilateral relations because they have to be alert for the power bases and interest of third actors (being either allies or enemies). We will follow here the data-analysis of Kleinnijenhuis and de Vries (1994) on so-called *dyads: relations between states at given time points*. Dyadic analysis is a specific form of time series analysis.

The question that Kleinnijenhuis and de Vries (1994) try to answer is which factors affect the dyadic relationships within a network. There are several factors that might have influence here: the role of a third party or characteristics of the network itself (like characteristics of the multilateral interaction pattern), characteristics of the dyad itself (like differences in power resources), characteristics of the individual actors (like their preferences, policy choices).

The *hypothetical-deductive method* is applied here on the bilateral relationships between the Soviet Union and the United States. Hypotheses are formulated about the factors which influence the external relationships. The hypotheses give alternative explanations for the variations and trends in bilateral relationships within multilateral networks. These explanatory factors are as follows.

- A new President may pursue a different policy.
- The programmatic emphases and preferences of the President or cabinet parties may matter for the relationships in the network.
- The degree to which the power relations are in balance affects the readiness for cooperative behavior (a power balance favors cooperation, whereas the absence of this balance does hamper cooperation).
- A tit-for-tat reaction of the USA may be expected in case of *direct* actions of the Soviet Union (SU).
- If third actors support the SU, the USA will be more cooperative toward the SU. The USA will give a tit-for-tat reaction to indirect actions of the SU towards the USA. In cases of inconsistent direct and indirect relations (the so-called divergence), the USA will react cooperatively as the divergence can be interpreted as a way out of adversarial relationships.

In the next step the concepts are operationalized in ways that fit with the available data. Data on bilateral relations are sometimes called *events-data*. Each event is specified by information on:

- *i* the actor
- *j*, the target actor
- *t*, the time factor.

In this section we focus on two quantitative aspects of the (i, j, t) relations:

- C^t_{ij}, the degree of cooperation of the action of *i* toward *j* on time point *t*;
- f^t_{ij}, the intensity or saliency or frequency of an action of *i* towards *j* during period *t*.

Data on successive Presidents need no further operationalization. The same goes for the bilateral tit-for-tat-hypothesis: $c^{t-1}_{ji} \rightarrow c^t_{ij}$. The policy preferences of the President are operationalized by means of the pro-military policy stance of the party of the President (see Chapter 7 for an introduction to the Manifesto data).

The power balance is operationalized by the number of military personnel, expressed by the indicator P^t_{ij} ($0 =$ balance, $-1 =$ SU preponderance, $+1 =$ US preponderance). Since 1969 the Russians had been developing such a conventional superior strength extent that we expected the Americans to seek to counterbalance this by all means.

Finally, the concepts relating to the multilateral interaction pattern need operationalization. We distinguish between the direct and indirect relations:

- the average degree of cooperation of indirect relations of actor *i* during period *t* toward actor *j* (range $[-1 \ldots +1]$);
- divergence of all possible pathways (direct relation plus all indirect relations) of actor *i* toward actor *j* during period *t* (range $[0 \ldots 1]$).

The third step examines the available data. The dependent variable is the degree of cooperation and intensity of dyadic interactions. For this the events data of E. E. Azar are used: 'When does who what to whom?' (the Conflict and Peace Data Bank: COPDAB). The COPDAB data base comprises 347,749 actions of sovereign states and supranational organizations in the period 1948–1978. The data base is based on the analyses of news reports in seventy English-speaking journals. The degree of cooperation is coded on a 15-point scale. This division covers (after transformation to the interval $-1 \ldots +1$) voluntary integration of two states $(+1)$ to full-scale war (-1). Verbal actions are coded between $1/3$ and $-1/3$. The intensity of a verbal action is therefore less than a diplomatic or military step.

The COPDAB data are aggregated on a half-year basis. For all asymmetrical relations between the 27 most frequently mentioned actors, the action frequency f^t_{ij} and the average degree of cooperation c^t_{ij} are computed. On the basis of these data transformations, the direct tit-for-tat relationships are plotted in Figure 9.5.

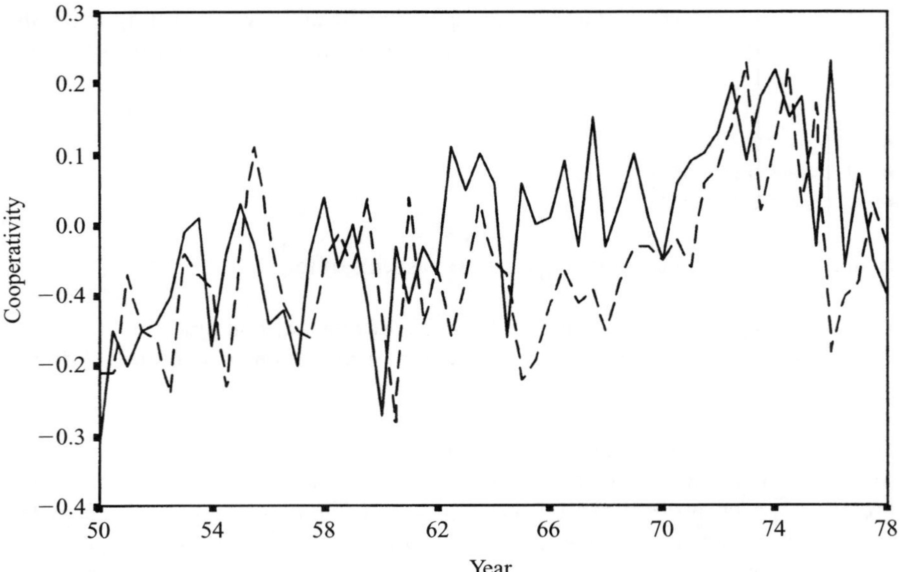

Figure 9.5 *The direct tit-for-tat relationships between the USA and the Soviet Union (SU) (1950–1978): solid line, USA → SU; broken line, SU → USA. Source: Kleinnijenhuis and De Vries (1994: 224)*

Finally, we need data on the power resources of nation-states that are derived from the data base of Singer 'Correlates of War' (1979). Now we are in a position to test the hypotheses by means of regression on dyads, the so-called dyadic analysis. The first hypotheses referred to the role of a new President. Analysis of variance, as explained in Subsection 5.5.2, is used to examine to what extent the degree of cooperation between the SU and the USA is influenced by the President holding office. The ANOVA analysis (Table 9.22) shows that foreign policy of the USA regarding the SU correlates with the changing of the President at 59 per cent ($\text{eta}^2 = 0.59$). The results indicate that every president after Truman has improved the relationship with the SU gradually.

Table 9.22 *Degree of cooperativity per American President (ANOVA)*

Truman	−0.19
Eisenhower	−0.08
Kennedy	−0.01
Johnson	0.02
Nixon	0.08
Ford	0.08
Carter	−0.03

$\text{eta}^2 = 0.59$; $F\,(6{,}51) = 12.33$.

Source: Kleinnijenhuis and de Vries (1994).

The next step will examine to what extent the structural factors are more important (see Table 9.23). The null-hypothesis was that there is no variation in the hostile relationship between the SU and the USA. This hypothesis is rejected by the regression analysis that includes the variables power imbalance, direct support in the direct and indirect relations, and divergence. The hypothesis that the pro-militarism of the party that supports the president matters is also refuted. The other hypotheses are more or less supported by the results.

9.9 CONCLUSIONS

In this chapter we have illustrated several Research Designs related to the output and/or performance in the socio-economic, democratic and international domains. Most designs have in common that they are looking for the variations in performance given different sets of actors, institutions and conditions. In this chapter we have used several designs, such as: a most-similar design ($n = 12$) based on one time point (the year 1900) in §9.3; a most-similar design ($n = 18$) for three aggregated time periods in §9.4; a pooled time series analysis on 18 countries and 26 time points in §9.6; a most-different design (based on the Gastil democracy index) in §9.7; a time series analysis based on one country in §9.8; a dyadic time series analysis based on multilateral networks in §9.9.

The ways in which the sections are summarized in Table 9.24 are, of course, simplifications of the Research Question, the Research Design and the Research Answer. Yet, in general, it is important that one is able to summarize in one or two sentences the main steps that are taken in any research.

The importance of the Research Design for the results of the research has several implications:

1 Two researchers, asking the same question, may come to different results because of a different Research Design;
2 the Research Design leads one to the answer, and by manipulating the design one may direct the research to one particular answer, mostly the one that confirms the Research Question.

Table 9.23 *Determinants of the cooperativity of the USA towards the Soviet Union (b coefficients)*

	b	*t*
Direct support (M_QIO)	0.7	4.9
Cooperative direct relations (MW_QL1)	0.37	3.6
Change of cooperative indirect relations (MW_QCD)	1.06	3
Divergence (MW_DC1)	7	2.9
Power imbalance (SD_P1)	0.26	3
Constant	−0.23	

Source: Kleinnijenhuis and De Vries (1994). Regression statistics: $DW = 1.76$; $R^2 = 0.70$.

Table 9.24 *Overview and examples of the main stages in comparative research on types of policy outputs and performance*

Research Question	Research Design	Research Answer
§9.3 To what extent do actors (parties, unions) affect socio-economic policy-making?	Conceptualization and operationalization of (in)dependent variables and selection of cases, time period and statistical techniques	The influence of parties and unions depends on the time period and the institutional environment
§9.4 What role do institutions play in socio-economic problem-solving?	Idem. A special problem is the discrepancy between the theoretical and empirical variance of many institutional variables	Institutions affect the type and degree of socio-economic interventionism, but the 'fit' is moderate
§9.5 Do governments affect their re-election prospects by means of incidental or strategic policy-making?	Design of a cross-national and longitudinal test of public expenditures before and after elections	There is no cross-national generalizable evidence on the manipulation of the re-election results
§9.6 To what extent does the degree of democracy depend on the economic welfare?	Conceivable are, by example, a most-different test on a model that includes democracy and welfare indicators and also a most-similar test on the democratic performance of consensus and majoritarian democracies	The most-similar test shows a strong correspondence between democracy and welfare, but the model specification affects the result significantly. The most-similar test shows a (slightly) better performance of consensus democracies, but again, the choices made by the previous steps matter for the results
§9.7 Under which political-institutional conditions do we find a firm connection between 'party pledges' and 'pledge fulfillment'?	Conceptualization and operationalization of the 'mandate model'	Majoritarian democracies offer better conditions for 'pledge fulfillment'. All forms of power-sharing (also within majoritarian democracies) hamper 'pledge fulfillment'
§9.8 Which factors affect the evolving relationships between the USA and the USSR (both situated within multilateral networks) during the Cold War?	Conceptualization and operationalization of a dyadic model based on hypotheses	The objective conditions (power balance) are important determinants. The preferences of Presidents hardly matter here

The first implication is rather common and even crucial for making progress in political science, as it stimulates discussion and critical evaluation. In Section 9.8 we have seen an example which relates to the mandate theory. The second implication is more problematic. To solve this problem, there are several rules which have to be followed in order to make the research plausible and reliable:

1 The model should be correctly specified, and the assumptions of statistical analysis should not be violated.
2 Alternative insights, results and explanations should be discussed during all the steps which are taken during the research.
3 All the steps should be presented in such a way that others can replicate the research as it is done.

These three conditions for scientific research also form a check list which can be used to check the overall validity and reliability of the results which are reported in papers and publications.

9.10 ENDMATTER

Exercises

The purpose of the following exercises is to get acquainted with the empirical and technical aspects of data-analysis on socio-economic policy output and performance. The exercises correspond with the subsequent sections. The rough working may help the student through a possible impasse, but first come up with your own solution before looking at the working.

EXERCISE 9.1: WELFARE RELATED OUTPUT AND OUTCOMES

File: nias.sav.

1 Compute the WEDC-scale with the help of factor analysis on the variables dtax, sscap, sscwo, ed, he, trans.
2 Compute the TEDC-scale with the help of factor analysis on the variables def, tax, pe, ssc.
3 Both examine and correct for autocorrelation in a model that tries to explain the variations in the WEDC and TEDC variables. Split the model into cross-time and cross-sectional components and report the results.
4 Also determine what difference it makes whether the WEDC and TEDC scales are measured on the basis of time series or on the basis on separate years. How do you explain this difference?

Suggested steps: 1. Calculate the two scales both per year and on the basis of the pooled time series data. 2. Construct a model that includes cross-sectional variables like corporatism and leadership and with time series variables (like the openness of the economy, trade union density, the share of left votes). 3. Perform a PCSE and a

OLS regression on WEDC. 4. Split the country and year variables into dummy variables and incorporate them into two separate models. 5. Report on the results.

Background reading: Keman (1993b).

EXERCISE 9.2: ACTORS AND SOCIO-ECONOMIC PROBLEM-SOLVING

File: nias.sav.

Design a test for the 'social democratic model' in the periods before and after the crisis by means of time series analysis. Why is the performance of this model declining?

Suggested steps: 1. Specify a social democratic model. Note that the social democratic model does not prescribe particular dependent or independent variables. 2. Use the 'select if'-statement to differentiate between the periods before and after the crisis. 3. Study the regression results and report on them.

Background reading: Esping-Andersen and van Kersbergen (1992).

EXERCISE 9.3: INSTITUTIONS AND SOCIO-ECONOMIC PROBLEM-SOLVING

File: pol4.sav.

In general we may predict that corporatism, consociationalism and a cooperative style of political leadership enhance state interventionism in the socio-economic realm. Apply residual analysis in order to examine the exceptions to this 'rule'. What are the theoretical implications of this test?

Suggested steps: 1. Study the relevant dependent and independent variables and their intercorrelation. 2. Perform the regression analysis. 3. Study (plot) the residuals. 4. Interpret the results.

Background reading: Peters et al. (1977).

EXERCISE 9.4: ELECTORAL CYCLES AND MACRO-ECONOMIC POLICY

File: nias.sav.

Design a test for the Lessmann-model in which you incorporate alternative explanations for variations in tax levels and expenditures.

Suggested steps: 1. Determine the alternative explanatory variable for both the tax levels and the public economy. 2. Integrate this new variable into the Lessmann-model. 3. Test the model with the help of regression and report on the results.

Background reading: Lessmann (1987).

EXERCISE 9.5a: DEMOCRATIC PERFORMANCE (1)

File: vanhanen.sav.

Perform a regression of the Index of Democracy on the Index of Power Resources as included in the Vanhanen data set and include the residuals and the ID estimates. Report on how well the regression equation estimates the ID values for single countries and which countries are the most deviating cases.

Suggested steps: 1. Perform a regression analysis that includes the residual scores. 2. Study and discuss the results (see also Vanhanen's discussion of these residuals, pp. 97–9).

Background reading: Vanhanen (1990).

EXERCISE 9.5b: DEMOCRATIC PERFORMANCE (2)

File: Widlak.sav.

It is conceivable that the theoretical assumption that economic development enhances democratic performance (and/or democratization) can be turned around. Suppose that more democracy and more freedom are the preconditions for more economic development. Even when one accepts that in the old days democracy was a consequence of liberal capitalism, it is still possible that nowadays democracy is a precondition for economic development. Elites in autocratic regimes have no interest in prosperity for the people; they merely extract capital from the economy for their own use. Elites in autocratic countries will respond differently to economic crises, since the elite itself does not really suffer from it. Elites in democratic countries will feel the consequences of a crisis and they either respond effectively or have to resign after the elections. The exercise is meant to test both hypotheses. Suggested steps: 1. Construct a time lag of five years. 2. Run two regressions 3. Interpret the results.

Background reading: Doorenspleet (1997).

EXERCISE 9.6: PARTIES AND ACCOUNTABILITY

Budge and Hofferbert have applied several models, like the competitive, the consensus, the complementary and the control model in order to uncover the influence of parties on the policy-making process. Test the Budge and Hofferbert mandate models for any country for which you have relevant data. Note that a test of the mandate model is also possible without any Manifesto-data. You may have a look at the Dutch data in the file elfrso.sav.

Suggested steps: 1. Make an overview of the Budge and Hofferbert models and specify the underlying hypotheses. 2. Specify the models for a particular country (given the party systems and the presence/absence of a president). In the case of a multi-party system: simplify the models! 3. Specify the models for that particular country. 4. Use regression analysis to test the models. 5. Compare the results with Budge and Hofferbert's results.

Background reading: Budge and Hofferbert (1990); Royed (1996).

EXERCISE 9.7: OUTPUTS AND OUTCOMES IN THE INTERNATIONAL ARENA

File: Havana3.sav.

What factors determined the degree of cooperation of the Soviet Union towards the USA? Construct a model, test it and report the results.

Background reading: Azar and Ben-Dak (1975).

Topics highlighted

The effects of the interactions between political institutions and actors on socio-economic policy formation are explored by means of the following Research Questions (the prevailing techniques are Boolean analysis, regression analysis, factor analysis, ANOVA and discriminant analysis).

- To what extent do actors (parties, unions) affect socio-economic policy-making?

- What role do institutions play in socio-economic problem-solving?
- Do governments affect their re-election prospects by means of incidental or strategic policy-making?
- To what extent does the degree of democracy depend on the economic welfare?
- Under which political-institutional conditions do we find a firm connection between 'party pledges' and 'pledge fulfillment'?

Further reading

- *General*: Keman, 1993a; Pennings, 1995.
- *Specific*: Esping-Anderson and van Kersbergen,1992; Doorenspleet, 1997.

Notes

1 One rule of thumb is that one needs more than five cases per variable. Thus, in strict statistical terms, a number of 18 cases is not just 'small', but too small!

2 In our view this is not fully correct. Regression with a dichotomous variable is strictly statistically speaking equivalent to discriminant analysis.

3 It was introduced there as a nominal variable. In this chapter it is presented as an ordinal variable: the higher the score, the more socio-economic state intervention we expect. This is not self-evident, as the two mid-between categories can only be placed in such a rank-order by stating that it is harder to achieve consensus on social interventionism than on economic interventionism (and thus a supermarket regime is nearer to an interventionist regime than to a monetarist regime). See Keman (1988).

4 We wish to thank the Dutch student Arjan Widlak for gathering and analyzing the data on democratization and its determinants.

Appendix
Statistical tables

Statistical probabilities for Tables 1–4 have been calculated using PCalc 2.1.

Table A.1 *Cumulative standard normal distribution*

Z	0.00	0.01	0.02	0.03	0.04	0.05	0.06	0.07	0.08	0.09
0.0	0.5000	0.5040	0.5080	0.5120	0.5160	0.5199	0.5239	0.5279	0.5319	0.5359
0.1	0.5398	0.5438	0.5478	0.5517	0.5557	0.5596	0.5636	0.5675	0.5714	0.5753
0.2	0.5793	0.5832	0.5871	0.5910	0.5948	0.5987	0.6026	0.6064	0.6103	0.6141
0.3	0.6179	0.6217	0.6255	0.6293	0.6331	0.6368	0.6406	0.6443	0.6480	0.6517
0.4	0.6554	0.6591	0.6628	0.6664	0.6700	0.6736	0.6772	0.6808	0.6844	0.6879
0.5	0.6915	0.6950	0.6985	0.7019	0.7054	0.7088	0.7123	0.7157	0.7190	0.7224
0.6	0.7257	0.7291	0.7324	0.7357	0.7389	0.7422	0.7454	0.7486	0.7517	0.7549
0.7	0.7580	0.7611	0.7642	0.7673	0.7704	0.7734	0.7764	0.7794	0.7823	0.7852
0.8	0.7881	0.7910	0.7939	0.7967	0.7995	0.8023	0.8051	0.8078	0.8106	0.8133
0.9	0.8159	0.8186	0.8212	0.8238	0.8264	0.8289	0.8315	0.8340	0.8365	0.8389
1.0	0.8413	0.8438	0.8461	0.8485	0.8508	0.8531	0.8554	0.8577	0.8599	0.8621
1.1	0.8643	0.8665	0.8686	0.8708	0.8729	0.8749	0.8770	0.8790	0.8810	0.8830
1.2	0.8849	0.8869	0.8888	0.8907	0.8925	0.8944	0.8962	0.8980	0.8997	0.9015
1.3	0.9032	0.9049	0.9066	0.9082	0.9099	0.9115	0.9131	0.9147	0.9162	0.9177
1.4	0.9192	0.9207	0.9222	0.9236	0.9251	0.9265	0.9279	0.9292	0.9306	0.9319
1.5	0.9332	0.9345	0.9357	0.9370	0.9382	0.9394	0.9406	0.9418	0.9429	0.9441
1.6	0.9452	0.9463	0.9474	0.9484	0.9495	0.9505	0.9515	0.9525	0.9535	0.9545
1.7	0.9554	0.9564	0.9573	0.9582	0.9591	0.9599	0.9608	0.9616	0.9625	0.9633
1.8	0.9641	0.9649	0.9656	0.9664	0.9671	0.9678	0.9686	0.9693	0.9699	0.9706
1.9	0.9713	0.9719	0.9726	0.9732	0.9738	0.9744	0.9750	0.9756	0.9761	0.9767
2.0	0.9772	0.9778	0.9783	0.9788	0.9793	0.9798	0.9803	0.9808	0.9812	0.9817
2.1	0.9821	0.9826	0.9830	0.9834	0.9838	0.9842	0.9846	0.9850	0.9854	0.9857
2.2	0.9861	0.9864	0.9868	0.9871	0.9875	0.9878	0.9881	0.9884	0.9887	0.9890
2.3	0.9893	0.9896	0.9898	0.9901	0.9904	0.9906	0.9909	0.9911	0.9913	0.9916
2.4	0.9918	0.9920	0.9922	0.9925	0.9927	0.9929	0.9931	0.9932	0.9934	0.9936
2.5	0.9938	0.9940	0.9941	0.9943	0.9945	0.9946	0.9948	0.9949	0.9951	0.9952
2.6	0.9953	0.9955	0.9956	0.9957	0.9959	0.9960	0.9961	0.9962	0.9963	0.9964
2.7	0.9965	0.9966	0.9967	0.9968	0.9969	0.9970	0.9971	0.9972	0.9973	0.9974
2.8	0.9974	0.9975	0.9976	0.9977	0.9977	0.9978	0.9979	0.9979	0.9980	0.9981
2.9	0.9981	0.9982	0.9982	0.9983	0.9984	0.9984	0.9985	0.9985	0.9986	0.9986
3.0	0.9987	0.9987	0.9987	0.9988	0.9988	0.9989	0.9989	0.9989	0.9990	0.9990
3.1	0.9990	0.9991	0.9991	0.9991	0.9992	0.9992	0.9992	0.9992	0.9993	0.9993
3.2	0.9993	0.9993	0.9994	0.9994	0.9994	0.9994	0.9994	0.9995	0.9995	0.9995
3.3	0.9995	0.9995	0.9995	0.9996	0.9996	0.9996	0.9996	0.9996	0.9996	0.9997
3.4	0.9997	0.9997	0.9997	0.9997	0.9997	0.9997	0.9997	0.9997	0.9997	0.9998

Table A.2 *Values of χ^2 corresponding to p*

df	$\chi^2_{0.005}$	$\chi^2_{0.01}$	$\chi^2_{0.025}$	$\chi^2_{0.055}$	$\chi^2_{0.10}$	$\chi^2_{0.90}$	$\chi^2_{0.95}$	$\chi^2_{0.975}$	$\chi^2_{0.99}$	$\chi^2_{0.995}$
1	0.000039	0.00016	0.00098	0.0039	0.0158	2.71	3.84	5.02	6.63	7.88
2	0.0100	0.0201	0.0506	0.1026	0.2107	4.61	5.99	7.38	9.21	10.60
3	0.0717	0.115	0.216	0.352	0.584	6.25	7.81	9.35	11.34	12.84
4	0.207	0.297	0.484	0.711	1.064	7.78	9.49	11.14	13.28	14.86
5	0.412	0.554	0.831	1.15	1.61	9.24	11.07	12.83	15.09	16.75
6	0.676	0.872	1.24	1.64	2.20	10.64	12.59	14.45	16.81	18.55
7	0.989	1.24	1.69	2.17	2.83	12.02	14.07	16.01	18.48	20.28
8	1.34	1.65	2.18	2.73	3.49	13.36	15.51	17.53	20.09	21.96
9	1.73	2.09	2.70	3.33	4.17	14.68	16.92	19.02	21.67	23.59
10	2.16	2.56	3.25	3.94	4.87	15.99	18.31	20.48	23.21	25.19
11	2.60	3.05	3.82	4.57	5.58	17.28	19.68	21.92	24.73	26.76
12	3.07	3.57	4.40	5.23	6.30	18.55	21.03	23.34	26.22	28.30
13	3.57	4.11	5.01	5.89	7.04	19.81	22.36	24.74	27.69	29.82
14	4.07	4.66	5.63	6.57	7.79	21.06	23.68	26.12	29.14	31.32
15	4.60	5.23	6.26	7.26	8.55	22.31	25.00	27.49	30.58	32.80
16	5.14	5.81	6.91	7.96	9.31	23.54	26.30	28.85	32.00	34.27
18	6.26	7.01	8.23	9.39	10.86	25.99	28.87	31.53	34.81	37.16
20	7.43	8.26	9.59	10.85	12.44	28.41	31.41	34.17	37.57	40.00
24	9.89	10.86	12.40	13.85	15.66	33.20	36.42	39.36	42.98	45.56
30	13.79	14.95	16.79	18.49	20.60	40.26	43.77	46.98	50.89	53.67
40	20.71	22.16	24.43	26.51	29.05	51.81	55.76	59.34	63.69	66.77
60	35.53	37.48	40.48	43.19	46.46	74.40	79.08	83.30	88.38	91.95
120	83.85	86.92	91.58	95.70	100.62	140.23	146.57	152.21	158.95	163.64

Table A.3 *Values of t for v degrees of freedom and* $p = 1 - \alpha$

v \ $1-\alpha$	0.75	0.90	0.95	0.975	0.99	0.995	0.9995
1	1.000	3.078	6.314	12.706	31.821	63.657	636.619
2	0.816	1.886	2.920	4.303	6.965	9.925	31.598
3	0.765	1.638	2.353	3.182	4.541	5.841	12.941
4	0.741	1.533	2.132	2.776	3.747	4.604	8.610
5	0.727	1.476	2.015	2.571	3.365	4.032	6.859
6	0.718	1.440	1.943	2.447	3.143	3.707	5.959
7	0.711	1.415	1.895	2.365	2.998	3.499	5.405
8	0.706	1.397	1.860	2.306	2.896	3.355	5.041
9	0.703	1.383	1.833	2.262	2.821	3.250	4.781
10	0.700	1.372	1.812	2.228	2.764	3.169	4.587
11	0.697	1.363	1.796	2.201	2.718	3.106	4.437
12	0.695	1.356	1.782	2.179	2.681	3.055	4.318
13	0.694	1.350	1.771	2.160	2.650	3.012	4.221
14	0.692	1.345	1.761	2.145	2.624	2.977	4.140
15	0.691	1.341	1.753	2.131	2.602	2.947	4.073
16	0.690	1.337	1.746	2.120	2.583	2.921	4.015
17	0.689	1.333	1.740	2.110	2.567	2.898	3.965
18	0.688	1.330	1.734	2.101	2.552	2.878	3.922
19	0.688	1.328	1.729	2.093	2.339	2.861	3.883
20	0.687	1.325	1.725	2.086	2.528	2.845	3.850
21	0.686	1.323	1.721	2.080	2.518	2.831	3.819
22	0.686	1.321	1.717	2.074	2.508	2.819	3.792
23	0.685	1.319	1.714	2.069	2.500	2.807	3.767
24	0.685	1.318	1.711	2.064	2.492	2.797	3.745
25	0.684	1.316	1.708	2.060	2.485	2.787	3.725
26	0.684	1.315	1.706	2.056	2.479	2.779	3.707
27	0.684	1.314	1.703	2.052	2.473	2.771	3.690
28	0.683	1.313	1.701	2.048	2.467	2.763	3.674
29	0.683	1.311	1.699	2.045	2.462	2.756	3.659
30	0.683	1.310	1.697	2.042	2.457	2.750	3.646
40	0.681	1.303	1.684	2.021	2.423	2.704	3.551
60	0.679	1.296	1.671	2.000	2.390	2.660	3.460
120	0.677	1.289	1.658	1.980	2.358	2.617	3.373
∞	0.674	1.282	1.645	1.960	2.326	2.576	3.291

Table A.4 *Values of F for $\alpha = 0.05$ and ν_1 and ν_2 degrees of freedom for numerator and denominator*

ν_2 \ ν_1	1	2	3	4	5	6	7	8	9	10	12	15	20	24	30	40	60	120	∞
1	161.4	199.5	215.7	224.6	230.2	234.0	236.8	238.9	240.5	241.9	243.9	245.9	248.0	249.1	250.1	251.1	252.2	253.3	254.3
2	18.51	19.00	19.16	19.25	19.30	19.33	19.35	19.37	19.38	19.40	19.41	19.43	19.45	19.45	19.46	19.47	19.48	19.49	19.50
3	10.13	9.55	9.28	9.12	9.01	8.94	8.89	8.85	8.81	8.79	8.74	8.70	8.66	8.64	8.62	8.59	8.57	8.55	8.53
4	7.71	6.94	6.59	6.39	6.26	6.16	6.09	6.04	6.00	5.96	5.91	5.86	5.80	5.77	5.75	5.72	5.69	5.66	5.63
5	6.61	5.79	5.41	5.19	5.05	4.95	4.88	4.82	4.77	4.74	4.68	4.62	4.56	4.53	4.50	4.46	4.43	4.40	4.36
6	5.99	5.14	4.76	4.53	4.39	4.28	4.21	4.15	4.10	4.06	4.00	3.94	3.87	3.84	3.81	3.77	3.74	3.70	3.67
7	5.59	4.74	4.35	4.12	3.97	3.87	3.79	3.73	3.68	3.64	3.57	3.51	3.44	3.41	3.38	3.34	3.30	3.27	3.23
8	5.32	4.46	4.07	3.84	3.69	3.58	3.50	3.44	3.39	3.35	3.28	3.22	3.15	3.12	3.08	3.04	3.01	2.97	2.93
9	5.12	4.26	3.86	3.63	3.48	3.37	3.29	3.23	3.18	3.14	3.07	3.01	2.94	2.90	2.86	2.83	2.79	2.75	2.71
10	4.96	4.10	3.71	3.48	3.33	3.22	3.14	3.07	3.02	2.98	2.91	2.85	2.77	2.74	2.70	2.66	2.62	2.58	2.54
11	4.84	3.98	3.59	3.36	3.20	3.09	3.01	2.95	2.90	2.85	2.79	2.72	2.65	2.61	2.57	2.53	2.49	2.45	2.40
12	4.75	3.89	3.49	3.26	3.11	3.00	2.91	2.85	2.80	2.75	2.69	2.62	2.54	2.51	2.47	2.43	2.38	2.34	2.30
13	4.67	3.81	3.41	3.18	3.03	2.92	2.83	2.77	2.71	2.67	2.60	2.53	2.46	2.42	2.38	2.34	2.30	2.25	2.21
14	4.60	3.74	3.34	3.11	2.96	2.85	2.76	2.70	2.65	2.60	2.53	2.46	2.39	2.35	2.31	2.27	2.22	2.18	2.13
15	4.54	3.68	3.29	3.06	2.90	2.79	2.71	2.64	2.59	2.54	2.48	2.40	2.33	2.29	2.25	2.20	2.16	2.11	2.07
16	4.49	3.63	3.24	3.01	2.85	2.74	2.66	2.59	2.54	2.49	2.42	2.35	2.28	2.24	2.19	2.15	2.11	2.06	2.01
17	4.45	3.59	3.20	2.96	2.81	2.70	2.61	2.55	2.49	2.45	2.38	2.31	2.23	2.19	2.15	2.10	2.06	2.01	1.96
18	4.41	3.55	3.16	2.93	2.77	2.66	2.58	2.51	2.46	2.41	2.34	2.27	2.19	2.15	2.11	2.06	2.02	1.97	1.92
19	4.38	3.52	3.13	2.90	2.74	2.63	2.54	2.48	2.42	2.38	2.31	2.23	2.16	2.11	2.07	2.03	1.98	1.93	1.88
20	4.35	3.49	3.10	2.87	2.71	2.60	2.51	2.45	2.39	2.35	2.28	2.20	2.12	2.08	2.04	1.99	1.95	1.90	1.84
21	4.32	3.47	3.07	2.84	2.68	2.57	2.49	2.42	2.37	2.32	2.25	2.18	2.10	2.05	2.01	1.96	1.92	1.87	1.81
22	4.30	3.44	3.05	2.82	2.66	2.55	2.46	2.40	2.34	2.30	2.23	2.15	2.07	2.03	1.98	1.94	1.89	1.84	1.78
23	4.28	3.42	3.03	2.80	2.64	2.53	2.44	2.37	2.32	2.27	2.20	2.13	2.05	2.01	1.96	1.91	1.86	1.81	1.76
24	4.26	3.40	3.01	2.78	2.62	2.51	2.42	2.36	2.30	2.25	2.18	2.11	2.03	1.98	1.94	1.89	1.84	1.79	1.73
25	4.24	3.39	2.99	2.76	2.60	2.49	2.40	2.34	2.28	2.24	2.16	2.09	2.01	1.96	1.92	1.87	1.82	1.77	1.71
26	4.23	3.37	2.98	2.74	2.59	2.47	2.39	2.32	2.27	2.22	2.15	2.07	1.99	1.95	1.90	1.85	1.80	1.75	1.69
27	4.21	3.35	2.96	2.73	2.57	2.46	2.37	2.31	2.25	2.20	2.13	2.06	1.97	1.93	1.88	1.84	1.79	1.73	1.67
28	4.20	3.34	2.95	2.71	2.56	2.45	2.36	2.29	2.24	2.19	2.12	2.04	1.96	1.91	1.87	1.82	1.77	1.71	1.65
29	4.18	3.33	2.93	2.70	2.55	2.43	2.35	2.28	2.22	2.18	2.10	2.03	1.94	1.90	1.85	1.81	1.75	1.70	1.64
30	4.17	3.32	2.92	2.69	2.53	2.42	2.33	2.27	2.21	2.16	2.09	2.01	1.93	1.89	1.84	1.79	1.74	1.68	1.62
40	4.08	3.23	2.84	2.61	2.45	2.34	2.25	2.18	2.12	2.08	2.00	1.92	1.84	1.79	1.74	1.69	1.64	1.58	1.51
60	4.00	3.15	2.76	2.53	2.37	2.25	2.17	2.10	2.04	1.99	1.92	1.84	1.75	1.70	1.65	1.59	1.53	1.47	1.39
120	3.92	3.07	2.68	2.45	2.29	2.17	2.09	2.02	1.96	1.91	1.83	1.75	1.66	1.61	1.55	1.50	1.43	1.35	1.25
∞	3.84	3.00	2.60	2.37	2.21	2.10	2.01	1.94	1.88	1.83	1.75	1.67	1.57	1.52	1.46	1.39	1.32	1.22	1.00

Table A.5 *Critical values of Kolmogorov–Smirnov test (two-sided test)*

sample size n	$p = 0.10$	$p = 0.05$
1	0.950	0.975
2	0.776	0.842
3	0.642	0.708
4	0.564	0.624
5	0.510	0.565
6	0.470	0.521
7	0.438	0.486
8	0.411	0.457
9	0.388	0.432
10	0.368	0.410
11	0.352	0.391
12	0.338	0.375
13	0.325	0.361
14	0.314	0.349
15	0.304	0.338
16	0.295	0.328
17	0.286	0.318
18	0.278	0.309
19	0.272	0.301
20	0.264	0.294
25	0.24	0.27
30	0.22	0.24
35	0.21	0.23
>35	$\frac{1.22}{\sqrt{n}}$	$\frac{1.36}{\sqrt{n}}$

Source: Adapted from W.L. Zijp (1974) *Handleiding voor statistische toetsen*. Groningen: Tjeenk Willink. p. 247.

Table A.6 *Durbin–Watson Statistic (upper (d_U) and lower (d_L) critical values for a test at the 5% level of significance)*

	Number of explanatory variables									
	1		2		3		4		5	
T	d_L	d_U	d_L	d_U	d_L	d_U	d_L	d_U	d_L	d_U
15	1.08	1.36	0.95	1.54	0.82	1.75	0.69	1.97	0.56	2.21
16	1.10	1.37	0.98	1.54	0.86	1.73	0.74	1.93	0.62	2.15
17	1.13	1.38	1.02	1.54	0.90	1.71	0.78	1.90	0.67	2.10
18	1.16	1.39	1.05	1.53	0.93	1.69	0.82	1.87	0.71	2.06
19	1.18	1.40	1.08	1.53	0.97	1.68	0.86	1.85	0.75	2.02
20	1.20	1.41	1.10	1.54	1.00	1.68	0.90	1.83	0.79	1.99
25	1.29	1.45	1.21	1.55	1.12	1.66	1.04	1.77	0.95	1.89
30	1.35	1.49	1.28	1.57	1.21	1.65	1.14	1.74	1.07	1.83
40	1.44	1.54	1.39	1.60	1.34	1.66	1.29	1.72	1.23	1.79
50	1.50	1.59	1.46	1.63	1.42	1.67	1.38	1.72	1.34	1.77
75	1.60	1.65	1.57	1.68	1.54	1.71	1.51	1.74	1.49	1.77
100	1.65	1.69	1.63	1.72	1.61	1.74	1.59	1.76	1.57	1.78

Source: Adapted from R. S. Pindyck and D. L. Rubinfeld (1991) Econometric Models and Economic Forecasts. New York: McGraw-Hill. p. 568.

Bibliography

Abrams, P. (1982) *Historical Sociology*. Ithaca, NY: Cornell University Press.

Alber, J. (1982) *Vom Armenhaus zum Wohlfahrsstaat: Analysen zur Entwicklung der Sozialversicherung in Westeuropa*. Frankfurt a.m.: Campus Verlag.

Allison, P.D. (1984) 'Event history analysis', *Quantitative Applications in the Social Sciences*, 46.

Almond, G.A. (1968) 'Comparative politics', *International Encyclopedia of the Social Sciences*, (13): 331–6.

Almond, G.A. (1990) *A Discipline Divided*. Boston: Little and Brown.

Almond, G.A., Powell, B.G. and Mundt, R.J. (1993) *Comparative Politics: A Theoretical Framework*. New York: Harper Collins College Publishers.

Althusser, L. (1983) 'Schets van het begrip historiese tijd', *Te Elfder Ure*, 31: 341–80.

Antal, A.B., Dierkes, M. and Weier, H. (eds) (1987) *Comparative Policy Research: Learning from Experience*. Aldershot: Gower.

Apter, D.E. and Andrain, Ch.F. (1972) *Contemporary Analytical Theory*. Englewood Cliffs, NJ: Prentice-Hall.

Armingeon, K. (1989) 'Arbeitsbeziehungen und Gewerkschaftsentwicklung in den achtziger Jahren: ein vergleich der OECD-Länder', *Politsches Vierteljahresheft*, 30 (4): 603–28.

Atkinson, A.B., Rainwater, L. and Schmeeding, T.M. (1995) *Income Distribution in OECD Countries: Evidence from the Luxembourg Income Study*. Paris: OECD.

Austen-Smith, D. and Banks, J. (1988) 'Elections, coalitions, and legislative outcomes', *American Political Science Review*, 82: 405–22.

Axelrod, R. (1970) *Conflict of Interest: A Theory of Divergent Goals with Applications to Politics*. Chicago: Markham.

Azar, E.E. (1982) 'The Conflict and Peace Data Base', Ann Arbor: International Consortium for Political and Social Research, data base I7767.

Azar, E.E. and Ben-Dak, J.D. (1975) *Theory and Practice of Events Research: Studies in Inter-Nation Actions and Interactions*. New York: Gordon and Breach.

Barrington Moore, Jr (1966) *Social Origins of Dictatorship and Democracy*. Boston, MA: Beacon Press.

Barry, B.M. (1978) *Sociologists, economists and democracy*. Chicago: University of Chicago Press.

Bartotini, S. (1992) 'On time and comparative research'. Working Paper. University of Trieste.

Bartolini, S. (1995) *Electoral Competition: Analytical Dimensions and Empirical Problems*. San Domenico, Italy: European University Institute.

Bartolini, S. (1998) 'Coalition potential and governmental power', in P. Pennings and Jan-Erik Lane (eds), *Comparing Party System Change*. London: Routledge. pp. 40–61.

Bartolini, S. and Mair, P. (1990) *Identity, Competition and Electoral Availability. The Stabilisation of European Electorates, 1885–1985*. Cambridge: Cambridge University Press.

Beck, N. and Katz, J.N. (1995) 'What to do – and not to do – with time-series-cross-section data in comparative politics', *American Political Science Review*, 89: 634–47.

Bendix, R. (1977 [1959]) *Weber: An Intellectual Portrait*. London: Allen & Unwin.

Bendix, R. and Lipset, S.M. (eds) (1977) *Class, Status and Power: Social Stratification in Comparative Perspective*, 2nd edn. New York: The Free Press.

Bergman, T. (1995) *Constitutional Rules and Party Goals in Coalition Formation. An Analysis of Winning Minority Governments in Sweden*. Umeå: Umeå University.

Berg-Schlosser, D. and Müller-Rommel, F. (eds) (1987) *Vergleichende Politikwissenschaft*. Opladen: Leske & Budrich.

Berg-Schlosser, D. and Quenter, S. (1996) 'Makro-Quantitative vs. Makro-qualitative Methoden in der Politikwissenschaft-Vorzüge und Mängel Komparativer Verfahrensweisen am Beispiel der Sozialstaatstheorie', *Politische Vierteljahresschrift*, 37: 100–18.

Berndt, E.R. (1996) *The Practice of Econometrics: Classic and Contemporary*. Reading, MA: Addison-Wesley.

Berry, W.D. (1993) 'Understanding regression assumptions', *Quantitative Applications in the Social Sciences*, 92.

Bingham Powell, G. (1982) *Contemporary Democracies: Participation, Stability and Violence*. Cambridge, MA: Harvard University Press.

Blalock, H.M. Jr (ed.) (1972) *Causal Models in the Social Sciences*. London: Macmillan.

Blalock, H.M. Jr (1979) *Social Statistics*, 2nd edn. Tokyo: McGraw-Hill.

Blondel, J. (1981) *The Discipline of Politics*. London: Butterworths: 173–8.

Bogdanor, V. and Butler, D. (eds) (1983) *Democracy and Elections: Electoral Systems and their Consequences*. Cambridge: Cambridge University Press.

Bohrnstedt, G.W. and Knoke, D. (1982) *Statistics for Social Data Analysis*. Ithaca, NY: F.E. Peacock.

Bollen, K.A. (1994) *Structural Equations with Latent Variables*, 6th edn. New York: Wiley.

Bollen, K.A. and Jackman, R.W. (1985) 'Political democracy and the size distribution of income', *American Sociological Review*, 50: 438–57.

Braudel, F. (1977) *Capitalism and Material Life 1400–1800*. London: Fontana.

Braun, D. (1995) 'Handlungstheoretischen Grundlagen in der empirisch-analytischen Politikwissenschaft. Eine kritische Übersicht', in A. Benz and W. Seibel (eds), *Beiträge zur Theorieentwicklung in der Politik- und Verwaltungswissenschaft*. Baden-Baden: Nomos.

Browne, E.C., Frendries, J.P. and Gleiber, D.W. (1988) 'Contending models of cabinet stability: a rejoinder', *American Political Science Review*, 82: 930–41.

Bryce, J. (1929) *Modern Democracies*. New York: Macmillan.

Bryk, A.S. and Raudenbush, S.W. (1995) *Hierarchical Linear Models: Applications and Data-analysis Methods*. Newbury Park, CA: Sage.

Budge, I. (1993) 'Rational choice as comparative theory: beyond economic self-interest', in Hans Keman (ed.), *Comparative Politics: New Directions in Theory and Method*. Amsterdam: VU University Press.

Budge, I. and Farlie, D.J. (1983) *Explaining and Predicting Elections: Issue Effects and Party Strategies in 23 Democracies*. London: Allen & Unwin.

Budge, I. and Keman, H. (1990) *Parties and Democracy: Coalition Formation and Government Functioning in Twenty States*. Oxford: Oxford University Press.

Budge, I. and Laver, M.J. (eds) (1992) *Party Policy and Government Coalitions*. Basingstoke: Macmillan.

Budge, I. and Hofferbert, R.I. (1990) 'Mandates and policy outputs: US party platforms and federal expenditures', *American Political Science Review*, 84: 111–31.

Budge, I., Robertson, D. and Hearl, D. (eds) (1987) *Ideology, Strategy and Party Change: Spatial Analyses of Post-war election Programmes in 19 Democracies*. Cambridge: Cambridge University Press.

Burkhart, R.E. and Lewis-Beck, M.S. (1994) 'Comparative democracy: the economic development thesis', *American Political Science Review*, 88 (4): 903–10.

Busch, A. (1995) *Preisstabilitätspolitik. Politik and Inflationsraten im internationalen Vergleich*. Opladen: Leske and Budrich.

Cameron, D.R. (1984) 'Social democracy, corporatism, labour quiescence and the representation of economic interest in advanced capitalist society', in J.H. Goldthorpe (ed.), *Order and Conflict in Contemporary Capitalism*. Oxford: Clarendon Press. pp. 143–78.

Castles, F.G. (1978) *The Social Democratic Image of Society*. London: Routledge & Kegan Paul.

Castles, F.G. (ed.) (1982) *The Impact of Parties. Politics and Policies in Democratic Capitalist States*. London: Sage.

Castles, F.G. (1985) *The Working Class and Welfare in Australia and New Zealand*. Wellington: Allen & Unwin.

Castles, F.G. (1987) 'Comparative public policy analysis: problems, progress and prospects', in F.G. Castles, F. Lehner and M.G. Schmidt (eds), *Managing Mixed Economies*. Berlin: de Gruyter. pp. 197–224.

Castles, F.G. (ed.) (1989) *The Comparative History of Public Policy*. Oxford: Polity Press.

Castles, F.G. (ed.) (1993) *Families of Nations: Patterns of Public Policy in Western Democracies*. Aldershot: Dartmouth.

Castles, F.G., Lehner, F. and Schmidt, M.G. (eds) (1987) *Managing Mixed Economies*. Berlin: de Gruyter.

Castles, F.G. and Mair, P. (1984) 'Left–right political scales: some "expert" judgements', *European Journal of Political Science*, 1 (12): 73–88.

Castles, F.G. and McKinlay, R.D. (1979) 'Does politics matter? An analysis of the public welfare commitment in advanced democratic states', *European Journal of Political Research*, 7 (2): 169–86.

Cawson, A. (1986) *Corporatism and Political Theory*. Oxford: Basil Blackwell.

Chilcote, R.H. (1994) *Theories of Comparative Politics: the Search for a Paradigm Reconsidered*. 2nd edn. Boulder, CO: Westview Press.

Choi, Kwang (1983) 'A statistical test of Olson's model', in Dennis Mueller (ed.), *The Political Economy of Economic Growth*. New Haven, CT: Yale University Press.

Coleman, J.S. (1991) *Foundations of Social Theory*. Cambridge, MA: Harvard University Press.

Collier, D. (1993) 'The comparative method', in A.W. Finifter (ed.), *Political Science: The State of the Discipline II*. Washington, DC: APSA. pp. 105–19.

Collier, D. and Mahon, J.E. (1993) 'Conceptual "stretching" revisited: adapting categories in comparative analysis', *American Political Science Review*, 87 (4): 845–55.

Connolly, W.E. (1988) *Political theory and modernity*. Oxford: Blackwell.

Crepaz, M.M.L. and Lijphart, A. (1995) 'Linking and integrating corporatism and consensus democracy: theory, concepts and evidence', *British Journal of Political Science*, 15 (2): 281–8.

Crewe, I. and Denver, D. (eds) (1985) *Electoral Change in Western Democracies: Patterns and Sources of Electoral Volatility*. New York: St Martin's Press.

Crouch, Colin (1985) 'Conditions for trade union restraint', in Leon Lindberg and Charles S. Maier (eds), *The Politics of Inflation and Economic Stagnation*. Washington, DC: The Brookings Institution. pp. 115–39.

Czada, R. (1983) 'Kondensbedingungen und Auswirkungen neokorporatistischer Politikentwicklung', *Journal für Sozialforschung,* 23: 421–40.

Czada, R. (1987) 'The impact of interest politics on flexible adjustment policies', in Hans Keman, Heikki Paloheimo and Paul F. Whiteley (eds), *Coping with the Economic Crisis. Alternative Responses to Economic Recession in Advanced Industrial Societies*. London: Sage. pp. 20–53.

Czada, R., Héritier, A. and Keman, H. (eds) (1998) *Institutions and Political Choice: on the limits of Rationality* (revised edn). Amsterdam: VU Press.

Daalder, H. (1966) 'The Netherlands: opposition in a segmented society', in R.A. Dahl (ed.), *Political Oppositions in Western Democracies*. New Haven, CT: Yale University Press. pp. 188–236.

Daalder, H. (1974) 'The consociational democracy theme', *World Politics*, 26: 604–21.

Daalder, H. (1993) 'The Development of the Study of Comparative Politics', in H. Keman (ed.) *Comparative Politics: New Directions in Theory and Method*. Amsterdam: VU University Press. pp. 11–30.

Daalder, H. and Mair, P. (1983) *Western European Party Systems: Continuity and Change*. Beverly Hills, CA: Sage.

Dahl, R.A. (1963) *Modern Political Analysis*. Englewood Cliffs, NJ: Prentice-Hall.

Dahl, R.A. (1966) *Political Oppositions in Western Democracies*. New Haven, CT: Yale University Press.

Dahl, R.A. (1971) *Polyarchy, Participation and Opposition*. New Haven, CT: Yale University Press.

Dalton, R.J. (1991) 'Comparative politics of the industrial democracies', in W.J. Crotty (ed.), *Political Science*. Evanston, IL: Northwestern University Press. pp. 5–43.

Debets, P. and Brouwer, E. (1989) 'Mokken Scale Analysis', version 1.50. Groningen: ProGamma.

Derbyshire, J.D. and Derbyshire, I. (1990) *Political Systems of the World*. Edinburgh: Chambers.

Dierkes, M., Weiler, H. and Antal, A.B. (eds) (1987) *Comparative Policy Research: Learning from Experience*. Aldershot: Gower.

Dogan, M. and Pelassy, D. (1990) *How to Compare Nations: Strategies in Comparative Politics*, 2nd edn. Chatham, NJ: Chatham House.

Doorenspleet, R. (1997) 'Political democracy: a cross-national quantitative analysis of modernization and dependency theories', *Acta Politica*, 32 (4): 349–74.

Downs, A. (1957, 1965) *An Economic Theory of Democracy.* New York: Harper & Row.

Dunleavy, P. (1991) *Democracy, Bureaucracy and Public Choice: Economic Explanations in Political Science*. Englewood Cliffs, NJ: Prentice-Hall.

Dunleavy, P. and Margetts, H. (1995) 'Understanding the dynamics of electoral reform', *International Political Science Review,* 16 (1): 9–29.

Duverger, M. (1968) *The Study of Politics*. London: Routledge.

Easton, D. (1965) *A Systems Analysis of Political Life*. New York: Wiley.

Eijk, van der C. (1993) 'Comparative studies of elections and political science', in H. Keman (ed.), *Comparative Politics*. Amsterdam: VU University Press. pp. 59–78.

Ersson, S. and Lane, J.-E. (1998) 'Electoral instability and party system change in Europe', in P. Pennings and J.-E. Lane (eds), *Comparing Party System Change*. London: Routledge. pp. 23–39.

Esping-Andersen, G. (1990) *The Three Worlds of Capitalism*. Cambridge: Polity Press.

Esping-Andersen, G. (1996) *Welfare States in Transition. National Adaptations in Global Economies*. London: Sage/UNRISD.

Esping-Andersen, G. and Kersbergen, K. van (1992) 'Contemporary research on social democracy', *Annual Review of Sociology*, 18: 187–208.

Evans, P., Rueschemeyer, D. and Skocpol, T. (eds) (1985) *Bringing the State Back In*. Cambridge: Cambridge University Press.

Everitt, B.S. (1993) *Cluster Analysis*, 3rd edn. London: Heinemann.

Flora, P. (1974) *Modernisierungsforschung: Zur empirischen Analyse der gesellschaftlichen Entwicklung*. Opladen: Westdeutscher Verlag.

Flora, P. and Heidenheimer, A.J. (eds) (1981) *The Development of Welfare States in Europe and America*. New Brunswick: Transaction Books.

Fox, J. (1991) 'Regression Diagnostics', *Quantitative Applications in the Social Sciences*, 79: 619–28.

Fox, J. (1997) *Applied Regression Analysis*. London: Sage.

Frendreis, J.P. (1983) 'Explanation of variation and detection of covariation: the purpose and logic of comparative analysis', *Comparative Political Studies*, 16: 255–72.

Frendreis, J.P., Gleiber, D. and Browne, E. (1986) 'The study of cabinet dissolutions in parliamentary democracies', *Legislative Studies Quarterly*, 11: 619–28.

Gallagher, M., Laver, M. and Mair, P. (1995) *Representative Government in Modern Europe*, 2nd edn. New York: McGraw Hill.

Geer, J.P. van de (1986) *Introduction to Linear Multivariate Data Analysis*. Leiden: DSWO Press.

Gerth, H.H. and Mills, C.W. (eds) (1968) *From Max Weber*. London: Macmillan.

Gibbons, J.D. (1993) *Nonparametric Statistics: an Introduction*. Newbury Park, CA: Sage.

Giddens, A. (1971) *Capitalism and Modern Theory: An analysis of the Writings of Marx, Durkheim and Weber*. Cambridge: Cambridge University Press.

Goodin, R.E. and Klingemann, H.-D. (1996) *A New Handbook of Political Science*. Oxford: Oxford University Press.

Greene, W.H. (1997) *Econometric Analysis*, 3rd edn. London: Prentice-Hall.

Grofman, B. (1982) 'A dynamic model of protocoalition formation in ideological n-space', *Behavioural Science*, 27: 77–90.

Hague, R., Harrop, M. and Breslin, S. (1992) *Comparative Government and Politics: an Introduction*, 3rd edn. Basingstoke: Macmillan.

Hardy, M.A. (1993) 'Regression with dummy variables', *Quantitative Applications in the Social Sciences*, 93.

Heywood, A. (1997) *Politics*. Basingstoke: Macmillan.

Héritier, A. (1993) 'Policy network analysis: a tool for comparative research', in: Keman H. (ed.), *Comparative Politics. New Directions in Theory and Method*. Amsterdam: VU University Press.

Hoel, P.G. (1971) *Introduction to Mathematical Statistics*. New York: Wiley.

Holsti, O.R. (1969) *Content Analysis for the Social Sciences and Humanities*. Reading, MA: Addison-Wesley.

Holt, R.T. and Turner, J.E. (eds) (1970) *The Methodology of Comparative Research*. New York: The Free Press.

Huber, J. and Inglehart, R. (1995) 'Expert interpretations of party space and party locations in 42 societies', *Party Politics*, 1 (1): 73–111.

Inglehart, R. (1990) *Culture Shift in Advanced Industrial Society*. Princeton, NJ: Princeton University Press.

Inglehart, R. (1997) *Modernization and Postmodernization: Cultural, Economic, and Political Change in 43 Societies*. Princeton, NJ: Princeton University Press.

Jaccard, J., Turrisi, R. and Wan, C.K. (1990) 'Interaction effects in multiple regression', *Quantitative Applications in the Social Sciences*, 72.

Jackson, J.E. (1996) 'Political methodology: an overview', in R.E. Goodin & H.-D. Klingemann (eds), *A New Handbook of Political Science*. Oxford: Oxford University Press. pp. 717–48.

Janoski, T. and Hicks, A.M. (1994) *The Comparative Political Economy of the Welfare State*. Cambridge: Cambridge University Press.

Kalleberg, A.L. (1966) 'The logic of comparison: a methodological note on the comparative study of political systems', *World Politics*, 19: 69–82.

Kanji, G.K. (1994) *100 Statistical Tests*. London: Sage.

Katz, R.S. and Mair, P. (1992) *Party Organizations: a Data Handbook on Party Organizations in Western Democracies, 1960–1990*. London: Sage.

Katzenstein, P. (1985) *Small States in World Markets: Industrial Policy in Europe*. Ithaca, NY: Cornell University Press.

Keman, H. (1988) *The Development Toward Surplus Welfare: Social Democratic Politics and Policies in Advanced Capitalist Democracies, 1965–84*. Amsterdam: CT-Press.

Keman, H. (1990) 'Social democracy and welfare statism', *The Netherlands Journal of Social Sciences*, 26 (1): 17–34.

Keman, H. (1993a) 'Proliferation of the welfare state. Comparative profiles of public sector management, 1965–90', in K.A. Eliassen and J. Kooiman (eds), *Managing Public Organizations*. London: Sage. pp. 13–33.

Keman, H. (1993b) 'The politics of managing the mixed economy', in Hans Keman (ed.), *Comparative Politics. New Directions in Theory and Method*. Amsterdam: VU University Press. pp. 161–89.

Keman, H. (1993c) 'Comparative politics: a distinctive approach to political science?', in Hans Keman (ed.), *Comparative Politics. New Directions in Theory and Method*. Amsterdam: VU University Press. pp. 31–57.

Keman, H. (ed.) (1993d) *Comparative Politics. New Directions in Theory and Method*. Amsterdam: VU University Press.

Keman, H. (1995) 'The Low Countries: confrontation and coalition in segmented societies', in J. Colomer (ed.), *Political Institutions in Europe*. London: Routledge. pp. 211–53.

Keman, H. (ed.) (1997) *The Politics of Problem-Solving in Postwar Democracies*. Basingstoke: Macmillan.

Keman, H. (1998) 'Political institutions and public governance', in R. Czada, A. Héritier, H. Keman (eds), *Institutions and Political Choice. On the Limits of Rationality*. Amsterdam: VU University Press. pp. 109–33.

Keman, H. and McDonald, M. (1996) 'Accountable and responsible policy-making through democratic party-government. An explorative analysis of 16 OECD Nations (1972–1991)'. Paper presented at the Joint Sessions of the ECPR, Oslo.

Keman, H. and Pennings, P. (1995) 'Managing political and societal conflict in democracies: do consensus and corporatism matter?', *British Journal of Political Science*, 25 (2): 271–81.

Kersbergen, K. van (1995) *Social Capitalism: a Study of Christian Democracy and the Welfare State*. London: Routledge.

Kim, H. and Fording, R.C. (1998) 'Voter ideology in Western democracies, 1946–1989', *European Journal of Political Research*, 33 (1): 73–97.

Kim, J-O. and Mueller, C.W. (1978) 'Factor analysis', *Quantitative Applications in the Social Sciences*, 14.

King, G., Alt, J.E., Burns, N.E. and Laver, M. (1990) 'A unified model of cabinet dissolution in parliamentary democracies', *American Journal of Political Science*, 34 (3): 846–71.

King, G., Keohane, R.D. and Verba, S. (1994) *Designing Social Inquiry*. Princeton, NJ: Princeton University Press.

Kleinnijenhuis, J. and Vries, M.S. de (1994) 'Dyadenanalyse', in L.W.J.C. Huberts and J. Kleinnijenhuis (eds), *Methoden van Invloedsanalyse*. Amsterdam: Boom. pp. 211–34.

Klingemann, H.-D., Hofferbert, R.I., Budge, I. (1994) *Parties, Policies and Democracy*. Boulder, CO: Westview Press.

Korpi, W. (1983) *The Democratic Class Struggle*. London: Routledge & Kegan Paul.

Krämer, J. and Rattinger, H. (1997) 'The proximity and the directional theories of issue voting: Comparative results for the USA and Germany', *European Journal of Political Research*, 1 (32): 1–29.

Kriesi, H. and Koopmans, R. (1995) *New Social Movements in Western Europe: A Comparative Analysis*. London: UCL Press.

Krippendorff, K. (1985) *Content Analysis: an Introduction to its Methodology*, 5th edn. Newbury Park, CA: Sage.

Krouwel, A. (1998) '*The catch-all party in Western Europe 1945–1990: a study in arrested development*'. PhD Thesis, Amsterdam: Vrije Universiteit.

Lane, J.-E. and Ersson, S.O. (1986) 'Political institutions, public policy and economic growth', *Scandinavian Political Studies*, 9 (1): 19–34.

Lane, J.-E. and Ersson, S.O. (1990) *Comparative Political Economy*. London: Pinter.

Lane, J.-E. and Ersson, S.O. (1994a) *Politics and Society in Western Europe*, 3rd edn, London: Sage.

Lane, J.-E. and Ersson, S.O. (1994b) *Comparative Politics: an Introduction and New Approach*. Cambridge: Polity.

Lane, J.-E. and Ersson, S.O. (1997) *Comparative Political Economy. A Developmental Approach*, 2nd. edn. London: Pinter.

Lane, J.-E., McKay, D. and Newton, K. (1997) *Political Data Handbook OECD Countries*. Oxford: Oxford University Press.

Lange, P. and Meadwell, H. (1991) 'Typologies of democratic systems: from political inputs to political economy', in Howard J. Wiarda (ed.), *New Directions in Comparative Politics*. Boulder, CO: Westview Press. pp. 82–117.

Lasswell, H.D. (1968) 'The future of the comparative method', *Comparative Politics*, 1: 3–18.

Laver, M. (1983) *Invitation to Politics*. Oxford: Robertson.

Laver, M. (1995) 'Party policy and cabinet portfolios in the Netherlands', *Acta Politica*, (1): 3–28.

Laver, M. and Budge, I. (1992) *Party Policy and Government Coalitions*. Basingstoke: Macmillian.

Laver, M. and Hunt, W.B. (1992) *Policy and Party Competition*. London: Routledge.

Laver, M. and Schofield, N. (1990) *Multiparty Government. The Politics of Coalition in Europe*. Oxford: Oxford University Press.

Laver, M. and Shepsle, K.A. (1996) *Making and Breaking of Governments. Cabinets and Legislatures in Parliamentary Democracies*. Cambridge: Cambridge University Press.

Lehmbruch, G. (1984) 'Concertation and the structure of corporatist networks', in J.H. Goldthorpe (ed.), *Order and Conflict in Contemporary Capitalism*. Oxford: Clarendon Press. pp. 60–80.

Lehner, F. (1988) 'The political economy of distributive conflict', in F.G. Castles, F.

Lehner and M.G. Schmidt (eds), *Managing Mixed Economies*. Berlin: De Gruyter. pp. 54–96.

Lessmann, S. (1987) *Budgetary Politics and Elections: An Investigation of Public Expenditures in West Germany*. Berlin: de Gruyter.

Lewis, P.G., Potter, D.C. and Castles, F.G. (eds) (1978) *The Practice of Comparative Politics: A Reader*. London: Longman.

Lijphart, A. (1968) *The Politics of Accommodation: Pluralism and Democracy in the Netherlands*. Berkeley, CA: University of California Press.

Lijphart, A. (1971) 'Comparative politics and the comparative method', *The American Political Science Review*, 65: 682–93.

Lijphart, A. (1975) 'The comparable cases strategy in comparative research', *Comparative Studies*, 8 (2): 158–77.

Lijphart, A. (1977) *Democracy in Plural Societies: A Comparative Exploration*. New Haven, CT: Yale University Press.

Lijphart, A. (1984) *Democracies. Patterns of Majoritarian and Consensus Government in Twenty-One Democracies*. New Haven, CT: Yale University Press.

Lijphart, A. (1994) 'Democracies: forms, performance, and constitutional engineering', *European Journal of Political Research*, 25 (1): 1–17.

Lijphart, A. (1997) 'Dimensions of democracy', *European Journal of Political Research*, 31 (1-2): 195–204.

Lijphart, A. and Crepaz, M. (1991) 'Corporatism and consensus democracy in eighteen countries', *British Journal of Political Science*, 21: 235–46.

Lipset, S.M. (1963) *Political Man: The Social Bases of Politics*. New York: Doubleday Anchor Books.

Lipset, S.M. and Rokkan, S. (1967) 'Cleavage structures, party systems, and voter alignments: an introduction', in S.M. Lipset, and S. Rokkan (eds), *Party Systems and Voter Alignments: Cross-national Perspectives*. New York: The Free Press. pp. 1–64.

Long, J.S. (1983) 'Confirmatory factor analysis', *Quantitative Applications in the Social Sciences,* 33.

MacIntyre, A.C. (1978) 'Is a science of comparative politics possible?', in P.G. Lewis, D.C. Potter and F.G. Castles. (eds), *The Practice of Comparative Politics: A Reader*. pp. 266–83.

Mackie, T.T. and Rose, R. (1991) *The International Almanac of Electoral History*. London: Macmillan.

Macridis, R.C. (1955) *The Study of Comparative Government*. New York: Random House.

Macridis, R.C. and Brown, B.E. (1986 [1961]) *Comparative Politics: Notes and Reading*. Homewood, IL: Dorsey.

Macridis, R.C. and Burg, S.L. (1991) *Introduction to Comparative Politics: Regimes and Change*. 2nd edn. New York: HarperCollins.

Mair, P. (1996a) 'Party systems and structures of competition', in Lawrence LeDuc, Richard G. Niemi and Pippa Norris (eds), *Comparative Democratic Elections*. Beverly Hills, CA: Sage. pp. 83–106.

Mair, P. (1996b) 'Comparative politics: an overview', in R.E. Goodin and H. Klingemann (eds), *A New Handbook of Political Science*. Oxford: Oxford University Press. pp. 309–35.

Mayer, L.R. (1972) *Comparative Political Inquiry*. Homewood, IL: Dorsey.

Mayer, L.R. (1989) *Redefining Comparative Politics: Promise Versus Performance*. Beverly Hills, CA: Sage.

Merritt, L. and Rokkan, S. (eds) (1966) *Comparing Nations: The Use of Quantitative Data in Cross-National Research*. New Haven, CT: Yale University Press.

Miles, M.B. and Huberman, M.A. (1994) *Qualitative Data Analysis*. Thousand Oaks, CA: Sage.

Mill, J.S. (1872) *System of Logic*, reprinted in *John Stuart Mill on Politics and Society*. London: Fontana, 1976. pp. 55–89.

Mokken, R.J. (1971) *A Theory and Procedure of Scale Analysis*. The Hague: Mouton.

Mueller, Dennis (ed.) (1983) *The Political Economy of Economic Growth*. New Haven, CT: Yale University Press.

Muller, E.N. (1995) 'Economic determinants of democracy', *American Sociological Review*, 60: 966–82.

North, D.C. (1990) *Institutions, Institutional Change and Economic Performance*. Cambridge: Cambridge University Press.

Olson, Mancur (1982) *The Rise and Decline of Nations: Economic Growth, Stagflation and Social Rigidities*. New Haven, CT: Yale University Press.

Ostrom, E. (1990) *Governing the Commons. The Evolution of Institutions for Collective Action*. Cambridge: Cambridge University Press.

O'Donnell, G.A. (1979) *Modernization and Bureaucratic Authoritarianism: Studies in South American Politics*. Berkeley, CA: Institute of International Studies/UCLA.

Paloheimo, H. (ed.) (1984) *Politics in the Era of Corporatism and Planning*. Helsinki: Finish Political Science Association.

Pennings, P. (1995) 'The impact of parties and unions on welfare statism', *West European Politics*, 18 (4): 1–17.

Pennings, P. (1997) 'Consensus democracy and institutional change', in H. Keman (ed.), *The Politics of Problem-Solving in Postwar Democracies*. Basingstoke: Macmillan. pp. 21–42.

Pennings, P. (1998a) 'Party responsiveness and socio-economic problem-solving in Western democracies', *Party Politics*, 4 (3): 119–30.

Pennings, P. (1998b) 'The triad of party system change: votes, office and policy', in P. Pennings and J.-E. Lane (eds), *Comparing Party System Change*. London: Routledge: 79–100.

Pennings, P. and Keman, H. (1994) '"Links" en "Rechts" in de Nederlandse Politiek', in *Jaarboek 1993 van het Documentatiecentrum Nederlandse Politieke Partijen*. Groningen. pp. 118–44.

Pennings, P. and Lane, J.-E. (eds) (1998) *Comparing Party System Change*. London: Routledge.

Peters, B.G., Doughty, J.C. and McCulloch, M.K. (1977) 'Types of democratic systems and types of public policy', *Comparative Politics*, 9 (3): 237–55.

Petrocik, J.R. (1996) 'Issue ownership in Presidential elections, with a 1980 case study', *American Journal of Political Science,* 40: 825–50.

Powell, B.G. (1982) *Contemporary Democracies. Participation, Stability and Violence*. Cambridge, MA: Harvard University Press.

Pridham, G. (ed.) (1986) *Coalitional Behaviour in Theory and Practice: An Inductive Model for Western Europe*. Cambridge: Cambridge University Press.

Pryor, F.L. (1968) *Public Expenditures in Communist and Capitalist Nations*. London: Allen & Unwin.

Przeworski, A. (1987) 'Methods of cross-national research, 1970–1983', in A.B. Anthal, M. Dierkes and H. Weiler (eds), *Comparative Policy Research: Learning from Experience*. Aldershot: Gower.

Przeworski, A. and Teune, H. (1970) *The Logic of Comparative Social Inquiry*. New York: Wiley Interscience.

Rabinowitz, G. and Macdonald, S.E. (1989) 'A directional theory of issue voting', *American Political Science Review*, 89: 93–121.

Ragin, Ch.C. (1987) *The Comparative Method. Moving Beyond Qualitative and Quantitative Strategies*. Berkeley, CA: University of California Press.

Ragin, Ch.C. (ed.) (1991) 'Issues and alternatives in comparative social research', *International Studies in Sociology and Social Anthropology*, 56: 1–9.

Ragin, Ch.C. and Becker, H.S. (eds) (1992) *What Is a Case?: Exploring the Foundations of Social Inquiry*. Cambridge: Cambridge University Press.

Ragin, Ch.C., Berg-Schlosser, C.D. and Meur, G. de (1996) 'Political methodology: qualitative methods', in Robin E. Goodin and Hans-Dieter Klingemann (eds), *A New Handbook of Political Science*. Oxford: Oxford University Press. pp. 749–68.

Ravallion, Martin (1994) *Poverty Comparisons*. Chur, Switzerland: Harwood Academic Publishers.

Richardson, L.F. (1960) *Statistics of Deadly Quarrels*. Pittsburg: Boxwood Press.

Riggs, F.W. (1994) 'Conceptual Homogenization of a Heterogeneous Field. Presidentialism in Comparative Perspective', in Mattei Dogan and Ali Kazancigil (eds), *Comparing Nations. Concepts, Strategies, Substance*. Oxford and Cambridge: Blackwell. pp. 72–152.

Riker, W.H. (1962) *The Theory of Political Coalitions*. New Haven, CT: Yale University Press.

Roberts, C.W. (1997) *Text Analysis for the Social Sciences: Methods for Drawing Statistical Inferences from Texts and Transcripts*. New York: Erlbaum.

Roberts, G. (1978) 'The explanations of politics: comparison, strategy, and theory', in P.G. Lewis, D. Potter and F.G. Castles (eds), *The Practice of Comparative Politics*. London: Longman. pp. 287–305.

Rogowski, R. (1993) 'Comparative politics', in A.W. Finifter (ed.), *Political Science: The State of the Discipline II*. Washington, DC: APSA.

Rokkan, S. (1970) *Citizens, Elections, Parties: Approaches to the Comparative Study of the Processes of Development*. Oslo: Universitetsforlaget.

Romein, J. (1971) *Historische lijnen en patronen*. Leiden: Querido.

Royed, T.J. (1996) 'Testing the mandate model in Britain and the United States: evidence from the Reagan and Thatcher eras', *British Journal of Political Science*, 26 (1): 45–80.

Rueschemeyer, D., Huber, E. and Stephens, J.D. (1992) *Capitalist Development and Democracy*. Cambridge: Polity Press.

Sartori, G. (1970) 'Concept misformation in comparative politics', *American Political Science Review*, 64: 1033–53.

Sartori, G. (1976) *Parties and Party Systems: A Framework for Analysis*. Cambridge: Cambridge University Press.

Sartori, G. (1994) *Comparative Constitutional Engineering: An Inquiry into Structures, Incentives and Outcomes*. New York: New York University Press.

Sartori, G. et al. (1991) *Rethinking Democracy*. Oxford: Blackwell.

Sayrs, L.W. (1989) 'Pooled time series analysis', *Quantitative Applications in the Social Sciences*, 70.

Schmidt, M.G. (1982) 'Does corporatism matter? Economic crisis, politics and rates of unemployment in capitalist democracies in the 1970s', in G. Lehmbruch and P.C. Schmitter (eds), *Patterns of Corporatist Policy-Making*. London: Sage. pp. 237–58.

Schmidt, M.G. (1987) 'The politics of labour market policy', in F.G. Castles, F. Lehner and M.G. Schmidt (eds), *Managing Mixed Economies*. Berlin: de Gruyter. pp. 4–53.

Schmidt, M.G. (1989) 'Social policy in rich and poor countries: socio-economic trends and political-institutional determinants', *European Journal of Political Research*, 17 (6): 641–59.

Schmidt, M.G. (1992) 'Regierungen: Parteipolitische Zusammensetzung', in Dieter Nohlen (ed.), *Lexikon der Politik*. Munich: Beck. pp. 393–400.

Schmidt, M.G. (1995) 'Germany: the grand coalition state', in J. Colomer (ed.), *Political Institutions in Europe*. London: Routledge. pp. 62–98.

Schmidt, M.G. (1996) 'When parties matter: A review of the possibilites and limits of partisan influence on public policy', *European Journal of Political Research*, 30 (2): 155–83.

Schmitter, Ph. C. (1974) 'Still the century of corporatism?', *Review of Politics*, 26 (1): 85–131.

Schmitter, Ph. C. (1981) 'Interest intermediation and regime governability in contemporary Western Europe and North America', in Susanne Berger (ed.), *Organizing Interests in Western Europe: Pluralism, Corporatism and the Transformation of Politics*. Cambridge: Cambridge University Press. pp. 285–327.

Schmitter, Ph.C. and Lehmbruch, G. (eds) (1982) *Patterns of Corporatist Policy-Making*. London: Sage.

Schneider, F. and Frey, B.S. (1988) 'Politico-economic models of macroeconomic policy: a review of the empirical evidence', in Thomas D. Willett (ed.), *Political Business Cycles. The Political Economy of Money, Inflation, and Unemployment*. Durham, NC: Duke University Press. pp. 240–75.

Schuur, W.H. van (1984) *Structure in Political Beliefs. A New Model for Stochastic Unfolding with an Application to European Party Activists*. Amsterdam: CT Press.

Schuur, W.H. van (1993) 'Nonparametric unidimensional unfolding for multicategory data', *Political Analysis* (4): 41–74.

Schuur, W.H. van and Kiers, H.A.L. (1994) 'Why factor analysis often is the incorrect model for analyzing bipolar concepts, and what model to use instead', *Applied Psychological Measurement*, 18 (2): 97–110.

Shalev, M. (1983) 'The social democratic model and beyond: two generations of comparative research on the welfare state', *Comparative Social Research*, 6: 316–31.

Sigelman, L. and Yough, S.N. (1978) 'Left–right polarization in national party systems: a cross-national analysis', *Comparative Political Studies*, 11 (3): 355–79.

Singer, J.D. (1979) *The Correlates of War*. New York: Free Press.

Skocpol, T. (1979) *States and Social Revolution: A Comparative Analysis of France, Russia and China*. Cambridge: Cambridge University Press.

Skocpol, T. (1985) 'Bringing the state back. Strategies of analysis in current research', in P. Evans, D. Rueschemeyer and T. Skocpol (eds), *Bringing the State Back In*. Cambridge: Cambridge University Press. pp. 1–45.

Skocpol, T. and Somers, M. (1980) 'The use of comparative history in macrosocial inquiry', *Comparative Studies of Society and History*, 22: 174–97.

Small, M. and Singer, J.D. (1982) *Resort to Arms: International and Civil Wars 1816–1980*. Beverly Hills: Sage.

Smelser, N.J. (1976) *Comparative Methods in the Social Sciences*. Englewood Cliffs, NJ: Prentice-Hall.

Smith, D.A. and White, D.R. (1992) 'Structural position in the global economy: network analysis of international trade 1965–1980', *Social Forces*, 70: 857–93.

Spector, P.E. (1992) 'Summated rating scale construction', *Quantitative Applications in the Social Sciences*, 82.

Stinchcombe, A.L. (1968) *Constructing Social Theories*. New York: Harcourt, Brace & World.

Strom, K. (1985) 'Party goals and government performance in parliamentary democracies', *American Political Science Review*, 79: 738–54.

Strom, K. (1990a) 'A behavioral theory of competitive political parties', *American Journal of Political Science*, 34 (2): 565–98.

Strom, K. (1990b) *Minority Government and Majority Rule*. Cambridge: Cambridge University Press.

Swaan, A. de (1973) *Coalition Theories and Cabinet Formation*. Amsterdam: Elsevier.

Tacq, J. (1997) *Multivariate Analysis Techniques in Social Science Research*. London: Sage.

Taylor, C.L. and Jodice, D.A. (1977) *World Handbook of Political and Social Indicators*, 3th edn. New Haven, CT: Yale University Press.

Vanhanen, T. (1990) *The Process of Democratization. A Comparative Study of 147 States, 1980–1988*. New York: Crane Russak.

Vasquez, J.A. (1993) *The War Puzzle*. Cambridge: Cambridge University Press.

Visser, J. (1989) *European Trade Unions in Figures*. Deventer: Kluwer.

Volkens, A. (1994) *Programmatic Profiles of Political Parties in 27 Countries, 1945–92: Dataset CMP94*. Berlin: WZB.

Von Beyme, K. (1985) *Political Parties in Western Democracies*. Aldershot: Gower.

Wallerstein, I. (1974–1989) *The Modern World System*. New York: Academic Press, 3 vols.

Ware, A. (1996) *Political Parties and Party Systems*. Oxford: Oxford University Press.

Warwick, P. (1994) *Government Survival in Parliamentary Democracies*. Cambridge: Cambridge University Press.

Weaver, R.K. and Rockman, B.A. (eds) (1993) *Do Institutions Matter? Government Capabilities in the United States and Abroad*. Washington: The Brookings Institution.

Weber, M. (1972, [1918]) *Wirtschaft und Gesellschaft: Grundriß der verstehenden Soziologie*, 5th edn. Tübingen: Mohr-Siebeck.

White, L.G. (1994) *Political Analysis: Technique and Praxis*. Belmont: Wadsworth.

Whiteley, P.E. (1986) *Political Control of the Macro-economy*. London: Sage.

Wiarda, H.J. (1991) *New Directions in Comparative Politics*. Boulder, CO: Westview Press.

Wijck, P. van (1991) *Inkomensverdelingsbeleid in Nederland: over Individuele Voorkeuren en Distributieve Effecten* (Income distribution in the Netherlands: on individual preferences and distributive effects). Tilburg: Tinbergen Institute Research Series, 19.

Wijers, G.J. (1998) 'Vernieuwing door Vergelijking', *Economisch Statistische Berichten*, 30 (1): 73–6.

Wilensky, H. (1975) *The Welfare State and Equality: Structural and Ideological Roots of Public Expenditures*. Berkeley, CA: University of California Press.

Windhoff-Héritier, A. 'Policy network analysis: a tool for comparative political research', in H. Keman (ed.), *Comparative Politics. New Directions in Theory and Method*. Amsterdam: VU University Press. pp. 143–60.

Woldendorp, J. (1997) 'Neo-corporatism and macroeconomic performance in eight small west European countries (1970–1990)', *Acta Politica*, 32 (1): 49–79.

Woldendorp, J., Keman, H. and Budge, I. (1993) 'Political data 1945–90: party government in 20 democracies', *European Journal of Political Research*, 1 (24): 1–120.

Yin, R.K. (1996) *Case Study Research. Design and Methods*. Thousand Oaks, CA: Sage.

Index